CRIP
GENEALOGIES

ANIMA: Critical Race Studies Otherwise

A series edited by Mel Y. Chen, Ezekiel J. Dixon-Román, and Jasbir K. Puar

Duke University Press Durham and London 2023

CRIP GENEALOGIES

EDITED BY MEL Y. CHEN, ALISON KAFER,
EUNJUNG KIM, AND JULIE AVRIL MINICH

with a foreword by therí a. pickens

Printed in the United States of America on acid-free paper ∞
Typeset in Garamond Premier Pro and Din by Westchester Publishing Services

Library of Congress Cataloging-in-Publication Data
Names: Chen, Mel Y., [date] editor. | Kafer, Alison, editor. | Kim, Eunjung,
[date] editor. | Minich, Julie Avril, [date] editor. | Pickens, Therí A., writer of
foreword.
Title: Crip genealogies / edited by Mel Y. Chen, Alison Kafer, Eunjung Kim,
and Julie Avril Minich ; with a foreword by Therí A. Pickens.
Other titles: ANIMA (Duke University Press)
Description: Durham : Duke University Press, 2023. | Series: Anima | Includes
bibliographical references and index.
Identifiers: LCCN 2022040977 (print)
LCCN 2022040978 (ebook)
ISBN 9781478019220 (paperback)
ISBN 9781478016588 (hardcover)
ISBN 9781478023852 (ebook)
ISBN 9781478093725 (ebook/other)
Subjects: LCSH: Disability studies. | Critical pedagogy. | Feminist criticism. |
People with disabilities—Political activity. | People with disabilities in literature. |
BISAC: SOCIAL SCIENCE / People with Disabilities | SOCIAL SCIENCE /
Ethnic Studies / General
Classification: LCC HV1568.2 .C75 2023 (print) | LCC HV1568.2 (ebook) |
DDC 362.4—dc23/eng/20230106
LC record available at https://lccn.loc.gov/2022040977
LC ebook record available at https://lccn.loc.gov/2022040978

COVER ART: Sandie Chun-Shan Yi, *Skinny*, 2014. Human skin flakes, silk
organza, sewing thread, embroidery thread, and lotion. Made in collaboration
with Rahnee Patrick. Courtesy of the artist.

Open access of this book was made possible by the support of the University of
Texas at Austin, the University of California, Berkeley, and the College of Arts
and Sciences at Syracuse University.

For Christopher M. Bell and Stacey Park Milbern

Contents

Acknowledgments

This project has been nourished by the words and the work of too many people to name here, and we are grateful to all of them. We wish to recognize, in particular, Courtney Berger and Sandra Korn at Duke University Press, who believed in this project and also kept us accountable. We are deeply grateful to all of our contributors for trusting us with their work and believing in this project. We thank Therí A. Pickens and two anonymous readers for their labor of reviewing this manuscript during the pandemic and providing thoughtful suggestions and support. Finally, we send much love to our families.

DESCRIPTION OF THE COVER: The image on the cover is a detail of Sandie Chun-shan Yi's artwork titled *Skinny* (2014–2019), made in collaboration with Rahnee Patrick. The color photograph consists of a close-up view of two small sacs made with silk organza resting on a white background. One sac takes up the lower half of the image while the other sac appears to float above it. Both sacs contain pieces of human skin flakes and have clusters of embroidery stitches in dark red and ivory colors. The book title, *Crip Genealogies*, sits in between the sacs. The editors' names—Mel Y. Chen, Alison Kafer, Eunjung Kim, and Julie Avril Minich—appear in smaller font and in all capital letters above the book title, to the right. The bottom right corner features the text "with a foreword by therí a. pickens" in lowercase letters.

Sometimes being reader #1 is awesome. Reading this manuscript was one of those times. I received the call for papers (CFP) for *Crip Genealogies* in December 2016. At the time, I was working on what would become *Black Madness :: Mad Blackness*. I was also at the beginning of a prolonged crisis with myasthenia gravis that, when it was done, had resulted in the following: five hospital stays longer than three weeks, including a stint in a nursing home and rehabilitation center; six other hospital stays for recurring pancreatitis; three emergency surgeries and one preplanned surgery; several rounds of chemotherapy; and innumerable doctors' appointments. And that was just my medical life.

I disclose this information because I write in the tradition of Black feminists who believe my specific location influences my analysis. It matters that I am disabled and Black and woman and more. I also believe Anna Julia Cooper: to paraphrase, when and where I enter, others enter as well. In this case, I enter where the ramp is, usually at the back or on the side of a building, if it is there at all.

The editors of this volume (authors and luminaries each in their own right) understood the necessity of a collection that perturbs readers interested in the history of what the American academy calls "disability studies." Their call for papers read, "In this anthology, we want to push back against the expectation of a coherent narrative of disability studies, one without contradictions, and its limited and limiting approach to race. In its place, we want stories of a disability studies very much entwined with, and indebted to, the fields of feminist studies, queer studies, postcolonial studies, and race and ethnic studies. We want to think through alternative intellectual histories and genealogies. We suggest that offering critical genealogies, ones that recognize critical race theorists' and theory's contributions to disability studies, counters hegemonic genealogies and in so doing remakes the field."

Returning to the discipline (!) of English, I offer comments on form and function. Chen, Kafer, Kim, and Minich knew that this type of inquiry required a collection. You need a cacophony of voices to have this conversation, and an edited volume does the trick. Further, this type of inquiry—a usefully cranky one—pushes against the possibility of cohesion because it asks readers and writers to deliberately consider the places where the narrative refuses cohesion. In Matthew Salesses's work in *Craft in the Real World*, the accepted stories of a culture rely on forms of erasure. Salesses opines, "Any story relies on negative space, and a tradition relies on the negative space of history.... Some readers are asked to stay always, only, in the negative. To wield craft responsibly is to take responsibility for absence" (19). These editors asked, who is left out of a field that champions itself as the most marginalized? They curated the essays you now hold, which fill in the gaps and retell the dominant and, heretofore accepted, narratives about disability the world over. I would be remiss if I did not add that their introduction defies the formal expectations of an introduction by asking questions, being transparent, and opening up conversations rather than foreclosing them through forced cohesion.

When I received the first iteration of *Crip Genealogies*, I was thrilled to be reader #1. For those who are unfamiliar, publishers typically choose two experts in the field to read a manuscript and approve it or decline it for eventual publication. The running joke is that reader #2 tends to be the most irritable. I have no idea whether this is true for this volume, but I will say that irritability is rather a standard state for many academics. In my case, I felt negatively implicated by the reading—*Why had I not considered the issues raised here? What the hell was I doing, such that I could not answer the CFP?*—but also buoyed and represented by it. This emotional mélange of need and chagrin made music as it shivered up my spine.

In 2009, I saw Christopher Bell for the last time at the Rocky Mountain MLA conference in Snowbird, Utah. Michelle Jarman and I spoke with him about disability over sandwiches. We each had our own misgivings about the field: it did not feel wide enough for the people we were most interested in honoring. Characteristically, Chris abruptly ended the conversation and pushed Michelle and me into a picture. Now, when I see our faces smirking from the photo, I can only envision Mel Chen, Alison Kafer, Eunjung Kim, and Julie Avril Minich in the frame with us, Chris and other crip ancestors behind the lens, a different SOS, come in, wherever you are, urgent, calling you, calling all of us, come in, y'all, come on in.

INTRODUCTION

Crip Genealogies

MEL Y. CHEN, ALISON KAFER, EUNJUNG KIM,
AND JULIE AVRIL MINICH

We open with a feeling of welcome and generosity, eager for the company of others.

This book is for those of you

who have had your hearts broken after years of engaging with disability studies;

who keep returning to disability studies, even with a broken heart, even though it sometimes leaves you sharply wanting and exhausted;

who have wanted to engage with disability studies but haven't felt welcomed or supported in doing so;

who have left disability studies (but are still hopeful for the possibility of return);

who have dismissed disability studies altogether, assuming it is only white disability studies, or Western/Northern disability studies, or disability with a capital "D";

who seek affirmation that anti-ableist and antiracist theorizing is not separate and can coexist;

who are committed to finding knowledge away from traditional academic routes;

who labor in academic institutions and are committed to finding ways to make them livable;

who yearn for an opening that welcomes your presence in all of these endeavors;

and who seek company and crip camaraderie in doing so.

This book is our incomplete offering and our invitation.

> **Sticky Note:** This introduction is much longer than is typical for a book like this. We have divided our introduction into mini-chapters for ease of reading, and we invite you to read in whatever way is accessible for you. Read out of order, pick and choose the sections you need now, go at your own pace.
>
> —Crip Feelings
> —Metaphors of Genealogies, Genealogies of Metaphors
> —Methodically Crip: More Crip Feelings
> —White Disability Studies and Access Exceptionalism
> —Transnational Disability Studies
>
> At the end of the introduction, we have included a brief overview of the book as well as some concluding thoughts.

The four of us—Alison, Eunjung, Julie, and Mel—first came together around shared feelings: a wish for histories and recognitions to be held differently; a love for movements and orientations seldom recognized as part of disability studies; a commitment to *crip* as a form of praxis; and a belief in the transformative possibilities of knowledge, regardless of whether it is part of an academically recognized field or discipline. All of these feelings inform what follows, including the decision to begin this introduction with a focus on *crip*—the word, its histories, and our shifting orientations to it—less a genealogy of crip than a mapping of its movement into, through, and against the academy (and us).

Crip Feelings

I love hearing this word, *crip*, come out of your mouths, in reference to us.
I'm writing about *crip* but feelings come in.

The praxis of crip is about being in relation to each other in such a way that risks a falling out with disability studies. In naming this anthology, we used the word "crip" instead of "disability studies" to signal our investment in disrupting the established histories and imagined futures of the field. If *crip* indexes a wide range of positions, orientations, subjects, and acts, not all of them academic, then *disability studies* hews more closely to notions of academic discipline. In the spirit of honoring more complex genealogies, we wanted to keep questions of institutionality and disciplinarity afloat.

Due in part to its distance from diagnosis and legal recognition, the term *crip* has the potential to remain open, allowing for disabilities and illnesses not yet marked as such; for traumas, health histories, and other "unwellness" that rarely register as "disability"; for nonnormative ways of being that have historical and contemporary resonances with "disability"; and for political orientations, affiliations, and solidarities still emerging.[1] *Crip* is less tethered to the structures of academia than *disability studies*, not yet defined or contained within university governance structures or funding cycles, and, unlike *disability*, it has not yet been incorporated into bureaucratic mechanisms of "inclusion" or "accommodation." *Crip* instead can signal a refusal of social and bureaucratized systems of classification, and *crip theory* and *crip politics* tend to recognize the limitations and exclusions of rights-based claims on the state. As Aimi Hamraie reminds us, the goal of those kinds of initiatives, such as the Americans with Disabilities Act, "was not to foster crip culture but to reintegrate disabled [white] men into the realms of productive labor and consumption," fostering "inclusion in exchange for contributions toward national productivity."[2]

I was recently asked to weigh in on the disability language in a draft "Diversity and Inclusion Statement" at my university: "The university is dedicated to attracting highly qualified students, faculty and staff, of all races, ethnicities, peoples, nationalities, religious backgrounds, sexual orientations, gender identities/expressions, socioeconomic statuses, and regardless of disability, marital, parental, age, or veteran status."

"Thank you for asking," I responded, and then suggested that "moving 'disability' before the 'regardless' would send a stronger and more affirming message. In the current version, disability and disabled people might register more as something/someone that we are willing to tolerate but aren't especially interested in attracting. Moving 'disability' to the list with 'races, ethnicities' also makes room for an acknowledgment of ableism in ways that the 'regardless' phrase does not. Adding 'health' is important, too, especially given the current state of things. So it could read something like: 'The university is dedicated to attracting highly qualified students, faculty and staff, of all races, ethnicities, peoples, °nationalities, religious backgrounds, sexual orientations, gender identities/expressions, socioeconomic statuses, disabilities and health histories, and regardless of marital, parental, age, or veteran status.'"

But the committee pushed back. If they agreed to move "disability" out of the list of things that the university will accept ("regardless of") and into the list of things the university wants to attract ("all races, ethnicities, sexual orientations"), then they wanted to replace "disabilities" with "abilities."

Note that the institution was fine with the language of disability when it came after "regardless," but once we moved from tolerance to desire, "disability" no longer worked. People "of all abilities" are welcome, but "disability" is not (well, people of "all" abilities are welcome as long as they are also "highly- qualified," which is another disavowal of disability). The rhetoric of "regardless of," common to antidiscrimination policies, builds on the presumption that each of the named conditions—disability, marital, parental, age, or veteran status—can only have a deleterious effect on one's performance, qualifications, and abilities. They can be accounted for—accommodated—but never desired.

> **Sticky Note:** Throughout this introduction, we leave many stories, such as the one above, unattributed, although readers who know basic details about the four of us—like the names of the institutions where we work—might imagine that they know whose stories they are. In sharing these stories collectively, untethered to a particular person's experience or institution, we are accentuating the pervasiveness of these experiences, making clear their ongoing repetitiveness across multiple institutional locations.

Academia, ableist to its core, rejects *disability* in its love for *abilities* (read: merit, excellence, rigor, achievement, productivity, and so on), a preference so strong that disability is lost and, with it, sick and disabled people. Ableism dictates the very conditions under which diversity and inclusion are allowed into the university, with both increasingly framed and justified in terms of how they boost "performance" and increase "capacity." Disability is to be tamed through the expectation of "reasonable accommodations" as conceived within the narrow bounds of legislation like the ADA (Americans with Disabilities Act) and its amendments. The typical negative framing of disability—as aligned against, opposed to, and the absence of ability—reveals abledness as the liberal foundation of equality. But we also want to highlight how, as evidenced by the institution's quick recoil in the story above, *disability* is potentially no less radical than *crip*. If *crip* allows for expansiveness and openness, then *disability*'s force of negativity disavows any attachment to "abilities" and exceeds the limits of "reasonableness." It can and does disrupt, and has done so. We want these disruptions to continue.

Crip is not free of its own contradictions, and in choosing this term, we also commit to its ongoing examination. *Crip*'s political openness has long been complicated by its stronger association with mobility impairments than with chronic illnesses or mental and cognitive disabilities. As M. Remi Yergeau points out, "Crip histories largely elide the neurodivergent, privileging rhetors who are critically conversant and academically able, constructions that often silence those with cognitive disabilities."[3] Moreover, *crip* is a site of tension in its very refusal of rights and recognition, as it cannot capture or honor ways of engaging with disability that might include a demand for rights that have been denied. Some uses of *crip*—and some crips—are able to note the limitations of rights-based politics precisely because their critiques are issued from a position of legal security. For those whose documentable disabilities are accommodated within existing legal structures, or for those whose intersections of race, ethnicity, nationality, caste, gender conformity, and class position offer protection, challenging the limitations of rights-based policies might feel more possible because one's rights are not otherwise in jeopardy.

But other uses of *crip*–and other crips—situate themselves within a disability justice agenda that, in Jina B. Kim's words, "orients its politics around the most marginalized within disability communities," namely those "for whom legal rights are inaccessible."[4] As documented in *Skin, Tooth, and Bone: The Basis of Movement Is Our People*, a primer published by Bay Area (California, USA) arts organization Sins Invalid, the call for disability justice emerged out of frustration with the limitations of the mainstream disability rights movement. Building on prior and ongoing organizing by disabled people of color and/or queer and trans disabled people, activists developed a set of principles and practices for approaching disability organizing from a different center. Leah Lakshmi Piepzna-Samarasinha explains that the term *disability justice* was "coined by the Black, brown, queer, and trans members of the original Disability Justice Collective, founded in 2005 by Patty Berne, Mia Mingus, Leroy Moore, Eli Clare, and Sebastian Margaret."[5] While "disability justice work is largely done by individuals within their respective settings," groups such as Sins Invalid and the Disability Justice Collectives based in New York City, Seattle, and Vancouver have been and continue to be instrumental in shaping the movement.[6] The tenets of disability justice include challenging ableism as entangled with white supremacy, settler colonialism, racism, capitalism, and heteropatriarchy and emphasizing collectivity and solidarity in building sustainable movements for justice and liberation. Disability justice has pushed many progressive communities to challenge their own ableist assumptions about bodies, behaviors, and abilities, particularly insofar as they require productivity, speed, and efficiency in their activists. It also has pushed for disability studies and disability rights movements to abandon a single-issue approach to disability (one often centered only on particular physical disabilities) grounded in white liberal individualism. Such approaches, Sins Invalid explains, erase "the lives of disabled people of color, immigrants with disabilities, disabled people who practice marginalized religions (in particular those experiencing the violence of anti-Islamic beliefs and actions), queers with disabilities, trans and gender non-conforming people with disabilities, people with disabilities who are houseless, people with disabilities who are incarcerated, people with disabilities who have had their ancestral lands stolen, amongst others."[7] The leadership of queer and trans disabled people of color, disabled people of color, and queer and trans disabled people has been the consistent emphasis of disability justice theorizing and organizing.

Too often, however, mainstream white-majority disability organizations and those working in white disability studies have taken up the language of disability justice without actually transforming their leadership, frameworks, and agendas as would be required to address capitalism, racism, classism, heterosexism, and transphobia within disability communities or even to reckon with the exclusions and failures of rights-focused initiatives such as the ADA. Berne criticizes this trend of adding "the word 'justice' onto everything disability related—from disability services to advocacy to disability studies, . . . as if adding the word 'justice' brings work into alignment with disability justice. It doesn't."[8]

Mere citation does not accomplish it; neither does representational "coverage" as the measure of substantive engagement. Isolated moves to cite, publish, or invite-to-keynote more scholars of color, Indigenous scholars, or non-US-based scholars have not sufficiently dislodged a persistent white US/settler orientation in the field. Instead, such moves have resulted in a dynamic in which the same people are tasked with "representing," even as representation itself is substituted for meaningful reorientation. Prominent women of color with histories of disability and illness, such as Audre Lorde and Gloria Anzaldúa, are often cited in extractive and reductive ways, incorporating them into the bureaucratic and normative operations of disability rights/disability studies rather than fully engaging with the radical changes that their work and disability justice require.

Sticky Note: Our critique of reductive and extractive citational practices results in a challenge to the field that this volume, by itself, cannot fully answer. And our resistance to mere representation does not justify or excuse this volume's gaps, some of which we recognize and some of which we have yet to understand. While we hope that we are doing the work of reorientation—and making room for more important work to come—we nonetheless acknowledge this insufficiency.

One such change might be admitting the limits of exclusively defining *crip* as equivalent to *queer*.[9] While we continue to be moved by the frictions and reverberations between both terms, we also want to reaffirm the work of scholars and activists who have, both independently and collectively, worked to chart alternate genealogies for crip, not (only) via (white) queerness but through critical theories of race, ethnicity, and indigeneity, as well as Black feminism, Black music, and queer of color critique. Leroy Moore, of Sins Invalid and Krip-Hop Nation, aligns his use of the word *Krip* with Black music history: "We're also using it in a way that connects to history because there were a couple blues artists that named themselves 'Crippled.' So we're taking it, twisting it, and putting it back out there. . . . That's what I want to get out there: Dig deeper. Open your eyes and find out about black deaf history, black blind blues history. It's so rich."[10] For Moore, part of that richness is about linking disability culture and activism to histories of organizing for racial and economic justice, organizing that is less focused on making claims on the state. According to Jina B. Kim's formulation, a crip-of-color critique reveals how "the state, rather than protecting disabled people, in fact operates as an apparatus of racialized disablement, whether through criminalization and police brutality, or compromised public educational systems and welfare reform." Nirmala Erevelles makes similar moves, drawing on *crip* to interrogate the racist, ableist, and classist logics of the school-to-prison pipeline, as does Liat Ben-Moshe, who casts "crip/mad of color critique" as central to analyses of incarceration and decarceration. *Crip* in these formulations allows us, as Ben-Moshe puts it, to refuse "approaches that look at violence and discrimination as related to individual acts and instead focus, through an intersectional lens, on systemic issues and structural inequalities."[11]

Doing so might mean acknowledging another significant history of the term *crip*, namely its use in designating members of the gang/underground economic organization that first arose in Los Angeles. This connection is often dismissed as merely coincidental; yet Erevelles reminds us that the experiences of those who "becom[e] disabled as a result of gang violence and who are often also confined in incarcerated spaces like prisons" compel genealogical attention.[12] The possibilities, effects, costs, and implications of living with disabilities are deeply entangled with ongoing histories of racism, classism, disenfranchisement, violence, and geopolitics, suggesting that the link between Crips and *crip* is no mere coincidence. We do not want to repeat a sweep of *crip* that simply distances the word from the gang or acknowledges this history only to appropriate or romanticize it. Rather, we want to ensure that people whose lives have been most directly shaped by these histories—the development of gangs as well as social responses to them, both sites of potential violence—have a place in the investments of the field in their lived fullness: not as antagonists to *crip*, not as separable from *crip*, and not as mere metaphors for *crip*, because each of those moves renders affected lives and deaths tangential or disposable. This is particularly so at a moment when a humanitarian crisis facing Central American migrants at the US-Mexico border has been overdetermined by rhetoric that assumes the need to exclude gang-affiliated migrants and by questions about whether fear of gang violence constitutes political persecution.[13] Such exclusions are happening at the same time that disabled militia members and some disabled veterans are embracing ultranationalist politics and urging (para)military interventions.[14] How does the hypervisible criminality of gangs serve to obfuscate state, privatized military, and police operations by marking them as fundamentally different? We want to suggest that the proximity of *crip* to *crip* urges us neither to uphold the existing line of distinction between "cripplers" and the "crippled" nor to aim for a definitive or monolithic position in exploring the connections between violence and disabilities.[15]

Even within disability-centered communities, *crip* and *cripples* have not always been used with a consistent political or ideological orientation. As suggested by our brief gloss, and as evidenced by the work in this collection, activists and scholars draw on multiple origin stories for these words and use them toward different goals and to different effect. Moreover, reclaiming *crip* is neither the only option nor an isolated phenomenon: users of other languages have taken up other words typically considered outdated or derogatory in order to signal intimacy, nonconformity, and a political commitment to radical social transformation.

Disability justice foregrounds crip ways of thinking, feeling, doing, interacting, and loving, and it centers crip ways of resisting normativity, recognition, rights, and incorporation.[16] *Crip* also urges us to leave open the meanings of each of these terms, as well as notions of "justice," "community," and "sustainability." What are the historical, material, philosophical, cultural, and political origins, assumptions, and effects of such orientations? How might *crip* itself need to shift meanings in a political context in which identities are understood as community-based rather than as matters of self-determination? Or in situations in which ideals of collectivity have been based on romanticized histories or majoritarian understandings of liberation? Could *crip* shift meanings in such contexts, working in opposition to rigid understandings of community or expectations of collectivity? How might any of these frames limit our imaginations and transformations?

I started my first tenure-track job in 2008, at a time when disability studies was still difficult to explain to search committees (maybe it still is?). Then *crip* cleared a path for me that I wasn't entirely comfortable with. Colleagues who seemed to get anxious around the term *disability studies*—too stodgy, too mired in dated versions of identity politics—were suddenly receptive to crip theory. I was supposed to feel validated, I think, but I was terrified. At the time I still considered myself nondisabled, unaware of (or unwilling to acknowledge) my cognitive disabilities, and being attached to *crip* felt like posing, like appropriating, like stealing an insider term. Has my relationship to the word changed only because I no longer identify as "nondisabled"? Or is there something else in me, in the word, that makes me feel right using it now?

In the process of academic branding, at least in some scholarship produced in the United States, *crip* underwent an aestheticization that often took the form of a separation from—or a superficial gesture toward—ethical and political investments in anti-ableism. *Crip* and *cripping* as theory and method began to flourish in spaces where sick and disabled people could not. Rather than an intersectional and cross-movement analysis of how norms of achievement, productivity, competence, fairness, and development continue to function to surveil the boundaries of the academy, *cripping* too often came to focus narrowly on pushing the boundaries of interpretation and intervening at the level of the individual or interpersonal.

This dynamic is one in which our title participates, and we are writing from within US institutional locations that have often been eager to claim crip theory as their own. But what genealogies are erased or effaced in that appropriation? Claiming crip in ways aligned with disability justice would require grappling with the relentless consumption of ideas in the academy, namely the taking up of crip as a *more* aesthetic, *more* theoretical, *more* high, *more* edgy term (as well as the assumption that being *more* of any of these things is itself desirable). Such positioning, we argue, accentuates *crip*'s proprietary whiteness. Attaching itself to the concept of *crip* as a tool, white disability studies invests in carving out agendas concerned with disability alone and turns away from intersectional ways of being, from lives and communities that trouble access to insidiously class- and race-dependent expectations, such as "worth," "pride," "dignity," "rights," "privacy," and more. This amounts to a usage of *crip* that runs counter to its nominal purpose of troubling recognition and rights, instead reconsolidating whiteness and a proprietary relationship to ideas, rights, and power itself.

Note that as many "academics" insist that disability justice requires positioning crip not as an identity but only as an analytic or method, many disability justice "activists"—that is, the very group the academics are often name-checking—have long used and encouraged *crip* as identity. This disjuncture suggests the need for continued engagement with identity and identification, and we are reminded here of Cathy Cohen's call for the "destabilization, and not the destruction or abandonment, of identity categories."[17] In Cohen's reminder that only by "recognizing the many manifestations of power, across and within categories, can we truly begin to build a movement based on one's politics and not exclusively on one's identity," we find an important precursor to the kind of theory and praxis we yearn for.[18]

Like the four of us, the individual contributors to this volume make different choices about using the word *crip* and route it through different genealogies. Lezlie Frye uses a conceptualization of *crip pasts* to critique a "whitewashed, victorious narrative of disability rights as the apex of civil rights in the United States" that "conceals the presence and labor of disabled people of color, namely Black activists." In Frye's formulation, these crip pasts have the potential to disrupt established disability histories. Magda García's analysis of Noemi Martinez's zines positions both Martinez and her zines as crip in order to elaborate how a crip position illuminates logics of debilitation in the Rio Grande Valley. Natalia Duong uses *crip* in its verb form, describing a relational sense of chemical kinship tied to Agent Orange that "crips the transnational export of neoliberal legal and social discourses of disability in contemporary Vietnam." Suzanne Bost grapples with the implications of using the word to describe the interventions of a cultural worker (Aurora Levins Morales) who does not use the term herself, even as she acknowledges that "Levins Morales's contributions to the performance project Sins Invalid resonate with the radical disability pride associated with the term crip." Leah Lakshmi Piepzna-Samarasinha and Stacey Park Milbern use the term enthusiastically and extensively, in ways that capture the very multiplicity and complexity of the term that we explore here: to define themselves as crips, but even more as a way of marking radical forms of solidarity, community, resistance—being a crip elder, practicing crip wisdom, experiencing crip grief and bitterness. Translating the Korean word *bulgu* to *crip*, Tari Young-Jung Na explains that *crip politics* enables expansive solidarities among minorities without resorting to the very language of identity categories deployed by social institutions. Crip politics instead signals the potential for a unified abolition movement, one opposed to practices of institutionalization that encompass many different forms of segregation, isolation, and incarceration. Sony Coráñez Bolton raises a question about the meaning of *crip* in *supercrip*, arguing that the role taken up by an ill, disabled, colonized, Indigenous woman in a feminized national space—one where indigeneity is associated with disability—is that of a supercrip. Kateřina Kolářová positions crip as inseparable from and materialized with race and racialized understandings of ethnicity. Kolářová takes on the articulation of crip genealogies directly "from the point of homosexual, nonreproductive, non-straight, unwholesome, paid-for, virus-infected, across-the-borders sex acts" so that she does not reproduce whiteness through, in Sara Ahmed's terms, "good genealogical straight lines."[19]

Yet even as all of these authors offer more meaningful and sustaining uses of *crip*, we also want to suggest that this book as a whole seeks to let go of didactic obligations such as a drive for completion or definitiveness, even or perhaps especially around *crip*. As Jasbir K. Puar notes in her chapter, even though "crip theorizing about care webs, resisting productivity, and embracing the collectivization of slow life" is "capacious and frankly life-saving," we cannot ignore "the epistemological foreclosures of this lexicon in settler colonial contexts such as Palestine, where mass impairment is a predominating source of disability." Crip remains incomplete, as do any of its genealogies.

Though we are aware of the sneaky centering weight of US-based modes of thought, we note that this multiplicity of genealogies also hints at the impossibility of limiting crip to something that singularly originated in Anglo-American contexts. As authors of these chapters write across geopolitical contexts (what Keguro Macharia calls "the geohistories of location") about what crip can create and connect and how it may disrupt, crip begins to escape singularity in its origins and meanings. How might we read this escape in relation to the presumed portability of disability justice across borders, a portability that typically divorces the movement from its origins and even the principles attached to it.[20]

And so, while we find ourselves with some kinds of longing for more work to be included in this volume, and as we urge our readers to note the incomplete "coverage" of topics and geopolitical "sites" in this volume, we simultaneously urge detaching from the violence of such spatial models, particularly the ones inherited from area studies and its own inheritance of imperialist investments. We also point to the limited understanding of transnationality as only manifest when multiple locales are addressed. It is our view that geopolitical analysis of disability cannot be done only by looking at "flows" and "undoing borders" without attending to *how* borders have participated in ideas about specific locations, as well as their tangled histories of transnational power struggles and interactions. This lengthy introduction serves partly as our effort to extend that critique.

Metaphors of Genealogies, Genealogies of Metaphors

Scholarship, as a privileged form of currency among intellectuals, is a site through which power is articulated in ways that deeply impact genealogies.[21] Scholarship's normative praxis traditionally involves notions of canon, inheritance, filiality, gatekeeping, citation, property, credit, kinship, and more. It is further structured by affects, such as paternalism, indebtedness, and "aboutness": a training of the intuitive life of the academy in which a given field is understood—implicitly or explicitly—to be about a specific set of possible objects, methods, individuals, and geopolitical areas. Aboutness enables a distinctly arboreal genealogy in that it cuts off transversal affinities and rejects rather than welcomes uncommon archives, unexpected coalitions, tangential conversations, and mixed methods. It rejects muted, but crucial, presences.

> **Sticky Note:** The notion of "aboutness" surfaces throughout this introduction. It is a concept from Kandice Chuh's essay "It's Not About Anything." Chuh writes, "I have for some time been attuned to my irritation with 'aboutness,' partly because of the regularity and normativity of the practices organized by and around it. . . . It seems to me that the determination of what something (a novel, a field of study, a lecture) is 'about' often is conducted as a way of avoiding engagement with difference, and especially with racialized difference. I'm pointing attention to how aboutness functions as an assessment of relevance, and within the racialized economy of academic knowledge (canonical knowledge reproducing whiteness continues to center the US academy and thus ensures that higher education maintain its long tradition of con-

tributing to the reproduction of social inequality), preserves the (racist) epistemologies of (neo)liberalism through a reproductive logic that is utterly unqueer."[22]

As disability studies attracts more readers, researchers, activists, students, and teachers, a narrow account of its history and status has been gaining ground. According to this narrative, the field initially formed in alliance with disability rights movements in the United Kingdom and the United States, became more intersectional in its engagement with race, class, gender, and sexuality, and finally grew increasingly diversified and global. This account is reliant on a particular set of metaphors: after "emerging," the field has finally "arrived"; the "second wave" of the field is "flourishing" or even giving way to a newer "third wave."

But this celebratory rhetoric obscures the unevenness of the field's growth, as well as the conditions that promote it. What effects does this rhetoric have on our thinking? How are our conceptualizations of disability studies—and thus of disability itself—bound up in or even bound by the frameworks we use to describe it? How do the concepts and frameworks we use to describe the field orient our thinking in some directions but not others, or align the field with some projects rather than others?

Although these kinds of questions are urgent, they are not new. Narrations, articulations, theorizations, and enactments of a differently centered disability studies have long been and continue to be developed among communities of scholars and activists, some of which have circulated widely, others of which have remained more closely grounded. All of this scholarship contains provocations, interventions, and insights pertinent to all of our work, and we are learning much from the resonances and frictions we have found in scholarship calling for "transnational disability studies," "global disability studies," "southern disability studies," and more.[23] Part of what feels important to remember here, in this discussion of genealogies and lineages, is that the namings of "disability studies" found in this scholarship includes vital histories and overviews of "the field," including an identification of key tenets and developments, but that field is often described quite differently than in readers and textbooks edited by academics in the United States. Quite simply, other ways of naming, describing, and teaching disability studies—keywords and timelines emerging from different and multiple centers and margins—exist.[24]

Thus, one of our motivations for this anthology is to make apparent, to problematize, to interrogate, question, trouble, and disrupt the scholarly habits of the field. To note not only the whiteness of the field but also the ways in which it both stays white and perpetuates whiteness. Informed by the work of transnational feminism and women of color feminism, we want to suggest that among those mechanisms of whiteness is not only this language of "field development" but also the assumption that "development" (and thus also growth, expansion, institutionalization, and so on) is what we are all working toward.

The wave habit is a habit of whiteness. We are arguing for an installation of new habits, ones that refuse the law of coherence in order to make more pathways for present and future work.

Naming the existence of a prior "first wave" of disability studies gives the field a history and legacy, suggesting a legitimacy conferred by years of struggle. The "first wave" then serves as a repository, a location in the past for those theories that we have moved beyond, that have outlasted their usefulness, that are no longer relevant. As Therí A. Pickens notes, "to reach backward for intellectual forebears and trace a clear line of thought" positions whatever "theory emerges as not only useful, but inevitable."[25] The wave metaphor also signals that the field has a future: if we are in the second wave now, surely the third (or fourth) wave is coming. The wave model thus positions scholarship as linear, as progressing neatly from one wave to the next, with each wave constituting separate and discrete lines of thought. One manifestation of this way of thinking is the still common assertion in white disability studies and activism that it is disability's turn in the spotlight, that it is time for disability studies now that "we've done race/ gender/sexuality." But as that example suggests, determining what counts as first or second wave, or which inquiries had to happen first and are now "over," is a political move, rife with assumptions about the field and its subjects of study. The wave model thus serves as a mechanism for canonizing white disability studies texts as foundational to whatever scholarship comes "next," insisting on the primacy of that scholarship (the "first wave") to more recent disability scholarship, even though the latter might be more attuned to work in ethnic studies, queer theory, or queer of color critique. As feminist theorists such as Michelle Rowley and Kimberly Springer have long noted, the wave metaphor is an assimilating logic, reserving legibility for those theories and movements framed in relation to white Western ideas and positions. It obscures the fact that theory outside of the white Anglo-American context, outside of white Anglophone imaginaries, has unfolded along different chronologies, temporalities, and taxonomies.[26]

But waves are not the only naturalistic metaphor to trouble, that trouble. Think of how trees have been drawn into the very discourses disability studies aims to resist: "Like a tree, eugenics draws its materials from many sources and organizes them into an harmonious entity," reads the caption on an infamous eugenic tract below a line-drawing of a large, sprawling tree. Sociology, anthropology, history, and biology constitute some of the roots of this eugenics tree, right alongside mental testing and anthropometry.[27] "The self-direction of human evolution," namely the upward thrust and spread of the tree, explicitly relies on disciplinary systems of knowledge-making. What crip work might we make of this investment in a single line of ownership going all the way back, much like the grab of universality? How do attempts to ground disability studies in disciplinary histories, to trace the lineages of our thoughts back to earlier sources, replicate this move to "draw materials from many sources and organize them into an harmonious entity"?

Feelings continue to swirl. If one is inspired to give "credit" where credit is due— one way to extend lines of recognition to genuine moments of inspiration and the people who made them possible—is it possible to disentangle gratitude from aligning with only and always genealogical gratitude? Is it enough to queer ancestry if the arboreal ancestry has been a violent heteropaternalism?

Even if genealogy can be revised to mean not only (an imagination of) arboreal descent but instead something having "no beginning and end" with "each point [a]s the center"—as in the videopoem in Natalia Duong's essay in this volume—or something even more coincidentally generative and unconnected to evolutionary time, it is still worth asking the questions: To what extent is one still functioning in a settler colonial and imperial model of attribution, property, and personhood? What does one do when facing genealogy as a mode of obligational aboutness, which necessarily constitutes those who can arbitrate? Is it possible to continue in the face of a genealogy that legitimizes defensive acts of violence on individuals whose very work or presence would defang that genealogy? How does one manage to enact a metaphysics of presence, rather than absence, in order to be recognized as "doing the work" to "advance" a field, a contravening subfield, or a cause of some kind? Must one disengage, and how? Can we also imagine undoing, relinquishing, shrinking, and unsettling the field—or certain aspects of it—as opposed to doing, acquiring, expanding, and occupying it? If crip genealogies rely on disconnect and incomprehensibility as much as connection, translatability, and persistence, then what kinds of metaphor enable us to think about transversality or about coincidental happenings that bubble up in different places? What imaginations would allow us to presume the presence of multilingual expressions?

Alternative metaphors can sometimes be ones that attempt to re-naturalize nature; a famous one is Deleuze and Guattari's metaphor of the rhizome, a spatialization (and to some degree temporalization) of thought that is multilineal, multidirectional, and multiple rather than binaristic, and horizontal rather than strictly vertical. Rhizomatic entities, such as some fungi, are said to operate in mutualistic ways rather than unidirectional feeding, which would seem to liberate a more toxic rendering of labor. The affective rehearsal is seen over and over again in an exchange in the classroom: "Well, but what if we look at it outside of a linear model of inheritance? What about a rhizome?" followed by smiles of pleasure and relief. But the question must be asked: Does anyone really know how all kinds of rhizomes grow, and do they all simply evacuate dominance? What does horizontality actually mean? Horizontality can also be a site of violence and encroachment; horizontality can imply discreteness as much as connection. The rhizome doesn't eliminate the possibility of single-source growth from iconic, dubious schematic origins, and it does not remove the fantasy of territorial growth from its fantasy of distribution of knowledge. Even the rhizome can be colonial.

And metaphors of waves, trees, and even rhizomes can be tools not only of white disability studies, but also of settler and imperial disability studies. Let's add the notion of *field* itself to the mix. In its reliance on developmental models of scholarship, "field" inscribes colonial temporalities and spatialities into our conceptions of scholarship. Lineages are claimed; scholars and texts are flagged as belonging (or not belonging) to the field; borders are demarcated; pioneers of the field are named and celebrated. The "field" begins to resemble a sovereign nation-state in which one needs to be qualified as a citizen for legitimacy and presence. Within such logics, growing, expanding, and incorporating more territory into the field are largely unquestioned goals; so, too, is the institutionalization of disability studies itself into departments, programs, centers; curricula and degree requirements; budgets and governance structures.

We have encouraged or been part of some of these moves ourselves, urging the field to move in new directions or participating in initiatives to seed disability studies across our universities; this very introduction could be read in that light. Institutionalization can help make our research practices, theoretical insights, and pedagogies legible to funders, or hiring committees, or reviewers and evaluators. But we also want to trouble the move to institutionalize, making plain that the two different definitions of institutionalization—integrating a field of study into the structure of the university and confining people into highly restricted and surveilled spaces—are not as fully distinct as one might imagine. Confining knowledge, separating it from the communities most affected by it; using institutional power to sort, label, regulate, and surveil: naming such habits, technologies, and practices helps surface the disciplining power of the institution. What might it tell us about "disability studies" that it simultaneously offers deep critiques of the practice of institutionalization even as it argues for its own institutionalization within the academy?

Yet our feeling is that we cannot simply reject academic spaces and scholarship as a whole, even as we disavow their historical roots and continued investment in legacy building, settler colonialism, and white supremacy. Yearning brought us to the academy and to disability studies, and yearning keeps us there: yearning for the love of and connection to kindred thinkers; for the joy found in teaching and creating intellectual work; for the possibility of shared rebellion and transgression, however small it is; and for the hopefulness of what academic spaces might allow us to explore. We remember, too, that oppression and privilege are not monolithic: institutional legitimacy has not always been made available to disability studies, even as many declare that disability studies has "arrived." Students have difficulty finding curricula that speak to their experiences and often meet resistance from faculty when they propose projects, readings, and methods informed by disability/disability studies. Instructors face gatekeeping at multiple scales: curriculum committees refuse to allow *crip* in course titles and descriptions; committees approve disability courses only as electives or supplements to the "core" program; and institutions keep disability studies scholars / disabled scholars in contingent positions, allowed in only as visitors or adjuncts to the scholarly community. Sick and disabled faculty, staff, and students continue to face access barriers at every level of the institution, with one of the most stubborn of those barriers being the presumption that these are personal (and personnel) problems rather than structural ones.[28] Most people who want to learn and practice disability studies have to find their place in conventional disciplines with rigid methodologies and canons that undergird ableism, racism, sexism, and imperialism by default. The establishment of degree-granting programs in disability studies has been slow, and job opportunities in disability studies are limited, often requiring faculty to identify other "homes" for the purposes of tenure and promotion, "homes" that may be ignorant of or even hostile to the work of disability studies. And the place of disability studies in academic institutions is made even more precarious when other interdisciplinary critical studies, such as critical ethnic studies and gender and women's studies, have been subject to mergers, reductions, and closures under the strategic divestment plans of universities.

As the four of us worked on this project, other metaphors (about epistemology, knowledge organization, communities, and oppressions) arose in our conversations. Grids: a regulated, measured layout of intersecting axes that may potentially have centers. Networks. Assemblages. Webs: with and without centers and margins. Frequencies? Might they make room for simultaneity and concurrence, or asynchrony and disconnect, without linear notions of succession, causality, lineage, and connectivity?[29] We also thought about metaphors for aquatic life: the life underneath the waves, the beings that do not survive after emerging above water. What is the signal when something smells fishy and when we are on the same wavelength? Digestion, indigestion, and ingestion also came up: the notion of being forced to ingest certain ideas, the notion of being digested into the field, feeling sick.

We wonder: What are radically different ways of building crip space within, around, or across academia without reinforcing normative criteria for credentials, degrees, evaluation, pedagogy, methodology, and genealogy? What makes possible subversive existences undetected by the radar of the bureaucratic university, and how can they become more radically and transformatively crip? Our universities' perpetuation of violence and their insatiable investments in white supremacy, capitalism, and imperialism urge us to continue pursuing certain studies precisely because they have been marginalized and discredited as irrelevant, unreasonable, unuseful, and unpractical. Use value has long been used as a cudgel against minoritized knowledges and the people who produce them, both valued only insofar as they serve racial capitalism. How can we, together, rethink what is valued as knowledge, or dislodge the institution from the work produced within it?

Never forget the knowledge that does not emerge to the sight of institutional knowledge management, that escapes its notice. The knowledge that has to be hidden for survival. Theory in the flesh.[30]

As part of our collective writing exercises, we each wrote short reflections on our own intellectual histories and genealogies, tracing the multiple and idiosyncratic paths that continue to inform our approaches to, understandings of, hopes for, and feelings about our investments in disability studies. In our conversations that followed, Mel shared a toad gesture, or "something about honoring and remembering what is here and has been here." Eunjung told the story of an "immigration bag" in which she carried books from Seoul to Chicago to study disability studies, a bag that had to be dragged through airports because its wheels stopped turning. What might we learn about crip genealogies in their moves? This question is partly one of citation practice and formatting: How do the structures and conventions of academic "style" assume that our scholarly influences are contained in—and limited to—texts? Can we think instead about recognizing the hold, the pull, the influence of objects or entities or feelings? In asking this question, in making room in citation practices for toads, gestures, bags and baggage, we affirm other ways to connect to crip that are not bound up with humanness, with the idea of a recognizable self, or stabilized as an expected positionality or vow. We feel resonances here between these kinds of intellectual moves and the tension between a relationally identifiable crip (like "a queer," perhaps) and the simultaneous desire for an incoherent sense of self unbound by that nominalization.

Claiming ancestors is hard, or rather, having claimed ancestors is hard (which is necessary for someone to write what ancestors they "have"). It requires, to me, turning to human ancestors implicitly (I know not everyone will take it this way), and perhaps also being human. It takes something that many folks don't quite have or necessarily even want. Ancestor is an essentially natalist, heterosexualist concept that to me can't be fully queered (maybe because it relies on generations implicitly— elders doesn't cause the same conniption), and so, fending with diaspora, queerness, my own adoption-rich family, inhumanness, I lose power rather than gain it. But I fully acknowledge: this is also about me, and how difficult it is to claim things, identities, lineages, groups, and the like.

Methodically Crip: More Crip Feelings

It is incumbent on those of us thinking about crip genealogies to address one means of mapping genealogy: through mappings of method; tracing how things are thought, how things are done. (As in, a mode of thinking is preserved because one can trace lines of thinking *in a particular way* through history.) How is thinking and theorizing done? What are its objects, and what is supposed to happen to those objects in the shifts of knowledge that constitute study? How is disability made use of as a meaningful category?

Sticky Note: As a collective of disabled authors with different access needs, our writing together has, of necessity, involved explicit attention to the process of writing: working across different modalities (writing both synchronously and asynchronously, blending typing with dictation, translating spoken ideas and stories into written sentences), different locations (meeting both online and in extended in-person writing sessions), and shifting temporalities (typing and thinking both fast and slow). Over time, we have learned how to write directly into each other's sentences, finishing each other's thoughts, sharing words and ideas and feelings. Writing collectively became a deeply speculative experience, a form of time travel, in which we always ended up in places we hadn't foreseen. Together.

We understand method as a kind of doing. And to the extent that one can refer to "a" method, it is a kind of package of doing, a script for action. At the same time, we note that a given method can also constitute an undoing. That is, method can easily work, against evidence, to undo what is already there: relation, coalition, possibility, care. (This is why something called "queer method" has developed, as a way to refuse the willed perceptions and exclusions of standard perspectives and lines of connection.) "Rigor"—the demand for a "rigorous" method—can thus double as violence as it undoes other relations than those canonized or already known to be consequential, linear, within reason.

Thus, the four of us found the method of our work always and necessarily informed not only by the scholarship that preceded us but also by the feelings that brought us to do this work, separately and together. That is to say: Articulating, naming, thinking through "crip genealogies" is not just a mode of *doing* but also a mode of *feeling*. The kind of work we are hoping to see, the methods and orientations and moves we want and desire, are both about doing and about feeling.

This work radiates out: we want to do "disability studies" (for lack of a better term at this moment) in particular ways, and we feel particular ways about that doing; we feel particular ways about other people's doing of disability studies and want to do things about their doings; we think that other people's doings of disability studies is also about their feelings; and we are frustrated (a feeling!) by being asked or expected to do disability studies in particular ways as a way of protecting other people's feelings about disability studies.

We want to acknowledge and learn from all of these feelings. One reason among many would be a recognition (a queer recognition, a feminist recognition) that scholarship affects us—scholarship is about incorporation, or an expectation of incorporation, and we have feelings about that (expectation of) incorporation.

I don't want to read those people because I don't have the digestive system to ingest those kinds of words.

Much of our work together on this volume required us to voice our feelings (gut feelings) about whom to read, about which words to take in. This crip genealogical project does therefore attend to "the politics of citation," but it recognizes that such politics is not merely about refusing canons and citing sources. It is also about recognizing that who and what we cite shifts us, changes us, feeds us, depletes us, isolates us, situates us, makes expectations on us. (And yes, our citation practice both determines who the "us" is and who that "us" becomes.)

Who are we becoming in relation to what we don't read, or in relation to those whom we turn away and turn away from? Turning toward, turning away, turning away from: all are meaningful.

We are thinking not only of recognizing and practicing feelings as a kind of method, but of attending to, paying attention to, how a method will be felt and by whom. That construction—how will X be felt—acknowledges that methodologies have effects (and affects) and pushes us toward being more responsible along those lines. It has the potential to trouble a move toward instrumentalism.

In this spirit, we offer you some of the feelings that guide our method:

Crankiness

X makes me cranky.
—JULIE/EUNJUNG/MEL/ALISON, often and repeatedly, at different moments of our work together, with the value of X shifting and changing.

Crankiness about the field, about experiences we have all had in the field, with people in the field, with descriptions of and orientations to and away from the field. Might crankiness be a crip method? What if the cranky feeling is a sentry? A way to feel navigation, a repulsion away from something about which we have to decide whether to tell it, "I don't want you, you have done wrong" first?

In naming our crankiness, we remember Audre Lorde's "The Uses of Anger." Anger and crankiness are not identical, yet much in that essay feels related to the feelings we expressed to each other under the name of crankiness: "I cannot hide my anger to spare you guilt, nor hurt feelings, nor answering anger; for to do so insults and trivializes all our efforts," Lorde writes. And later adds, "When we turn from anger we turn from insight, saying we will accept only the designs already known, deadly and safely familiar. I have tried to learn my anger's usefulness to me, as well as its limitations." Our method in this volume—the feelings we bring to this volume—led us away from the "designs already known," at once both deadly and safe.[31]

As four people thinking together, part of what makes us cranky is the drive to *complete*: the drive to turn disability into a kind of totalizing narrative ("master trope"), the drive to make "disability" always the central category that illuminates everything about all the other categories, the drive to have answers at the ready for all the questions we want to pose and with which we want to linger. The imperative to *do something* leaves unchallenged the notion that the only thing that matters is action, that one's impulse to act, to do, to answer, is a good one. One might do the wrong thing, but that can be fixed. There's a melding of doing and intention here, so that neither doing nor intending are questioned in and of themselves; both are often tools of ableist white supremacy. But/and we can therefore think of a methodological undoing as a move away from this assertion of completion, of closure, of successor narratives, of universality, of "application," of comprehension, of achievement, of intervention, of correction, of omniscience, of action.

NOTICE: **these are all words of white ableist productivity.**

Sticky Note: The idea of the master trope appears in a number of widely cited disability theory texts. It refers to the idea—one that troubles us, that we hope to trouble—that disability functions as a sort of guiding principle of oppression, that social hierarchies of all kinds are at root hierarchies of ability.

As much as crankiness is pointing outward, it is also entangled with our commitment to being where we are, the place where disability does not just appear in passing or in the "etc." Crankiness is yearning for more.

Obligation/disloyalty

The feeling of "having to" cite someone. The sense that certain people "have to" be cited for work to be legible as disability studies. The sense that we need to perform certain kinds of gratitude to those in the field who preceded us. Wanting to name names. Wanting to *not* name names.

Responsibility

To whom do we feel responsible?

Responsibility as method. Responsibility as accountability, as recognizing the people and stories we want to hold in this volume.

Responsibility as responsiveness. Responsiveness to the voices we want to center/amplify/lift, responsiveness to pervasive problems/injustices in the world at large as well as in the field.

Natalia Duong's essay in this book offers *dance* as one possible model for the kind of responsibility/responsiveness we feel and want to enact. "For in dance," Duong writes, "the weight exchange between bodies molds force into something to be received and traded rather than unidirectionally imposed. Each body is responsible, and enabled to respond. Perhaps the threat of unpredictability looms; however, it is mediated by the premise that every action is always already being received by another, new, consequent action."

Joy

Our love for each other is generative for our work. Feeling good about the work we know is happening out there and in this book, feeling good about the work because we feel good about the people, in this volume and elsewhere, doing the work. The four of us feeling good about each other, about coming to this work together.

Expansiveness

The feeling that so many possibilities for disability studies—for what the field can be and do—keep getting shut down because of narrow ideas of "what disability is," "what disability studies is," who gets to "be" disability studies and who gets to "speak for" disability studies. The feeling of expansiveness when those possibilities are welcomed and nourished instead of shut down.

When disability studies scholars expand our understanding of what constitutes disability politics, understanding that disability politics can be enacted by those who might never call their work disability activism or identify themselves as disabled, then we can begin to build a stronger understanding of how disability activism and anti-ableist thinking has occurred historically within a wide range of activist and community spaces, especially among racialized and other oppressed groups.
—SAMI SCHALK, in this volume

Complicity

The work of compiling this volume and cowriting this introduction has forced us to grapple intensely with how aligned with whiteness the field of disability studies is and has been.

I am part of this field too. I can't disavow my role in perpetuating its whiteness.

I am complicit not only in the field's whiteness, but also in the institution's (and the field's) ableism.

Desire

Are all "good" feelings ones that promote desire, or align desire? What are the dangers of desiring disability, as much as uttering those words can be, and promote, good feelings? Is it also hard to allow ourselves to do precisely and only what we desire, given the configurations of labor and power that position us and that provide an interpretive framework for our actions? In other words, does the formation of a network of desire *for* disability studies (both in the sense of *within* and in the sense of *what is being served*) make desire itself suspect? Or, as with any discourse of aboutness, does such a network of desire presume, require, and consolidate desirable centers and undesirable margins?

What is understood as "goodness" can be ambiguous between how a body feels and the value system that has told us what is good and what is bad. (Hence, the desirability for "bad subjects" among Foucauldians.) Forms of violation, whiteness, master moves, helping others, are made to feel good/desirable in ways that feel undeniable and verifiable in the body's experience of the feeling.

Lezlie Frye's contribution to this volume uses the phrase "desirable discord" to trouble a well-established narrative that treats the US-based disability rights movement as an extension or outgrowth of the Black civil rights movement. Here Frye aligns desire not with "feeling good" but with tension, contradiction, dissent. Desire becomes not an affirmation of what is already presumed good but a mechanism for opposing a narrative that, as Frye argues, both "maintains the whiteness of disability studies" and "haunts contemporary social justice movements predicated on coalition work." Might Frye's use of *desire* orient us away from desiring disability even as it moves us into the terrain of crip desire?

The Unnamable, Uncategorizable Feelings

Some feelings, like the pain in my back that I know is there but that I cannot quite feel, are not quite nameable: they require periphrastic language, or they simply make us feel "off." What of those?

"Yikes!" is another feeling!
—MEL

Nonalignment/disidentification

Developed by Latinx queer theorist José Esteban Muñoz, *disidentification* is a term now widely associated with queer method—a way of *doing* that acts both within and against available theoretical currents. Yet, as Sami Schalk points out in her essay "Coming to Claim Crip," disidentification is also a *feeling*: "I find myself, a minoritarian subject, disidentifying with disability studies, a minoritarian field of research, because although the field's resistance to the pathologization of non-normative bodies appeals to me as a nondisabled, fat, black, queer woman, the shortage of substantive race analysis within the field and the relatively minor attention given to issues of class and sexuality trouble me deeply and disallow me any direct Good Subject identification. . . . Despite the disjuncture I experience in the field as it currently exists, I still have a deeply personal, *emotional* affinity with disability studies scholar and activist communities."[32]

Using this term—disidentification—puts us in a queer genealogy that starts with Muñoz and flows through Schalk. To describe our relationship with disability studies as *disidentification* means coming to disability not via the usual paths but via queer of color critique and a Black feminist disability theorist. And yet, as Schalk herself reminds us, "Disidentification is not, however, the only useful minoritarian political strategy and may not be appropriate or effective for all subjects or situations." Disidentification is one way to structure the feelings that animate the crip genealogy we seek to trace, but there are others.

Another way to describe our relationship to or feelings about disability studies comes to us via—and note, enforcers of aboutness, this turn is neither unusual nor "flighty"—the Non-Aligned Movement of African and Asian countries in 1961, which understood nonalignment as an anti-Western/Northern, anti-imperialist, and interdependent practice of refusal.[33] We take both the gesture of nonalignment and the history of people turning away from Western/Northern dominance and toward each other as meaningful to this project. Nonalignment immediately calls to mind thoughts of bodies, minds, and bodyminds that don't "align." But rather than misalignment, which suggests a mistake that can perhaps be fixed, nonalignment points to a refusal of the norm altogether.

And yet: there are things, bodies, presences, entities, theories, orientations, movements, and gestures toward which or even with which we do want to align, no? Nor can we disavow the ways in which the word *align* associates with perfect matches and straight lines; the ways in which nonalignment itself associates with a Cold

War history in which a nation-state is forced to choose one of the two superpowers to survive or the countries who have created an alliance based on not aligning themselves with the superpowers. We note our ambivalence about nonalignment as a way of marking that no descriptor is without its potential problems and pitfalls.

What the term *nonalignment* gives us, via the history of the Non-Aligned Movement, is a way to speak to the need for affiliating differently, for developing practices of anticoloniality, collectivity, copresence, and touch that can make nonalignment with power possible. Here we invoke Jina B. Kim's proposal for a reading practice that looks for patterns and practices of care and support rather than assertions of resistance: "Rather than reading for evidence of self-ownership or resistance," Kim suggests reading "for relations of social, material, and prosthetic support—that is, the various means through which lives are enriched, enabled, and made possible."[34] Might this be a way of decentering not just disability studies but canon and field-defining work in general, as well as assumptions of geographic consolidation in the West? Can we think of ways of naming nonalignment and disidentification not as forms of resistance (because resistance implies against or to something, such that the orienting object remains *white disability studies*, for example), but as forms of support, care, and relation that instead *take no heed* of existing consolidations of majoritarian power?

There are years that ask questions and years that answer.
—ZORA NEALE HURSTON, *Their Eyes Were Watching God*

Incomplete

We have questions. In many cases, we are offering questions without offering answers. This, too, is a method: a way toward incompleteness. Centering questions can be a way of shifting energies: *not this but that*. Centering questions might also require shifts: we must think differently for a question to register as a question. One of our early readers noted that we are offering "questions and challenges in [our] introduction that the volume seems unable to address in some contexts." We agree! As the four of us worked together on this introduction, we succumbed more and more (individually at times and collectively at others) to bouts of concern that we were raising too many questions and challenges for which we did not have immediate answers. We found ourselves persistently thinking through what a question is asking of us, what it is asking us to do. We became more committed to the challenges even as adequate answers seemed increasingly elusive. Our questions—leaving them in some cases unanswered—are a crucial aspect of our intervention. We invite you to continue asking, thinking, and feeling—incompletely—with us.

Sticky Note: Lists appear throughout this introduction. Although we did not originally intend to keep these lists (they initially appeared only as drafts, as places in the text to return and expand our thinking), their repetition and recurrence as a form finally made us take notice. We came to see them not only as a form of access, allowing readers to pick up ideas in a different format, but also as a way of marking some of our influences. While Christopher Bell's "Modest Proposal" is widely cited for its argument about the whiteness of disability studies, a key element of its structure—the top ten list of "do nots"—is rarely mentioned. We felt its echoes as we created our own lists of how white disability studies works and of scholarly habits to avoid. But inspired, too, by the more recent work of Angel L. Miles, Akemi Nishida, and Anjali J. Forber-Pratt, we have also included lists of habits to cultivate: lists of feelings, orientations, and practices that help us think DS otherwise.

Can lists also resist completion? Is there something about their form that makes more allowance for incompleteness because other points can be added without requiring significant revision to what came before . . . or might lists, especially lists of do's and do not's, generate the dangerous expectation of prescriptions as a way out?

White Disability Studies and Access Exceptionalism

As many of us know, there are those who have left and continue to leave SDS [the Society for Disability Studies] and disability studies because they feel the effects of racism—they feel unsafe, even as others continue to name SDS as the only place they feel safe, feel home; multiple affective responses circulate. Part of being in relation is to acknowledge these affective ruptures and not paper over them; to not insist on a single story or experience of disability studies but rather to see all of these orientations and affects as part of the genealogy of disability studies, as determining what disability studies and its gatherings like SDS can become. Attention to affect and archive, in our view, might inform an alternate law of cohesion—one more fleshed out than a sheer

cynical application of "intersectionality" in which race can be "done." We know this is no panacea; and yet, race is not done, and no one has arrived. This might be a bad feeling worth working for.
—MEL AND ALISON, Critical Ethnic Studies Association Conference, 2013

We begin this section with questions not of "whether," but of "how." *How* does a mandate for coherence in disability studies serve whiteness, white supremacy, and forms of cultural or intellectual imperialism? *How* does the insistence on a single, coherent narrative of disability studies (and perhaps of disability itself) allow, above and beyond mere disciplinarity, the whitewashing of disability studies, of disability histories, and of histories of disability studies in classrooms and bibliography sections and beyond? *How* do we challenge the persistent impulse to deny the fact that disability has primarily been politicized in terms of whiteness (at least in white-dominant societies), which has fostered the proliferation of analogies between disability and nonwhite racial formations? *How* might we begin to recognize the capacious and generative possibilities of a disability studies that is less interested in "incorporating" race and more interested in engaging deeply with the fields, practices, and knowledges of critical race and ethnic studies and related areas? *How* do metaphors restrain and open up these endeavors?

Whiteness is constituted through various enactments of the power to declare that what is understood as *race* exists only in nonwhite bodies. If whiteness is exceptional to or "free of" racialization, it is thought to reveal the impact of disability more clearly, rather than showing how whiteness and figures of disability work together. "Single-issue politics"—say, accounts of disability that are thought "simpler" from the perspective of white narration—are actually masked intersections of privilege and oppression (white disabled people) that don't receive as much attention as marked intersections of minoritization or disadvantage (disabled people of color). One of the manifestations of this constitution is that whiteness confers on itself the sole ability, capacity, or right to talk about, comprehend, and define both whiteness/white people and "everyone else." Whiteness comes to function as consumption, incorporation, omniscience, omnipotence. Whiteness has a global currency (global white supremacy) in which white people hold the power to legitimize and evaluate someone or something's quality. Whiteness and light skin color as a currency is at work even in nonwhite majority nation-states that view nonwhite people as the default group of citizenship, yet still seek white approval of their sovereignty and performance. Whiteness has enabled access to material resources and cultural and identitarian representations as well as grievances and legal reparations.

And yet: as late capitalist austerity measures continue to threaten the survival of people with disabilities, many white disabled people seem to assume that white privilege and ableist precarity cannot coexist, as if living under one threat means you cannot simultaneously be protected from others. It is this refusal to acknowledge whiteness as a shield that allows one to separate disability-based oppression from other systems of oppression. By calling attention to these dynamics, we are not arguing for a denial or minimization of the measures that threaten the survival of disabled people, but rather for being more attentive to the differential effects and impacts of these threats.

Moreover, naming the whiteness of disability studies can be a way of effectively preserving that whiteness; to begin and end with a statement about dominance, as do opening disclaimers about limited authority on the basis of one's positioning as white—only to go on with a limited perspective of a white genealogy of scholarship—further obscures the work that has always been there, albeit ignored by a proprietary genealogy of whiteness. Are there not moments when we might best be served by assuming that the field has *not* always been already and only white, because it might push us to expand our notions of what counts as disability studies?

White disability studies, the term coined by Christopher Bell, has become a frequently invoked term, used to distinguish one's intellectual work from work that does not attend to whiteness (even when engaging with nonwhiteness). We note, then, the need to distinguish *white disability studies* from the claim that "disability studies is white." In an effort to take this distinction seriously, we have decided to examine "white disability studies" in an effort to provincialize it, to assert that white disability studies is not and never has been the only disability studies, to make plain that one can do disability studies without doing white disability studies.

Sticky Note: Chris Bell's essay was first published in the second edition of the *Disability Studies Reader* (edited by Lennard Davis, 2006). It was retitled in the third and fifth editions of the reader (2010, 2017), after Bell's death in 2009. The essay was omitted from the fourth edition (2013) when it was mistakenly thought that the essay's call was no longer needed.

"Introducing White Disability Studies: A Modest Proposal."
2nd edition, 2006

> "Is Disability Studies Actually White Disability Studies?" 3rd edition, 2010
>
> 4th edition, 2013
> "Is Disability Studies Actually White Disability Studies?" 5th edition, 2017

What are some of the attributes of white disability studies? We offer an incomplete list here, and we do so noting that the "moves" named below are ones in which we have participated; we are not seeking to claim our own innocence or disavow our own involvement in white disability studies.

—Aiming to have disability recognized as a valuable human difference (as a self-sufficient abstraction) without attending to how other forms of difference fundamentally reconfigure binaries of disability/ability and reshape human/nonhuman relations. Do we really want to use "human being" as the central mode of political thought, as if the human itself is "a natural organism"?[35] Or to deploy a sweeping register of "diversity" centralized around the human figure? Cripping can also mean recognizing nonhumanity as a posture and as an intervention.

—Instrumentalization. Disability scholars are often deeply attentive to the ways in which disabled people, positions, materials, and archives—as well as the enterprise of "crip theory"—have become instruments for others' theorizations and arguments. But in what ways have we as disability scholars participated in the instrumentalization of others' knowledge (and "other" knowledges)? Can we know in advance the difference between instrumentalism and mutual or complex engagement? How have we ("we" as a field, as well as "we" as the scholars who have put this anthology together) failed to be self-critical as regards our own desire to engage with other/different/"exotic" knowledges?[36]

—Rhetorical surveillance. In their theorization of a Black feminist disability studies framework, Moya Bailey and Izetta Autumn Mobley highlight issues of language and rhetoric as an urgent site of analysis, noting that "Black people are often singled out and critiqued for the use of ableist language" without more nuanced attention to the ways in which "Black cultural production is often rearranging the original meaning and use of words for specific anti-racist purposes."[37] Hershini Bhana Young's work similarly reveals the nuanced depictions of illness, disability, and "differential movement" present in African diasporic cultural production that are lost to scholars who refuse to engage with performances of disability by artists "without" disabilities. Indeed, an extensive archive of art and activism by disabled cultural workers of color has been excluded from analysis by disability scholars because the language it deploys to explore disability experience does not conform to that used by white disability activists.

—**Access washing**. Stacey Park Milbern warns us about *access washing*, when institutions and dominant groups "leverag[e] 'accessibility' as justification to harm communities of color and poor & working class communities," such as when counties in Georgia moved to close polling places in majority Black neighborhoods by claiming they were inaccessible to disabled voters.[38] Other examples include policies that increase gentrification and displacement; Milbern mentions a "city government implementing anti-homeless measures under the guise of making streets more accessible to people with disabilities, with no consideration that those most harmed by this—houseless community members losing access to public space without alternative safety nets— are people [with] disabilities themselves."[39] Laura Jaffee offers a transnational conceptualization of access washing, with a focus on US and Israeli settler colonialisms. She defines access washing as "rhetoric and practices that render visible and valuable to the state particular, relatively privileged (namely white, settler, straight, cis-male) disabled people while leaving unmoved a state structure premised on the production of disability injustice (in particular, through settler-colonialism and imperialism)."[40] Her concern resonates with Aimi Hamraie's interrogatory approach to access: access for whom, access to what?[41] Jaffee turns these questions to an event that provided "access" but violated the Palestinian-led movement for Boycott, Divestment, and Sanctions (BDS) against Israel. Access—as "indexed by the provision of ASL and CART—was a mechanism to recruit a larger audience to an event that normalized Israeli settler-colonialism and violated an international call for academic boycott by Palestinian people."[42]

Milbern and Jaffee's *access washing* often conspires with a practice we are calling *access exceptionalism,* or the prioritizing of access above all other dimensions of justice, thereby narrowing down what constitutes access itself.

—**Access exceptionalism: the use of access as a tool of exerting whiteness and severing disability access from broader social justice**. In discussing access exceptionalism, we are hoping to open a conversation about the ways in which (a dominant and dominating understanding of) "access" operates as a tool of whiteness and white supremacy. When "access" is understood in individualized ways, as something with which to comply, it frequently functions as a deployment of whiteness; conversely, access understood in this way can be deployed in service of white supremacy. Access washing is a prime example of such deployment of whiteness, by highlighting access provisions in a way that aids and hides injustice against nonwhite communities. Exceptionalizing access manifests in calling out what is *perceived* as access failure, particularly "failures" by people of color or others living at or aware of lives at the intersections. The idea that certain accommodations, often those institutionally funded, must first be implemented in a prioritized, efficient, and seamless way—above other measures that might allow for intersectional approaches and solidarities—enables aggressions against BIPOC as the easy target in grievances of access failures. In other words, in both access washing and access exceptionalism, access is used as a tool of violence against people of color.

The center I direct at Berkeley, the Center for the Study of Sexual Culture, was set to host Sami Schalk for a talk on the Black Panther Party's involvement in disability activism. As we prepared for the event, we set up disability access standards, including scent access, that are considered standard for disability studies events, but we added nourishing food as our own internal standard for providing for economically imperiled participants. This was in recognition of the undeniable fact that uc Berkeley has been rocked by dynamic and growing precarities: costs of living that have become unsustainable and labor practices that fob off questions of food, housing, and employment security to individuals ill equipped to manage.

Six days in advance we learned that on the day of Schalk's scheduled talk, a uc-wide one-day strike had been scheduled by the American Federation of State, County, and Municipal Employees (afscme), which at the uc includes 24,000 service workers, half of whom are Latinx and a supermajority of whom are people of color. They were being pushed out of what meager measures of security they had because the uc was looking to hire lower-wage private contractors in their stead. In solidarity with the strike, and understanding the entanglement of service work with occupational disability, as well as disability with poverty (though those "content" relations are not necessary to act on supporting workers of any kind), we immediately moved to find a location off campus. The Labor Center, already off the central campus, was itself counted as a strike location; we kept looking. Then I recalled a privately owned café that had once warmly welcomed my class when it sought an off-campus location when helicopters flew overhead during the campus's militarized, backpack-searching, gun-wielding defense of the free speech of alt-right speakers. It was owned by the Muslim brother of an important Berkeley scholar of Islamophobia. I contacted him about using the café as an alternative location; he asked about the content of the talk as what I imagined would be a protective measure for the café; he offered a low rental cost; and I decided that cssc would buy a generous amount of Middle Eastern food for attendees to increase our monetary gratitude.

There were so many ways in which this move "felt right," felt like solidarity, felt like a symbolically meaningful intervention in the congealing of race, class, nation, and disability in ways that facilitate harmful and life-threatening combinations of oppression. Only later did I realize, with a start, that there was no elevator to provide access from the event down the stairs to the bathroom. In a panic, we sent out a quick announcement that we were working out the details for access to the bathroom and would offer more information as soon as possible. We got immediate feedback. The center's only other staff, a wonderful graduate student researcher, told me that someone on the mailing list for the event had written an immediate response even before we sent out a relieved email an hour later that there was a ramp external to the café by which one could easily reenter at the bathroom level. The indignant, angry email read, *Shame on you! The BPP would never do this!*

I told the graduate student researcher I didn't want to know who it was, that this was a form of community that was painful to experience. I felt a moment of shame, but then I felt anger. I did want to know whether the student could identify the person as white, given the kind of relationship I had observed—remarkably consistent—between a certain form of hostile surveillance "on behalf of people of color" and whiteness. Indeed, she confirmed that the person was white. I still don't know who it is, and I can't bear to know. I had been steeled, in my introduction, to publicly say, "I'm just going to give your shame politics right back to you," if the person again came forward. This is wasted and harmful energy.

What kinds of access come first—the most institutional, the most templatic, the most "obvious" to those with established power (at the very least, that power endowed by whiteness, not necessarily class) within a community? What does it mean when someone with power—myself, as director of a unit nevertheless run on a shoestring—perceives and supports one institutionally suppressed form of access before the other, conventional one, in spite of my institutional and neoliberal training?

Needless to say, Schalk's story of the Black Panther Party was one with complexity and negotiation about disability—at the very least, it was not a story of "nevers."

Which bodies are made available for blaming and shaming for structural access failures, and which bodies are shielded from blame/shame? What are the ways in which calls for access or, especially, criticisms of inaccessibility, have been used to assert white privilege and dominance? Who surveils access perfection before any conversation about racism can occur? We are describing structures of privilege and affect that involve a kind of "muscularity" associated with white and Western settler supremacy.

Aimi Hamraie notes that the notion of barrier-free design—a core component of access—emerged from the US polio epidemic in the late 1940s, when "legible polio outbreaks in predominantly white communities led to the creation of new architectural and urban spaces, premised upon the right of (white) citizens to access public space"; the first access guidelines in the United States were developed on the campus of a university (the University of Illinois at Urbana-Champaign) where only 0.01 percent of students were African American. Hamraie thus concludes, reviewing this history, that barrier-free design as a measure of access comes into existence "against the backdrop of systemic racial exclusion and violence in the Jim Crow era."[43] An examination of the logic of "but for," deployed by well-resourced, well-positioned people with recourse to recognition, is telling: "but for this access barrier, I would be able to access the power, recognition, and resources afforded me and to which I am entitled by my white skin/citizenship/gender normativity."[44] Removing that one narrowly described access barrier thus becomes the apex of disability politics (and the point of origin extended metonymically from the individual to the entire disability movement, since *this* individual is a proper representation of that movement and entitled to take that role).

These access aggressions are also about the reassertion of economic dominance. The structure of a combined intersectional economic-ethnic privilege of "white people of modest means" is (ironically) taken to reassert a supremacy in relation to other intersectional positions. The need to prioritize access for white people of modest means—who have, moreover, earned the entitlement because it is they who "carry disability studies forward"—*before* imagining significant shifts in who does the scholarship, who can populate the conference, who can work in the university, or who can attend the meeting exemplifies an ableist quantification of access in which some kinds of access are just "too much": unreasonable not only under the law but also to the good disabled subject and well-meaning ally. Here we mean the "other kinds of access," those outside of the realm of ADA definability, including chemical sensitivity, often resulting from labor-related chemical injury, and economic access: we first ensure that those with ADA-recognized disabilities are served *before* ensuring that those from economically racially suppressed communities subject to environmental injustices have any opportunity for remedy or reparation, or access to affordable food, as if there are no overlaps between these groups, as if providing one type of access necessarily forecloses another—access as zero-sum game. Note that these entitlements are secured often by the very same people who will pronounce the interest of the field in "diversity and inclusion." And the emphasis on reinforcing via whiteness, rather than via broadening, access to such "resources" as land (redlining), buildings, conferences and events (scholarship, knowledge forms), and jobs (ADA) suggests a lurking stability to a history of the *settler* assertion of "whiteness as property," a phrase made vividly palpable by the legal scholar Cheryl Harris.[45] Whiteness functions as property, Harris demonstrates, and in so doing consolidates the legal imagination of property securely with whiteness. Understood as a particular lens on the securing and expansion of property, ownership, and capital, then, the fact that access exceptionalism bears essential marks of whiteness in the examples we observe should not be a surprise, but an expectation.

In conjunction with the above forms of prioritized *securing* of continued or increased access for some, there are both outwardly hostile and liberally mild forms of *refusal* for others. The hostile form marks particular bodies as too loud ("distracting"), as too "smelly"—such that inaccessibility becomes something that sticks to particular kinds of racialized (and classed, lending an irony to the "modesty" of the white bodies above) bodies. Those bodies, because they are racialized, can't by definition be disabled in the entitled sense above. At best, they can occupy incommensurable, unrecognizable, abject forms of debility and wrongness and thus fall outside of the anointed zone of rehabilitatability or reclaimability for disability pride. They can then in turn never have their own access needs or requests, can never face their own access barriers ("about disability" or otherwise) because they are by definition themselves inaccessible. The liberal form of refusal isn't a sheer "no," but is experienced as the effect of a "soft no," a shrug, "sorry, try next time," or the echo of a civil rights "wait, we will get to you if you wait," or "keep coming and maybe we'll consider you next time," when it's clear that this time has already foretold the structuring failure of that future. Hostile or liberal, the aggressive surveillance of these targeted (in every sense) accusations of inaccessibility is what allows for the larger structures of inaccessibility and exclusion (*including ableism*) to go unchallenged. Access as a tool of whiteness links to the facile marking of disability as diversity. The consolidation of a "charmed circle" (to use Gayle Rubin's term in a distinct, if overlapping, context) of access is directly linked to the removal, erasure, and whitewashing of all other histories and structures as either invisible or subordinate to this one.[46]

In sum: if we quantify access in certain preferential ways, not only will legal mechanisms like the ADA (and those recognized in its language) continue to mark (and limit) the horizon of our politics, but in addition, a continuous population of white disability studies scholars of modest (and perhaps increasing) means is guaranteed. It is possible then to understand how access can be used as a litmus test. If X movement/event doesn't meet a particular version of access, then it isn't worth engaging. A particular form of community is maintained *against* other forms of community-making, which renders the idea of disability community into a kind of selective lie. And yet, at the same time, intersectionality—the idea of living at multiple intersections on the "underside" of difference—can be used to shut down the conversation: if attention to racialized policing is rejected as legitimate disability studies, it's because the injury occurs at an intersection of race and disability that doesn't minimally and essentially include white disabled people of modest means. Access vigilance is thus also a mode of field-defining and boundary making, another iteration of "aboutness." Aboutness materializes in the regulation not only of what counts as "access" and inaccessibility, but of what counts as a legitimate access claim, of who is seen as able to make access claims.

We want disability studies to be a place for developing language that can help us navigate, challenge, and refuse this whole operation of access surveillance. Disability studies should be a site where access is constantly imagined and reimagined, with the goal of making access as radically comprehensive and transformational as possible—not one where compliance with the minimum standards of the ADA is "the best we can do" and therefore all we strive for and imagine. Puar (this volume) prompts such a transformational reimagining of access as she juxtaposes how the term is deployed by US disability rights advocates against its meanings in Palestine: "For example," she writes, "bus and taxis drivers are conjuring constantly shifting 'access maps' through monitoring and assessing impromptu checkpoints, divided highways, the violence of the Israeli occupation forces, the presence of settlers, increasing drone surveillance, unexplained road closures, protest and mass demonstrations, spontaneous parades that welcome released prisoners, and house demolitions." Access in this framing, of necessity, "foregrounds the intermeshed matrices of settler colonialism, empire, and infrastructures of disablement that cut across otherwise self-apparent geographies."

Is *access exceptionalism* the right term for the aggression we describe? What do we seek instead? We reproduce here notes from our discussion of this question. We want to keep thinking.

Access exceptionalism
Access supremacy
Supreme access
Access as the most important marker
. . . for the largest minority / the most marginalized
. . . the last/next/best/most timely group

Unsettling access
Collective access[47]
Access intimacy[48]
Radical collective care
Access indignation
Access crankiness
Access incompleteness
Access animacies
Access reciprocity
Access grace
Access solidarity

Access exceptionalism hinders relationality and solidarity; it renders all encounters antagonistic and competitive. In fall 2019, Leah Lakshmi Piepzna-Samarasinha joined an academic conference by Zoom for access reasons. The conference had allowed this only after insisting Zoom was too complicated, if anyone Zoomed then everyone would, and the Hilton conference center might not "be able to handle" Zoom. Pre-pandemic, video conference technologies frequently used by disabled organizers were regularly disallowed by institutions as a mode of access. Technology problems occurred at the event, and the chair of the panel apologized repeatedly, to the degree that Piepzna-Samarasinha began to feel unwelcome, as if their participation had become a burden. In stark contrast, they explain, disabled BIPOC communities anticipate technological glitches and access gaps, providing room for mistakes. When access is approached from this position, such that failures become opportunities for improvisation and negotiation, then access can be a means toward greater solidarity, community, and relationality, rather than obligation, competition, and requirement.

We navigate clashing access needs every day in our lives and relationships. We find cooperative solutions that could never be dreamed in abled imaginations.
—STACY PARK MILBERN

Transnational Disability Studies

Deciding to have a separate section on "the transnational" and "transnational disability studies" was not a decision we made lightly, and it remains a source of unease and ambivalence. Structurally, it continues the very habits we are trying to undo, namely assuming (always unmarked) English-language, US-based, white disability studies to be universally applicable while "transnational disability studies" is an optional add-on, a "new" or "emerging" subfield, a specialty relevant only in particular (always marked) contexts and only to particular (always marked) locales, people, and "populations," the subject of special issues and conference tracks tangential to the larger trajectories of the field.[49] "Disability studies" thereby remains intact and fully separable from this Other mode of engagement, such that the decision not to engage with transnational scholarship (or not to contextualize one's own scholarship in a specific location) is itself removed from analysis. But if we are really attempting to provincialize "disability studies"—perhaps in part by naming it not only as white, but also as Anglophone, Western, Global Northern, US/Canadian/British, or settler—then why have a separate section titled "Transnational"?

Our concern is that, in much white/Anglophone/Western/imperial/settler colonial/Northern disability studies, race and nation are often discussed in tandem, with little attempt to disentangle them or map their relations, while ethnicity and nationality disappear. As a result, "whiteness" often comes to stand in for all forms of domination, flattening out and obfuscating other forms of power and other genealogies of dominance. Scholars can then condemn "white disability studies" without attending to the ways in which their/our analyses continue to assume unmarked geopolitically situated perspectives. The field's origins in British and US empires are obscured.

Disabled communities in the United States—and especially "the disabled community" in the United States—continue to be described in and through nationalist imaginations. For example, in another iteration of the "but for" dynamic, the experience of being disabled in an ableist society is sometimes framed as the denial of citizenship to an otherwise entitled citizen. Although there are systematic barriers to exercising citizenship for people with disabilities, framing citizenship as the prerequisite for rights suggests that our concerns about these barriers are limited only to those people with legal citizenship status rather than advocating for the removal of those barriers for all. Similarly, anti-ableist politics is sometimes expressed in nationalist terms, as a yearning for a disability nation or for a recognition of disability as a kind of ethnicity. Think, for example, of one of the iconic photographs of the US disability rights movement, in which a disability activist holds a flag of the United States, but with the stars aligned in the shape of a person in a wheelchair. This realignment signals a clear desire for disabled people (or those disabled people legible within the wheelchair icon) to have access to the power of the nation-state, for a disabled person (or at least a wheelchair user) to be imaginable as the national subject. But the easy reliance on and recourse to the flag, especially its symbology of incorporated Indigenous territories into one unified shape, reveals how an imagination of the disabled community as a nation with a shared culture and identity depends on the logics of settler colonialism: territorial access, renaming and replacing, and possession.[50]

How might we instead acknowledge the harms and hazards of collapsing disability into nationality and cultural difference, while still recognizing the desire for collectivity? Can we forge transnational connections that are not simply subsumed under nationalism? Or that aren't subsumed under post- and anticolonial resistances that also wield hegemonic and majoritarian violence, erasing internal hierarchies, dissents, differences, and disabilities? What would such spaces of connection—beyond meetings at the UN and international conference gatherings—look, feel, sound, or smell like? What do we want to see instead of these assumptions that collectivity can take only the form of the nation with its attendant exclusions based on citizenship and documented belonging?

Simple references to ableist nationalism and imperialism too often fail to address the sub-empires that serve as brokers or mediators between empires and sites of exploitation. Sub-empires seek approval from white empires and aspire to join their rank by expanding the network of military and capitalist alliances to maximize their expropriation and exploitation. Moreover, provincializing white/imperial/settler colonial/Western/Northern disability studies—a move against unmarked generalization and monopolization of disability studies— also requires grounding it within the spaces of Anglo-American settler colonial societies. Doing so allows for the exploration of ableism's entanglements not only with racism but also with settler colonialism. It is problematic, in other words, to challenge the whiteness of disability studies without reckoning with the field's own attachments to settler futurities (e.g., claiming access only for disabled citizens within the US nation-state, assuming access to territory is an uncomplicated good and national right, and so on).[51] Finally, we are interested in tracking the field's global traffic outward from the imperial centers and the effects of its passing as universal. Decentering and dethroning whiteness is not necessarily sufficient in challenging this selective geopolitical positioning, especially if "whiteness" and "nonwhiteness" are defined solely through US/UK histories and parameters.

What are the costs to our theories and practices of not questioning nation-states as independent self-contained entities, as if they can exist outside of transnational rubrics of relationality? Or, to put it differently, as scholars continue to flesh out methodologies of disability studies and disability studies as methodology, what does a transnational disability studies make possible, what does it do, what are its orientations and investments and aims? What does an attention to disability as more than mere consequence of injustice reveal about settler colonialism, neocolonialism, ethnicism, racism, colorism, caste-ism, and nationalism? These oppressions have taken shape differently and interactively through transnational constructions of global white abledness as a normative entity and its supplemental hierarchies, materialities, and ideological manifestations—all of which are typically unmarked. Being more precise about the historical contexts of cooperations and oppositions, rather than blurring them all together or listing them in one breath, will also help us theorize disability differently, without simplifying and homogenizing the meanings of disabled lives. What has happened/happens/will happen to bodies that have become/are becoming/will become disabled? What do disabled lives need? What do disabled people desire?

By forwarding these questions we are calling for critiques that are reciprocal and multidirectional. For flows of knowledge that do not move only one way. For theories that do not announce themselves as universally applicable. For scholarship that does not presume a concept that works in one context will work in another context without attending to the specificities of its emergence. For scholars who recognize that permission to speak in universal terms has always only been available to some. Tari Young-Jung Na's essay in this volume offers a generative model here, as it focuses explicitly on questions that have emerged in South Korean contexts (and as it recognizes that "South Korean contexts" are not monolithic, singular, or contained within national borders) in order to respond to urgent questions of deinstitutionalization but without aiming to write a generalized and generalizable theory. Yet, through its careful and grounded accounting, Na's analysis does have resonance in other locations in its expansive conceptualization of what constitutes an institutionalized life. Offering other transnational approaches, Natalia Duong's and Sony Coráñez Bolton's essays generate knowledge from (by grounding their stories in) colonial legacies that are ongoing. By transposing and defamiliarizing disability critiques of individual rights and supercrips, they generate, in Bolton's terms, transnational understandings of disability "located within the historical and cultural detritus of the colonial." In so doing, they offer potential responses to Adria L. Imada's question, "How might decolonization projects differ in their relationship to disability?"[52]

Is "transnational disability studies" just an Anglophone knowledge-making project about the rest of the world? Or is the question of cripping transnationalism even the right question, given how *crip* is considered to be grounded in US theoretical practices, activist histories, and knowledge bases? How does a research project on disability in the United States with a transnational approach differ from one that doesn't engage with transnational dynamics in which the United States richly partakes? Transnationality seems to recognize borders and nations as products of geopolitical histories and their differences, yet it aims not to be delimited by borders in other ways, such as understanding the connectedness of human and nonhuman beings. It also aims to acknowledge the struggles to have borders and nationhood be recognized by international entities.

Academic conferences—and not only in the United States and United Kingdom—are commonly held exclusively in English, a commonplace that often goes unmarked, unmentioned, and assumed. Associations, their boards, and their members too often overlook the discrepancy between their desire for "more" international participants or "more" transnational analysis and their unquestioned assumption that everything will transpire in English. Other languages may be "welcomed," but only through participants' own labor, networks, and time, or cordoned off into "social" time. (Sign language users will undoubtedly recognize these logics at work in the hegemony of spoken and written language in the academy, as conferences and institutions continue to provide access to sign language only on a limited basis, if at all.)

Please note: English and ASL are the two main languages in use at SDS; if you have other language needs, please indicate such on your proposal and we will try to assist you in obtaining accommodations.
—CALL FOR PAPERS, Society for Disability Studies, "Cosmopolitan? Disability Studies Crips the City," 2008

The Society for Disability Studies' Call for Papers for its conference in New York City demonstrated some awareness of the linguistic dominance of English and ASL and the existence of other language needs. But such recognition can often serve only to defend and reinforce current linguistic practices. In its willingness to assist "in obtaining accommodations," SDS transferred its responsibility to the individual, obscuring what assistance could be provided and the process by which accommodations could be obtained. Yet we also want to highlight how its acknowledgment of language needs as a whole, without separating them based on proximity to disability, suggests a broader crip praxis of language justice, potentially allowing multiple linguistic practices to coexist alongside other kinds of access practices.

To enable broad transnational communications and to share scholarship and activist works, translation services are necessary. Thinking of translation services as different from sign language interpreter services ignores the entanglement of the colonial erasure of spoken languages with the ableist/audist erasure of sign languages. Centuries of linguistic imperialism establishing and enforcing the hegemony of English have made most scholars who work only in English fully unaware of scholarship and activism that don't take place in English or the other frequently translated European languages. This unawareness and assumed absence allows these scholars to claim an idea as unprecedented and prevents them from noticing the wide range of anti-ableist consciousness and practices already / long happening outside of the privileged locations of the United States/North/West. And this unawareness often means that when such scholars do engage other locations, they recognize only violence, or debilitation, or ableism, and not the histories, presents, and futures of resistance, art, lifeways, and cultures. It is also worth noting in this context that, to the extent it is provided at all, ASL too can occupy a hegemonic position; rarely do academic conferences in the United States offer interpreters for signed languages other than ASL. It too is assumed that ASL would be accessible by and to all deaf people and sign users.[53] This linguistic hegemony intersects with temporal and phonetic norms that marginalize nonverbal communication, machine- and people-assisted communication, speech marked as slow or fast, consecutive interpretation, and nondominant accents.

What we are suggesting, then, is that conversations about accessibility be broadened to include language and communication. We know that we are moving far beyond what counts as a "disability" in legal terms (and we are most definitely not arguing that an inability or unwillingness to use English constitutes a disability), but that is precisely our point. The unquestioned assumption of access to English testifies to a continued reliance on rights- and accommodation-based models in the United States, even among many of those scholars who critique them. Falling back on the legal requirements of the ADA without addressing their limitations, or adhering to the constraints disability law places on what an entity must legally provide, means that we can bracket language use as not a disability issue and therefore not an access issue. Deaf people's advocacy of sign language as a minority language similarly supports such an expansion of access to include language use; they are calling for solidarity among minority language users in a given space without legally privileging one over the other.

At the same time, by framing language translation as a matter of access, we don't mean to suggest that it is not also, simultaneously, a matter of language justice; we aren't arguing for a universalizing model of access in which all issues of inequity or redistribution become subsumed under notions of accessibility, thereby flattening out the workings of imperial, settler disability studies. Language justice, as an approach, might also make room for thinking through the ramifications of communications among people who have no common empirical and cultural backgrounds; translation alone cannot ensure access in a context of unquestioned ethnocentrism.[54]

We also want to recognize the vibrant and ongoing activisms that can occur at the site of such failures, the meaningful engagements that can happen via the improvised efforts that often animate transnational encounters. When a request for language accommodation is denied, for example, improvised peer-to-peer access labor often erupts. How, then, have moments of incomplete access often led to moments of connection? These moments too are an important part of crip genealogies. What kinds of access experiences, including access failures, catalyze or animate relationality? And can those failures be responded to with creativity, solidarity, and grace? What possibilities for unexpected connection are lost when we focus solely on institutionally funded professional services and architectural designs? If "the revolution will not be funded," as INCITE! teaches us, what (re)imaginations are required in building access animacies into the revolutionary work?[55] Through improvisation and direct engagement, access animacies both generate and rely on the embodied knowledges that are crucial to broader changes.

Transnational disability studies exceeds the parameters set for it, and we yearn for the radical (or potential) possibilities of encounters toward transnational crip/disability solidarity, frictions, and transnational crip/disability activism. At the same time, it is not about simply transcending borders and passing through borderlands, but also about dwelling in historical specificities and spaces demarcated by the complex imperial effects of fragmentations and partitionings.

Sticky Note: In many parts of this introduction, pronouns fail us. "I" am writing to myself, reminding myself to do and think differently, while "you" are writing to me, modeling other ways of thinking. "We" are a collective of writers, thinkers, and editors, but "we" are not equally positioned or equally situated in relation to the questions and the lists that appear in this introduction. Some of "our" work ("my" work) could be used to illustrate the DO NOT list below, while other ones of "us" are creating scholarship and engaging in world-making practices that move the DOs into being. Or, to put it differently: what violences and erasures am "I" enacting by writing as if "my" understanding of these insights predated learning them from "you"?

Habits of thinking, ways of orienting, practices of feeling, modes of practice to undo—or, what we don't want to do:

- Proceeding from the assumption that "we" are bringing or teaching or extending disability rights to the Global South, thereby
  - obscuring the leadership of those in the Global South in international disability rights work within the human rights frame (e.g., the UN Convention on the Rights of Persons with Disabilities)
  - ignoring how "disability rights" has different histories, functions, roles, and meanings in different contexts
  - re-centering the Global North even in/under the cover of "transnational analysis"
- Treating transnational analysis as only a matter of addition and citation, such that the fundamental arguments and assumptions of the work and the field remain unchanged by the work newly incorporated (digested, consumed, commodified) into it
- Reducing transnational scholarship to a matter of mere "coverage": adding scholars from X location (or who "work on" Y region) to the panel/keynote/anthology without considering the geopolitics of the panel/keynote/anthology itself
- Treating *intersectional analysis* and *transnational analysis* as fully separate and separable, or as if "intersectional" is for work "within" the United States and "transnational" for work "outside" of it[56]

- "Translating" the work of disability activists and theorists in the Global South into concepts and terms created by theorists working in Anglophone white settler societies
  - as if the ideas are the "same"
  - as if the ideas, though the same, nonetheless work better once expressed in terms more familiar to Anglophone white settler scholars
- Using the work of disability activists and scholars from the Global South while simultaneously apologizing for their "failure" to use the "correct" terminology, to cite the "canonical" sources, to engage in "properly rigorous" modes of scholarship; and for their "awkward" syntax, which is then attributed to their use of English as a "second language"
- Cordoning "transnational analysis" away from accounts of disability, debility, and ableism *within* imperial centers
- Reifying the value of independent living without considering the transnational labor market that makes independent living available
- Defining "ablenationalism" only as a subset of ableism, obscuring the complicity of disability studies and disability rights in nationalist projects and imaginaries
- Conflating colonialism, settler colonialism, and imperialism (and transnational, postcolonial, and decolonial)
- Approaching transnational disability studies as a mode of extraction, mining the intellectual/political/emotional/material labor of disability activists and scholars in the Global South for "answers" to problems in the Global North
  - as if that work were important only to the extent that it addresses questions generated in and by those in the Global North, or
  - as if that work can only shape the trajectory of the field if first vetted by scholars working in English from within the Global North
- Celebrating "disability pride" without considering questions of health care access, vulnerability to violence, labor conditions, or different cultural connotations of pride and the individual
  - more: mandating forms and expressions of "disability pride" easily recognizable as such by white Western observers
  - more: illustrating or defining "disability pride" only through recourse to the nation
  - more: using "disability pride" as an indication of a movement's health, stage of development, consciousness, criticality, or progress

- as if health, developmental stages, and progress were not themselves concepts deeply steeped in ableism (and targets of disability critique in other contexts)
- Urging the activists and scholars in the Global North to "pay attention" to the realities of disabled people in the Global South in the name of human rights and to save them from their cultural and social practices that are considered "barbaric" and "unthinkable in the Global North," thereby concealing the violence and abuse of disabled people in the Global North
- Using colonialism and imperialism as metaphors for white disability experiences in the ableist world, unaware of and disinterested in the histories, experiences, and existence of disabled people under colonial and imperial exploitation
- Assuming disability justice, critical race theories, critical ethnic studies, queer theories, and feminist theories have the same or similar resonances across all locations
- Assuming the same disability yields the same experiences and solidarity across the globe
- Supporting and participating in imperialist knowledge projects that legitimize and justify military intervention and economic exploitation in the name of disability inclusion, accessibility, human rights, or humanitarianism

Habits of thinking, ways of orienting, practices of feeling, modes of practice we want to cultivate—or, what we want to do:

This list is a lot harder to write and that means something . . .

- Acknowledging complicity in settler colonialism, imperialism, nationalism, war, and state violence
  ◦ examining how "disability rights" is deployed in the service of these phenomena
  ◦ recognizing that having a disability or identifying as disabled does not necessarily preclude support for these phenomena
- Reading, rereading, seeking, translating, and citing disability activists and scholars who are not based in the United States/Canada/United Kingdom and/or whose work wasn't originally written in English
- Recognizing that models of disability activism grounded in liberal principles (such as independence, individuality, and rights) are not the only models and do not have universal meanings and manifestations

- Understanding differences as sites of and for ingenuity and creativity
- Being open to terms, feelings, orientations, and priorities that you/I/ we don't recognize, or feel comfortable with, or feel hailed by
- Sharing frameworks and strategies of disability resistance that arise in different places
- Collaborating to formulate transnational agendas and solidarities, even if they may not have "disability" at the forefront of their agenda
- Acknowledging the presence of power dynamics and the persistence of assumptions about gender, culture, nation, religion, race, ethnicity, and indigeneity in inter- and intranational encounters
- Attending to geopolitics and entangled histories
  ◦ recognizing that international policies and diplomatic practices shape disabled people's lives
  ◦ exploring the parts of the world too often skipped over or homogenized, those occupying an ambiguous middle between the Global North and the Global South (e.g., Northeast Asia, Eastern Europe, Middle East)
- Holding governments, militaries, corporations, and supranational organizations in the Global North accountable for systematic injustice, exploitation, and violence
- Seeking feedback from the people who are studied and portrayed in the research, bringing the research back to them, and making it accessible and accountable to all
- Attending to the effects of maps, photos, and journalistic descriptions of scenes that are unfamiliar to targeted readers
- Critically engaging with representations of disability that are presented as and assumed to "be" signs of suffering and that give no attention to strategies of survival, resistance, and solidarity
- Being equally critical of disability representations that romanticize conditions of community with no acknowledgment of structural hierarchies and conflicts.

We note that everything in this section is much more easily said than done. For example, as we revised this introduction, we frequently found ourselves asking whether we had cited robustly enough from beyond the US academy, and the answer was always an emphatic no. How then might we resist the temptation of attempting to remedy the limitations of our analysis through mere strategic citation? What does it reveal about the concept of "the transnational" that many of the "transnational disability scholars" recommended to us—and that we ourselves have recommended to others—have PhDs from and/or jobs at US, Canadian, Australian, or UK institutions? Is it possible to ever fully know the difference between citing amply and citing tokenistically?

We keep these lists open, incomplete, and ongoing; we continue to ask questions.

Although these two lists are not the only ones contained in this introduction or even in this volume, we are uneasy about our turn to the form in this particular section. We know that even as lists can make content accessible and declarative (lists are how some of us think), they can also reduce, freeze, and leap. The genre of the list has played a prominent role in global disability studies scholarship, which often features long litanies of "realities"—implicitly and explicitly contrasted to "theories"—such as war, displacement, malnutrition, detention and incarceration, environmental degradation, and absent or inadequate resources. These descriptions are frequently accompanied by statistics broken down by nation-states or regions. All of this data is necessary and vital, and too little of it has been recognized or addressed by white imperial disability studies. Yet when offered in the form of lists—without careful explanations of historical and geopolitical intricacies, without reference to the multiple analyses generated from *within* those contexts—then those lists serve to simplify entire nations and regions. Lists often fail to convey internal hierarchies and differences; they obscure the stories of community, pleasure, relationality, and creativity that exist alongside and beyond suffering, loss, and survival. They can serve the colonial project by offering imagery of the "rampant sufferings in the third-world" that need to be alleviated by external intervention. All the nuances, textures, desires, experiences, imaginations, and resistances that emerge from disability and illness experiences disappear in those "sobering" realities of "war-torn" countries filled with suffering and wounded bodies. Transnational feminist scholars have long criticized this materializing trope of the Third World that fuels the very white saviorism that produces and justifies further (disabling and debilitating) "interventions." Details about the material conditions of the Global South can serve to conceal and abstract as much as they reveal.

Overview of the Book

The essays collected in this volume do not all accumulate to a singular argument about the field; their authors do not share a single relationship to it. Just as we committed to incompleteness in the introduction, we did not strive to select essays that would tell a singular narrative or that would collectively add up to a "complete" perspective. At the same time, the contributors to the volume do share an interest in the overlapping themes and ideas described here. Authors take up related questions, draw on the same sources, use similar words. We hope you will find the resonances and gaps within and across texts illuminating in thinking through your own crip genealogies.

Another point of generative friction among the essays is the question of style, or the recognition of different audiences. Many of the pieces anticipate readers familiar with debates within academic disability studies, while others are more closely conversant with the work of disability activists or scholars immersed in other fields. Some authors lean heavily into the terminological and methodological habits of their disciplines and areas of study, and some have chosen to write more broadly, to share a conversation, or to tell stories. We hesitate to use the language of accessibility, marking some chapters as more accessible or readable than others, because such attributions often mark deep assumptions about inside/outside and academic/activist; they can also be used to reify narrow understandings of neurodiversity, neuroqueerness, communication, and cognition. A mandate to write "accessibly"—especially if the histories, contexts, and meanings of "accessible writing" are left unspoken or unexplored—can serve as yet another taken-for-granted expectation that serves to mark some texts as inappropriate, or incorrect, or unworthy, thereby further constraining the kinds of voices present in the academy. Given that any one kind of writing is never accessible to all, we welcomed writers with varying degrees of, approaches to, and modes of accessibility to find their readers, leaving open questions of what constitutes an accessible text (accessible to whom? accessible for what?). To put it differently: some chapters will speak more directly, or more clearly, or more urgently, to you than others, but part of the work of this volume is to trouble the suggestion that we can know in advance (not to mention claim on your behalf) which chapters those are. Texts become accessible and inaccessible to various readers—and writers—in unexpected ways, ways not limited to one's location in (or distance from) the academy or one's experiential and cultural knowledges.[57]

Rather than attempt to represent all possible subject positions and experiences of marginalization, the volume overall includes an effort to lend particular specificity to the modes of disability attendant to Asian and Asian American lives, particularly given a legacy of the racialization of Asians as subject to, or people of, illness and disease.[58] Several chapters thus focus on the experiences of Asian subjects living with illnesses and disabilities (produced) under capitalist, colonial, and imperial dominations.

Part I, **Mobilization and Coalition**, examines how disability justice activists move and work in concert with other social justice projects. **Tari Young-Jung Na** explores how the deinstitutionalization movement in South Korea can offer a radical vision for liberation. From a postcolonial perspective, Na reconsiders the problem of institutionalization, which became full-fledged in South Korean society with the birth of the modern state, searching for an epistemology of deinstitutionalization at the intersections of the disability liberation movement, feminist movement, and queer movement in South Korea. **Lezlie Frye** traces the legacy of US disability rights through and against Black civil rights and Black power. Combining close readings of interviews, ephemera, and activist and scholarly articles and monographs, Frye critically reorients the presumed origins of this social movement, focusing instead on the racial dimensions of the political trajectory it has pursued. Through conversation, **Stacey Park Milbern and Leah Lakshmi Piepzna-Samarasinha** discuss what they call "crip doulaship," or the process of coming into disabled identity and awareness through caring, mentoring, and modeling community relationships. The crip lineages they outline, which include forms of relation such as "being closer to the dead than the living," attune to the particularities of QTBIPOC lives and histories, allow for grief and longing, and assert the primary importance of intersectional forms of liberation. **Jasbir K. Puar** outlines the different issues that arise when studying disability in the Global South, suggesting that a diversification of critical disability studies winds up reinforcing the US boundaries of the field, while relegating southern disability studies as an Other that gestures toward a transnational and global frame.

Part II, **Crip Ecologies and Senses**, considers crip environments. **Natalia Duong** examines how dance can articulate a different relational experience of disability. She highlights an ethics of care and kinship through her analysis of the dancefilm *Rhizophora,* which disrupts the trope of other documentary portrayals of Agent Orange by depicting a community of people who come together through their relationship with disability. **Suzanne Bost** stages a dialogue between posthumanist theory and the writings of Aurora Levins Morales, a Latina feminist whose recent works examine the social and environmental dimensions of chronic illness and disability. Bost proposes an other-than-humanist approach to disability ethics that is not derived from the lineages of Western thought. **Magda García** elaborates how the cultural worker and zinester Noemi Martinez has expansively contributed to discussions of queerness, sexuality, and illness over the course of two decades. Her essay focuses on Martinez's *South Texas Experience Zine Project* (2005) and *South Texas Experience: Love Letters* (2015), which present a sensual and affective encounter and confrontation with the geopolitical location that is South Texas and its colonial markings.

Part III, **Genealogies**, considers what it means to refuse concepts of lineal descent. **Faith Njahîra Wangarî** narrates the process of growing into disability and learning to trust her body. In telling her story, she shows that there are no neat lines; we can honor the experiences, the people, and the places without seeking hierarchical and professional validations of any form. **Kateřina Kolářová** turns to the postsocialist geopolitical and temporal context of Eastern Europe, and specifically to Czechoslovakia/Czech Republic, as a location that bears witness to the complex and complicated transnational translations of disability theory. She thinks with the cinematographic oeuvre of Wiktor Grodecki, a US-based Polish émigré who was drawn back to Eastern Europe in the mid-1990s by the subject of MSM sex work. **Sami Schalk** argues that the Black Panther Party's material and ideological solidarity with 504 activists can be read as a genealogical precursor to disability justice today. By connecting concepts in disability justice to the BPP, Schalk argues that disability studies must not only expand our understanding of what constitutes disability politics today, but also what constituted disability politics in the past, especially within Black and other oppressed populations.

Part IV, **Institutional Undoing**, broadly rejects assimilatory urges toward institutional coherency, recognizing the implicit violences they comprise. **James Kyung-Jin Lee** explores the characteristics of recent Asian American illness memoirs, such as Paul Kalanithi's *When Breath Becomes Air*, evidencing, cynically, "a new structure of feeling in watching model minorities get sick and sometimes die." He ultimately arrives at the possibility of unique, iconoclastic Asian American memoir, rejecting the contiguity of model minoritarianism and all it engenders. **Sony Coráñez Bolton** recuperates the figure of the "Filipina supercrip," reading mestizo Filipino author José Reyes's *Novela de la Vida Real* (1930) to catalogue the ways that representations of illness, impairment, and disability are aligned to consolidate the power of an elite literary culture through the rehabilitation of Filipino Indigenous subjects. **Mel Y. Chen** considers the widespread unmarked of racialized disability within the bounds of the university, and the ways that it takes an integral part in a broad, emergent counterforce, not necessarily intellected or composed, that Chen calls "agitation." Chen explores a recent installation by Australian-Badtjala artist Fiona Foley in relation to what Snaza and Singh call the necessary potency of "educational undergrowth," showing that agitations work across the physical-mental divide and move against the disciplining forces of entangled educational, security, and medical systems.[59]

Conclusion

Although this introduction focuses on the promises and failures of disability studies and crip theory, we have each spent most if not all of our academic careers in feminist/women's/gender/sexuality studies departments and programs in the United States, and everything that we say here has been influenced by those locations. In marking that trace, we mean to acknowledge our intellectual, political, and psychic ties to feminist, queer, and trans scholarship and activism, particularly queer of color critique, transnational feminism, and women of color feminisms. But we also want to acknowledge the ableism of some of that work, and to underscore that many of the critiques detailed above have also been and continue to be directed to feminist and queer scholarship and activism (we have learned much from those critiques). Or, to put it differently, part of the work of crip genealogies is to read the oppressive and liberatory practices of one field in relation to others, rather than simply determining one field as better or worse than another. Disability studies, in other words, is not a singularly oppressive field any more than disability is a singularly oppressed condition.

Although those two attributions—disability studies as most oppressive, disabled people as most oppressed—seem to run counter to each other, they both share a removal of disability from larger historical contexts, an assumption that the problem of disability/disability studies can be discussed in isolation. But as the COVID-19 pandemic continues to unfold and decimate, it is ever more vital to write against these removals and not just in terms of white/nonwhite dyads. The conjunction of anti-Black racism, ableism, and sanism in the extrajudicial murders of Black men, women, nonbinary folks, and children (adding to the judicial forms of death and slow death within the prison industrial complex); the marking of sick, disabled, and old people, of people confined in institutions, and/or of Black, Indigenous, Pacific Islander, and Latinx people as "high-risk" and therefore inevitable or acceptable losses to COVID-19; the cynical use of "preexisting conditions" as a cover for the deadly effects of policing and a racially and economically stratified health-care system; the insistence on "reopening" economies on the backs of low-income service workers, most of whom are immigrants and/or people of color; the attacks on Asian people as presumptively sick *and* contagious, which makes impossible to imagine the vulnerabilities faced by certain intersectionalities within the disaggregated API populace: all of these must be viewed as integral rather than incidental to the questions we pose around crip genealogies.

We began writing together, in various forms and to different ends, in 2013; some of that writing appears here. During the intervening years, and especially in the time period when work on this collection began in earnest, different configurations of us have experienced intensifications of illness, changing relationships to mental and cognitive disabilities (and diagnoses), "high-risk" pregnancy, inadequate and discriminatory health care, cancer and other "scares," pain and fatigue of unknown etiology, illnesses and deaths of family members, shifting work accommodations and access failures, along with the stress of keeping pace with changing policy in the universities where we do much of our work. These experiences of ableism and healthism are also entangled with racism, sexism, homophobia, transphobia, and anti-immigrant vitriol, and occurred both beyond and within the borders of the universities where we nevertheless have a limited if precious form of security of employment. Continuing to learn about the workings of these forces, and in particular making sense of them in collaboration, lent fire to this project, and also gave us opportunities to find new forms of wisdom, fury, peace, and dedication. If it's obvious that our experiences have not been the "same," what is critically important in this context is that there have been resonances across and through them: temporal, embodied, emotional, intellectual, and political, the navigation of which potentiates, as we understand it, crip being. In the midst of these lives, and in sharing them, we have drawn great sustenance from each other and from doing this work together. Perhaps we could even say that the crip time of curating and assembling this project had to do with love as much as any hardship. All of this is part of our crip genealogies.

So, too, are you.

NOTES

1   Mimi Khúc has developed a pedagogy of "unwellness" that "starts with the radical recognition that we are all differentially unwell." Khúc explains, "I not only teach about unwellness—mental health, race+racism, structural violence—I teach with the assumption that we are all shaped by structural unwellness and that the purpose of the classroom space is to learn the contours of that unwellness and discover how to live through it." https://www.mimikhuc.com/teaching.

2   Hamraie, "Mapping Access," 461.

3   Yergeau, *Authoring Autism*, 84.

4   Kim, "Disability in an Age of Fascism," 267.

5   Piepzna-Samarasinha also mentions "disabled queer Black and brown writers and activists" Stacey Park Milbern, Aurora Levins Morales, and Billie Rain as integral to this work. Piepzna-Samarasinha, *Care Work*, 15.

6   Sins Invalid, "What Is Disability Justice?," in *Skin, Tooth, and Bone*, 15. This chapter was adapted from Patty Berne's 2015 essay, "Disability Justice: A Working Draft."

7   Sins Invalid, "What Is Disability Justice?," 15.

8   Sins Invalid, "What Is Disability Justice?," 10. This kind of appropriative move is all too common in the academy, as many feminists of color have long noted. The Cite Black Women project, for example, arose out of a frustration with the erasure of Black women's voices and a claiming of their ideas by (white, male) others without appropriation or acknowledgment. Sins Invalid and Cite Black Women are both, in different ways, challenging the extractive approach of the academy to the intellectual labor of BIPOC activists and scholars. https://www.citeblackwomencollective .org/.

9   The move to use *crip* and *queer* interchangeably can point to important coalitional impulses within crip and queer activism and theory. However, it can also—as Ellen Samuels notes in a different context—risk reifying single-issue politics: "What we risk losing sight of when we substitute one term for the other in our analytical framework is the necessary evolution of those frameworks beyond a single-term approach." Samuels, "Critical Divides," 65.

10 Lisa Hix, "Interview with Leroy Moore."

11 Kim, "Toward a Crip-of-Color Critique"; Erevelles, "Crippin' Jim Crow"; Ben-Moshe, *Decarcerating Disability*, 28.

12 Erevelles, "Crippin' Jim Crow," 81. Erevelles notes that her analysis builds on that of Robert McRuer; consult his *Crip Theory*, 65–70.

13 For example, consult Saldaña-Portillo, "Violence of Citizenship," 1–21.

14 For example, consult Aciksoz, *Sacrificial Limbs*.

15 With thanks to Hershini Bhana Young for the notion of "cripplers."

16 Sins Invalid, *Skin, Tooth, and Bone*; consult also Clare, *Brilliant Imperfection*; and Stacey Park Milbern and Leah Lakshmi Piepzna-Samarasinha, "Crip Lineages, Crip Futures: A Conversation," in this volume.

17 Cohen, "Punks, Bulldaggers, and Welfare Queens," 479.

18 Cohen, "Punks, Bulldaggers, and Welfare Queens," 479.

19 Ahmed, *Queer Phenomenology*, 121.

20 Macharia, "On Being Area-Studied," 184.

21 Alexander, *Pedagogies of Crossing*.

22 Chuh, "It's Not about Anything," 127.

23 Consult, for example, Nguyen, "Critical Disability Studies," 2–25. Nguyen and the Decolonial Disability Studies Collective center an "alternative body of knowledge, theory, and praxis that aims to unsettle hegemonic forms of knowledge production in Western disability studies."

24 Journals such as *Disability in the Global South* and the new *Indian Journal of Critical Disability Studies* offer deep dives into more expansive disability studies, but we are thinking especially here of recent anthologies and the important work their introductions and tables of contents do in framing the field. Consult, for example, edited volumes by Falola and Hamel, *Disability in Africa*; Soldatic and Johnson, *Global Perspectives on Disability Activism*; Chappell and de Beer, *Diverse Voices*; and Grech and Soldatic, *Disability in the Global South*. For an earlier influential collection, consult Parekh's "Intersecting Gender and Disability Perspectives."

25 Pickens, "Blue Blackness, Black Blueness," 95.

26 Rowley, "The Idea of Ancestry"; Springer, "Third Wave Black Feminism?" Springer's text feels especially important to highlight here, given that one of her critiques of feminist texts that rely on wave metaphors is that they fail to account for disability.

27 https://www.wisconsinhistory.org/Records/Image/IM101667.

28 All of these are means by which academic institutions, as Moya Bailey reminds us, "play a critical role in the exacerbation and creation of disability and delimiting of life." Bailey, "Ethics of Pace," 288 (cf. Bailey 2017).

29 We are thinking alongside José Esteban Muñoz here, and his evocation of "the receptors we use to hear each other and the frequencies on which certain subalterns speak and are heard or, more importantly, felt." Muñoz, "Feeling Brown, Feeling Down," 677.

30 Cherríe Moraga and Gloria Anzaldúa define a "theory in the flesh" as "one where the physical realities of our lives—our skin color, the land or concrete we grew up on, our sexual longings—all fuse to create a politic born out of necessity." *This Bridge Called My Back*, 19.

31 Lorde, *Sister Outsider*, 130, 131.

32 Schalk, "Coming to Claim Crip," np (emphasis added).

33 Established in 1961, the Non-Aligned Movement arose out of the 1955 Bandung (Indonesia) Conference, where Asian and African states refused to align with imperial powers and formed an independent Third World alliance focused on peace and disarmament, economic development, and social justice. Prashad, *Darker Nations*. For a theorization of Indigenous practices of refusal, consult, for example, Simpson, "On Ethnographic Refusal," 67–80.

34 Kim, "Toward a Crip-of-Color Critique."

35 Consult Wynter, "'No Humans Involved.'"

36 Pickens, *Black Madness :: Mad Blackness*.

37 Bailey and Mobley, "Work in the Intersections," 30.

38 Milbern, "Notes on 'Access Washing.'" Also consult National Disability Rights Network, "Blocking the Ballot Box: Ending Misuse of the ADA to Close Polling Places," 2020, https://www.ndrn.org/resource/blocking-the-ballot-box/.

39 Milbern, "Notes on 'Access Washing.'"

40 Laura Jaffee, "Access Washing," 15.

41 Hamraie, *Building Access*.

42 Jaffee, "Access Washing," 15–16.

43 Hamraie, *Building Access*, 72.

44 Kimberlé Crenshaw writes about the implicit grounding of white femaleness in the "doctrinal conceptualization of sex discrimination. For white women, claiming sex discrimination is simply a statement that *but for* gender, they would not have been disadvantaged." "Demarginalizing the Intersection of Race and Sex," 144 (emphasis added).

45 Harris, "Whiteness as Property," 1707–91.

46 Rubin, "Thinking Sex."

47 Mia Mingus, "Reflections on an Opening: Disability Justice and Creating Collective Access in Detroit," *Leaving Evidence* (blog), August 23, 2010, https://

leavingevidence.wordpress.com/2010/08/23/reflections-on-an-opening-disability
-justice-and-creating-collective-access-in-detroit/.

48 Mia Mingus, "Access Intimacy, Interdependence and Disability Justice," *Leaving Evidence* (blog), April 12, 2017, https://leavingevidence.wordpress.com/2017/04/12 /access-intimacy-interdependence-and-disability-justice/.

49 For those scholars tempted to assume that transnational perspectives on or approaches to disability are "new" or part of "the next wave" of disability studies, it might be helpful to remember that disability activists around the world have spent decades building transnational collaborations in order to pressure governments to enact policies and legislations upholding the human rights of disabled people.

50 Laura Jaffee and Kelsey John importantly state, "Indigenous struggles for national sovereignty challenge the uncritically assumed desirability of access/inclusion and suggest that decolonial disability justice necessitates that Indigenous peoples' land ought to be inaccessible to or non-inclusive of (disabled and nondisabled) settlers." "Disabling Bodies of/and Land," 1418.

51 For a range of analyses of ableism in relation to settler colonialism, including attention to the deep relations between bodies and lands, consult Larkin-Gilmore, Callow, and Burch, "Indigeneity and Disability."

52 Imada, "Decolonial Disability Studies?"

53 Other sign languages in use in North America include BASL (Black American Sign Language), LSM (Lengua de Señas Mexicana), and LSQ (Langue des signes québécoise).

54 Sins Invalid's recent articulation of language justice as integral to disability justice marks a similar concern, noting that "language justice isn't *just* about access" but also requires a commitment to "flatten hierarchies." Sins Invalid, "La justicia de lenguaje."

55 INCITE!, *The Revolution Will Not Be Funded.*

56 Jennifer C. Nash challenges this kind of bifurcation in her careful exploration of the rifts, ruptures, and possibilities of Black feminist theory. Nash, *Black Feminism Reimagined.*

57 Our thinking about the importance of naming access practices and specifying how they affect one's scholarship has been informed by a wide range of disability studies scholars and disability activists and cultural workers, many of whom are cited here. As Lydia X. Z. Brown notes, questions of style are never only or purely stylistic: "Forced conformity to arbitrary standards of 'better' language usage has a violent and oppressive history, especially targeting poor people, those for whom English is not a first language, cognitively disabled people, and uneducated people (which is often related to class, race, and disability)" ("A Note on Process," ix). For another generative example of such an access statement, one that recognizes financial cost and lack of library access as forms of inaccessibility, consult Burch, *Committed.*

58 For additional theorizations of illness, disability, and Asian America, consult James Kyung-Jin Lee's special issue of *Amerasia,* "The State of Illness and Disability in Asian America"; Lee's *Pedagogies of Woundedness*; Mimi Khúc's curation of "Open in Emergency: A Special Issue on Asian American Mental Health," *Asian American Literary Review*; as well as the work of The Asian Americans with Disabilities Initia-

tive, https://www.aadinitiative.org/. There is extensive scholarship on disability in Asian contexts, including a continued and necessary caution against homogenizing approaches that create a monolithic "Asia" (or, for that matter, "South Asia," "East Asia," and so on). As Fiona Kumari Campbell explains, for example, "South Asian disability studies is not a monolith of equal partnerships; instead, there is the dominance of a regionalised Indian disability studies and relatively little disability studies research and conceptual development produced in other countries, especially in English, such as in Bhutan, the Maldives and Sri Lanka." Campbell, "Indian Contributions," 23.

59   Snaza and Singh, "Introduction," 1.

Part I
MOBILIZATION AND COALITION

1. INSTITUTIONALIZATION, GENDER/SEXUALITY OPPRESSION, AND INCARCERATION WITHOUT WALLS IN SOUTH KOREA

Toward a More Radical Politics of the Deinstitutionalization Movement

TARI YOUNG-JUNG NA

TRANSLATED BY YOO-SUK KIM

In this chapter, I reflect on whether the disability rights movement currently underway in South Korean society, or, more specifically, the deinstitutionalization movement, can constitute more radical politics for the liberation of minorities. In particular, in order to raise the problem of gender/sexuality oppression caused by institutionalization and to reveal the voices of people who have been excluded and isolated socially due to gender/sexuality oppression, including those of "people living with HIV/AIDS" (PLWHA), I pose questions on the ways in which the deinstitutionalization movement must proceed. These questions are very urgently placed before me and my colleagues, who live as activists participating in the disability liberation movement, feminist movement, and queer movement.

Becoming active in earnest in the 2000s, the independent living (IL) movement for people with disabilities in South Korea continued into the deinstitutionalization movement, whose key arguments were the self-determination and social integration of people with disabilities.[1] Through the powerful and tenacious struggles of the disability rights movement, social perceptions of independent living and deinstitutionalization of people with disabilities have changed, and these issues, becoming mainstream to a certain extent, have been accepted by social welfare experts and government agencies. However, the transformation of claims that previously resounded in the streets into the language of law and policy simultaneously produces beings and spheres outside the law. Now, the value and orientation of deinstitutionalization have come to reveal profound differences, depending on whether the subject speaking of them is the government or the movement. For example, whereas the social integration aimed at by the disability liberation movement is for the eradication of isolation and exclusion, the social integration presented by the government as a disability policy is the demand that people with disabilities assimilate into mainstream society.

The key concepts of the IL movement in North America and Northern Europe were presented as "self-determination, consumerism, and advocacy," and the need for deinstitutionalization was presented with the goal of social integration.[2] The movement took on the "characteristic of intermixing human rights and a service-centered management model."[3] Though the IL movement in the West ideologically started with resistance against professionalism and with the determination of life according to the positions and needs of people with disabilities, it gradually became mainstream policy and came to be closely linked to an emphasis that people with disabilities were purchasers and users of social welfare services. This resonates with the neoliberal principle that rights can be possessed as commodities and that the allocation of rights differs according to one's purchasing power. Scholars who, in opposition to such disability rights movements and policies, criticized the normalization model and consumerism stressed broader social transformation instead.

The methodology of the American IL movement began to be concretized in South Korea from the end of the 1990s onward. Initiating exchange with the Japanese IL movement for people with disabilities, which had been deeply influenced by the United States, South Korea's disability rights movement actively embraced the methodology of the IL movement implemented in Japan. The Korea-Japan Seminar on Practicing Independent Living was held in Seoul in 1998, the Japanese movement invited four South Korean leaders with disabilities in 1999 and provided IL training, and, with support from the Japan Council on Independent Living Centers, IL centers were established in Seoul and Gwangju in 2000, for the first time in South Korea.[4] With the South Korean government's pilot support for their operation, IL centers embarked on the path to legalization starting in 2005. Subsequently, the grounds for the installation of IL centers on the district (gu) level nationwide were established through legalization, and the government's support of budgets began.

The ideology and direction of the IL movement for people with disabilities, "imported" and applied at the end of the 1990s, had profound influence on the disability rights movement in South Korea and served as a significant reference regarding ideas of what constituted "rights" and the ways in which services were to be designed as well. In addition, undergoing the Asian financial crisis (1997) at the time, South Korea received relief loans from the International Monetary Fund, US government, and Wall Street according to the neoliberal principles of the Washington Consensus.[5] During the process of the economic crisis, social welfare services in spheres such as childcare and caregiving finally came to establish the "voucher" system, which saw the objects of services as consumers/clients.[6] Concepts such as choices according to one's abilities, consumer rights, and normalization encompassed by the paradigm of the IL movement tallied well with this voucher system.

From the position of activists who have been leading the IL movement as a part of the disability liberation movement, such conditions have been disconcerting. They perceive the danger that the demands for rights of the disability rights movement—with the slogan "[There's to be] nothing about us without us" confronting the power of expert groups—will be reduced to the right merely to be consumers, to pay the price for services directly or be subsumed under mainstream norms that hitherto have isolated and excluded people with disabilities. Consequently, fellow activists and I have engaged in struggles for antidiscrimination and social justice, participating not only in the disability rights movement that critically intervenes in values surrounding normalization and consumerism alike and pursues social change based on Marxism but also in the feminist movement and the queer movement.

The Moon Jae-in administration has declared "inclusive nation" as its principle of national governance.[7] The Moon Jae-In administration's policy on the independent living of people with disabilities likewise has been arranged under this principle. However, the reality, where, in fact, neoliberal values are stressed, consists of detailed moments at which agencies implementing IL policies are evaluated by the state. For example, as for people with disabilities who are the beneficiaries of deinstitutionalization support policies, those already equipped with the ability to live independently are selected because selection is linked to performance indicators. In addition, some of the IL centers implement projects promoting heterosexual dating and marriage or, in trying to emphasize people's self-reliance, use promotional phrases that describe disabilities negatively as well.[8] The possibility for the deinstitutionalization movement to develop into a movement seeking radical change depends on how the limitations of the bureaucratic system and heteropatriarchal ableism can be surmounted.

Meanwhile, critical reflections on the movement and policies regarding deinstitutionalization are linked to examinations of points at which gender/sexuality oppression and oppression due to institutionalization intersect in a complex manner. Institutions have locked in particular groups, yet how can those who have been forced to live in de facto isolation outside such institutions

FIGURE 1.1. On April 27, 2006, the Solidarity against Disability Discrimination (Preparatory Committee) sponsored a struggle in which more than fifty people with severe disabilities crossed the Hangang Bridge at their respective paces, demanding the institutionalization of the activity assistant system. As a result of the six-hour-long struggle, three participants became exhausted and were taken to the hospital in an ambulance. Courtesy n_m.

participate in the deinstitutionalization movement? Answers to this question will become possible when we direct our attention to the structures that have deprived queer people, PLWHA, and sex workers of places where their lives can unfold as well as to "normality," that have branded them with sexual stigmas, and that have enforced their "incarceration without walls." I raise questions about the contexts and genealogies through which the ideologies of both the IL movement and the deinstitutionalization movement have been created and the circumstances under which these movements have been understood in South Korea. I seek to expand the deinstitutionalization movement into a movement for the liberation of nonnormative beings in society. The failure hitherto to analyze thoroughly and to challenge the effects of the ideologies of consumerism and "normality" on human rights and rights, people with disabilities, racialized and ethnicized minorities, queer people, and violators of sexual norms/labor norms seeking to reject normative temporality has caused their exclusion from being the subjects of rights. Moreover, the deinstitutionalization movement has consciously or unconsciously disregarded such agendas.

The effects of colonization cannot be limited to the transmission and establishment of imperialist rule through individual national systems alone. Unless the ideology of the IL movement is also committed to transnational solidarity based on grassroots organizations, only the needs and arguments of those occupying mainstream positions in so-called advanced nations are transmitted selectively. Most of the new policies created in South Korea are justified based on precedents in "advanced" countries, and the national and mainstream accomplishments of "advanced" states are already in tune with the dominant order such as neoliberalism.

What does it mean to think of and to implement the deinstitutionalization movement from a postcolonial perspective? I examine the histories of detention and incarceration in institutions that have been implemented in South Korean society as a main means of oppression and domination. In the process, the history of people with disabilities cannot be singled out. This is because people who have led institutionalized lives, those who have been placed in institutions for people with disabilities, are not limited to people with disabilities registered in the Act on Welfare of Persons with Disabilities or those who have identified themselves as people with disabilities.[9] The task of agitating the boundaries of identity will, I hope, decentralize the discourse of rights created by the First World and challenge the system where rights are allocated in accordance with identities approved by state power. In addition, there are people who, though not physically placed in residential institutions and detention facilities, have been forced to lead institutionalized lives while living in so-called local communities. The lives of PLWHA and women living in red-light districts teach the deinstitutionalization movement about the ways in which sexual stigmas have created incarceration without walls. In addition, strategies of resistance will become valid if and when the methods and contents of the ways that sexual stigmas have operated are identified concretely through historical and cultural analyses and reconstructed based more on the reality.

New Understandings of the Genealogies of Crip

Going beyond stating that institutionalization is oppressive and engaging in a deinstitutionalization movement, it is necessary to ask how the histories of people with disabilities and incapacitated beings, who have been detained and incarcerated in institutions in South Korean society because they are considered "seditious," "useless," and "abnormal," can be remembered and genealogized.[10] This is a task not of accepting the history of the IL movement as an imported movement and an ideology of "advanced" nations but of linking oppressions based on exclusion and isolation—which have been imposed ever since the beginning of the Republic of Korea (1948) following Japanese colonial domination (1910–45), the liberation (1945), and national division into northern and southern Koreas (1945)—to crip resistance and solidarity, as well as to the movement for independent living for people with disabilities in response to that oppression.

In South Korea's history, both the Omura Immigration Detention Center (present-day Omura Immigration Center) in Japan, created during the occupation of southern Korea by the United States Army Military Government in Korea (1945–48), and the residential facilities on Sorokdo, established during the Japanese colonial era to isolate Hansen's disease patients, can be seen as the starting points of the problem of institutionalization.[11]

Installed in 1950 in Nagasaki Prefecture in Japan, the Omura Immigration Detention Center detained Korean stowaways who had received deportation orders for violations of Japan's Immigration Control and Refugee Recognition Act up to the 1970s and thus was dubbed the Auschwitz of Japan by Korean residents in Japan.[12] Seung-ki Cha points out that, immediately after its defeat in World War II, Japan forced Koreans violating its territory and laws to go through the Omura Immigration Detention Center before deporting them to southern Korea, occupied by the US Army. He explains that not only so-called stowaways—including Koreans who had either crossed over to mainland Japan without authorization following Japan's defeat in the war or returned to the Korean Peninsula but gone back to Japan—but also Korean residents in

Japan who had violated Japanese laws had to be deported from Japanese territory through this "illegal entrant detention center." In addition, Cha posits that the Omura Immigration Detention Center "was expected to protect [the Japanese people] safely by excluding aliens, above all, from Japan's labor, hygiene, and public security."[13] If prisons create a virtual image of a society in which violence is governed by law by isolating "criminals," he argues, detention centers create a virtual image of a protected community by isolating and excluding elements who may cause racial (ethnic), labor, political, or ideological unrest.[14] Simultaneously, the Omura Immigration Detention Center had the effect of firmly establishing the borders of the state of Japan and of constructing ethnic Koreans, who had crossed over because of the impact of colonial rule and for socioeconomic reasons, as "lawbreakers." As "one of the technical apparatuses that replaced the history of the colonial empire and its responsibilities with the problem of 'eliminating criminals,'" the Omura Immigration Detention Center is positioned in the genealogy of racial and ethnic discrimination against and hatred for Korean residents in Japan that continue to this day.[15]

Since the Japanese colonial era, Hansen's disease patients in (South) Korea have been placed mainly in the Sorokdo Rehabilitation Center. Human rights violations against the affected people ranged from the forced worship at Shinto shrines that took place during the Japanese colonial period to the forced isolation, forced internment, forced labor, forced sterilization and abortion surgeries, hunger, and cadaver dissections that continued even after the liberation. Jae-hyeong Gim points out that vagrants with "leprosy" became symbols threatening modernization and health.[16] Here, "vagrancy" and "leprosy" were perceived as identical threats to society. Jung-Gie Choi points out that, during the Japanese colonial period, the colonial government mobilized administrative power across the territory both based on the perception that society must be protected from the socially pathological phenomenon of Hansen's disease patients and in the name of urban "beautification projects." At the time, the goal was not to treat the patients but to prevent the transmission of the disease and to protect society. Consequently, to hunt down patients, the colonial government adopted the method of categorical inspections and crackdowns across the colony through the use of the police and administrative officials, and when affected people were discovered in this process, they were immediately sent to and forcibly interned on Sorokdo.[17] Following the liberation, the South Korean government continued to maintain the policy of isolating patients. Patients with particular diseases such as Hansen's disease and AIDS are isolated regardless of medical needs and are criminalized based on the ways in which crip bodies are governed.

Under military regimes from the 1960s onward, as represented by the Park Chung-hee regime (1963–79), how would patterns of institutionalization have changed as the population began to be understood scientifically and life and rights began to be rearranged actively for economic development? Ministry of Home Affairs Directive No. 410 was an administrative order regarding "the reporting, regulation, detention, protection, return of vagrants to hometowns, and follow-up management," announced by the South Korean government on December 15, 1975, under the Yusin (Restoration) system, which had forcibly dissolved the National Assembly (South Korean legislature). This directive provided a strong foundation for judging and detaining certain beings as "vagrants." A vagrant detention center established in Busan based on Ministry of Home Affairs Directive No. 410, Brothers Home, operated from 1975 to 1987.

Represented by Brothers Home, "vagrant protection facilities" demonstrate the effective operation of administrative power that the dictatorial regime exercised while pursuing economic growth and social control. At the same time, "vagrant protection facilities" fully demonstrate the structure wherein, once state subsidies to civilian welfare facilities were established, people considered "appropriate" for these facilities were captured like prey and exploited to enrich the power of the social welfare authorities. Both the government and society overall targeted not only children and women who were perceived to be free from "protection" by male heads of families but also the homeless and even, at times, people simply standing in the streets as vagrants who "harm healthy society and urban order."[18] Brothers Home was closed after the 1987 exposé of the deaths of its inmates, and Ministry of Home Affairs Directive No. 410 was discarded in the same year. However, the Brothers Home Oral History Recording Team has pointed out that the power that seeks to "cleanse" people who threaten social safety or have negative influence on society is still alive and well.[19]

The logic that created spaces and times of incarceration in the Omura Immigration Detention Center, Sorokdo Rehabilitation Center, and Brothers Home has yet to be settled. In order to protect the boundary of the state, "wrong" beings who are in "wrong" places have been targeted, interned, and isolated through the establishment of the ruling order and through social perceptions of disease and infection, with the assumption that they "impede" national development and other people's safety. Eugenics, an ideology and a praxis that justified both the provision of welfare to those whose lives had to be promoted and the isolation of those whose lives had to be weeded out, emerged and spread from the West at the turn of the twentieth century. Through the genealogy of incarceration politics implemented in the names of social integration and the maintenance of order, political and social interpretations of why

FIGURE 1.2. South Korea regulates and indefinitely incarcerates unregistered aliens who have simply stayed in the country beyond their respective periods of sojourn. In 2021, a form of torture called "shrimp bending" was committed at the Hwaseong Immigration Detention Center. The victim of this torture has complained, dubbing the Hwaseong Immigration Detention Center "Hwaseong Guantanamo," and a movement to close down immigration detention centers and to mitigate human rights violations has been under way. The photograph shows a participant holding up a piece of cloth that reads, "Shut down immigration 'protection' [crossed out] detention centers" (the word "protection" is a part of the Korean-language name for these facilities) at a press conference held on February 10, 2022, in commemoration of the fifteenth anniversary of a disastrous fire at the Yeosu Immigration Detention Center. Source: Tari Young-Jung Na.

people with disabilities have been institutionalized become possible. Residential institutions nominally are social welfare facilities and "protective" facilities. However, explanations positing human rights violations occurring in residential institutions solely as malfunctions in social welfare or as evil deeds committed by South Korean society's dictatorial regimes are insufficient. Hyun-Chul Kim stresses "incarceration as a temporal-spatial process" and suggests that, "instead of viewing the incarcerated subjects simply as 'bare life' separated from 'quotidian society,' [adopting the perspective of carceral geographies] is to see them as beings who undergo 'becoming' amidst the violence, intimacy, and caregiving that arise in the process of incarceration."[20]

The legacy of the Omura Immigration Detention Center continues to this day in South Korea in the form of immigration detention centers. When aliens become unregistered simply because they have stayed in the country beyond their respective periods of sojourn, they are subjected to regulation and incarceration. The South Korean government thus advertises its own activities at these facilities regarding aliens: "We ensure that, immediately before leaving South Korea, [the inmates] will be able to cherish good memories and images [of the country]." In these immigration detention centers, however, illegal torture and human rights violations have been committed amid indefinite incarceration. The inmates are made to receive diagnoses and examinations off the premises and are restrained with handcuffs and ropes when ill; they are in a chronically unhygienic and malnourished state, and most of those who have been incarcerated for six months or more suffer from grave mental crises. One individual, incarcerated in a windowless solitary cell for over five months on the pretext of being an HIV infectee, has not even been allowed time for exercise.[21]

Meanwhile, though many people have been debilitated by such internment, they have not been included among the beneficiaries of disability welfare services because many of their disabilities often are medically undiagnosed. In recent years, the disability rights movement has struggled to bring about the abolishment of the disability rating system, which classifies people with disabilities according to the degree of "impairments" based on the medical model and allocates welfare services according to these ratings. The disability liberation movement must be able to reply also to the question of whether struggles for the abolishment of the disability rating system should not only get rid of the hierarchy among people with disabilities but also be linked all the way to the deconstruction of the boundaries between people with disabilities and people without disabilities.

Discussions on incarceration politics from the perspective of gender/sexuality have been very insufficient in academic and activist circles in South Korea as well. Completed during the Park Chung-hee regime, the Resident Registration Act (1962) and the Military Service Act (1949; wholly amended in 1970 after a series of partial amendments) have functioned as apparatuses indispensable to the organization of society that imposes gender binarism. Issued during the Japanese colonial era to ferret out "seditious" elements, the citizen card has changed into the resident registration number, or a serial number containing a gender code assigned to every citizen under the Resident Registration Act, which continues to this day. Minorities who do not match the gender codes in the Resident Registration Act inevitably become beings in discord with the establishment and are subject to oppression by institutionalization, which exists both inside and outside institutions.[22] When detained in correctional facilities, transgender people suffer greatly because they are not acknowledged according to self-identified genders and cannot easily obtain medical treatment necessary for gender transition or the undergarments of their choice.[23] Under South Korea's conscription system, the armed forces likewise are immense facilities that forcibly detain the male body. In addition, because the military system constitutes power that defines "maleness," implementing naked physical checkups, grading all citizens who have been classified as "male," and detaining these "males" in facilities that are managed in accordance with the military order for certain duration, the gender effect of the conscription system must be analyzed closely from the perspective of institutionalization as well.[24] South Korea's Military Criminal Act punishes consensual sexual acts between male members of the armed forces as "disgraceful conduct" (Article 92(6)). In its decisions on two cases (2002 and 2011), the Constitutional Court of Korea declared the article constitutional: "Acts of sexual gratification that objectively arouse revulsion among the general public and run counter to the sound sense of sexual morality, [same-sex acts] signify the violation of the healthy life and military discipline of the armed forces community." The logic that, presuming the position of "objective" members of the "general public," sexual rights may be violated for the maintenance of "healthy life" is one that applies not only to the military but across detainment and incarceration. In the next section, I will examine the patterns of oppression that incarceration politics and institutionalization have created through the order surrounding gender/sexuality.

"Incarceration without Walls" Created by Gender/Sexuality Oppression

How can gender/sexuality oppression be problematized in the genealogies of "inappropriate" people subject to institutionalization, or those who are forced to become "normal" citizens through institutionalization? The histories of internment in so-called institutions for women requiring protection targeted women who lacked male heads of households ("masters") under the household head system including war widows, women who had run away from their homes, women defined under the regulations of the Prevention of Prostitution, Etc. Act (1961), and unmarried mothers. Though licensed prostitution was abolished after the liberation, the state allowed exceptions, seeking to restrict sex workers to particular spaces to protect both the general public and "normal" homes.[25] In particular, with the creation of the Prevention of Prostitution, Etc. Act, military camp towns for US soldiers were formed, and the tendency to control sex workers was further strengthened. In addition, though created under the pretext of protecting homeless women and women sex workers, the Seoul Municipal Shelter for Women was implemented under the Park regime's principle of "social cleansing," and when particular red-light districts were closed, this shelter quite often accommodated more than six hundred women even though its capacity was three hundred. Such "moral guidance" projects manifested themselves also as marriage projects, and the women at the shelter were mobilized for forced marriage with forcibly interned young males in the Seosan Reclamation Group as well.

Such a history has yet to be settled properly even to this day, and red-light districts are disappearing, one by one, because of redevelopment. Before the legislation of the Act on the Prevention of Commercial Sex Acts and Protection, Etc. of Victims in 2004, red-light districts were places explicitly acknowledged and managed by the state. A hierarchy and a division of labor existed among the diverse people living in these places, and the content and degree of stigma, too, differed according to one's position on that hierarchy. In my view, striving to understand the lives of sex workers—who were restricted to these areas and had to lead difficult lives, separated from "society at large," even though red-light districts had been formed at transportation hubs—in terms of institutionalization helps to expand our resistance movement against institutionalization. Furthermore, when the workers were driven out without any rights, much less property right to the land, with the closure of red-light districts, sex workers embarked on new lives in the "'residential' neighborhoods" that had excluded them. In her research on the migration experiences of middle-aged and elderly women following the closure of the Yongsan red-light district in Seoul, Mi-Hae Won explains, "In the histories of those who have lived within the particular enclosures of red-light districts for decades, the meaning of migration lies between 'expulsion' and a 'challenge' at a new life." However, Won continues, the degree of crisis experienced because of such drastic change varied for each individual, based on their experiences of the outside world and of control over spaces as well as their life goals and initiative beyond material resources.²⁶ Won argues that, in order to separate red-light districts from society, mainstream society has branded women in red-light districts with sexual stigmas and created a hierarchy. To ignore the reasons for their difficulties in forming peer relationships with their neighbors in "mainstream" society after their departure from red-light districts and to turn them into people who need social adjustment is to isolate them, once again, within "residential" neighborhoods.

The processes through which red-light districts closed down provide the disability deinstitutionalization movement with important questions. How should power relations within institutions change in order for us to envision post-deinstitutionalization life? While living in institutions, how should people contact those outside? How can institutionalized people intervene and participate in decision making in the process of becoming deinstitutionalized? In addition, after these people's deinstitutionalization, how should we acknowledge their previous unique histories and relationships? Whom should we hold responsible for these people's isolation and exclusion, and how should we settle this past? The answers to these questions will become important criteria for making post-deinstitutionalization life possible.

People who have been victimized by crimes and received a certain degree of protection from the state cannot be free from the workings of "normality." Although shelters and treatment/rehabilitation programs for victims of "violence against women" (women victims of sexual violence, domestic violence, and prostitution) exist, long-term housing support and income support are not provided. Such facilities exist as places to prepare these women for "return to society," not as places for living. Even though policies designate victims of violence as objects of treatment and recovery, there is no proper society to which these women—who are no longer the same as before their victimization—can return, either. More questions regarding the relationship between institutionalization and gender/sexuality have to be raised in the deinstitutionalization movement in order to challenge institutionalization in South Korean society. Revealing this relationship is clearly necessary for exposing the essence of institutionalization, uncovering hidden populations, and resisting the discrimination and oppression they have experienced, as well as making their experiences count.

The problems of gender/sexuality oppression and incarceration without walls have become concrete since Women with Disabilities Empathy, an organization of which I am a member, began to visit institutions to support deinstitutionalization. When we started to visit residential facilities for people with visual disabilities, people with developmental disabilities, and people with severe physical disabilities, we noticed that the numbers of women residents were incomparably small. The reasons for such a situation were difficult to discover. However, we came to learn with certainty that statistics on the facility inmates' numbers and duration of stay were insufficient for understanding excluded and isolated existence and lives. If so, then where are women with disabilities? In particular, now that deinstitutionalization has been included in legal policies, those who have not been placed in institutions are not eligible for deinstitutionalization support policies and face difficulties socially representing themselves. Though women with disabilities who are living in local communities with their parents experience various forms of violence and control and thus have experiences similar to those who live in institutions, their experiences and plans for independent living are not treated as important by either the IL movement or the deinstitutionalization movement. One gender-nonconforming person with severe disabilities who is a member of Women with Disabilities Empathy and suffers from domestic violence has been continuously subject to violent restrictions of gender expression including forced head-shaving for the convenience of care by their parents. However, because only residents of institutions are eligible for independence support services provided by deinstitutionalization policies, people first have to choose to live in institutions if they are to receive such services.

That family members play the role of institution in the community becomes clear considering the fact that children, senior citizens, people with disabilities, patients, and full-time housewives—all of whom are perceived as objects of economic support and protection within the family system—engage in labor both inside and outside their homes. The value of such labor or the fact that they work itself is concealed. In addition, when these people free themselves from their homes, they are not seen as having become "independent" but as having "run away from home," which constitutes a social problem. The fact that they are then placed in facilities proves that homes are merely another form of such facilities. Such cases lead to the necessity for the deinstitutionalization movement to recognize people who live in a state of incarceration without walls within their families and, once again, to delve into the problem of institutionalization, which cuts across the spaces of homes, local communities, and institutions. A state of incarceration without walls overlaps with a state in which one has been deprived of housing rights and labor rights. Institutionalization is justified in the name of protecting those who are homeless and lack the ability to work, while the very unequal conditions that deprive one of housing rights and labor rights are the very mechanism that maintains institutions. Such points inevitably expand the horizons of the deinstitutionalization movement and, once more, prompt the movement to join with various other movements for social justice.

In 2020, Women with Disabilities Empathy published the book *Institutionalized Society*. This work raises issues regarding how people—including not only women with disabilities but also single mothers, youths who have left homes, PLWHA, refugees, homeless people, Korean adoptees abroad, people with mental disabilities, and survivors of gender violence—can live in an institutionalized state even without being confined to physical facilities. Since 2018, the twenty-one authors who participated in creating the book have continued to meet and to search for avenues for joint action to challenge the oppression imposed by incarceration.

Eradication and Elimination: A Virus as a Metaphor for the Political

Though the number of people living with HIV/AIDS (PLWHA) in South Korea is smaller than that of patients who are diagnosed as having rare, incurable diseases, the "AIDS phenomenon" surfaced in the 1980s as a major social reality, to the extent that it could be dubbed a "sex panic," which has gradually intensified along with homophobia. However, the narratives of "lives with HIV/AIDS" that the acronym PLWHA consciously seeks to reveal have yet to be properly publicized in South Korean society.[27] Ever since "homosexuals from the West" and women working at entertainment business establishments were pointed out as transmitters of the disease in the 1980s, AIDS has become a powerful symbol of the fear of and stigma on sex itself. The panic, which began without full-fledged social discussions on sexual freedom and sexual liberation, came to be directed toward social punishments for sex that does not contribute to the reproduction of the patriarchal family system.

This social perception of AIDS still wields considerable power. In 1987, two years after the emergence of the disease in South Korea, the Prevention of Acquired Immune Deficiency Syndrome Act was legislated. The need for a unified law on a single disease was a social, not a scientific, one. The legislation stemmed from the need to codify policies for regulating and controlling people who "harbored" HIV rather than from the need for the government and society to control the virus and effectively treat people who were affected. The law still includes clauses criminalizing PLWHA's sexual acts, restricting these people's employment, and allowing the protective placement (forced detention) of those who do not receive treatment. Interestingly, the HIV/AIDS policy is the basis for the only budget allocation that acknowledges the existence of non-heterosexual, non-cisgender beings among South Korean citizens. The government has specially allocated a budget for gay men and men who have sex with men (MSM) and implemented campaigns and educational projects focusing on them. However, this budget designates the objects of the policy only as a vulnerable group and a high-risk group, never stipulating their empowerment and rights.

Minorities unwelcome within a democratic system often do not have access to channels to represent and speak for themselves, and their existence has been socially concealed. Minority groups are depicted in the names of diseases, in medical language such as *Mycobacterium leprae*, poliovirus, and HIV. The World Health Organization established a plan to eradicate polio by 2000, and South Korea, where no case has been reported since 1983, is classified as a nation that has eradicated polio. People with disabilities caused by polio in South Korea are mostly in their middle age now. My colleagues who live with these disabilities and I have discussed what it feels like to know that the world no longer has people with disabilities like their own. It is a good thing yet makes them feel lonesome, they have told me. Because people with disabilities will continue to exist in this world, for them, "eradication" does not seem like a term that respects people with diverse disabilities who once lived in the past and continue to live in the present. The eradication and elimination of this virus, which gives rise to social phenomena precisely because it affects living people, are executed through the existing social order based on discrimination and exclusion.

I redirect my attention to this rhetoric of eradication and elimination because, in 2017, a picket stood out from the crowd at a rally held against the Seoul Queer Parade, an annual LGBT pride parade held in the city. Reading "Exterminate homosexuality! Eliminate homosexuality! A clean [South] Korea (♡), hallelujah (♡)," this picket was carried by a middle-aged-looking man wearing a white dress shirt and a necktie. The anti-LGBT movement of right-wing Christians became active in 2007, when first efforts were made to enact an umbrella antidiscrimination law. Ever since, it has positioned itself as a movement to save both homes and the nation from depravity and disease, through propaganda such as "homosexuality = AIDS = death." After seeing a slogan to the effect not of "exterminate HIV, eliminate AIDS" but of "exterminate and eliminate homosexuality," I have come to pay attention to the fundamental, anti-human-rights violence reflected by the terms *eradication* and *elimination*. The will to equate an identity (homosexuality) with a disease (AIDS) manifests itself in concrete strategies that seek to pathologize people with a homosexual identity and to criminalize AIDS. In other words, the logic is that homosexuality causes misery because it creates AIDS, and AIDS is evil because it is caused by homosexuality. In this logic, homosexuality itself

FIGURE 1.3. On June 24, 2017, some groups organized to oppose the Daegu Queer Culture Festival (pride festival), held near the Dongseong-ro area in the city of Daegu, and carried pickets reading, "Exterminate homosexuality! Eliminate homosexuality! A clean [South] Korea (♡), hallelujah (♡)." Courtesy Minsoo Kim.

becomes a contagious disease that must be exterminated; both homosexuality and AIDS become objects of punishment and isolation.

I argue that this logic of isolation and extinction is completed by the denial of sexual rights and reproductive rights. Though the state allows those considered to be socially incompetent and contaminating society with evils to sustain lives on the minimal level—and, at the same time, to die slowly—and occasionally provides support for their survival, it denies them a future by not ensuring their sexual and reproductive rights.[28] The state's denial of these people's sexual and reproductive rights conveys its wishes for the absence of such citizens in future generations. Not only people with disabilities and PLWHA but also other minorities are similarly portrayed as citizens who are no good, citizens who are undesirable, and citizens who only burden the nation. This is linked to the idea that these people therefore cannot be depicted as representing the citizenry and are not represented in the media as individuals with opinions and that only a very small number of them who have "succeeded" and "overcome" their circumstances selectively become beings capable of inspiring the public. When the "reproductive futurism" that Lee Edelman has elaborated is taken into consideration, minorities, especially people with disabilities, PLWHA, and migrants, are erased from reproductive futurism, and this process is expanded to measures including the Mother and Child Health Act, which has served as a ground allowing the state to intervene in "inappropriate" reproduction, the Prevention of Acquired Immune Deficiency Syndrome Act, which deprives PLWHA of sexual rights, and the employment permit system, which categorically expels migrant workers after a designated duration.[29] While the rights of minorities who are living at present are restricted through a refusal to distribute resources right now, such exclusion is justified as a measure for the future.

Currently, PLWHA are eligible to receive basic life benefits and to apply for low-cost public rental apartments because they lack the ability to work and have been cut off from their families. Since the Asian financial crisis, South Korea's welfare policies have been rearranged and re-signified within a neoliberal order. Considerable administrative power and budget have been poured into verifying people's ability to work, while forcing on them requirements for productive welfare and self-supporting labor, and into strengthening the screening procedures to determine welfare beneficiaries while imposing on families the responsibility for livelihood.[30] Even though the social provisions have helped PLWHA to survive with minimal living conditions through social welfare services, because the policy's goals have been set for public health rather than for the human rights and equality of PLWHA, such policy has produced the effect of incarceration without walls. In my view, HIV/AIDS policies that are implemented without the will to eliminate discrimination by medical institutions, employment discrimination, and social stigmas experienced by PLWHA produce institutionalized lives even outside institutions. Because PLWHA are still seen as dangerous beings threatening both society and homes, policies are not designed to integrate them as family members, neighbors, colleagues, and citizens. Social policy support for PLWHA in the future must have clear goals transcending such fear, stigmas, and exclusion. I argue that the intention behind the subsumption of PLWHA under residual welfare systems through special clauses, instead of expanding universal welfare, has the effect of depriving PLWHA of the conditions under which they can maintain their labor rights and preinfection lives. Resonating with policies of monitoring and controlling PLWHA, this effect has led PLWHA who can no longer live alone in low-cost public rental apartments to move to nursing homes.[31] However, most nursing homes refuse to take PLWHA, not for medical reasons but for social reasons. The series of processes institutionalizing certain people in domestic spaces and local communities gradually occur in this way.

To resolve such problems, the Korean Network of PLWHA (KNP+) decided in 2020 to implement a new project, in which PLWHA would take care of one another in local communities. This is meaningful in that the HIV/AIDS movement has initiated action reflecting the orientation of the deinstitutionalization movement. KNP+ has thus initiated activities to find PLWHA who are forced to live in sanatorium hospitals because it is difficult for them to live alone in local communities and to forge relationships with such people so that they may continue their lives in society.

The Construction of an Epistemology of Deinstitutionalization

Why do PLWHA live in pain? Why are those who nurse and provide care to PLWHA invisible? Why are the deaths of PLWHA not treated as meaningful? If experiences, emotions, memories, and relationships of sexual pleasure cannot be included in narratives of being ill, passing away, or providing care to others, then the entire stories of the lives of PLWHA become invisible. AIDS patients are not provided with care because it is not possible for people to say that they are providing care to AIDS patients. Mourning chambers for deceased AIDS patients cannot be set up when these people are incarcerated in institutions without walls during their lives and therefore unknown.[32]

The questions that are necessary now should be "What contents and forms must social policies take on to make the lives of PLWHA livable?" "How can we establish concrete methods for these people so that they will not die in nursing homes, which function as detention facilities?" and "Who are the subjects and colleagues of the movement for the liberation of PLWHA, who have lived in a state of incarceration without walls due to sexual stigmas?" Currently, continuing efforts are made to fight the medical discrimination experienced by PLWHA through the Act on the Prohibition of Discrimination against Disabled Persons, Remedy against Infringement of Their Rights, Etc. It is very meaningful, through such efforts, to expand the category of "disabilities" and to prompt society to perceive discrimination experienced by PLWHA as one of "universal discrimination." However, the acknowledgment of discrimination experienced by PLWHA as discrimination against people with disabilities is not in itself the goal or the destination of the movement. Rather than seeking the stability of certain people's lives simply by having one group include another group, I would like to recognize together the connection among the foundations, which have led people to die slowly in their respective locations in isolation. I would also like to explore how we can become a part of the movement to challenge such foundations.

When the lives of PLWHA intervene in feminism against gender/sexuality oppression and the reality of disability politics, more expanded questions are raised. If the pain of illness and death is considered to arise from sexual pleasure, can people from various groups join in the efforts to make their voices heard by society without disregarding their sexual pleasure? We must further explore the kinds of chemical changes that can take place when the politics involved in practices such as chemsex and barebacking are linked to the perspectives of disease and death. How can the deinstitutionalization movement discuss the meaning of impairments created by sex?[33] I feel that it is necessary to explore the meaning of impairments, debilitating labor, aging, and death rather than the value of birth, reproduction, and future claimed by normativized sex. I believe that, through such questions, institutionalized lives—the lives of those who live in a state of incarceration without walls and are subjected to gender/sexuality oppression—will be revealed in more meaningful ways, positioning these people as important colleagues and subjects of the deinstitutionalization movement.

Such a movement constructs an epistemology of deinstitutionalization that makes possible new interpretations of rights, temporality, locationality, and sexual praxis. Solidarity created based on this epistemology challenges "normality" and smashes the patterns of endowing rights according to state-approved identities based on one's ability to pay taxes and to consume, as well as on one's citizenship status. By rewriting the genealogies of crip from a postcolonial perspective, such solidarity newly organizes peer relationships for resistance. In my view, such solidarity will make it possible to understand modes of gender/sexuality oppression and the cemented intertwinings of institutionalization and to create the ideology and praxis of the deinstitutionalization movement based on this understanding. This process consists of times and places for inquiring into the Eurocentrism, white-centrism, male-centrism, heterocentrism, nationalism, and neoliberal conformity that formed the catalyst of the IL movement and for searching for other paths. The epistemology of deinstitutionalization argued for in this chapter poignantly challenges the meaning of the politics of inclusion, which is the ideology of independent living for people with disabilities in this era and the national governance principles of the administration headed by the neoliberal reformer President Moon. This epistemology of deinstitutionalization constitutes valid politics for resistance at this moment because it drives a fundamental challenge to the rights and laws approved through the neoliberal mainstream order; reveals that the governing strategy of detention and incarceration in institutions has been a mechanism for depriving people of homes and workplaces; and elucidates that the structures of gender/sexuality oppression have been devices not only justifying isolation and exclusion but also effectively implementing incarceration without walls. An epistemology of deinstitutionalization reveals that the politics of inclusion conspires with the maintenance of incarceration without walls. What we need is not assimilationist social inclusion but the separation of our lives from the mechanism of institutionalization, which started out together with imperialism and the nation-state, by exposing the times and sites of incarceration. The task of writing history anew in order for oppressed people to become one with the future has never been completed but has never stopped, either. If this writing of history can be merged with the everyday struggles for deinstitutionalization, there will be no need to worry about a monolithic future.

NOTES

I am grateful to my colleagues in Women with Disabilities Empathy, HIV/AIDS Activists Network Korea, and Oryu-dong Queer Seminars who share the problematics of this chapter and engage in activism together. Moreover, my thoughts on "incarceration without walls" existing in South Korean society have been influenced by diverse social movements including the disability justice movement, which has forged solidarity with the Palestine liberation movement. Pointing out that the Palestinians have been placed in a state of open-air imprisonment by ceaseless military attacks and the blockage of food, water, and medical treatment and therefore harbor permanent disabilities, an organization called Sins Invalid proposes joint resistance for the liberation of people who are in an "incarcerated" state: https://www.youtube.com/watch?v=w_jre3409jA.

1 Publications surveying the ideology and policies of the IL movement in South Korea are as follows: 정종화, 주숙자, *자립생활과 활동보조서비스*; 김종인, 김재익, *자립생활실천론*; 조영길, 김정미, 노경수, *장애인자립생활개론*.

2 조영길, 김정미, 노경수, *장애인자립생활개론*.

3 이익서, 최정아, 이동영, "장애인 자립생활모델에 대한 탐색적 고찰," 61.

4 정종화, 주숙자, *자립생활과 활동보조서비스*, 30–31.

5 김성구, *신자유주의와 공모자들*.

6 Eun-gu Ji has pointed out that though the voucher system is based on a user-centered model, its key lies in the reduction of state welfare and marketization through for-profit institutions' infiltration into social welfare. 지은구, "바우처와 사회복지서비스."

7 The basic conditions of the "inclusive nation" presented by President Moon are: (1) a nation where the people can rest assured within social safety nets and welfare; (2) a nation where fair opportunities and just results are guaranteed; and (3) a nation where not even a single citizen is subjected to discrimination. The home page of the South Korean government, http://www.korea.kr/special/policyCurationView.do?newsId=148855401&pWise=main&pWiseMain=D1.

8 Consult 조미경, "장애인 탈시설 운동에서 이뤄질 '불구의 정치'간 연대를 기대하며," 279–89.

9 Ji-seong Hwang has argued, "Created based on Western Caucasian-centered society, the conceptual category of 'disability' fails to reflect the contradictory positions of gendered, criminalized, racialized, and disabled bodies—i. e., countless bodies that must undergo colonialism, war, gender discrimination, and the violence of globalized capitalism." 황지성, "건강한 신체와 우생학적 신체들," 240.

10 Though *bulgu*, or *crip*, was a term in South Korean society denigrating people with disabilities, Women with Disabilities Empathy proposed *crip politics* in the declaration commemorating the twentieth anniversary of its establishment. This is because we believed that *crip politics* could play the role of an alternative linguistic locus for solidarity with other minorities without subsuming the experiences and resistance of oppressed beings under the language of institutions.

11 Sorokdo is an island under the jurisdiction of Doyang-eup, Goheung, South Jeolla Province. Medical treatment was provided to Hansen's disease patients on the island mainly through the Sorokdo Charity Clinic created by the Government-General of Korea, the Japanese colonial government, in 1916, and a sanatorium for patients established by Western missionaries in 1910. These facilities were combined and renamed the Sorokdo Rehabilitation Center in 1934, and, from this time onward, both the Japanese colonial authorities and, following the liberation, the South Korean government began to forcibly intern Hansen's disease patients there. 정근식 외, *한센인 인권 실태조사*.

12 Consult 이정은, "'난민' 아닌 '난민수용소'; 오무라(大村)수용소," 323–48.

13 차승기, "수용소라는 안전장치," 164.

14 차승기, "수용소라는 안전장치," 166.

15 차승기, "수용소라는 안전장치," 169.

16 Consult 김재형, *질병, 낙인*.

17 최정기, 감금의 정치, 54–56.

18 Ji-hye Gim has pointed out that though people who do not fit the mainstream order are driven out from public space and rendered invisible, when such nonnormative beings have difficulty securing private space (space free from state power, commonly imagined as the "home") as private land because of their economic status, they are forced to lead a form of life deprived of privacy (김지혜, lecture "'프라이버시와 차별,'" unpublished, 장애여성공감, March 12, 2019). In particular, those possessing private spaces are presumed to be "normal" citizens, and "normality," constructed with a focus on nondisabled, heterosexual, adult males, destabilizes the positions of beings who do not belong to these categories. Questions regarding who are pointed out as vagrants and detained in facilities are linked to such a structure.

19 형제복지원구술프로젝트, 숫자가 된 사람들, 8.

20 김현철, "'감금'에서 '감금지리'로."

21 Choi, "South Korean Activists."

22 Consult 루인, "번호이동과 성전환," 25–46.

23 In 2010, a judicial judgment partly acknowledged the state's responsibility regarding a case where a trans woman confined in a correctional facility had severed her genital with scissors and attempted suicide after the authorities' rejection of her demands for measures for gender transition and after her exposure to hate speech and violence within the facility. However, the responsibility of the authorities acknowledged by the court was limited to their neglectful management of self-harm and suicide attempts with scissors. 천주교인권위원회, 공익인권법재단공감, 한국게이인권운동단체친구사이, 한국성적소수자문화인권센터, 구금시설과 트랜스젠더의 인권 토론회 자료집.

24 For further details, see Na, "South Korean Gender System," 357–77.

25 After liberation from Japanese colonial rule, southern Korea (present-day Republic of Korea or South Korea) saw the beginning of a ruling system under the US Army Military Government in Korea. Though the US military government abolished the licensed prostitution system created by the Japanese colonial authorities, at the same time, it conducted medical checkups for sexually transmitted diseases on "professional entertainers" (gisaeng; akin to the Japanese geisha), "bar girls," and "waitresses" in order to manage military camp towns for American soldiers instead. Women who failed to pass health checkups had to be forcibly detained and receive treatment. 박정미, "식민지 성매매제도의 단절과 연속," 199–238.

26 원미혜, "보이지 않는 '경계'에서," 247–48.

27 박차민정, "AIDS패닉 혹은 괴담의 정치," 12.

28 Eunjung Kim has argued that, as in Alison Kafer's expression, "future without disabilities," the state has controlled the reproductive process in order to produce particular future versions of humans called "normal bodies" through medical interventions and policies. Kim, *Curative Violence*, 44.

29 Legislated in 1973, the Mother and Child Health Act was created to implement state-led population control policies (birth control, eugenic policies) in a situation where abortion had been defined as a crime in the Criminal Act. In a situation where abortion is illegal in the Criminal Act, the clause permitting induced abortion stipulated by the Mother and Child Health Act serves as the standard for the

types of abortion permitted by the state. In addition, Article 19 of the Prevention of Acquired Immune Deficiency Syndrome Act stipulates, "No infected person shall perform any act of carrying and spreading AIDS to another person through blood or body fluids." This clause prohibiting acts of carrying and spreading AIDS makes it possible to punish HIV-positive people criminally if and when they either do not inform sexual partners of the fact of their own infection or do not use condoms. In the case of the employment permit system, migrant laborers are permitted to work for up to three years but are prohibited from inviting their spouses to South Korea, and children produced after three years, when laborers have become unregistered migrants, are rendered stateless beings.

30 Emerging after the Asian financial crisis, the Kim Dae-jung administration established the cornerstone of human rights policies, on the one hand, but introduced neoliberal welfare policies on the other. Borrowing Michel Foucault's discussion, Jesook Song points out that, in liberal nations, only people who can work, purchase commodities, and pay taxes—that is, those who conform to the class system and, ultimately, can contribute to the maintenance of the capitalist liberal state—have been included in the category of "citizens." Song, *South Koreans in the Debt Crisis*.

31 In accordance with Article 3 of the Medical Service Act, "intermediate care hospital[s]," or nursing homes, are defined as "medical institution[s] in which a doctor, dentist or oriental medical doctor provides his/her medical services primarily to inpatients." Equipped with facilities accommodating thirty or more patients, these medical institutions are established for the purpose of implementing treatment mainly on inpatients needing long-term care. However, because any member of the general public who wants treatment at any time or rehabilitation treatment may be hospitalized there as well, a structure in which those needing care are hospitalized for prolonged periods has been created. This has the effect of pathologizing and medicalizing social problems, and long-term hospitalization has severed social relations, thus even leading to social isolation.

32 I have learned through HIV/AIDS human rights activist Miran Kwon that most family members who provide care to PLWHA are women and that their labor is even more concealed than are the lives of PLWHA themselves. Kwon has met, counseled, and pondered solutions with women from such families, who are wholly responsible for caregiving when PLWHA are expelled from or rejected by nursing homes.

33 *Chemsex* signifies the use of drugs including methamphetamine, mephedrone, ketamine, and/or GHB/GBL by MSM before or during sex. It takes place mainly in private homes or spaces for sex such as gay bathhouses. Because drugs prolong sexual functions, they enable users to participate in sex continuously with multiple partners for durations ranging from several hours to several days. Such situations leave participants vulnerable to STD, HIV, and hepatitis C infections and can lead to physical harm caused by drug overuse. Chemsex is linked to the complexity of sex by aspects including the loneliness experienced by gay men, the desire to connect with others, sexual stigmas, sexual norms, and HIV and STDs. Through the Research Group POP, I have been informed of the experiences of gay men and MSM practicing chemsex and have striven to create plans for harm reduction together with drug users.

2. TOWARD A FEMINIST GENEALOGY
OF US DISABILITY RIGHTS

Mapping the Discursive Legacies and Labor of Black Liberation

LEZLIE FRYE

The US disability rights movement has been thoroughly recounted through a rich set of autobiographies, images, ephemera, and activist and scholarly narratives.[1] This collected body of work is heterogeneous in nature, telling not a single, monolithic story but many, sometimes contesting, ones. Yet some paradigmatic discursive threads in disability rights historiography persist, particularly regarding the movement's presumed birth from and evolution out of Black civil rights. Indeed, the origin story of US disability rights is narrated almost unanimously as a direct, organic outgrowth of Black civil rights. Given the contradictory and vexed nature of this history, its relationship to Black civil rights is at once spectacularly obvious and at times violently obscured.

Because the US disability rights movement is often presumed as a fundamental precursor to the scholarly development of disability studies, lingering on this relationship illuminates the conditions of possibility for the "single, coherent" account of the field that *Crip Genealogies* resists. In keeping with this anthology's interrogation of temporal narratives such as "waves" or "arrival" of the field, I join a number of crip activist-scholars in critically revisiting the historical relationship between disability and Black liberation movements.[2] I approach this site as a crucial contradiction, one that maintains the whiteness of disability studies as well as it haunts contemporary social justice movements predicated on coalition work. Sustaining focus on the politics of race, gender, and labor that animated some early and influential white activists' rights claims might also produce desirable discord, dispersing our investments in how the history of US disability rights is told.

Just as the largely white leadership of the burgeoning US disability rights movement of the 1970s and 1980s deployed discourses of racial oppression, equality, and justice with the goal of integrating disabled people into US society and thereby making their struggle legible, so underexamined racial politics continue to underwrite scholarly attempts to integrate disability into US historiography and likewise to make disability studies institutionally legible. When disability rights is narrated primarily as a marker of liberal progress alongside (or, more frequently, following) struggles for racial equality, however, it is positioned against dominant regimes of power rather than complicit with them. Such analogic comparisons between activist struggles for disability rights and racial equality tend to signal the eclipse of incommensurable struggles against racial injustice and of anti-Black violence in the latter twentieth-century United States. The existing historiography thus impedes consideration of how precisely disability studies might have inherited or sustained broader investments in white supremacy, colonialism, and the related impulse to consume the labor of racialized others. More importantly, it drains (at worst) and deprioritizes (at best) the more radical threads of Black resistance politics that animate(d) disability rights.

This essay is part of a broader effort to trace the legacy of US disability rights through and against Black civil rights and Black power. Through close readings of oral histories, ephemera, activist and scholarly articles and monographs, it critically reorients to the presumed origins of the disability rights movement, focusing instead on the racial dimensions of the political trajectory it pursued. In particular, I examine a series of discursive threads that cohere in origin stories of US disability rights: narratives that frame disabled peoples' history and lived experiences in terms of slavery, critiques of disabled segregation that hinge on claims of apartheid and incarceration, and the formulation of disabled subjectivity through analyses of colonialism. These early articulations of the movement reveal constitutive failures to claim whiteness, insistence on figuring disability as racially neutral, and the politicization of disability against, if parallel to, Blackness. While disability justice activists and disability studies scholars alike have waged substantive critiques of such racial politics, their effects continue to resonate in foundational conceptualizations of the field.[3] In the following pages, I consider how investments in whiteness that underwrite US disability rights have been obscured and where the traces of this movement's racial legacy lie: What is the evidence of that forgetting and why has it been so effective?

By experimenting with feminist and antiracist approaches to caring for the legacy of this social movement, this essay gestures toward another genealogy of disability rights, one that exceeds celebratory commemorations of disabled people's advancement that necessarily center legislative achievements and approximations of normative citizenship. Sensing crip pasts that do not lend themselves to reclamation, I argue that the institutionalization of US disability rights was afforded in part by the *undertheorized, uncompensated labor* of Black activists, intellectuals, and cultural workers. I am referring to the discursive and narrative work that frames Black liberation struggles as well as to the political and legislative efforts that were used in service of the enfranchisement of disabled Americans, but that arguably consolidated the relationship between citizenship and whiteness. In other words, Black civil rights and Black power produced the very conditions of possibility for the development of US disability rights, and yet, as its origin stories reveal, deep investments in whiteness persist. Rather than read this movement's history exclusively through the rubric of liberal progress, early articulations of US disability rights must be interrogated for their compatibility with the project of racial capitalism, which normalizes the consumption of Black peoples' uncompensated labor, the theft of Black culture and thought, and the obfuscation of histories of anti-Black racism.[4]

This premise bears further scrutiny for the limits imposed on contemporary social justice movements, particularly those that focus on the reproductive labor of care/work or personal assistance. Likewise, it raises important questions for disability studies, which has inherited a legacy that limits both conceptualizations of the field and its material effects, a central inquiry of *Crip Genealogies*. If disability rights was indeed an outgrowth of Black civil rights and Black power, what intellectual and structural forms of accountability might surface from more sustained reckonings with its vexed relationship to Black liberation movements? By extension, what debt do disability studies practitioners sustain to Black radical politics and thought? Finally, what political possibilities, desires, or futures might come into sensation if our collective attention lingered on the racial politics of US disability rights historiography?

Disability Rights as the Apex of Progress

Activists and scholars alike recount how the early architects of US disability rights were inspired by the public recognition of African Americans' sustained confrontation with the US government, the movement's many local protests and unprecedented national presence, and the teachings of its leaders. Witnessing—and, no doubt, sometimes participating in—this growingly powerful movement, they recognized an opportunity to make visible the discrimination against disabled Americans. Coined by George Will as "the last great inclusion," US disability rights emerged as a strategic vehicle for transforming disabled people into a recognizable minority group, the legitimate claimants of the gains of civil rights struggles.[5] As Scott Rostron of the United

Handicapped Federation observed in 1977, "equality is coming to the Handicapped communities slowly, as it has for the black, women, elderly, and other sub-cultures in America."[6]

This paradigmatic temporal framing of disabled people as "behind" or "after" other American minorities, whose inclusion was already underway, threads throughout accounts of US disability rights. So too does the corresponding framing of this social movement as the "culmination of the civil rights era," its symbolic marking as the apex of progress.[7] In the strategic reclaiming of US history *as* disability history, for example, disability rights is positioned as a marker of liberal progress, a political project that works against earlier histories of exclusion and that leads to increased visibility and recognition in American society. For example, the period between the mid-1970s and the turn of the century is characterized as a "trailblazing crusade" of legislative triumphs,[8] a journey "from caste to class,"[9] "from segregation to integration,"[10] and "from charity to independent living."[11] It marks out the transition "from goodwill to civil rights" and "from the special needs category to the people category."[12] In short, these decades mark the path to "full" and "equal" citizenship.[13] Yet this emergent personhood took shape in complex relationship to African Americans as well as other racial-ethnic minorities, gays and lesbians, and women.

US disability rights leaders, indebted to "lessons . . . carried over from the 1960s black civil rights movement" variously related to Black civil rights as a precursor, an inspiration, a conflict resolved, or a parallel project.[14] More complex accounts hold that disability rights "intersected with and borrowed from" or "was energized by, overlapping with, and similar to other civil rights movements across the nation."[15] Susan Schweik's "Lomax's Matrix: Disability, Solidarity, and the Black Power of 504" presents a rare historical snapshot of coalition work—detailing the conditions that drew Black Panthers into proximity and shared struggle with Bay Area disability rights leaders leading up to the historic 504 sit-in. Others emphasize the ambivalence, tension, or distance that marked this relationship. For example, reflecting on his experience as the only Black man working at the Center for Independent Living in Berkeley in the mid-1970s— which he euphemistically characterizes as "kind of a bummer period"—Donald Galloway recounts that "our main focus was disability. We would draw from the civil rights movement, some of the principles of nonviolence and advocacy and protest. We would borrow some of that, and we would appeal to the black politicians on those levels." Even so, he distinguishes, "we were not actively involved in the black movement, in a conscious way, other than to use the similarity to bring about some empathy for our struggle."[16] Until the appearance of Sami Schalk's groundbreaking text, *Black Disability Politics*, such accounts figure only sparsely into the historiography of US disability rights and into its contemporary practices of remembering and commemoration. Poet and activist-scholar Leroy Franklin Moore Jr., for another example, directs attention to "the work of Black disabled activists during and after the 504 sit-in" that have been omitted from the formal record of disabled peoples' activist struggles and the corresponding legislative achievements.[17] This is, of course, due in part to the practice of "whitewash[ing] disability history, ontology and phenomenology," to cite the late Chris Bell's enduring critique of "white disability studies."[18]

Discursive Strategies: From Analogy to Appropriation

In contradistinction to such forgetting, much more visible are the repetitions of analogies, parallels, and comparisons among the positions of disabled people and "blacks and women," as well as more divisive ranking of oppressions, racial appropriation, and expressions of disability exceptionalism. For example, Justin Dart Jr., an influential architect of the ADA, reserved for disabled people that most coveted position of the "poorest, most oppressed group," also known as "the nation's largest minority."[19] Alongside claims that "the possibilities affording relief to others are not usually open" to disabled people—including formal attempts at reparations like affirmative action, no matter how limited their effects—some disability activists and thinkers implied that institutionalized racism had been at least partially resolved, that racial minorities were receiving disproportionate access to resources or occupied a relatively protected position in relation to the state.[20] Disabled people's exceptionality was presumably due to the failure of society to register their status as "second-class citizens" or their righteous claim to "equal rights." A blunter calculation: "If most [marginalized] persons are only half-visible, then the cripple, like the black man until recently, is wholly invisible."[21] Needless to say, it is "Blacks" who are made to occupy the fungible position of comparable other, the presumably discrete figure against which racially unmarked disability rights activists measured their position in society, the conditions of their lives, and their path toward "full citizenship."

Other influential white leaders claimed Black civil rights leaders, refrains, or imagery so as to make visible the plight of disabled Americans. "Using Rosa Parks as their icon," white disabled activist and editor of the disability magazine *Ragged Edge* Mary Johnson recounts, members of the militant disability rights group ADAPT (originally Americans Disabled for Accessible Public Transit) were "often appearing at protests with name tags reading 'My name is Rosa Parks'—trying to make the public connect their protest to the civil rights movement."[22] Another frequent refrain reasoned that "all the issues are the same." Reverend Wade Blank, a white founding member of ADAPT, argued just that: "The black movement wanted to ride the buses equally. The black movement wanted to eat at the lunch counters. The black movement wanted the right to vote. The black movement wanted the right to keep their families together. The black movement wanted the right to be integrated into the school system. That's what the disability rights movement wants, exactly."[23] Such comparisons obviously tend to imagine African Americans and disabled people as separate constituencies rather than considering their intersecting identities and complex social positions. They also suggest linear and discrete trajectories for these social movements, obscuring more fragmented, tense, chaotic, or promiscuous forms of political development.[24]

Slavery as Metaphor, Civil Rights as Corrective

In an attempt to politicize the dehumanizing conditions of isolation and abuse that structured many disabled peoples' lives, early activists sometimes invoked allegories of racist institutions, most notably slavery. Echoing the utterly ubiquitous use of the slavery metaphor in liberal discourse, they looked to abolition and other struggles for racial freedom to make the case for—arguably, to give birth to—a burgeoning disability rights movement that had yet to achieve a liberation akin to that of its political peer. For example, the independent living movement was narrated (as late as the early 1990s) as "freeing the slaves," including by Blank, who referred to the "exodus" of eighteen "severely disabled" people out of a nursing home and into what became the Atlantis Community of Denver, Colorado.[25] Disability advocate Bob Cooper extended this analysis further yet: "We may have freed the slaves—but all we did was take the chains off. We've left them on the plantation to become sharecroppers. Only those who are willing to insist that what was written on a piece of paper into law—who are willing to exercise their rights—have gotten them."[26] Here figuring the post-ADA landscape as "plantation" life for disabled Americans through a flattened critique of Reconstruction-era racial and economic conditions, Cooper's statement illuminates the instrumentalization of slavery as a means to dramatize discrimination against disabled people in the form of barred access to education, housing, and public accommodations.

The more specific equation of racial slavery with the institutionalization of disabled people (on the basis of disability and class but not, presumably, race) is also apparent in accounts from white disability rights activists and movement narrators. In the frequently cited history of the US disability rights movement, *No Pity*, Joseph P. Shapiro reasons that "as with slaves, people in institutions were regarded as 'inferior.' They, too, were cut off from their families, and their own possibilities for marriage." While institutions were not expressly designed to profit from disabled people's labor, he concedes, "they were put to work, often backbreaking work, for long hours and without pay. . . . [Institutionalization] exposed people to deficient diets; cheap, often ill-fitting, and inadequate clothing; and cramped, lightly furnished barracks where they slept with large groups of people." Shapiro extends the parallel to analyze the systemic incidence of sexual assault, since "there was inordinate cruelty, too, from 'masters'"—that is, doctors, nurses, and orderlies—"*just as* enslaved women were routinely considered the sexual property of their white owners and foremen."[27] Such comparisons necessarily obscure the history of slavery that undergirds racial segregation and that structures the very landscape of institutionalization to which Shapiro refers.

In addition to invoking the plantation, leading disability rights activists likened nursing homes to prisons and other racially segregated spaces as an attempt to make their cause visible to a national audience that might better recognize segregation in the aftermath of *Brown v. Board of Education*. Referring to King's later emphasis on economic injustice as a corollary to his own commitment to "the [disabled] people that don't have any money," Blank claims that "our ghettos are the nursing homes."[28] Cheryl Marie Wade names the privilege of living independently as conferred on those "who are on the outside."[29] Other disability rights activists referred to disabled people institutionalized in nursing homes as "locked up" or incarcerated.[30] This language, echoed in the iconic images of wheelchair users breaking apart hand shackles, sought to demonstrate the lack of agency afforded to those less-privileged disabled people (namely those who required substantive personal assistance) and to emphasize the brutality of their living conditions.[31] However, while they were all too willing to draw on abolitionist discourse and imagery, there is little record of these same white activists fundamentally opposing prisons—sites where Black people (disproportionately disabled) are the primary targets of institutionalization—so much as to attempt to differentiate the true criminals from the false ones.[32]

The use of precedents for ending segregation against African Americans took shape in an even more troublesome claim that disabled people occupied an American apartheid. For example, white disability historian Fred Pelka reports that "by the mid-twentieth century, then, Americans with disabilities lived under a system of virtual apartheid, in which those with discernible disabilities were most often hidden away in institutions, special schools, or . . . isolated in their homes."[33] Given the many ways "this isolation was reinforced by the physical infrastructure" and access barred to every dimension of public life, he repeats political scientist Jacqueline Vaughn Switzer's claim that "the word that best describes the historical treatment of persons with disabilities is *separation*."[34] In 1987, Robert Funk, a white disability rights lawyer and founder of the Disability Rights Education and Defense Fund—the national legal arm of the disability rights movement—goes so far as to call them a "dependent caste."[35] Funk, whom Shapiro describes as "one of the founding philosophers of disability integration," used this rhetoric to denounce "discriminatory programs, policies, and laws designed to deny disabled people's participation in organized society."[36] Yet, as with the equation of the social positions of "the cripple" and "the Negro" discussed below, these activists envisioned an American apartheid fundamentally structured by disability, displacing the very analysis of profound racial and class divisions that made such a claim even possible.

Similarly, some white disability rights activists echoed Black civil rights critiques of "separate and unequal" accommodations (in the arenas of education, housing, communication, transportation, and other public spaces), expressly invoking racial segregation in the Jim Crow era.[37] In her protest of inaccessible public toilets in New York City in 1992, Frieda Zames of Disabled In Action held that "the exclusion was as blatant example of discrimination as if the city had put up toilets and then hung a WHITES ONLY sign on each one."[38] When then-student Fred Fay "was told that [he] wasn't welcome" at a faculty canteen in the rehabilitation center at the University of Illinois in the 1960s, he pictured on "the front page of [the] student newspaper . . . a picture of some officials dressed up as Ku Klux Klan, saying, 'Disabled Keep Out.'"[39] Such comparisons served to make legible the segregation of (presumably non-Black) disabled people by calling up the segregation—and integration—of (presumably nondisabled) Black people. In addition to obscuring the multiplicity of social identity categories, they also reconsolidate the Black/white binary that erases a range of other racial ethnic positions. Finally, the discursive appropriations of slavery and racial segregation discussed here underscore the centrality of physical and mobility impairments to the racial construction of disability rights.

Literally by association with Black civil rights, reigning historiographies of US disability rights nonetheless forward a progress narrative that decidedly figures disabled people—and their burgeoning movement—on the side of freedom. In other words, it is the establishment of formal (albeit symbolic) rights for newly recognized disabled citizens that functions as a corrective to the ills of a bigoted society presumed to have, at least nominally, resolved inequity resulting from anti-Black racism. The examples above indicate that at least some influential disability rights leaders favored a vertical model of power that mapped Black and white onto disabled and nondisabled. Such painful gestures have the effect of divorcing disability rights from the politics of race to which the movement is indebted and, more specifically, from a critical history of the anti-Black violence that both preceded and followed the civil rights movement. As crip activist-scholars note, the whitewashed, victorious narrative of disability rights as the apex of civil rights in the United States also conceals the presence and labor of disabled people of color, namely Black activists. To cite Moore's poetic intervention in the false separation of Blackness and disability, "So many Krip-Soul Brothers / Put their sweat and time in / From activism, counseling to music."[40] Yet if the history of disabled people is framed in terms of slavery, their lived experiences of segregation in terms of apartheid and incarceration, and their subjectivity through analyses of colonialism, it becomes impossible to account for how disabled activists and scholars might participate in or benefit from those violent legacies.

Tracing Anti-Black Racism, From Negro to Crip

Such use of the discourses and imagery of Black civil rights and sometimes Black nationalism extended further to the analogue of identity encapsulated by "the cripple as Negro." In a 1969 article, white disabled author and college professor Leonard Kriegel argued that "no one can teach the cripple, can serve as so authoritative a model in the quest for identity, as can the black man."[41] Theorizing these parallel positions through a collapsed and decontextualized reading of Frantz Fanon's classic anticolonial text, Kriegel reasoned, "Just as Uncle Tom, in order to placate the power of white America, learned to mask his true self . . . so the cripple has the right, one is tempted to say the responsibility, to use every technique, every subterfuge, every mask, every emotional climate— no matter how false and seemingly put on—to alter the balance in his relation to the world around him."[42] That balance, it is worth mentioning, is to be established between the—decidedly masculine—cripple and the able-bodied world rather than between the overlapping communities of African American and disabled people. Therí A. Pickens forwards this critique in her assessment of how Kriegel's analogy fails, naming the "racist erasure" that necessarily results from a comparative and hierarchical understanding of the relationship between Blackness and disability.[43] For example, in response to an ill-advised city proposal regarding handicapped parking, Kriegel argues that "forcing a man who has great difficulty in walking to surrender his car, the source of his mobility, is comparable to calling a black man 'boy' in a crowd of white onlookers."[44] In defense of this identification with the misrecognition entailed in "being black in a psychologically white world," he insists that "the analogy is neither farfetched nor unusual. Uncle Tom and Tiny Tim are brothers under the skin."[45] While

Kriegel's essay may have lent itself to a counter-history of queer belonging lived through these figures—one he begins to approach in his meditation on the spatial politics of race, class, and disability at the Hospital for Joint Diseases in Harlem—it more nearly functioned in service of making visible "the cripple" while making invisible race, gender, sexuality, or any other axes of identity. Kriegel says as much in an admission that "whether this assessment of ["the Negro's"] situation is accurate is of no immediate concern, for what we are interested in is its validity as an analogy for the life of the cripple."[46]

While Kriegel's position should not stand in as a decisive or singular account of the place of Black politics in burgeoning disability rights activism, it resonates clearly with the political impulses I am tracing to the white majority of activists—so much so that disability historian Fred Pelka describes the article as "evidence of this new disability consciousness" of the late 1960s and early 1970s.[47] This consciousness might be understood as a series of claims: to identity, culture, and pride, but also to rights, citizenship, and national/domestic space. Such claims hinged on white activists' conceptualizations of disabled people through and against racialized—namely Black—noncitizens, dehistoricized and trans-spatial appropriations of identity that display the extractive dimensions of the path to disabled personhood, enduring at least into the 1990s.[48] Like Kriegel two decades earlier, white disabled poet-activist Marta Russell harshly critiques the "Uncle Tiny Tims" among disabled people, those who "are addicted to the charity—enslavement—mode of thinking." Instrumentalizing Malcolm X's critique, she offers "house Negroes" as their corollary: those who choose not to identify as disabled, who form their primary relationships with nondisabled people, and who prefer integration over building power for disabled communities.[49] In contrast, disability rights activists envisioned politicized, militant disabled people as "freedom fighters." "When we can love disability" like Malcolm and other "US-colonized black peoples," Russell posits, "then we will have a real movement."[50] In a parallel claim to disability culture, white disability artist and founder of the Wry Crips Disabled Women's Theatre group Cheryl Marie Wade writes, "We are more and more proud, we are freedom fighters, taking to the streets and the stages, raising our gnarly fists in defiance."[51] Among the "new definitions, new inflections," Wade presents "CRIPPLE . . . Dig it or not."[52] There is no question as to the enthusiasm and sheer possibility held in these articulations of pride, which express political hope for the world-making power of disability identity.

The claiming of the term cripple by politicized disabled people, certainly not widespread by the time of Kriegel's piece, might thus be more fully understood in direct relationship to the figure of the American Negro and within the context of Black power in the United States. In an effort to communicate the political project of self-definition that "compares the change to the civil rights movement's replacement of 'Negro' with 'black,'" white disabled poet and essayist Nancy Mairs suggests that "in reclaiming 'cripple,' disabled people are taking the thing in their identity that scares the outside world the most and making it a cause to revel in with militant self-pride."[53] Shapiro reports on a survey in the *Disability Rag*, the local-newsletter-turned-national-magazine that disability rights activist Mike Ervin called "the gimp-radical's bible," indicating that its readers preferred the term "cripple" by 1990 (notably during the very summer of the ADA's passage). Shapiro cites Irving K. Zola, commonly credited as a foundational figure in the academic field of disability studies, for reading this as "a sign of a new and thriving group identity."[54] This takes expression in *Rag* editor Mary Johnson's disdain for politically correct euphemisms like "differently abled" or "handi-capable" (authored by "nondisabled 'do-gooders'") because these words are devoid of disability culture, "like vanilla custard."[55] Cripple, Shapiro reports, holds "the requisite soul power."[56] It appears that Black power as well as civil rights made available the color, flavor, and "soul" that could invigorate a movement (and corresponding identity) that was primarily represented by white leadership.

In this way, the growing movement for Black power produced discursive possibilities for US disability rights, a resource that early activists ironically used in service of the fortification of white citizenship. I see an important distinction between this argument and the common recognition that, in the shared spirit of "identity exploration," disabled activists, "like feminists, African Americans, and gay and lesbian activists," claimed their disabled bodies as "sources of political, sexual, and artistic strength."[57] The former framing signals an element of extraction, and the latter emphasizes benign synergy. For the bold claim to disability pride was not merely emerging alongside or even through Black pride, but also sometimes against it. The arguably predictable 1969 appearance of the "cripple as Negro" and its iterations, explored above, prove a rich case in point. As Eli Clare notes, cripple, like queer ("cousins") are "words to help forge a politics."[58] Indeed, gay and lesbian rights movements also participate in this familial habit of extraction, repeating the broader pattern of absorbing Black liberation into the trope of progress narratives. Framing it as an artifact, Pickens argues that Kriegel's essay "clarifies how the Black power movements and civil rights gains of the 1950s and '60s *paved the way* for disability activism" that resulted in concrete legislative protections between the 1970s and the 1990s.[59] While disability rights activists and historians unanimously recognize(d) such legislative milestones as precedents, unlike Pickens, they offer neither critical examination of the racial politics of borrowing, exploiting, or stealing the rhetorics of Black civil rights and Black power nor assessments of where the politics of racial and economic justice live(d) in US disability rights.

If *cripple* indeed helped to forge a politics, then crip theory and epistemologies are among the offspring of such words and their surrounding political frameworks. *Crip* is, of course, an incomplete rubric that includes a range of unruly politics, praxes, and relations that the coeditors of this anthology skillfully survey. As they note, it is not merely a site of identity (a paradox, given its common genealogical routing through queer politics), a critical methodology or analytic, an "orientation" or a site of feelings, a justice-based politic expressed through a range of art and activism, and an affinity or kinship system of gangs founded by Black men in Los Angeles.[60] As has been remarked on both by implicated scholars and by artist-activists who resist appropriation of their intellectual and political work, it is also the basis for an increasingly marketable field of knowledge on which articles and books, curriculums, and even academic jobs rest (if precariously). Even as they resist the periodization of crip theory as a more sophisticated "successor" to disability studies—a move the coeditors argue "accentuates crip's proprietary whiteness"—some of its earlier descriptions in relative terms leave curious traces: more contestatory, risky, radical, textured.[61] Does there not live here some unintended historical echo, some sediment, of early and formative white disability rights activists' racial construction of cripple? This is not to disregard the deeply generative and confrontational materializations of crip theory, including but not limited to the queer practice Jina B. Kim calls crip-of-color critique and the many "alternative genealogies" this anthology offers.[62] There is little utility in (re)routing disability studies through or, worse yet, *to* Kriegel's failed (or is it painfully successful?) analogy. Yet, following the foundational scholarly intervention of Black feminist queer theorist Cathy Cohen, it is clear that the promise or potential of crip theory is foreclosed, impaired perhaps, by failures to fully trace (the labor of) this political project through Blackness, but also—more germane to this chapter—through histories of anti-Black racism.[63]

Approaching Feminist Genealogies of US Disability Rights: Caring for Legacy

Caring for the legacy of disability rights thus demands a more substantive account of the reproductive labor on which the very development of social movements, like academic fields, hinges. By gesturing toward a genealogy of US disability rights read through and against Black civil rights, my goal exceeds a mere rehearsal of anti-Black racism—particularly given the ongoing exclusion of disabled people from social justice movements composing the radical left. In addition to sparse acknowledgments from early activists, disability justice thinkers have thoroughly articulated such critiques—including Leroy Franklin Moore Jr., Patty Berne, Leah Lakshmi Piepzna-Samarasinha, Stacey Park Milbern, Mia Mingus, and many other activists. While racial appropriations and analogies for disability may be painfully familiar, the magnitude of their violence arguably endures. The formal historiography of US disability rights cannot accurately be characterized as collectively disturbed, nor can contemporary social justice organizers dismiss the accumulated cultural capital and political power of mainstream disability rights, which has yet to account for its organizing racial politics.

My purpose is rather to emphasize that Black civil rights and Black power— and thus the labor of Black activists, intellectuals, and cultural workers—were and remain an *underexamined, uncompensated resource* for articulating the parameters, needs, and desires of the US disability rights movement. In other words, disabled citizenship was afforded in direct relation to undertheorized forms of labor: that of African Americans whose collective efforts made such coveted legislative and political victories possible, their labor in giving shape to the story that could be told—then and now—about disability and civil rights, and the labor of personal assistants, caregivers, and all those whose physical, mental, and spiritual work enabled disabled people to organize politically and that continues to sustain many disabled people's lives today, crip theorists among them. These uses of labor correspond with the historic exploitation of Black—particularly women's—labor in the United States, a resonance that demands further scrutiny when it comes to social movements, understood here as missed opportunities for coalition, but also when it comes to the institutionalization of disability studies as a field.

These queerly curated examples speak to the discursive legacies of white supremacy, nationalism, and anti-Black racism playing out in disability activism and scholarship. But they also represent part of a broader effort to recover a crip past lurking inside the archive of US disability rights. The provisional tableau I offer here may prove undesirable to the extent that it fails to fully encapsulate the "true story" of US disability rights. It may incite what the co-editors of this anthology theorize as "crankiness," a methodologically lush, if sometimes repulsive, feeling. Yet there is something crucial to be gleaned from shifting the vantage point through which we view the history of this movement, placing into the foreground what is often relegated to the background, the already known. I see this approach as directly connected to the work of seeking moments of coalition in both the past and the present, moments which—when strung together—tell another important counter-story, one of solidarity, "fluidarity," and interdependence.[64] For example, public intellectuals and activist-scholars like Sami Schalk, Moore, Schweik, and Corbett O'Toole sustain this focus when they reexamine the relationship between disability rights and Black power leading up to the infamous Section 504 sit-in, in 1977.[65] "East Bay equaled Black disabled planet / Krip-Soul Brothers / On both sides of the Bay," Moore writes in a poem that theorizes Black disabled people at the center of this story.[66] Of course, they labor to (re)member these histories precisely because they have been "forgotten" and "obscured."[67]

By reorienting to the origin stories of US disability rights, I have turned to the absences, gaps, tense ties, and missed opportunities for coalition that remain, ones that rest uncomfortably with/in the radical histories these handful of scholars have begun to trace. Of course, the civil rights movement is itself narrated through a contesting set of stories that both reveals and obscures, that holds moments of solidarity and betrayal, and that elicits pride and embarrassment (or, it is worth adding, denial). There are some acknowledgments of the failure of Black civil rights leaders to address disability and access.[68] There are fewer historical examinations of the betrayals of disability rights when it comes to Black communities and politics, however. Given that Black civil rights and Black power produced discursive—as well as legislative—possibilities for the very development of US disability rights, important questions remain about this movement's accountability to contemporary Black liberation movements. What would it mean for the field of disability studies to take seriously its debt?

If the established histories and foreclosed futures of disability studies rest in part on the coherence of US disability rights historiography, then the *deinstitutionalization* of disability studies demands that activists and scholars (re)member a broader range of crip pasts. To do so is to risk displacing the habits of colonization, theft, extraction, and disinheritance that have enabled the development of the field, alongside and between its (more easily claimed) radical histories and presents.

NOTES

1   Frequently cited monographs include Fleischer and Zames, *Disability Rights Movement*; Shapiro, *No Pity*; Barnartt and Scotch, *Disability Protests*; and Percy, *Disability, Civil Rights, and Public Policy*. Commonly cited oral histories include Pelka, *What We Have Done*; and Orlansky, *Voices*. Notable archives include the Disability Rights and Independent Living Movement Collection at the Bancroft Library at the University of

California, Berkeley, and the Disability History Museum. The most frequently cited examples of disability press are the *Disability Rag*, *This Mouth Has a Brain*, and *Mainstream*. One collection of such articles can be found in Shaw, *The Ragged Edge*.

2 Schalk, *Black Disability Politics*; Schweik, "Lomax's Matrix"; Moore, "Black History of 504 Sit-In."

3 For critiques of racism in US disability rights and analysis of the centrality of race to disability justice, see Sins Invalid, *Skin, Tooth, and Bone*. For theorizations of the complex historical construction of Blackness and disability, including and exceeding critiques of the limits of white disability studies, see Erevelles, *Disability and Difference*; Bell, *Blackness and Disability*; Pickens, "Blackness and Disability" (2017); Pickens, "Blackness and Disability: This. Is. The. Remix" (2021); Bailey and Mobley, "Work in the Intersections," 19–40; Pickens, *Black Madness :: Mad Blackness*.

4 For discussions of racial capitalism and slavery, see Robinson, *Black Marxism*; Stephanie Smallwood, "Turning African Slaves into Atlantic Commodities," in *Saltwater Slavery*, 33–64; Melamed, "Racial Capitalism," 76–85; Glenn, *Unequal Freedom*. For further discussion of the global racialization of labor, see Chakravartty and da Silva, "Accumulation, Dispossession, and Debt," 361–85; Marable, "Blackness beyond Boundaries," 1–8. For analysis of the exploitation of Black women's labor under slavery that focuses on reproduction, see Morgan, *Laboring Women*. For texts that explore Black women and work following the formal end to slavery in the United States, see Hunter, *To 'Joy My Freedom*; Branch, *Opportunity Denied*; Hill-Collins, "Work, Family, and Black Women's Oppression," in *Black Feminist Thought*, 45–68. For a study of the denial of histories of anti-Black violence in the United States, see Vargas, *Denial of Antiblackness*.

5 Longmore and Umansky, *New Disability History*, 2.

6 Rostron, as cited by Nielsen, *Disability History*, 177.

7 This is Longmore and Umansky's interpretation of Will's quote (2). They object to the historical timeline. I am objecting to the progress narrative contained therein. Longmore and Umansky, *New Disability History*, 2.

8 Shapiro, *No Pity*, 339.

9 Funk, "Disability Rights," 7–30.

10 Rostron, as cited by Nielsen, *Disability History*, 177.

11 Shapiro, *No Pity*, 41. Robert Funk characterizes this development as a shift from "charitable care" to empowered, consumer-directed personal assistance. Funk, "Disability Rights," 10.

12 Scotch, *From Good Will to Civil Rights*; Rostron, as cited by Nielsen, *Disability History*, 177.

13 Nielsen, *Disability History*, 160; Funk, "Disability Rights," 23–28.

14 Hershey, "Wade Blank's Liberated Community," 149.

15 Nielsen, *Disability History*, 168, 160.

16 Donald Galloway, as cited by Pelka, *What We Have Done*, 222.

17 Moore, "Black History of 504 Sit-In."

18 Bell, "Introducing White Disability Studies," 275. In their analysis of deaf cultural history, Susan Burch and Hannah Joyner engage a similar critique, drawing on Toni

Morrison's concept of the "disremembered" past and the practice of "rememory" she explores in the novel *Beloved*. I join these lingering practices by gesturing hesitantly toward another "crip past." Burch and Joyner, "The Disremembered Past," 65–82.

19 Justin Dart Jr., as cited by Pelka, *What We Have Done*, 5; Shapiro, *No Pity*, 7. Chris Bell aptly problematized such characterizations of "the disabled community [as] a monolithic one, struggling against the same oppressors, striving for identical degrees of dignity, recognition and cultural representation." Bell, "Introducing White Disability Studies," 276.

20 For example, Shapiro claimed that African Americans were the beneficiaries of "a more consciously adopted societal goal." He cites as examples "affirmative action programs, minority set-asides, college scholarships, and other efforts to open up opportunities"— which, it is worth noting, were only provisionally secured and were subject to enormous backlash by the following decade. On the contrary, he argues, "integration has been more quirky and halting for disabled Americans." Shapiro, *No Pity*, 180–81.

21 Kriegel, "Uncle Tom and Tiny Tim," 5.

22 I found no documentation of a direct relationship between Rosa Parks and ADAPT activists, save for her "use" as a symbol of civil rights for disabled people seeking redress of inaccessible transit systems.

23 Blank, as cited by Hershey, "Wade Blank's Liberated Community," 151.

24 Schweik makes a parallel argument that histories of Black Power are obscured by less complicated—more "whitewashed"—stories about the 504 sit-in in San Francisco and the moments of coalition or overlapping movement work that must have preceded the protest. Schweik, "Lomax's Matrix," 6.

25 Blank, as cited by Hershey, "Wade Blank's Liberated Community," 151.

26 Cooper, as cited by Johnson, "The Power of One Person," 159.

27 Emphasis is mine. Shapiro concludes that just as slavery "robbed the Negro of his manhood, encouraged infantile and irresponsible behavior, and put a premium on docility," Shapiro argues "so, too, has institutionalization regarded adults with disabilities . . . removing their basic rights to choice, opportunity, and claim to community." Shapiro, *No Pity*, 159–60.

28 Blank, as cited by Hershey, "Wade Blank's Liberated Community," 153.

29 Wade, "It Ain't Exactly Sexy," 89.

30 Blank, as cited by Hershey, "Wade Blank's Liberated Community," 152.

31 One iteration of this image can be found on ADAPT's official website, www.adapt.org/.

32 Liat Ben-Moshe has thoroughly critiqued this distinction between the criminalization of incarcerated people and the exoneration of disabled people who are unjustly institutionalized in nursing homes or carceral spaces. See, for example, Ben-Moshe, *Decarcerating Disability*.

33 Pelka, *What We Have Done*, 17.

34 Pelka, *What We Have Done*, 17. Emphasis is Vaughn Switzer's.

35 Funk, "Disability Rights," 8.

36 Shapiro, *No Pity*, 103; Funk, "Disability Rights," 9.

37 For an illuminating discussion of how Jim Crow laws and the accompanying forms of racial violence shaped design standards that secured relative access for disabled people in the United States, namely by mobilizing narratives of whiteness and

productivity, see Hamraie, "All Americans: Disability, Race, and Segregated Citizenship," in *Building Access*, 65–94.

38 Shapiro, *No Pity*, 323.

39 Fay, as cited by Pelka, *What We Have Done*, 106–7.

40 This is an excerpt from Moore's poem "Krip-Soul Brothers." Moore, "Black History of 504 Sit-In."

41 Kriegel, "Uncle Tom and Tiny Tim," 2.

42 Kriegel, "Uncle Tom and Tiny Tim," 2. Kriegel is not unique in this instrumentalization of Fanon. Rather he demonstrates the problems of mistranslation that biographer David Macey argues "dislocates Fanon from a francophone context and . . . transforms him into the archetypal Negro from the American deep south." Max Silverman, "Introduction," in *Frantz Fanon's "Black Skin, White Masks,"* 2.

43 Pickens, *Black Madness :: Mad Blackness*, 2.

44 Kriegel, "Uncle Tom and Tiny Tim," 1.

45 Kriegel, "Uncle Tom and Tiny Tim," 1.

46 Kriegel, "Uncle Tom and Tiny Tim," 6.

47 Pelka, *What We Have Done*, 25.

48 For an example that does not exclusively center Blackness, consider Joanne Monroe's argument, featured in the 1980 inaugural issue of the *Disability Rag*, wherein she claims that disabled people in the United States occupy the status of refugees: "Our closest parallel is that of refugees, surviving through the activities and help of others—not at home even in our own land." As Pickens argues of Kriegel's essay, it "reinscribes the erasure[s] it originally promises to rectify"—in this case, indigeneity, forced migration, and imperial violence, in addition to Blackness (3). Monroe identifies with white settler coloniality even as she positions disabled people as "the most put upon, discriminated against, unemployed, ignored, undereducated, poorest minority in the United States." She concludes, "this country is as much ours by birthright as those who won it with their fists." As is perhaps obvious, this narrative of exceptional exclusion is animated by an outright claim to white citizenship—not just to the full rights and resources of the state and to the occupation of national space, but more nearly to what Jasbir Puar has theorized as "the right to maim." Like Kriegel's logic, it demonstrates Puar's argument that certain bodies (Black bodies, refugee bodies, bodies in occupied territories, among others) "are sustained in a perpetual state of debilitation precisely through foreclosing the social, cultural, and political translation to disability." Puar, *The Right to Maim*, xiv.

49 Russell, "Malcolm Teaches Us, Too," 13.

50 Russell, "Malcolm Teaches Us, Too," 14.

51 Wade, "Disability Culture Rap," 18.

52 Wade, "Disability Culture Rap," 15.

53 Mairs, as cited by Shapiro, *No Pity*, 34.

54 Shapiro, "In Search of a Word."

55 Johnson, as cited by Shapiro, *No Pity*, 33–34.

56 While Shapiro quotes Johnson as saying "these words have 'no soul' and 'no power'" in his monograph (34), he draws them together in the article version, reported two years prior. Shapiro, "In Search of a Word."

57 Nielsen, *Disability History*, 160.

58 Clare, *Exile and Pride*, 70.

59 Pickens, *Black Madness :: Mad Blackness*, 2. Emphasis is mine.

60 Julie Avril Minich, Jina Kim, and Sami Schalk staged a noteworthy dialogue about disability as a critical methodology in 2016–17. See Minich, "Enabling Whom?"; Kim, "Toward a Crip-of-Color Critique"; Schalk, "Critical Disability Studies as Methodology."

61 See, for example, Kafer, *Feminist, Queer, Crip*, 15, 183–84 (note 53); McRuer, *Crip Theory*, 35, 71–72; Sandahl, "Queering the Crip," 26–27, 34–35.

62 Kim, "Toward a Crip-of-Color Critique"; Kim, "Anatomy of the City," ix, 52–56.

63 Such an argument is also indebted to the scholars and activists who collaboratively articulate Black disability studies, many of whom are cited above. Among them, Anna Hinton, Sami Schalk, Moya Bailey and Izeta Autumn Mobley, as well as Jina Kim, have strategically traced the field through Black feminism and women of color feminisms, thereby rerouting the presumed origins of the field and reclaiming foundational historical thought-work and its constitutive labor. See Hinton, "On Fits, Starts, and Entry Points," 11–29; Dunhamn et al., "Developing and Reflecting."

64 Susan Schweik frames the historical period surrounding the Section 504 protest by employing Diane Nelson's theoretical framework of "fluidarity" rather than solidarity. Schweik, "Lomax's Matrix," 10.

65 Corbett O'Toole offers an account of the role Black Panthers played in the 504 sit-in and their impact on her in an oral history in Pelka's *What We Have Done* (271–75). It is worth noting Moore's critique of the limits of many accounts of the 504 sit-in, which tend to reduce the role of the Black Panthers to serving food. These are among few direct interventions in the formal story of the 504 sit-in, which more commonly presents as a race-neutral historic turn in disability rights activism.

66 Moore, "Black History of 504 Sit-In."

67 Schweik, "Lomax's Matrix," 1, 3.

68 For example, ADAPT activists report that Rosa Parks "shunned" them by refusing to participate in their protest of inaccessible buses in Denver in 1986. She allegedly opposed the "traumatic manner" of the protest and its effect to "cripple the city's present transportation system." See Shapiro, *No Pity*, 128; Johnson, "Rosa Parks and Access." Johnson's blog post the day after Parks's death presents a counter-memory, that of her betrayal of disability rights activists. It would seem that, despite (or perhaps because of) Parks being held up as a symbol of civil rights for disabled people, ADAPT did not build a relationship with her in the years leading up to the protest, which arguably might have contributed to a different outcome. Johnson and Shaw also provide an account of this incident that leaves a sliver of room for more interpretations of why Parks may not have been drawn to participate. Mary Johnson and Barrett Shaw, *To Ride the Public's Buses: The Fight That Built a Movement* (Louisville, KY: Avocado Press, 2001), 82–84. Finally, Susan Schweik takes account of Black Panther Party leaders' ableism alongside analyses of how health politics (and disability) figure into the history of Black power, the subject of Alondra Nelson's scholarship. See Nelson, *Body and Soul*.

3. CRIP LINEAGES, CRIP FUTURES

A Conversation by Stacey Park Milbern and Leah Lakshmi Piepzna-Samarasinha

STACEY PARK MILBERN AND LEAH LAKSHMI
PIEPZNA-SAMARASINHA

Leah: Stacey, remember that thing you posted about crip doulaing on Facebook? It blew my mind. You basically posited this whole new language around crips mentoring and assisting with birthing into disability culture/community, different kinds of disability, etc. as something we already do all the time but there is no language around in abledworld. Say more?

Stacey: Thank you, Leah. I see a lot of disabled people of color doing a ton of work in supporting people rebirthing themselves as disabled (or more disabled). This looks like a lot of things—maybe learning how to get medicine, drive a wheelchair, hire attendants, change a diet, date, have sex, make requests, code-switch, live with an intellectual disability, go off meds, etc., etc. The transition itself, of becoming disabled or moving along the ability spectrum, is frequently invisibilized, to the point that these changes do not even have a name. We do not have a way to talk about becoming disabled or more impaired. I feel like society not having language to describe this transition or the support it requires speaks to the ableism and isolation people with disabilities face in our lives. Of course there aren't yet words for this. Without crip intervention, we are frequently left alone to figure out how to be in our bodyminds and in this ableist world.

Crip mentorship/coaching/modeling at its best is "disability doulaship." We—you and I—are doulas. I am thankful for every person who has trusted me with the honor of supporting them through their journey and those who have supported me through the same. My survival and resilience has depended on it.

Leah: Yes. Yes. And that is such a huge paradigm shift—to view coming into disability identity as a birth, not a death, which is how the transition(s) are seen by ableist culture. To see it as a series of births, as our bodyminds evolve in their crip, neurodivergent, Deaf, sick identities over time—to name that there are life stages and rites of passage of becoming disabled, that this is not a static wound, these disabled bodyminds are creative, evolving strategies. Naming disability as a space we can be born into, not alone but supported and welcomed by other disabled people—and then again and again as we acquire new disabilities or discover words for things that have been there all along—that warm doulaed space creates a container that changes not only the entire way both individuals can experience disability but the ways disability communities can be formed.

And crip doulaing is both an interpersonal dynamic and one that creates new disability justice space. My moment where I was like, holy shit, I can actually feel myself a part of a politicized disability community, was around 2007, and I began to find sick and disabled QTBIPOC [queer and trans Black, Indigenous, and people of color] community around 2008, right? Now, a decade later, I see a younger generation of SDQTBIPOC [sick and disabled QTBIPOC] who both seem to have less struggle talking about ableism as a social justice and lived issue and who are creating new cultural spaces that blow my mind. The other day, I saw posts by some sick and disabled femmes of color who are creating BDSM [bondage and discipline, sadism, and masochism] parties with detailed access info in houses in Oakland. They're trying to create sexual cultures where discussing trauma, consent, desirability politics, and ableism is a norm, even if it's imperfect and struggling against a violent gentrification real estate market where finding accessible space is challenging. I haven't visited them in person yet, but I'm like, this is light-years ahead of the queer sex cultures I grew up in! (Which so often weren't accessible—not wheelchair or Deaf or fragrance accessible and also just in their assumptions that people have sex and how people have sex.) And I'm like, this happened because of the doulaing as organizing we did, the talking and supporting and hanging out and sharing articles and writing them. Or when I see QWOCMAP [the Queer Women of Color Media Access Project, an annual queer women of color film festival in the Bay Area] have this beautiful, warm, fragrance-free ask on their promotional material, coming from a working-class Black and Asian, middle-aged, partially disabled leadership, framed as being about collective love and support, I think about how some of that being there came from our loving, co-supportive relationships with each other. But I simultaneously am like, GREAT, and also like, is all this history of organizing going to get forgotten in a couple of years, because that's what happens to crip histories, period, but especially to grassroots, working-class Black, Indigenous, and brown sick and disabled femme organizing that flies under the radar and is not studied or noticed by abled POC or white crip land? And how do we prevent that from happening? What are our lineages? Who are the crip people and spaces who came before us who we call on, who are often not named in white disabled history?

Stacey: One of the hardest experiences about being disabled QTBIPOC for me is that there is little visibility or acknowledgment we exist, and we are left alone to figure out who we are and where we come from. That struggle to understand and create a genealogy that includes oneself is not necessarily unique to disabled people or queer people of color but nonetheless difficult. We may be the only one like us in our given and chosen family stories. There are so many stories of Deaf people who grow up in hearing families where no one signs. Or I think of my own story. I was the only disabled person in my immediate family, and they loved me but didn't have tools for conceptualizing my life outside of brokenness needing healing or bootstrap mentality about "overcoming" one's circumstance. My heart swells hearing about second- and third-generation families of disabled people, for example, a handful of friends who are people living with dwarfism or osteogenesis imperfecta [OI], who are proudly raising kids with dwarfism or OI.

I feel like I have spent lifetimes doing excavation work to find myself and my people, whether it is actively or passively, and most days I don't actually have a lot materially to show for it, except for the poetry of disability justice and relationships with crip queer beloveds. If you are a wheelchair user like myself, especially of color, a woman, a queer person riding gender borders, who are you supposed to see yourself represented in, Franklin D. Roosevelt or the kid from *Glee*? History frequently has not found our lives valuable enough to record-keep or tell our stories, and if it does, the narratives do not look like us, and if they by some miracle chance do, they are riddled with so much ableism that it is hard to separate out how the person with the impairment felt about their life and what is the story-keeper's ableist projections onto them.

It is frequently dangerous to seek each other out, even when we are alive in the same time period—disabled people face so much violence on the day to day—and admitting to having an impairment frequently can lead to losing one's parenting rights, bodily autonomy, employment, more. My friends Moya Bailey and India Harville, two Black, queer, disabled activists, and many other people, have done a lot of work to understand how the violent history of subjugation and chattel slavery shapes how Black communities may or may not relate to crip identity and being open about disability when it requires a person to "admit one has a compromised relationship to labor" (Bailey) within a system of ableism that has so often led to isolation, violence, and death.

At the same time, we know disabled people have been surviving, resisting, and leading communities from the beginning of time. We do this work of seeking ourselves out across time and planes, scribbling letters to each other in zines after helping disabled kiddos get through homework, calling out to ancestors while washing dishes, laughing over the ridiculousness of life via text and online groups, documenting our experiences with photos and microblogging, etc., etc. I know, Leah, that you've written about wondering if radical women of color ancestors would have claimed us with all the internalized ableism they faced. It is so hard to know. I wonder frequently what kind of conversation we would have if disability justice activists time-traveled back thirty, forty, fifty years ago and got to share an anti-ableism framework the same time the Combahee River Collective was forming or *This Bridge Called My Back* was penned. What kind of conversations would they have at the kitchen table with us? I want to speculate that the analysis of living in an environment of systemic oppression is functionally what creates disability would resonate with their understanding of intersectionality and oppression. I can also imagine that being open about disability, and some people even being proud of their disability identities, might not translate. That feels understandable, since we needed their work to build these ideas upon.

My own lineage is complicated. It includes my friends who have gone on, disabled friends who might not have politically shared a lot but who so very much wanted to live the life I live now and whom I live in honor of. It includes Korean ancestors I've not gotten yet to know fully. It includes some white disabled women, like Harriet McBryde Johnson and Laura Hershey. Their legacies all are important and a part of me.

Leah: Young abled people are always like, where are our queer elders? But it's pretty clear to me where we often are—someplace affordable where we can go to bed early—and what we gain in that move, and also what we lose. My neurodivergent brain and slow body really want some kind of accessible QTBIPOC rural community, but I also get really scared that if I'm not constantly out there as a performer, how fast I'll be forgotten.

We need to ask ourselves, what are the conditions that will allow disabled QTBIPOC elderhood to flourish? For me, some of those conditions are creating accessible community spaces. When I first moved to Oakland, I was struck by how some of the most popular dance nights for queer women of color happened in the afternoon. They were Black and Latinx queer spaces that went from two to eight p.m., they had free (or \$5) barbecue and lots of places to sit down. Those spaces had accessibility, even if no one used the word, that made it possible for me to go dancing. And while I was there, I saw women in their fifties and sixties—dancing and hanging out and being able to be part of a queer women of color social world there. When we really value ourselves as queer and trans disabled Black and brown people, the ways our spaces look are going to change—but shit like this proves we already've been doing it! We know how to refuse to forget about each other.

I both do and do not have disabled QTBIPOC elders in my life. Ancestors, yes. Elders, not as much. Elderhood is not a state that just happens. Disabled QTBIPOC elderhood is dependent on systems that support it being there—like affordable rent, neighborhoods that don't gentrify, social spaces that are accessible, Section 8 or social housing that exists and doesn't have a ten-year waiting list, guaranteed annual income, accessible work. When those things don't exist, it affects the likelihood that we'll get to elder.

In the last few years, since I turned forty, younger disabled QTBIPOC have started calling me "elder." While I'm honored that they see me as someone they respect and have maybe learned from, it also makes me feel a little desperate. I know that part of why they are naming me as an elder is because I'm the oldest disabled QTBIPOC person they know.

Many sick, disabled, Mad, and neurodivergent older people don't live to get really old. Sometimes that's because of progressive disability, but it's also because of systemic oppression. So many of my sick and disabled QTBIPOC elders are in trailer parks or living in a motel or moved back in with their shitty family because they didn't have a better option. When that class and location slippage happens, they become really invisible to younger hip queers really fucking fast.

Other elders I know have more choices but have withdrawn from the world as they've gotten older, because lack of access doesn't get easier when you get older. In our twenties and thirties, we might have forced ourselves to be visible to abled people, for them to care about us, by organizing and writing and pushing ourselves to be present in abled spaces. But then when we turn forty, we're like, fuck it; we're tired and we can't push ourselves like that in the same way anymore. Often our hearts are broken, or very, very tired, from twenty years of struggle—it really sucks to be having the Access 101 conversation you've been having since the late '80s, again. Our friends are dead, our neighborhood has gentrified, and everyone in the club is twenty-two and has no idea who that old lady/fag/butch is. Our bodyminds never fit that well into capitalism, and as we age we fit into it even less.

What are some moments of birthing ourselves we want to describe?

Stacey: Zora Neale Hurston said there are years that ask questions and years that answer. To be honest, I'm in a year right now of completely being undone. I'm having a hard time with higher levels of daily pain and faster bursts of my progressive neuromuscular disability advancing. I have always had a progressive disability and know what is needed to adjust myself to a big lifestyle change (e.g., becoming less ambulatory in sixth grade, becoming a powerchair user in tenth grade, getting a trach in twelfth grade, etc., etc.), but it is still so hard and painful, and this time it is harder. I find myself having moments where I am closest to all of these edges that I've spent my entire life avoiding—edges of grief, edges of pride or things I thought I'd never do, edges of shame—and somehow still hanging on, sometimes even dancing on the cliffs. Like the time last week when I was crying in a hospital bed and alone, and instead of having a pity party that none of the chaplains could relate to my experience, the Spirit found me and I preached to myself the words I needed to hear. Or also last week, when I was terrified to be alone after getting out of the ICU—instead of keeping my anxiety to myself and being in terror, I found my mouth telling people that truth (I'm so scared) and asking them to stay and sit, or stay and sleep. I had 24-7 support the first eighty-four hours after the hospital. The sense of being a burden still burns hot in my throat, but the necessity of the moment triumphs. There is nothing more crip than crip practicality. I'm riding an avalanche and won't know how things will land until I crash to a stop. That requires support. A lot of support.

Just as I'm learning to let myself have support and learning to be compassionate with myself, I'm learning to let myself grieve. I let myself go in the low. I give myself a window of time to stay there, and then I come to get me out. I also give myself reality breaks. I spend a lot of my time watching fantasy movies where people transfigure or get to leave their bodies via avatars. I watch them over and over. It's okay that that's my jam. These bodyminds of ours require a lot of us; we can be imperfect, we can cope with shitty things that get us through. I'm thankful for whatever help you get in this life.

Rebirthed me always has new priorities. I let them guide me. This time it's to live life with my disabled love as much as we can with the time and health we have and to let the Spirit transform me through this experience that I may be of use to my communities and people in a way I wasn't before. Everything else forms around those things. Pain and loss clarifies, refines. Sometimes crip life is crystal clear. I know how I want to live in this world. I fight to be here.

How have you found crip ancestors? Do your ancestors feel the same way about disability and ableism as you? What have you learned from them? What are you teaching them?

Leah: I stumbled upon them. I dug them up. I fought to find them. I dreamed them. Others shared them. I remembered them, like, oh, the woman who chosen-mothered me when I was eighteen. That was a disabled story because we were two crazy femmes mentoring each other. I think about questions like, what does it mean to claim Marsha P. Johnson and Sylvia Rivera as crip ancestors because they were both chronically ill, trauma-surviving, Mad trans women of color and sex work organizers? What doors open up then in terms of how we understand madness as power, Black and brown trans women's brilliant Mad political actions?

In my own lineage, for years I always said that I became disabled at twenty-two, the first in my family, but as I got older I remembered my mother's story of living with polio—a buried and a fiercely present story, because she closeted her disability to survive, but her pain and physical difference was all up in our house. So often, when we start telling the stories of disability, we realize they are woven into every thread of all our lives.

I don't know if these ancestors feel the same way about disability and ableism as I do. I don't know. Probably not! It's likely they had some wicked internalized ableism and isolation. Or maybe they thought all the same shit I do but it didn't get passed down or recorded/they didn't have anyone to speak it to/no one who cared was listening. Maybe they experienced disability in fundamentally different ways than I did that are not just internalized ableism. I don't know. I am making it up as I go along. I believe running back to look for our disabled ancestors is political work. I believe in sitting in the space of prayer, in the void of not always knowing who is disabled and what their legacy means as a disability justice space. I feel like we are passing knowledge back and forth, beyond the beyond. Being closer to the dead than the living is another kind of crip relationship. I think about the possibilities I am articulating in my life as ones that maybe they were or were not able to embody in their life—but either way, I would not be here without them. Their crip Black and brown queerness gets to breathe because of our storytelling and remembering.

And I wonder, with all our people who have been murdered or died early, this flood of ancestors, are they part of our crip wealth? We mourn our dead, we become our dead, but are our dead also weapons and resources, seed banks?

I also think a lot about crip futurity. It is radical to articulate that we have a past and lineages and cultures, in a world that says we are individual medical defects to be eliminated. AND it is also radical to dream a liberated future by and for sick and disabled, Deaf, neurodivergent, and Mad queer/trans/Black/ brown people, for the same reason. Ableism scarcity means we are often feeling like we're just fighting to survive another day, not be buried under erasure or lack of insurance or both—so it is FUCKING HUGE to imagine, what ARE disability justice revolutionary futures? Especially right now, when so many of us are in the throes of being like, here we go, it's early fascism and they're gonna come for the crips first, and none of the abled will notice. Fighting for basic rights—the ACA [Affordable Care Act] and ADA [Americans with Disabilities Act], not being eliminated, not being warehoused—means often we are panicking and terrified, frozen in reaction. All of that makes it difficult to imagine what we are for, not just what we are against. BUT this is precisely the time when it is the most important for us to imagine a radical disability justice future.

What element does disability justice play in your spiritual life and how does this connect to lineage for you?

Leah: I grew up the kid of lapsed Christians, both of whose families were forced to convert and faced a lot of violence in Christian spaces. They left but still retained a lot of scars from the Christianity they knew, and I wanted something else. As a survivor kid, I found solace and connected with spirit in running away to the woods and talking to the moon. And as I got older, I learned a lot about earth-based and ancestor-loving spirituality from multiple traditions, from library books about Wicca to other QTBIPOC friends who talked about ancestors and ways as South Asians we were trying to reconnect to our spiritual traditions without casteism, patriarchy, or Hindutva.

So I have crip ancestors on my altar, and I pray for them and to them. I ask them to help me—to help me figure out how to write something, be in right relation, deal with a problem or conflict in community, survive, deal with my having to interface with the medical-industrial complex. Right now, the people up there include Baba Ibrahim Abdurrahman Farajajé, Leslie Feinberg, Taueret Davies, Galvarino, Gloria Anzaldúa, Frida Kahlo, Audre Lorde, Emma Deboncoeur. They remind me that we are and have been here and heroic in complex ways; we have survived crazy shit and done crazy shit, dealt with complex questions, and not always had all the answers. They remind me that I come from somewhere, that we are not the first people to do DJ [disability justice] work, and that we get to do meaningful things as imperfect people. Too often, people in social justice spaces pedestalize ancestors as saints, and I think it's important to resist that. Disabled ancestors' crip ideas of ancestry, because concepts of perfection are ableist and we sure aren't "perfect!" And we're still valuable.

Stacey: I grew up evangelical Christian in the American South. I was all in. . . . My parents took me to every healing service in the Carolinas (there are tel-evangelist Benny Hinn videos with me on them). I taught Sunday school, and I was totally the nerd organizing prayer events at school. It really impacted my sense of self to hear that I was broken and unlovable by God because I was dis-abled and, then later, queer. Some people legit thought I was disabled because of some sin my mom must have done. I stopped being the same kind of Chris-tian as my parents when church bullies told me I hadn't been healed by God yet because I "didn't believe enough." We were all thirteen years old.

I have done a lot of work on my faith and, surprisingly, have come back to believing in God. My faith is a huge part of my resiliency practice because it an-swers a lot of my questions. I know disabled people are perfect as we are because I believe we were made by the same hand that made flowers, and mice and dogs and stars, and they are perfect as they are. I know God wants us to strive for jus-tice because God is love and "justice is what Love looks like in public" (Cornel West). I don't know why suffering happens, but I know it hurts God, and I feel the Divine's presence with me through loves who join me in the hard moments.

What does crip wealth mean to you?

Leah: I always go to generosity, and "crip kindness." Crip kindness is the wealth and skill where we notice each other's pain face and offer a chair, ask in a low-key way if we can help with a service task, sit without speaking, drop a bottle of tincture next to someone having a panic attack, raise thousands of dollars for someone to buy an accessible van, or mail a stranger our extra prescription. It's collective noticing and collective hustle. It's being witnessed. It's being allowed to relax, expand, just be.

It's also not automatic, which is a place where I want to deepen Mia Mingus's idea of "access intimacy."[1] Like many other sick and disabled queers, Mia's well-known essay "Access Intimacy" has been foundational to my disability justice knowledge in its naming the experience of crip-on-crip understanding of each other's access needs as a place of love and communion. But some of that essay reads to me like understanding each other's access needs is an automatic and magical process. I want to push back on that and say that while access intimacy is often a sophisticated disabled gift, and we are magic and make magic, I want to argue for access intimacy as a process and a learnable skill. I think it's dangerous when we believe that as disabled people we always "just know" each other's needs—I want us to acknowledge the ways that crips do have ways of knowing each other's "stuff" and how we also need to not assume, and ask each other what our needs are. I also think it's very important to state that abled people can and do commit to learning access intimacy, through asking and respecting our knowledge—because otherwise we'll be stuck in this place where we're the only ones who can do for us. I want everyone to have crip knowledge.

Crip wealth is also the gift of us being the normal. The gift of, yes, you can live in your sweatpants, you can change your ostomy bag in front of me, you can be really, really weird, the amount of time it takes for you to transfer to the toilet is normal. I see so many abled people running into disability or madness or illness and just being completely flummoxed by all of this, because the ableist shame everyone swims in is so deep. Not that I have shame beat—this is something that I've seen get thrown at us sometimes, "Oh, I'm not like you totally shame-free DJ people"—but I totally still grapple with shame all the time. But some of our wealth is creating these small spaces away from shame, where it is okay to have a disabled bodymind.

Stacey: Leah, this concept you introduced me to has totally been a paradigm shifter! Crip wealth. I'm not going to go into defining it but want to say that I feel like even thinking about crip wealth is so crip itself. I see disabled people every day thinking of ideas abled people never would have, primarily by focusing their time and efforts on using what they do have, and the space between, rather than putting their attention on the limitation or lack of ability. It sounds a little like inspiration porn, but we do come up with wildly imaginative solutions this way. I can ramp a three-inch step by taking off my sneakers and rolling over them. I've seen blind friends do wicked things with text to speech in their ear. My friend Leroy Moore taught me that one way Harriet Tubman was able to scout so many routes is by using her traumatic brain injury and talking aloud to herself; people brushed her off as a crazy woman. Texting, now used by everyone, was created as assistive technology for Deaf people. I save so much time sometimes letting strangers in public assume I can't speak. We have so much at our disposal and most of the world has no idea. It can give us a big toolbox to play with.

What haunts you about ableism?

Leah: Shit, Stacey. Thank you for using the word "haunted." I wouldn't have, but that word captures the ghosts and grief of ableism that haunt me, the corridors of my mind in the nights.

So much haunts me. I have so much crip grief around abled BIPOC organizing that cares about disability and ableism for a year or a few months or a season and then just ... forgets about it. I live in a city, Seattle, right now, where people go, OMG, that is heaven for SDQTPOC [sick and disabled queer and trans people of color]! and I'm like, laughing because what they think of as this "big disability justice scene" is like twenty people! Despite there having been disabled activism by people like Billie Rain, E. T. Russian, and many others here for decades, there's still a huge gap where abled queers are just, like, what? We're the ghosts, where, they wonder where we went, or they don't even wonder, they just think of us fleetingly now and then but don't hold enough cripworld knowledge to maintain relationships with us—which would mean making systematic change in how they run their lives and gathering spaces.

I am haunted by how I am forgotten by nondisabled activists of color. How most people won't give up the points and success they get from moving in abled time to be with us meaningfully. They'll do lip service about sustainability, but that's it. They will point at the three years disabled people were able to organize in a space they created as how committed they are to anti-ableism but erase the way they stopped supporting us that didn't allow us to continue.

There's also crip bitterness—something very few abled people understand that works to isolate us, because they can't deal with how "harsh" or "depressing" we are to be around and quietly stop working with us. The lack of understanding of the wear and tear of having to be stuck fighting for basic access after twenty-five years of work.

I am haunted by the question of, will all our work and lives be remembered and by who and how? Most DJ folks I know are really nervous about our work being co-opted and ripped off, for good reason, and I'm worried about that too, but I'm equally worried about us being deliberately erased. I believe that our work often thrives in the small scale, the ignored, the underground. I thrive in those cracks myself. But I want disabled QTBIPOC to find each other, find our work, our paradigms, our tools, our science, our hacks and art and love, and it just takes one huge personal relationship fallout to make a community inaccessible or erase years of work. There is no disability justice archive yet. (Another thing to work on.) I remind myself we are each other's archive. Anytime an SD person remembers each other and moments in movement history, we memorialize our history, we witness ourselves into being.

Finally, I am haunted by my dead. The first queer love I had was another suicidal femme, and I have loved Crazy femmes all my life, romantically, sexually, as friends. Many of them are not here anymore. I was organizing my storage closet yesterday and started to sift through my archives—all these piles of papers, zines, cards, event promo cards, of twenty years of QTBIPOC organizing—and when I said online, wow, 2010 sure was different, and someone asked me to explain, one of my first thoughts was of how many more people were alive then. I am haunted by the fact that I will continue to lose femmes I love, as much as I will fight to create and share tools that could help us stay here.

Stacey: I feel heavy with the weight of our longing. Sometimes it haunts me. All of the dreams of our ancestors, disabled people currently living, and disabled people to come. There is so much I want for us, that we want for ourselves and each other. Every person I ever met in an institution, a day program, a sheltered workshop, on the street, on the bus, anywhere has wanted and deserved so much that the world has not given. I feel immense privilege and responsibility for everything I have access to, and it haunts me how many disabled people do not share the same access, even to basic things like a person to talk to who cares about you or choosing the place you live, what you wear, eat, who puts their hands on your body, etc. When I first moved to the Bay, I had a lot of survivor's guilt. The life I was getting to live that loved ones I knew wanted and deserved just as equally but did not have.

Have you thought what you want your legacy to be? How have you held envisioning future, navigating trauma of past, surviving the present all at the same time?

Leah: Oh Christ, I don't know. Yes. Yes, I have thought about it. I write my obituary in my head often. I want to be remembered as the person who broke the cycle of abuse in my family. I want the messy, real, concrete ways I made this happen to be remembered, as one of many possibility models for ending abuse. I want to be remembered as a writer, storytelling performer, and grassroots intellectual—that by telling stories I helped change the world. I want the fragile and strong spaces where we came together as disabled BIPOC, the doorways coming and going, to be remembered. I want to be remembered as one of the many who hung out and lay down and laughed and texted each other ideas and did medical advocacy and did not forget each other and changed the world. Small and big changes that I pray will make a disability justice future. I want to be remembered as that femme cane dancing with you in your chair in the club, or hanging out on our couch plotting and laughing.

Stacey: I want my legacy to be loving disabled people. It has been my life story and work. Through loving disabled people, I get to love myself.

NOTES

This chapter is reprinted with permission from *Care Work: Dreaming Disability Justice* by Leah Lakshmi Piepzna-Samarasinha (2018).

1   Mia Mingus, "Access Intimacy, Interdependence and Disability Justice," *Leaving Evidence* (blog), April 12, 2017, https://leavingevidence.wordpress.com/2017/04/12 /access-intimacy-interdependence-and-disability-justice/.

4. CRITICAL DISABILITY STUDIES AND THE QUESTION OF PALESTINE

Toward Decolonizing Disability

JASBIR K. PUAR

The Question of Palestine

In April 2021, during a Society for Disability Studies plenary session on crip temporalities, Alison Kafer astutely noted that those who are afforded the indexing of a "before" the pandemic and an "after" the pandemic are already displaying a mark of bodies deemed worthy of care in contrast to those who persist through braided strands of debilitation.[1] What has been widely fetishized as "pandemic time" is actually what "crip time" has always been—never on time, waiting out time, needing more time, unable to keep up with time, forced time at home, too long a waiting time. While there is a renewed discovery of "care" as an ethics of conviviality and interdependency, North American disability justice organizing has long experimented with the praxis and pedagogy of sharing socially reproductive labor in order to counter the stratifying forces of biopolitics, akin to what Tithi Bhattacharya calls the communalization of forms of "life making."[2]

Crip theorizing illuminates the biopolitical consolidation of the "make live" vector not only in terms of populations but also in terms of praxis, in the quotidian of social reproduction, most pointedly of the social reproduction of the pandemic WFH white nuclear capital F family. That is to say, while we can easily demarcate the populations that inhabit and protect the make live vector—ruling elite classes, the 1 percent—the amplification of practices of self-preservation during the pandemic gives us a different mapping of the make live vector. Locating a Black feminist tradition of communal care in the work of Audre Lorde, crip theorists Jina Kim and Sami Schalk argue that disabled people do not have the luxury of atomizing social reproduction from reproduction; further, the labor of reproducing oneself is exponentially greater, and often reliant on the work of "femmes of color."[3] Sins Invalid, a leading disability justice movement organization for BIPOC queer, trans, and nonbinary disabled people, has developed an entire lexicon on para- and sub-state community "care webs," "pods," "spoons," centralizing the collectivization of slow time, the antinuclearization of care, and, as Heike Peckruhn argues, a philosophy of "access" that goes beyond accommodations by demanding "access to life."[4]

Even as we affirm the capacious and frankly life-saving thinking of North American disability justice movement work and crip theorizing about care webs, resisting productivity, and embracing the collectivization of slow life, we can also note the epistemological foreclosures of this lexicon in settler colonial contexts such as Palestine, where mass impairment is a predominating source of disability and there has been over the years the use of a "shoot to cripple" approach to disciplining and controlling the colonized. It is unclear that the terminology of *crip* disability studies is even resonant in a context where "shoot to cripple" is a settler colonial tactic. Additionally, concepts such as "ableism," "access," and "accommodation" are necessarily revaluated. Access and what is accessible in Palestine center relationships of occupied space and colonized mobility. For example, bus and taxis drivers are conjuring constantly shifting "access maps" through monitoring and assessing impromptu checkpoints, divided highways, the violence of the Israeli occupation forces (IOF), the presence of settlers, increasing drone surveillance, unexplained road closures, protest and mass demonstrations, spontaneous parades that welcome released prisoners, and house demolitions.

But this is not only a problem of terminology and its travels. Thinking through the limits of such frames provides an opportunity to theorize a geopolitics of disability knowledge production that does not reify Global North/South divides but instead foregrounds the intermeshed matrices of settler colonialism, empire, and infrastructures of disablement that cut across otherwise self-apparent geographies. I use the Global North/Global South framing provisionally to mark rather than resolve the messiness of geopolitics. Palestine is often conceived of and taught as part of the Global South, but it is no less part of the Global North given the Israeli settler colonial occupation and the financial and ideological global support that Israel enjoys. Further, the United States and Israel are co-entwined in the normalization of settler colonialism, a structure that requires "perpetual injury as genocide."[5] This entwinement can be thought of in several different ways, both conceptually and materially. Palestinian CDS scholar Yasmin Snounu argues that "contextualizing disability in

Palestine within the U.S. frame of reference is important because disability is strongly intertwined with the political involvement of the U.S. in Palestine."[6] In an article (coauthored with Phil Smith and Joe Bishop), Snounu notes that "the U.S. in particular, contributes to the disablement of Palestinian people by supporting colonial projects of the Israeli state. Then, the United States sends developing countries funding for disability projects."[7]

Highlighting the perverse circuits of injury and care, Snounu et al. situate the specific relevance of disability in Palestine for a critical disability studies that addresses US and Israeli settler colonialisms and American empire.[8] Edward Said's classic formulation of the "question of Palestine" has challenged the intellectual left in the United States since the 1970s and is just as salient today as when he first posed it.[9] Although Palestine is not quite the "third rail" of academia that it was even ten years ago, the broadening discussion on Palestine has been accompanied by greater repression of free speech through myriad tactics: smear campaigns, anti-BDS laws in numerous states, and a definition of anti-Semitism that includes any criticism of the state of Israel. These details about the status of Palestine in US academia are relevant because CDS has historically been hailed as an activist field and therefore aspires to be aligned with disability justice movement organizing. Numerous disability justice organizations have supported this anticolonial cause: as one example, Sins Invalid released a statement of solidarity with Palestine as well as a video titled "Disability Justice for Palestine" when the maiming of Gazan protestors began in 2018.[10]

Helen Meekosha's 2011 provocation that disability studies can act as a "form of scholarly colonialism" is a caution about the ways that disability studies may unwittingly function as a handmaiden to US empire if we do not interrogate the genealogies of the field that exist not despite the occluding of race and empire, but because of such elisions. Meekosha further argues that despite fears of pathologization and a return to the medical model, "scholars and activists need to confront as a central issue the production of impairment in the global South."[11] Sarah Orsak eloquently redirects the import of these fears by noting that "impairment here is not marginalized as incapable or lacking, but rather becomes a valuable resource that is productive for capital and empire."[12] While the production of impairment in the Global South has, over the years, been increasingly acknowledged, such acknowledgment is often accompanied by a liberal declaration of the value of disabled lives, as if critiques of colonial violence on their own terms are somehow implicitly ableist. Such a rhetorical turn misses the force of Meekosha's point, at worst acting as an apologia for imperial violence, and at best reenacting this scholarly colonialism by refusing to grapple with the possibility that for many in the Global South, the main concern may not be the return or pervasiveness of the medical model but rather the struggle to "end global violence in all its forms."[13] As Meekosha succinctly summarizes, "the key debates around disability and impairment, independent living, care and human rights are often irrelevant to those whose major goal is survival" (670). Disability justice organizing that recognizes that all colonized bodies are deemed unworthy and unfit actively works through these tensions by valuing and prioritizing the knowledges and experiences that disabled people bring to the struggles to end ableist state and imperial violence rather than reiterating this false binary.

It is of course crucial not to reify Global North and Global South as discrete entities, nor to minimize the violence of "war-prone dictators . . . ruling elites . . . and popular nationalisms" (675). Yet Meekosha's concerns about citational practices that ignore "non-metropolitan" literature, social theory, and medical anthropology scholarship remain deeply relevant. Decolonizing disability and decolonizing disability studies are inseparable from each other. A radical orientation toward Global South locations does not bracket the Global South and southern disability studies but takes seriously that no singular "disability analytic" exists. This acknowledgment begins with the impossibility of disaggregating disability as an epistemological project from the biopolitical ascendancy of whiteness.[14] Fields of study and disciplines are not benign formations; they are bred from and breed interpretations of global orders, social formations, and arrangements of power. One of the field's founding mandates is the study of how knowledge about disability is created and circulated, and this mandate necessarily implicates its own practices of doing so. The field of critical disability studies therefore must account for its relationship to perhaps one of the largest producers of mass disablement in the world: US empire. Meekosha's call to "decolonize disability" is an opportunity to interrogate the knowledge-production projects on disability that benefit from the very circuits of empire that enable the massification of disability.[15] Mass scale is one such circuit, according to Snounu et al.: "The crimes committed by the Israeli occupation increase the number of disabled people, resulting in Palestine having the highest percentage of disabled people of any country in the world. . . . The total number of persons with disabilities in Palestine is between 114,000 to 300,000, depending on which definition of disability is used."[16] Indeed, the question of Palestine has resounding relevance for CDS today, both as a disability justice issue and as a geopolitical nexus that propels a rethinking of the field and its assumption.

In the discussion that follows, I offer thoughts on preliminary research on disability in Palestine. A thorough discussion, however, of the local terms and parameters of disability activism in Palestine is beyond the scope of this chapter.[17] Meekosha reminds us that the "anti-colonialist politics of disabled people in the majority world have yet to be documented."[18] And it may also be the case that these politics surface less under the signs of disability rights, activism, and justice organizing; rather they transit through anticolonial resistance movements more generally (the formulation of "spatial justice" is one such possibility).[19] My main goal in this brief piece is to foreground the circuits of US empire and settler colonialism in order to vex a binary between critical disability studies and southern disability studies and a north/south binarization that obfuscates the interconnected relations of infrastructures of colonial rule.

Spatial Debilities in the West Bank

In 2018, with a fellowship from the Palestinian American Research Center, I was part of a team that met with people working at and attending disability and rehabilitation centers[20] in refugee camps in the Occupied Palestinian Territories.[21] While there is almost no literature focused specifically on disability in the camps, there is some work that addresses "health disparities" to draw upon, including advocacy research dispersed across various NGOs, governmental agencies, and public health institutes.[22] Due in part to the Bantustan fragmentation of the West Bank and the temporal schisms that result from mobility restrictions, there are multiple and often contradictory genealogies of disability in Palestine: for example, spatial concentrations of disability in the refugee camps do not necessarily resonate with NGO work foregrounding identity, disability rights, and the neoliberal politics of recognition and empowerment.[23] This project therefore brings together the spatial distribution of disability with the vast literature on mobility restrictions so as to contribute to the understanding of the workings of the occupation.

Snounu et al. point to the complexities of disability in Palestine, due, in part, to the "number of Palestinians who are maimed by Israel on a daily basis."[24] I would add that spatial segregation delimits access and also means that what disability is, and what its relationship is to the general debilitation endemic to life in the West Bank, is spatially overdetermined. The occupation imposes extreme spatial regulation through the restriction of movement as one of its prime technologies of settler colonial rule, which then reproduces segregation of Palestinian populations from each other.[25] It is important to acknowledge that some camps are spatially isolated or consolidated, but this may be unexceptional given the broader matrix of partitioning in the West Bank. Some camps are within or extensions of cities; others, while not gated off from urban centers, are produced as peripheral to local cities and villages. Divisions between inside the camp and outside the camp are tenuous at best, hazily demarcated by urban and nonurban geographies, density of population, and the vertical sprawl that characterizes camps (they grow upward since they cannot spread out). While keeping in mind the indeterminacy of the spatial and temporal boundedness of camps, in our interactions we came to understand that debility and disability are perceived as spatially concentrated in ways that may contribute to a sense of enclosure.[26] The concomitant rise of neoliberal development in the West Bank (Ramallah as a bubble, Rawabi as luxury housing and shopping complex) is also central to the spatial splintering of the occupation.[27] Snounu et al. write that "Palestine, for instance, mostly deals with issues of physical disabilities because of Israeli practices of violence, and also because of the lack of diagnostic tools, which makes it difficult to identify those with learning disabilities."[28] While this accords with my own observations, I would add that ratio and distribution of "physical [war] disabilities" and "other" disabilities is, again, spatially overdetermined, insofar as the camps are often subjected to violent daily raids by the IOF.

During this initial research phase I grasped two things: first, that the creation of "mobility disabilities" through corporeal assault but also through infrastructures are not only central to the calculus of the occupation; they are also linked logics of debilitation that complicate a binary distinction between disabled and nondisabled bodies. "Mobility disability," argues Celeste Langan, is the "diminished difference" between people who are mobility disabled and those able-bodied who need to move but cannot.[29] Interviews and conversations with disabled Palestinians in refugee camps in the West Bank explain that this "diminished difference" is a lived reality in a context where Palestinians live in close proximity to each other, where there is less nuclear-family domestic atomization. In addition, all Palestinians are subject to the "collective punishment" of movement restrictions—checkpoints, permit regimes, the apartheid wall, divided highways. I continue to wonder whether these diminished differences, especially as experienced by those living in spatially segregated camps that endure higher rates of war injuries, foster solidaristic relations through differentials of mobility rather than reiterate the parsing of a disabled/nondisabled binary. In effect I am arguing that seriously thinking through this "diminished difference" is an important entry point into the process of *decolonizing disability*.

The spectrum of mobility disabilities illuminates what Alison Kafer calls the "political-relational" life of the camps—the care webs and mutual aid networks that have developed over decades in response to the conditions of the occupation.[30] It also reflects how disability is often a transactional category embedded in humanitarian aid economies that may or may not resonate as an identity per se; it is an analytic deployed to access resources and participate in the NGO and UN lexicon of rights and empowerment discourses, the latter being an extremely delicate issue in the context of such social, economic, and political oppression. Many center directors explained that human rights frames, NGO organizations, and humanitarian relief are producing "disability" and related lexicon that are driven externally; in turn these emergent linguistic interfaces are reshaped by center employees and camp residents to create narratives of disability that feed into preordained frames of funding.

From our conversations we learned that war injuries in the camps are considered a form of punishment and thus markers of anticolonial resistance, suggesting that disability is an onto-epistemological facet of Palestinian resistance, an unexceptional state of becoming that informs the comportments of many Palestinian refugees. Disability is experienced as a consequence of resisting the occupation and also as merely living as occupied. In a field of chronic health conditions—high levels of diabetes and heart disease are typical—disability was not an inhabited identity, nor a distinct phenomenological orientation that distinguished certain bodies from other bodies. That is not to say that residents did not understand themselves or others as disabled, but that identification in this context does not fall neatly into being either "descriptively disabled" or "politically disabled."[31] Rather, disability, typically invoked as a descriptor and deployed as a transactional facet between funding opportunities, is incorporated into a spectrum of debilitation in densely populated camp life that demanded alternative networks of care, integration, and support. In other words, I gleaned that disability is lived as much, if not more so, as a communal process of coming to terms with and resisting the conditions of the occupation than an individual condition.

The second thing I grasped is that the calibrations of movement necessary to navigate the endless infrastructures of containment demand specific stretchings of space and time, what I call slow life. In conversation with Palestinian theorists of temporality, slow life refers to the colonial modulation of registers of time, and there are a couple of these: being fixed as forever in the past of historical/civilizational time, the "stealing of time" through the expansion of labor time (living labor), and the withholding of temporal simultaneity so coveted in our connective technologies that signal modernity.[32] Here I am interested in the cordoning off and the creation of space through time. This cordoning works through the architectural structures that are erected as obstacles to "free-flowing" speed, rhythm, and pace: checkpoints, circuitous highways, settlement locations, the partitioning of land and populations into Areas A, B, and C. As Rema Hammami and other scholars in Palestine studies have pointed out, the stretching of time—the West Bank is both smaller, because movement is short-circuited, and larger, because it takes longer to move from one place to another—is not a by-product of surveillance and securitization apparatuses; it is the point of them, more so than halting Palestinian movement "in toto."[33] Nothing ever happens "on time." Uncertainty becomes a primary affective orientation, a folded-into-the-flesh condition of possibility, an ontology of sorts. Radical uncertainty is the condition of being.

Slow life thinks about connections between how people are denied access to movement and/or are displaced (mobility); how disability and maiming are spatially produced, distributed, and contained (debility); and how people experience time in relation to spatial geographies (temporality).[34] Whether it be the time of spectacular violence that is part of disaster capitalism or the "afterlife" of violence that turns out to be no afterlife at all, the interwovenness of temporality, debility, and mobility are absorbed into the violence of the everyday. *Slow life*, I argue, is therefore a reckoning with the capitalist captures of uncertainty. And as a corollary argument, slow life refers to the collectivization of slow time that upends the distinctions between those with mobility disabilities and those able-bodied whose movements are circumscribed.[35]

Southern Disability Studies

For some time now I have situated my work on Palestine in conversation with the concerns animating the nascent field of southern disability studies (SDS). This field insists on the importance of mapping colonial and imperial violence and the effects of war, poverty, and mass impairment. Meekosha states in her 2011 challenge to the field, "Decolonising Disability," that the anticolonial, antiwar work of ending what she calls "mass impairment" must be central not only to disability studies writ large but must complicate what disability is in a global sense. Mass impairment connects the blinding of hundreds of insurgents in Kashmir with pellet bullets; the targeting of more than seven thousand lower limbs of protestors during the Great March of Return in Gaza in 2018;[36] the disablement of thirty thousand people a month in Syria; the recent use of "nonlethal" crowd control weapons such as rubber bullets (aka kinetic impact projectiles, or KIP) and tear gas at protests in the United States, France, Lebanon, Hong Kong, Catalonia, Argentina, and Chile. (Chile recorded more than three hundred ocular trauma injuries caused by police violence during the 2019 uprisings.) This incomplete list of episodic maiming does not even get into the layering of disability (for example, across the intifadas, the targeting of Gaza in 2008–9, 2014, 2018, and 2021, and the serial wars in Afghanistan and Iraq) and of generational epigenetic debilitation; both might be considered a process of primitive accumulation enacted through dispossession of the corporeal. Snounu notes the humanitarian aid–driven circuitry of double maiming embedded in US and Canadian funding of the occupation particularly through armaments sales only to fund efforts to repair the corporeal and infrastructural damage of war, the cycle of disaster capitalism. The anticipatory violence of the future haunts as well: Paul Rocher's work on the exponential global growth of the nonlethal weapons industry in the last decade, of weapons that don't kill—never mind that they debilitate, disable, and can eventually kill—points to the increasing consolidation of injury as a form of humane violence.[37]

The need for southern disability studies could not be clearer, which is why it is unfortunate when this burgeoning scholarship is channeled as an epistemological corrective instead of illuminating the entwinement of transnational debilitation. Despite the fine work of Global South scholars such as Anita Ghai; journals such as the *Indian Journal of Critical Disability Studies* and *Disability and the Global South*; North America–based scholars such as Eunjung Kim (also based in South Korea), Rachel Gorman, and Nirmala Erevelles, who insist on a transnational, materialist analysis of disability; and work on settler colonialism and disability, largely from Canadian scholars, such as Dian Million's *Therapeutic Nations* and Louise Tam's research on how asylee mental health support services function as indoctrination into Canadian settler subjectivity—despite all this work, SDS (as well as convivial literatures on settler colonialism and transnationalism) is often relegated to the place of epistemic difference and alterity.[38] If southern disability studies is demarcated primarily by a mandate to distinguish itself from "proper" disability studies, thereby centralizing CDS as the dominant site of knowledge production, then the North/South divide is reified into a self/other ontological difference that places the burden of explicating the debilitating effects of colonization onto the (post)colonized.

This is a problem taken up by a project I am part of, Disability Under Siege (DUS), which focuses on disability in Palestine, Jordan, and Lebanon.[39] Directed by Palestinian public health researcher Rita Giacaman of Bizeit University in the West Bank and Dina Kiwan of the University of Birmingham, the research aim of Disability Under Siege has two parts: first, to explore how knowledge about disability is produced in contexts of conflict, centering the geopolitics and archives of "conflict zones," in this case in the Middle East, that may not be legible through a North American or Global North "disability analytic" or a "disability approach." The archives foregrounded in southern disability studies posit disability as a quotidian and prolific element of life as a result of war and resistance to it. Conflict zones are also areas that do not attest to the binarization of resisting medicalization versus cure; rather, these are places and events wherein extreme corporeal assault is accompanied by few infrastructural resources, medical and otherwise, to attend to these assaults. The second aim is to put the notion of disability itself under siege, as an approach, following Meekosha, to decolonizing disability.

In the literature review on Palestine generated by DUS, Giacaman argues that there is a dire need for more work theorizing the entanglement of war, poverty, and disability.[40] Her own research, which elaborates a critique of "western models of mental illness and PTSD," reflects the effects of the absence of such theory in the face of global health structures that privilege an inadequate "social model" of disability. Writing that early NGO work in the 1980s and 1990s overdiagnosed nearly everyone with PTSD, severe depressive disorder, and other mental health disabilities, Giacaman states, "We questioned the utility of post-traumatic stress disorder as a diagnostic category that *framed distress and suffering due to violence as a psychiatric condition.* This approach depoliticized mental ill-health due to war by framing it as a biological phenomenon, turning the pain of living in war into a technical problem, and obliterating the fundamental issue of justice."[41]

Giacaman and coauthors argue that instead of a medical diagnosis of PTSD or a focus on the disabled mental state of children, what is needed are sociopolitical solutions, indeed solutions to end the occupation, that would address a wide population of youth who tend to present with PTSD symptoms but locate these symptoms as part of a broader trauma-scape of the occupation rather than isolated events of trauma that can be mitigated through therapy, psychotropic drugs, and other forms of medicalization.[42] This is to say, these researchers mark what they consider to be the overdiagnosis of PTSD and mental illnesses and how this overdiagnosis works in the service of eclipsing the political problem of the occupation. By addressing the effects of settler colonialism through a redistribution of the disabled/nondisabled binary, thus opening up new populations for medical treatment, the terrain of generalized debilitation experienced by an occupied population is collapsed into the more legible, and thus from a humanitarian and rights-based perspective, more "manageable," binarization of ability and disability. What these researchers are insisting—and this is important—is that disability as it is conceived of in Euro-American CDS, dispersed into human rights regimes, and central to NGO work, is *part* of the colonial structure of domination. Pace Frantz Fanon's thinking on medicalization as colonization, diagnosis functions as a form of enclosure, and describing a population as "traumatized" (as it often happens with children in Gaza) risks an extractive and, per Giacaman, depoliticized relationship to war and occupation.[43]

Giacaman and coauthors are currently developing what they call a "political model" of disability, one that indexes broader contexts of social suffering in war. One way to think about this is to dislodge the normativity/nonnormative framing of corporeality that situates ableism and an able-bodied world as the status quo. From the vantage of conflict zones, occupation, settler colonialism, permanent war, and debilitation, we do not live in an able-bodied world. Rather, what is normative are the practices and structures of violence that create systemic debilitation, thus entailing that normative/nonnormative binary is irrelevant at best and at worst a violent rupture both epistemologically and ontologically of lived bodily realities. The vantage of a/the geopolitical model—should we continue to insist on a model at all—proposes that disability is endemic, normative (but not in relation to nonnormative), and yet spatially regulated such that it is concentrated in places of disenfranchised populations, conflict zones, occupied territories, and the vestiges of colonialism.

The concept of "ableism," for example, necessarily intersects with race, imperialism, and the biopolitical weaponization of disablement. Yet in its increasing usage in disability rights and justice discourses as a transparent truism of infrastructure and of social attitudes—the world is an intrinsically and equally an ableist place, regardless of which place—ableism, by presuming a priori what disability is and how it is lived and marginalized, comes dangerously close to becoming an empty analytic, often weaponized as an accusation by white disabled people who privilege very specific bodily experiences, capacities, and normativities. The construct of ableism does not, in my experience of interacting with disability rights organizations, people with disabilities, and health-care practitioners in Palestine, resonate terminologically; it is not (yet?) a widespread discourse. That is to say, the conceptual apparatus and critique of ableism is not generally used to describe how people experience or account for discrimination toward people with disabilities. Nor does ableism, as I have encountered life in Palestine thus far, have a particular anchor as a structure of feeling in Palestine, as an ideological force that is guiding and overdetermining the qualities of bodies that are valued and devalued. That is not to say that discriminatory attitudes and policies toward disabled Palestinians do not exist, but rather to point out that ableism is inextricable from the racist, colonial conditions of the occupation and therefore may not be the primary discourse used to mark such confluences. While the Palestinian nationalist resistance movement unsurprisingly favors a masculinist body politic, parsing the demand to cease the bodily debilitation created by the occupation from phobia toward disabled people is a somewhat futile endeavor. One of the more insidious effects of the debilitating of bodies in Palestine is how it fosters internalizing bodily defect as intrinsic to an inferior population. The violent production of disability should not be instrumentalized as the reason to end conflict/war/occupation, but it is unclear how to separate out the end of maiming from the end of the occupation writ large.

In thinking through the limits of the North/South reification of absolute difference, which is often entangled with the necessity of counteracting colonial systems by mobilizing the specificity of the local, we encounter the differential applicability of "globality" itself. From the vantage of the North American academy, southern disability studies will never represent the field of disability studies, even though it literally addresses the global state of disability if we are to take seriously the oft-cited statistic that 80 percent of the world's disability is located in the Global South. This isn't resolvable through what I have elsewhere called an "epistemological corrective"—in other words, "including" more southern disability studies in any curriculum is great, but not the point. This is about the epistemic violence inhered in the categorization of disability itself.[44]

Decarcerating Disability

Formed in 2021, the US-based Abolition and Disability Justice Collective foregrounds "alternatives to policing based on disability justice." The vision for this activist initiative is derived in part from Liat Ben-Moshe's recent book, *Decarcerating Disability*, which beautifully lays out the stakes and power of the coalescing of disability justice and the movements for the abolition of prisons and police. Noting that disabled people are disproportionately incarcerated, and that incarceration induces mass disablement, Ben-Moshe traces the psychiatric deinstitutionalization movement, the closure of disability institutions and psychiatric hospitals in the United States in the 1950s and 1960s during the civil rights era. She notes this was the "largest exodus of people from carceral facilities in the twentieth century."[45] This history traces how deinstitutionalized disabled people were reinstitutionalized through the mass incarceration that began in the 1970s. But it also fosters a capacious utopian horizon of abolition that draws together this history and contemporary abolition organizing, which challenges anti-Blackness: it has happened already, and it can happen again. Most importantly, her focus on the relationships between disability and carceral spaces opens all sorts of connective tissues between different forms of confinement, whether of prisons, occupations, detention centers, reservations, reserves, refugee camps, militarized zones, blockades. Although Ben-Moshe's work is based entirely in the United States, her frame of decarcerating disability can take the lead of Angela Davis, who emphasizes that "the abolition movement . . . cannot simply occur in one country."[46] Writing about the need for movements to be intersectional, Davis states, "In the abolition movement, we've been trying to find ways to talk about Palestine so that people who are attracted to a campaign to dismantle prisons in the U.S. will also think about the need to end the occupation in Palestine. It can't be an afterthought. It has to be part of the ongoing analysis."[47] With Ben-Moshe and Davis in conversation, an anti-imperialist, internationalist abolitionist agenda comes into view, one that centralizes the principles of disability justice.

In response to the uprisings in Palestine that began in spring 2021, the Abolition and Disability Justice Collective released a statement in support of Palestine on May 20, 2021. The statement deftly tied together disability in the United States and Palestine through structures of mass incarceration and the "deadly exchange [of] Israeli weapons, military/police tactics, and technologies [that] cycle between Israel, the U.S. and Canada."[48] The statement foregrounds police violence in the United States and Palestine, the incarceration practices in Israel as well as the United States—the largest incarcerator in the world—and the entwined settler colonial regimes of all three states.

What I find so pedagogically useful here is the framing of disablement and maiming as a massive architecture of global governance. By highlighting carceral infrastructures that demobilize, rather than primarily reiterating the conventional focus on accessibility, universal design, identity, and rights, the conviviality of abolition and decolonization entails, in this case, the abolition of the carceral structures of occupation and the decolonization of Palestine. In line with disability justice organizations that have challenged the imbrications of the medical-industrial complex with the military-prison-policing industrial complex, abolish the police means abolish the military means abolish ICE means abolish the occupation. Finally, they issue a clarion call "for decolonization and Palestine liberation, anti-imperialism and anti-militarism to be a central part of disability organizing agendas."[49] The explicitly anti-Zionist politics of the Abolition and Disability Justice Collective is yet another reminder that movement-based knowledges and action-driven theory, whether from anticolonial uprisings in Palestine and Colombia, the farmers' protest in India, the Black Lives Matter movement, or Indigenous demands for land back, what we learn from and within movements must be at the core of any version of critical disability studies.

NOTES

My deepest thanks to Ayla McCullough for excellent research assistance; to Maya Mikdashi for her incisive comments (as always); and to Mel Chen, Alison Kafer, Eunjung Kim, and Julie Avril Minich for their gracious support, patience, and editorial feedback.

1 See Kafer, "After Crip, Crip Afters."
2 Bhattacharya, "Three Ways."
3 Kim and Schalk, "Reclaiming the Radical Politics," 338.
4 Peckruhn, "Tracing Debility and Webbing Resistance."
5 Fred Moten, "blackpalestinian breath."
6 Snounu, "Critical Ethnographical Exploration," 3.
7 Snounu, Smith, and Bishop, "Disability, the Politics of Maiming."
8 For recent and forthcoming work addressing this nexus, see Troeung, *Refugee Life-worlds*; Sibara, *Imperial Injuries*; Kim, *Curative Violence*; McRuer, *Crip Times*. For an overview of recent discussions, see Grech and Soldatic, *Disability in the Global South*.
9 Said, *Question of Palestine*.
10 Sins Invalid, "Disability Justice for Palestine."
11 Meekosha, "Decolonising Disability," 668.
12 Orsak, "How Disability Became White."
13 Meekosha, "Decolonising Disability," 668.
14 For further discussion on whiteness and disability studies, see Orsak, "How Disability Became White," 244: "White disability infuses disability studies. The field's whiteness and imperial circulation emerge from American disability studies' attachments to disability identity. Redressing white disability requires imagining a disability studies without disability as an object of study. Such efforts demand a different posture towards disability. In such a posture, disability is not as an object of study, an identity, an analytic. Instead, what is at stake is the scholar's relation to disability as it is made—through an exclusionary definition—to serve such functions. Moving away from white disability-as-identity allows for a reckoning with disablement as a violent process, a reimagining of disability scholars' approaches to racism, imperialism, the nation. If disability as a category is bound up in this violence, a different posture is required to account for these processes without reproducing them."
15 Meekosha, "Decolonising Disability."
16 Snounu, Smith, and Bishop, "Disability, the Politics of Maiming." See also Harsha, Ziq, and Giacaman, "Disability among Palestinian Elderly."
17 Explicit mention of disability in Palestine is most prevalent in educational and domestic settings, with an emphasis on rights and access, or social stigma as it surfaces in so-called biological disabilities like spina bifida. For instance, see MacKenzie et al., "Barriers to Effective, Equitable and Quality Education"; Nahal et al., "Palestinian Children's Narratives"; Zahaika et al., "Challenges Facing Family Caregivers." Otherwise, across the humanities, public health, and social sciences, terms like mobility/immobility come closest to signifying disability as the restriction of movement.
18 Meekosha, "Decolonising Disability," 677.
19 On "spatial justice" for women in the Jenin refugee camp, see Bleibleh, Perez, and Bleibleh, "Palestinian Refugee Women." See Shatha Abu Srour's discussion of a sit-in protesting the Palestinian Authority in "Social Action to Achieve a Dignified Life." See also Puar et al., "Disability Under Siege"; and Laura Jaffee, who reframes student social movements *as* disability justice movements in "Student Movements against the Imperial University."

20 The centers in the camps were by and large birthed in response to the mass injuries sustained during the first intifada from 1987 to 1993. Many were funded in the wake of Oslo (UN plus neoliberal and humanitarian aid money). The first intifada resulted in nearly 30,000 children requiring medical treatment for injuries caused by beatings, from 6,500 to 8,500 Palestinian minors wounded by live gunfire and/or sustaining bodily trauma while in administrative detention, and more than a thousand Palestinians killed. Many of these centers, especially during the late 1980s and early 1990s, were routinely raided, pillaged, and vandalized by the Israeli security forces. Those working to set up these centers, usually men who were disabled themselves during the first intifada, were often harassed, targeted for (further) injury, or otherwise retaliated against in order to destroy these burgeoning efforts. Center workers describe how this attention to war-injured disabled people led to a broader awareness of disability, a massive change in attitude toward disability of many kinds, and the greater integration of long-time homebound disabled people into the public life of camps. These injuries often connected generations of Palestinians, for example, those injured during the first intifada to those injured during the second intifada; many had accumulated injuries from both intifadas. For injury statistics during the first intifada, see Giacaman, "Reframing Public Health in Wartime."

21 The West Bank has approximately two dozen camps (nineteen official ones), with 775,000 registered refugees out of a total population in the West Bank of 2.8 million. Together with translators, we visited the following camps: Balata, Fawwar, Aida, Dhehishe, Jalazone, Aroub, Askar, Jenin, and Nour Shams. Camps all have their distinct reputations, political orientations, geospatial specificities, and levels of integration within humanitarian aid, research, and tourist/delegation networks, but in general, camps experience chronically high rates of diabetes, heart disease, high blood pressure, and the debilitating effects of chronic exposure to tear gas (Aida camp has been ranked as the most tear-gassed place in the world); they are also often sitting targets for daily IOF raids. These conditions occur within the contexts of deteriorating medical infrastructures, food insecurity, decreasing access to drinkable water, and few employment and educational opportunities. Some camps, such as Aida and Dheisheh, have had the resources, locational centrality, and politics necessary to hang in the circuitry of what is referred to as the "NGO-ization" of Palestine. But deeply radical camps such as Balata, near Nablus, or spatially remote camps, such as Fawwar camp, which is south of Hebron, struggle with basic necessities— drinkable water, health-care support systems, employment opportunities, electricity. On sensory perception of space in Balata camp, see Qzeih and Sani, "Sensory Perceptual Experience in Balata Refugee Camp." On water scarcity in Aida refugee camp, see Bishara et al., "The Multifaceted Outcomes of Community-Engaged Water Quality Management."

22 These English-language and translated studies amplify the geographic parameters of the camps, locating them as sites of chronic violence correlated with different health outcomes and what is not infrequently referred to as "low quality of life." For instance, see Marie et al., "Anxiety Disorders and PTSD in Palestine"; Fasfous et al., "Differences in Neuropsychological Performance." The health literature often

reinforces a trauma/resilience paradigm and access to infrastructure, demonstrating the ways in which these accounts remain underdeveloped from a critical humanities and social sciences perspective. See Mahamid, "Collective Trauma, Quality of Life and Resilience"; Veronese et al., "Spatial Agency." For emphasis on children's adaptive capacities as correctives to vulnerability and victimhood, see Veronese and Cavazzoni, "'I Hope I Will Be Able to Go Back to My Home City.'"

23 Rabie, *Palestine Is Throwing a Party*. See also Harker, *Spacing Debt*; Haddad, *Palestine Ltd.*

24 Snounu, Smith, and Bishop, "Disability, the Politics of Maiming."

25 Tawil-Souri, "Checkpoint Time"; Kotef, *Movement and the Ordering of Freedom*.

26 For discussion on "rhizomatic" approaches to camps and "camp afterlives," see Weima and Minca, "Closing Camps." On camp "spatial violations" and space-making, see Maqusi, "Acts of Spatial Violation." On im/mobility, temporality, and space in al-Am'ari refugee camp, see Woroniecka-Krzyzanowska, "Multilocality and the Politics of Space." On settler colonialism's "rapid spatial actions" in Palestine, see Katz, "Mobile Colonial Architecture." On historical political narratives of camp temporalities, see Abourahme, "'Nothing to Lose but Our Tents.'"

27 Rabie, *Palestine Is Throwing a Party*; Harker, *Spacing Debt*. For discussions on space, property, and practices and ideologies of possession and ownership, see Weizman, *Hollow Land*; Bhandar, *Colonial Lives of Property*, 29–31.

28 Snounu, Smith, and Bishop, "Disability, the Politics of Maiming"; see also Snounu, "Critical Ethnographical Exploration."

29 Langan, "Mobility Disability."

30 For an excellent discussion on Palestinian refugeehood as "multiscalar dispossession" from which specific ethos and politics of care are fostered, see Qutami, "'The Camp Is My Nationality.'"

31 Mia Mingus, "Moving toward the Ugly: A Politic beyond Desirability," *Leaving Evidence* (blog), August 22, 2011, https://leavingevidence.wordpress.com/2011/08/.

32 Berlant, "Slow Death," in *Cruel Optimism*, 95–120.

33 Hammami, "On (Not) Suffering," 4.

34 For extended elaboration of slow life, see Puar, "Spatial Debilities."

35 There has been prolific scholarly and political work thinking about what "slow" is in relation to normative metrics of time. Most often referenced include Rob Nixon's framing of environmental degradation as "slow violence" and Lauren Berlant's "slow death"; both provide contrasts to forms of incident-driven, spectacular violence that are represented in the enclosure of an event. More recently Jennifer Nash has written on "slow loss" to complicate paradigms of the psyche that privilege before-and-after ruptures. See Nash, "Slow Loss." Scholars of critical disability studies theorize "slow living" and "slow care" as well as "crip time" and "crip temporalities" to problematize the demands of social reproduction under capitalism that center on productive, purely capacitated bodies. In these conceptualizations, slowness is both constitutive of forms of violence as well as the basis for collective ways of living and being among that violence. Slow life contributes to the understanding in Palestine studies that slowness is also unto itself a form of violence, insofar as it is used as a colonialist tool

of control. At the same time, these frames, including my own, to a greater or lesser extent reify "slow" in opposition to "fast" or "speed," thereby inadvertently functioning as some capitulation to normative temporality. This is perhaps where Denise Ferreira da Silva's incisive work on the logic of time itself as a foundational violence of enlightenment suggests that all relations of time, whether slow or speedy, are subject to capture, extraction, and exploitation. See da Silva, "The Banalization of Racial Events." Her work prompts an articulation of slowness as a generative and differentiated mode of being that bypasses the measuring of speed altogether. Recent work in Black studies attests to the unworlding potentialities of such non-relations to capitalism's metric of time and of remaking time itself. For this discussion, see Lambert, "They Have Clocks." In Palestine studies, recent scholarship on temporality builds on the literature on the loss of time due to laboring and waiting by foregrounding nonlinear and noncapitalist temporalities outside and on the side of historical periodization. See Seikaly, "The Matter of Time"; Stamatopoulou-Robbins, "Failure to Build"; Jamal, "Conflict Theory"; Joronen et al., "Palestinian Futures"; Sa'di-Ibraheem, "Jaffa's Times."

36   See Puar and Abu-Sitta, "Israel Is Trying to Maim Gaza Palestinians into Silence"; Abu-Sitta, "There Is No International Community."

37   Rocher, "Shooting Rubber Bullets"; Anaïs, *Disarming Intervention*.

38   See Ghai, *Rethinking Disability in India*; Kim, "Specter of Vulnerability"; Gorman, "Disablement in and for Itself"; Erevelles, *Disability and Difference*; Million, *Therapeutic Nations*; Tam, "Agitation and Sudden Death." See also the recent issue of *Disability Studies Quarterly* on indigeneity and disability: Larkin-Gilmore, Callow, and Burch, "Indigeneity and Disability."

39   Disability Under Siege, The Disability Under Siege Network, https://disabilityundersiege.org.

40   Giacaman, "Conceptual Frameworks of Disability." With a similar concern regarding the need for more research on war injuries in Gaza, see Mosleh et al., "The Burden of War-Injury." It is worth noting that the use of the term "burden," rife in public health literatures discussing war and colonial disablement, does not reflect any pathologization of disabled people; rather, "burden" refers to the duress under which war-compromised medical infrastructures are unable to properly care for patients.

41   Giacaman, "Reframing Public Health in Wartime," 16–17. On the depoliticization of the occupation through the narrativization of trauma, see Fassin and Rechtman, *Empire of Trauma*, 210. See also Sheehi and Sheehi, *Psychoanalysis under Occupation*; Stryker, "Young People."

42   See Rabaia, Saleh, and Giacaman, "Sick or Sad?"

43   The West Bank is accustomed to lockdowns, forced closures, sheltering-in-place, quarantines, and stay-at-home orders, which begs the question, what is quarantine in a place already defined by containment? What is the effect of the pandemic in places where uncertainty is the condition of being, a collective uncertainty? Instead of "trauma," "triggering," "repetition of," "return to" the event, how does this resonance between enclosure and the pandemic refuse narratives of colonial trauma and

transform into forms of collective resistance? How do Palestinians de-privatize symptoms toward a collective anticolonial consciousness? For more on the pandemic in Palestine, see Qato, "Introduction."

44 Orsak, "How Disability Became White."

45 Quoted from book description on Ben-Moshe's personal website, "Decarcerating Disability," Liat Ben-Moshe, 2020, https://www.liatbenmoshe.com/decarcerating -disability.

46 Davis, "Dr. Martin Luther King Jr. Lecture."

47 Davis, *Freedom Is a Constant Struggle*. For elaboration and analysis of the intersectional, lateral diasporic solidarity politics of the Palestinian Youth Movement, see Salih, Zambelli, and Welchman, "'From Standing Rock to Palestine We Are United.'"

48 Abolition and Disability Justice Collective, "Statement of Solidarity with Palestine."

49 Abolition and Disability Justice Collective, "Statement of Solidarity with Palestine."

Part II

CRIP ECOLOGIES AND SENSES

5. *RHIZOPHORA*

Queering Chemical Kinship in the Agent Orange Diaspora

NATALIA DUONG

A camera peers down upon two women as they lay wrapped around each other on twin cots pushed together to create one bed. Their eyes are closed. A soft tinkling sound, like the first windup twists of a music box, and a bright whistling accompanies them. The women roll away from each other, then back toward each other, without attention to vertical or horizontal axes. Rather, the bed is flattened as the woman wearing pink creates a snow angel in the sheets. The viewer gazes in from this bird's-eye perspective. Each woman rolls about on her own, sometimes making contact with the other: a hand with an ankle, the bend of an elbow with a knee. Their eyes remain closed; as the music accelerates, so too do their movements. One woman mimes brushing her teeth while the other plays at yawning and drinking from an empty cup. The woman in orange thrusts a jacket at the woman in pink who puts it on, and she returns the gesture with her partner's sweater. They each continue to roll about the bed, reaching for more accessories—a headband, a skirt, a handbag—to complete their outfits. Finally, the woman in pink reaches for her partner, who nods as if to say "finished," before the two pedal their legs and feet in a running motion. The woman in orange waves to the camera as a smile illuminates her face. The scene fades.

This sequence is the first of a three-part triptych in a dancefilm titled *Rhizophora*. Described by its creators Davide De Lillis and Julia Metzger-Traber as a videopoem, the film depicts a community of people who inhabit the Vietnam Friendship Village outside Hanoi, Vietnam, with whom the creators collaborated to choreograph this portrait of daily life. The Vietnam Friendship Village (also refered to as the Vietnam Friendship Village Project USA) is a center founded by US veteran George Mizo in 1988 and opened in 1998, which aimed to provide housing and community support for veterans and children

FIGURE 5.1. Waking Up scene from *Rhizophora*. Two women, wearing orange and pink, are lying in a bed made up of two mattresses on the floor. They are surrounded by jackets, sandals, papers, and pens. Courtesy of Davide De Lillis and Julia Metzger-Traber.

affected by the chemical compound Agent Orange with the hopes of forging international "peace and reconciliation." The village is financially supported by nonprofit organizations in the United States, Canada, France, Germany, Japan, and Vietnam. As such, it has been a site for diplomatic visits and humanitarian tourism and has become a crucial stage for political and international performances of reparation between Vietnam and other nation-states.[1]

In the videopoem, images of sense-based improvisational movement within a forest are interwoven throughout, bookending each of the three scenes: *thức dậy*/waking up (described above), *ăn trưa*/lunch, and *thời gian trà*/teatime. This film is similar to other visual and filmic portrayals of people exposed to Agent Orange in that it follows a somewhat documentary structure featuring the daily activities of those living with the effects of herbicide exposure, however it departs from previous representations insofar as it relies on a politics of play rather than scopic observation, which, I argue, disrupts how knowledge about Agent Orange, and disability in Vietnam, is formed. Through the interweaving of scenes in a mangrove forest, the film portrays both human and nonhuman bodies as targets of chemical warfare and the potential for trans-species kinships to emerge between them. While the film also traffics in its own complicated ethics, often brought on by negotiations of power in artistic collaborations between artists and the subjects who are documented, I argue that dance within the film articulates an important intervention into the representation of Agent Orange by animating human and nonhuman ecologies of kinship to consequently offer an important critique of methodologies used to represent and negotiate disability in Vietnam.

This chapter considers how dance can articulate a different relational experience of disability to highlight an ethics of care and kinship.[2] I analyze how the dancefilm *Rhizophora* disrupts the trope of other documentary portrayals of Agent Orange, as it relies on neither a shocking portrayal of disfigurement nor a teleological "overcoming" narrative of a disabled child's success "despite" their disability. Instead, the film depicts a community of people who come together through their relationship with disability. Consequently, following the work of Vanessa Agard-Jones, who theorizes a multiscalar *chemical (kin)esthesia* and *chemical kinship* engendered in response to the spraying of insecticides and fungicides in Martinique, I suggest that *Rhizophora* imagines the possibility of queering and cripping chemical kinships that exist as alternatives to normative familial structures, which emerge from a shared experience of living in contaminated bodies. Moreover, the film relies on sensorial and sensual experiences that engage the portrayal of disability in ways that interrupt a scopic regime aimed at visually detecting and biopolitically managing disability. Instead, through dance, the film depends on touch, consumption, and play to reorient how the viewer becomes incorporated into crip worldmaking. The result is a dissensual experience that affectively attunes to a cosmos of trans-species kinship. As such, I turn to dance to provide a framework for theorizing an alternate economy of action and reaction, responsivity, and uses of force. This chapter asks how a relational *sense* of chemical kinship crips the transnational export of neoliberal legal and social discourses of disability in contemporary Vietnam.

Genealogies of Disability in Vietnam: Karma, War, and Sites of Care

Disability in Vietnam is a matter of genealogy. Though the globalization of medical understandings of disability have shifted how various impairments and bodily conditions are understood, the notion that disability is inherited through generations has always been central to a Vietnamese understanding of it. Despite increasing awareness of scientific approaches for identifying disability, many families maintain a hybrid belief that disability is an inherited trait that can be explained by both biological circumstance and karmic consequence. As anthropologist Tine M. Gammeltoft explains, disability in Vietnam is perceived to be a moral failure because of how it interrupts cultural, spiritual, and cosmological expectations about a child's ability to *care* for their biological family members as an expression of filial piety. Translating the work of social researcher Phạm Kim Ngọc, Gammeltoft explains, "Children with severe disabilities cannot but fail morally: since they are unable to 'perform their sacred responsibility of fulfilling duties to their parents and grandparents, looking after the worship of their ancestors,' they will never attain the full personhood that is acquired by fulfilling filial obligations."[3] Gammeltoft describes how Confucian values figure disability as an obstacle to the relational responsibility of filial care rather than as a biological or social circumstance that emerges within a singular body. This belief presumes that a disabled child cannot care for their parents, and as such cannot return the care given to them. Disability interrupts the cycle of care exchange in which parents are expected to become the recipients of care in their elder years and thus, according to Confucian beliefs, disability renders the child less than whole because the child is not capable of completing their caring duties.

Earlier conceptions of disability were formulated around a cultural and religious belief in karmic retribution, and later models focused on those disabled by war, while more recent conceptions of disability are founded on a liberal model of disability rights and empowerment through participation in a neoliberal workforce.[4] For this reason, Agent Orange in many respects has come to be synonymous with disability in Vietnam because of the ways it is passed through generations and interrupts expectant economies of care. As a material form, Agent Orange is a chemical compound that was used by the United States and its allies to defoliate millions of acres in Vietnam, and nearby Laos and Cambodia, during the wars in Southeast Asia, often colloquially called the Vietnam War in the United States. While the United States and Vietnam are often the only two countries named in the web of this compound's exchange, recent reports have shown how the compound's travel was facilitated by other countries (New Zealand, United Kingdom, Japan, Philippines) either in production or distribution at US Army bases. The chemicals' spread is consequently much greater than previously expected. The compound, made up of 2,4-dichlorophenoxyacetic acid (2,4-D) and 2,4,5-trichlorophenoxyacetic acid (2,4,5-T), contains trace amounts of the most toxic dioxin, 2,3,7,8-tetra chlorodibenzo-p-dioxin (TCDD), which has been correlated with increases in skin conditions, cancers, and other forms of cellular mutation. Its effects are often experienced multigenerationally, such that elevated dioxin levels have been measured in generations that were never directly exposed to the initial spraying. The "accidental" discovery of this chemical elixir occurred in a botany lab that was conducting an experiment to determine how to increase the speed of flowering for soybean plants with the hopes of increasing crop production. It is consequently important to mark how these technologies of warfare are co-constituted by a system of racial capitalism dependent on the productivity of human and plant bodies.

Consequently, Agent Orange, as a concept, is amply situated to intersect with all these various understandings of disability, as its effects can be traced to wartime exposure *and* its physical and visual manifestation often thwarts linear models of cause and effect, consequently materializing more mystic beliefs about disabilities' origins. In other words, Agent Orange satisfies those who employ empirical methods to seek medical and judicial reparation on behalf of those who were disabled "by" Agent Orange, and the chemical compound simultaneously fits into a schema of disability whose origins are not as easily identifiable but whose effects are understood to be passed through generations from ancestors to the present. In this way, a study of Agent Orange traces the simultaneous debilitation of communities through exposure to chemical warfare as a result of US imperialism, the cultural belief that disability is shared and inherited among biological kin, and also the continued hegemony of rehabilitation efforts premised on a belief in biomedicine and a linear teleology of cure.

In Vietnam, the 1986 economic reform Đổi Mới marked a shift from a centrally planned economy to a free market system, which consequently emphasized a greater cultural valuation of independence. This change occurred alongside a larger global shift toward the neoliberal management of disability, which has resulted in a greater emphasis on the right to inclusion for disabled individuals. Accordingly, the National Law on Disability in Vietnam, drafted in 2010, reiterates much of the language advocating for sovereignty for disabled people found in policies put forth by the United Nations Convention on the Rights of Persons with Disabilities and the World Health Organization. Centers that provide social support for people with disabilities in Vietnam often rely on vocational training or craft-making to cater to humanitarian tourists and further encourage investments in these circuits of "individual" labor. However, as anthropologists Gammeltoft and Xuan Thuy Nguyen have shown with their respective analyses of selective reproduction in Hanoi and the politics of inclusion for disabled persons throughout the country, these conceptions of disability, based on individual rights, directly contradict the ways in which disability is narrated as a *relational* process in Vietnam.

Because disability is believed to be inherited through one's ancestry, there is often a greater emphasis on, or expectation of, filial care for people with disabilities in Vietnam. Disability itself is conceived of as a condition that is shared among family members even though one member may be the only person who exhibits an "impairment." Experiences of disability are consequently deeply influenced by locally specific conceptions of the interrelationship between self and other, and self and nation. Programs that operate under a disability rights framework, proffered by institutions like USAID and the Disability Rights, Enforcement, Coordination and Therapies program that it cosponsors along with Vietnam Assistance for the Handicapped, focus on, as the organization's title suggests, the enforcement of the UN Convention on the Rights of People with Disabilities at the national level, while advocating for individual rehabilitation through the sponsorship of medical clinics and the expansion of a disability database in which disabled persons can be registered and surveilled.[5] These programs not only reproduce systems of surveillance established under colonial rule, they also presume an independent liberal subject as the recipient of "rehabilitative services," therefore faultily assuming an individualized experience of disability that is incongruent with what many in Vietnam articulate as their lived experience. For example, in her study of selective reproduction in Hanoi, Gammeltoft illustrates how the health of the individual body and the national body are intricately intertwined in the imaginary of Vietnam's mythic origins, socialist political foundations, and contemporary rhetoric about the standards of citizenship and subjectivity. Gammeltoft astutely considers how health—in particular reproductive health—is believed to be both a matter of individual (familial) responsibility and a project of state-controlled management of population "quality." She notes how following Đổi Mới, the family unit came to replace agricultural cooperatives or work units, such that women's roles were recast as that of nurturers and caretakers for their individual families. However, importantly, these individual families were imagined to be part of a larger mythos about Vietnam's origin, as a country birthed from the union of the dragon father Lạc Long Quân and the mountain fairy mother Âu Cơ, who produced an egg sac from which one hundred human children emerged. In other words, Gammeltoft constructs a compelling comparison between these two origins of collective responsibility, between Vietnam's mythic origins and its sociopolitical history, which she argues is fundamental to understanding collective approaches to health in the nation.

However, the third part of Gammeltoft's argument gives me pause, wherein she considers that community spirit (*tinh thần cộng đồng*) arises from what she describes as "collectively felt emotions of sadness, solidarity, and sympathy, in a joint conviction that something must be done" about Agent Orange exposure.[6] Gammeltoft considers Agent Orange to be an "important site of subjectivity-making in Vietnam," where the "national humanitarian emergency" allows the previously divided country to come together and experience a common empathy about Agent Orange's devastating effects.[7] And while I appreciate the opening that Gammeltoft creates for understanding disability in a relational and social context, her articulation of the chemical compound's effects denigrates those exposed to it as a humanitarian emergency to be solved. Instead, I suggest that those who live with exposure offer compelling strategies for navigating alternative experiences of sociality, community, and, indeed, family. For example, we might ask, what forms of care are valued in the economy of care exchange privileged by Confucian values? And might parents of disabled children also describe ways in which they *do* receive care, and *are* cared for, by their children? Moreover, how might these values extend beyond the forms of biological filial piety, to include kinship structures that rely on other forms of communal being?

Centers like the Vietnam Friendship Village exist throughout Vietnam, though the Vietnam Friendship Village remains one of the only centers created specifically for the care of those exposed to Agent Orange. They offer alternative care structures for individuals whose families either do not have the financial or medical resources to care for them, or who otherwise decide that the individuals would be better cared for in a center like the Vietnam Friendship Village. Unlike other institutions for disabled people that have historically housed individuals against their will, centers like the Vietnam Friendship Village are places where families elect to send their kin. Some families even view it as a privilege to be a part of the larger community, though, of course, each individual family navigates this decision differently. For some, the social stigma associated with caring for a disabled family member is too burdensome, and therefore the family might choose to bring their family member to the center to be cared for. Other families might lack the material and financial resources to care for their disabled family member and therefore celebrate the opportunity to have their family member cared for at the center, where basic needs like food, shelter, and accessible infrastructures are more readily available. For many, the decision is a complex set of affective and pragmatic negotiations often arbitrated by the elders of the family. Some centers are publicly funded by the Vietnamese government, such as the centers associated with hospitals, while others are independently run by nonprofit organizations sponsored by international grants and individual donations. It is also important to note that low socioeconomic status is common among families with people with disabilities, and that, as scholars of disability in the Global South like Helen Meekosha and Karen Soldatic have demonstrated, disabling events such as imperial warfare and colonization inextricably intertwine the impairment of bodies with the disablement of economic and social infrastructures, and, in turn, entire communities are debilitated.[8] In other words, disability in a global context cannot ignore the forces of global racial capitalism that further perpetuate the continued disablement of populations that are already underresourced. In the context of Agent Orange exposure, many of the families who were exposed came from a lineage of farmers. Those who worked the land were doubly exposed: first to the chemical residues in the soil, and second to land that would not reproduce new crops following herbicide dispersal. Consequently, centers like the Vietnam Friendship Village offer a temporary respite closer to urban centers where accessible infrastructure better supports the health and mobility needs of people with disabilities.

Though documentary narratives funded by individuals or organizations based in North America, Europe, and Australia often exhibit anti-institutional politics by depicting these centers as impersonal and overcrowded, these sites are also places where queer forms of care and kinship emerge. Given the history of deinstitutionalization and independent living movements in these Western geographies, it is not surprising that these portrayals are skeptical of centers focused on medical rehabilitation in which multiple people may share one sleeping space and "independent living" is not the main objective. As Nguyen reminds, French colonists established medical and educational institutions in Vietnam in the late 1880s to administer surveillance and social control, where bodily and behavioral deviance was monitored and quarantined. Two particular institutions that Nguyen cites were created for deaf and blind children who, by French colonial standards, were socialized into dichotomous gender roles and taught "productive" gendered activities such as knitting for the girls and learning to read and write Roman script for the boys.[9] Given this lineage of institutions for disabled people in Vietnam, including the geopolitical negotiations that led to the establishment of the Vietnam Friendship Village itself, contemporary deinstitutionalization can be seen as a decolonial process.

Yet, these community centers for people with disabilities often have newer, more accessible infrastructures that make mobility barriers less prohibitive for people that roll, hop, or traverse across space with varied rhythms. The structural supports, access to prompt medical care, and schooling at the centers often exceed the material means that families are able to provide in their rural hometowns. As residents are usually separated from their biological families, they forge new networks of care within these centers. The centers are thus both overtly medicalized—as some sites are literal extensions of hospital wings—and also a place of social gathering for people with disabilities who may otherwise be isolated from other forms of relationships because of persisting shame about disability's origins. Consequently, these centers importantly offer a place for disabled people to live together in community and to share important skills for navigating a social and political landscape that privileges ableist practices and beliefs. Skill-sharing ranges from pragmatic tasks like making clay flowers to sell to tourists to navigating the social dynamics of the canteen during lunch. Though individual experiences of the centers vary greatly based on each person's needs and expectations, the centers remain a pivotal space for fostering social bonds, both temporary and lifelong, outside the dominant social culture that can be isolating for disabled people because it continues to equate disability with shame.

Therefore, to crip a genealogy of disability in Vietnam is also to name the research methodologies still used to represent and manage disability as extensions of biopolitical control and discipline formulated within imperial logics. Though Agent Orange has been taken up by various studies as a discussion of the epidemiological inheritance of trauma, often these studies fail to articulate how calls for medical reparation of disability enact normalizing imperatives that further debilitate the communities these studies aim to benefit. Alternatively, I think with and against technoscientific frameworks, eloquently questioned by Michelle Murphy, when resisting the reenactment of what she terms "damage-based research," often perpetuated by ecology, epidemiology, and toxicology that, according to Murphy, eugenically differentiates between lives "worth" living or not.[10] Moreover, access to these forms of medical rehabilitation is reserved for the types of bodies who can become emblematic of recovery—children, or young adults who are infantilized in media portrayals and made to represent narratives of the potential for cure. And, as Eunjung Kim reminds, imperatives toward cure can further perpetuate violent treatments on bodies who do not otherwise meet standards for normative inclusion.[11] So, while efforts to portray disabled children as evidence of wartime atrocities have resulted in some legal reparations for those exposed to Agent Orange in the form of monetary recompense, and I do not weigh lightly how monthly stipends aid the families navigating the aftereffects of the chemical compound, I am also interested in shifting epistemic methods for engaging with exposure toward sensory capacities that consider how kinship arises from multiple exposures, rather than focusing only on the "cost" of disability. In doing so, I do not aim to reify all forms of kinship as innately liberating, as the application of the term *kinship* has itself resulted in the naturalization of certain forms of relationality and further denigration of relations that exist outside these normative standards.[12] However, I gesture toward an assemblage of relations, what Anna Tsing terms "contaminated diversity," in order to consider the types of porous intertwining that occur because of "histories of greed, violence, and environmental degradation" alongside the interpersonal relations that are affectively assembled in places of cohabitation.[13] Kinship is the term that, temporarily, aims to work against the economies of aesthetic representation, and of biomedical and legal reparation, that portray individual disabled bodies as isolated sites of damage. Rather, kinship aims to materialize the affective bonds that sustain the lives of those living in community at the Vietnam Friendship Village. Building on Leah Lakshmi Piepzna-Samarasinha's description of "care webs," formed through intersectional and interdependent disability justice frameworks within disabled communities in the San Francisco Bay Area, I am interested in how rhizomatic forms of care emerge in these communities of co-caring.[14] In other words, I want to hold these two realities in productive tension with each other: How might we understand the debilitation of communities exposed to Agent Orange as creating greater economic and social burdens for families who do not have the material resources to support their daily needs, respect their identification with medicalized forms of impairment as a political mechanism used to negotiate for reparation from the United States, and also acknowledge how exposure to Agent Orange opens up avenues for nonnormative kinship structures and affinities?[15] The friction among these multiple realities is the opening I experience when engaging with *Rhizophora*'s intervention into cultural conceptions about Agent Orange and disability in Vietnam.

Scopic Regimes of Contamination: A Genealogy
of Visual Representations of Agent Orange

Early visual representations of Agent Orange in Vietnam, which I purpose-fully choose not to reproduce in this chapter, took the form of spectacular photographs aimed at shocking the viewer into a response. In an attempt to reveal the harmful effects of the herbicide on human populations, documen-tary photographers portrayed the most visually evocative forms of disability as indexes of war trauma induced by the United States' and its allies' deployment of Agent Orange. The photographs depicted the subjects in anguish. They re-mained unnamed, appeared in dimly lit spaces, with exaggerated dark shad-ows, and, more often than not, the photographers portrayed them through the barred windows of their living quarters to emphasize the metaphorical and physical quarantine of their bodies. Many were photographed in their beds—some were even tied to their beds with cloth restraints. As visual documenta-tion of the Vietnam War proved to have such profound historical and political import, these photographs served the purpose of visually and affectively reveal-ing another afterlife of imperial violence that the US government denied. These portrayals objectified the bodies exhibited within them to mark them as per-ceptible evidence that could be used in legal claims for reparations. Although the majority of this genre of photographic documentation emerged in the early 2000s, there are certainly examples of photographs that predate the twenty-first century, and examples of this evidentiary framing that continue to appear in popular news sources at the time of this writing.[16]

Diane Niblack Fox, an anthropologist who has closely surveyed the cultural and legal rhetoric of Agent Orange in Vietnam, succinctly summarizes how shocking pictures deployed portrayals of suffering as visual evidence of con-tamination and institutional neglect. She writes,

> In the pictures shown around the world of children from families such as these, Agent Orange has become a symbol of innocent suffering, in-tensified and perpetrated by the refusal of those who caused the suffer-ing to take responsibility for their actions. These pictures have taken on a symbolic meaning that exceeds the literal truth claims of these images as representations of the effects of Agent Orange on individual bodies, pointing beyond the physical suffering of individuals to a more general malaise in the body of modern society as well as to the social forces that caused that suffering and shape responses to it.[17]

Fox argues that the affective force of the images, which draws on the image of a suffering child, has moved beyond the particular representation of the effects of Agent Orange to, instead, point toward the larger structural circumstances that reproduce suffering. The photos provide "truth claims" regarding the United States' use of herbicides but also document the lack of responsive action taken once the chemicals' effects were identified. Fox employs the term "malaise" to describe "modern society's" response because malaise, by definition, also has an unlocatable cause or source. The inability to verify a specific and singular result of Agent Orange exposure has also been cited as the main obstacle in securing definitive legal reparations from the US government and chemical manufacturing companies. The diffuse and "unlocatable" nature of the chemical compound's spread mirrors the movement that Fox describes in her description of the photos: from the individual body to a general affective discomfort felt at the level of the wider population. Visual indices thus become diffuse in their circulation despite attempts to ascribe causation between contamination and suffering. The floating signifier of "suffering" ultimately leads to the assumption that disability should be medically or reparatively fixed.

In the 2010s, another form of documentary emerged that featured a descriptive narrative of the daily activities of a disabled person in rural Vietnam. These documentaries tend to traffic in a *National Geographic* aesthetic, one that exotifies racialized bodies and enables an affective awe that results from the observation of disabled people "overcoming" their perceived limitations. At play in these visualizations are questions of affective response, which employ a presumed empathy between the viewer and the viewed that is meant to universalize the humanity of the persons portrayed and, consequently, universalize vulnerability to contamination.[18] In an effort to garner empathy, the documentaries depict suffering and overcoming as the only two possible experiences of disability. Often these representations reaffirm the exotification of disabled bodies or reify certain types of disability that are recuperable into routines of normative life and exclude bodies and behaviors that deviate from this expectation. Usually, the "recuperation" of a person's disability culminates in a heterosexual marriage ceremony in which the person's desirability is confirmed by their reinscription into heteronormative familial structures. No doubt this second genre of documentary emerged in response to the dehumanizing photographs that dominated the scopic field before them. Nevertheless, they contribute to the hierarchical privileging of certain forms of disability over others (often physical disability over neurodivergence) and portray inclusion into (re)productive life as the only reasonable desire for those exposed to chemical warfare.

Furthermore, many studies about the representation of Agent Orange unfortunately reiterate and reinforce ableist beliefs about the types of disability that can or should be visually represented. Historian Lisa Reagan, in an article comparing two documentary films about Agent Orange, maintains that the films act as testimonies reinforcing truth claims about the chemical's effects on bodies. In her description of the bodies that are portrayed, Reagan employs language that describes the films' protagonists as "lying on the floor, rolling around, their mouths open, feet twisted" with "missing eyes," or another as with "his mouth open, his mind apparently impaired."[19] In her attempts to contrast the more-graphic film with another film that Reagan deems more complimentary in its portrayal, she unfortunately reveals her own assumptions about how one is meant to equate these physical states—such as "an open mouth"—with "apparent impairment." In citing this comparison, I am particularly interested in Reagan's discussion of bodies rolling on the floor, for the ways her description mirrors my own description of the two women portrayed in the Waking Up scene in *Rhizophora* that I open this chapter with. While Reagan's conclusion is dependent on the assumption that rolling around on the floor is an indication of impairment, *Rhizophora* reinterprets this image into a playful and aesthetic representation of relational companionship.

In a similar fashion, communication studies scholar Jennifer Peeples conducts a visual analysis of Agent Orange representations in media and research studies and similarly replicates a rhetoric that ties certain bodily states to "obvious physical and mental disabilities." In Peeples's effort to summarize the types of images she noticed, her language reflects her own ableist anxieties about normative bodily structures and behaviors. She writes, "Roughly half of the images I collected for this time period were photographs of Vietnamese children with obvious physical and mental disabilities. Missing limbs, hydrocephaly, cleft palates, fused eyelids, deformed and twisted bodies, and vacant stares fill the frames of these images."[20] Peeples's description of bodies again links certain physical states to what she deems "obvious" disabilities; yet, I question this type of diagnostic language, which has often further perpetuated violence onto nonnormative bodies, particularly in circumstances in which disability is eugenically selected against after such visual identification takes place. How might these methods of visual analysis used in research also inadvertently replicate strategies of medical diagnostics that privilege normative bodies?

In addition, a politics of visualization is crucial not only to the representation of Agent Orange in media forms, but also to how medical establishments in Vietnam—both those funded by the Vietnamese state and others funded by supranational NGOs—treat disability. Gammeltoft describes in detail how the

Vietnamese state invested in prenatal screenings through 3D ultrasonography, with the hope of minimizing the future births of disabled persons. Gammeltoft recounts how midwives at a hospital "protect mothers and families from knowing about birth defects and protect them from the related fear and shame."[21] Similarly, Reagan describes a mother from the documentary in her research who recounts how the hospital staff and her family members did not allow the mother to *see* her child after he was born because he was, in their opinion, "deformed." Thus, the visuality of disability—both interpersonally and its mediatized representation—is representative of not only how conceptions of disability are produced within culture, but also how medical systems uphold the invisibilization of disabled people. Moreover, as these examples illustrate, studies that engage with the scopic regime of contamination that Agent Orange produces can further enact ableist distinctions between certain bodily states and what their visual natures suggest. It is within this genealogy of visual representation, both within media representations and the medico-political management of bodies, that I return to *Rhizophora*.

Dance as Intra-active Responsivity

Rhizophora is a genus of tropical mangrove trees that grow in Vietnam. It is one type of tree that was targeted for defoliation by the US military during its spraying of chemical herbicides. It tends to grow in brackish intertidal zones, which has resulted in the species developing plasticity to mercurial and harsh environments, where access to water and varying levels of salination would otherwise eliminate floral growth.[22] The mangrove tree's resilience and adaptability, along with the sonic resonance its name shares with rhizomes, inspired cocreators Davide De Lillis and Julia Metzger-Traber to name their videopoem after it. The film does not merely aim to describe life narratively; instead it offers a place for play, where the senses challenge the sensible.

The sixteen-minute videopoem begins with a textual description of the *Rhizophora* plant. It reads,

> Rhizophora is a tree that grows in forests along the coasts of Vietnam.
> Its roots are called Rhizomes.
> If a Rhizome is separated into pieces, each piece can create a whole new plant.
> Rhizomes spread in all directions simultaneously.
> There is no beginning or end.
> Every point is the center.[23]

This introductory description illustrates forms of proliferation that exist outside of linear narratives. The allusion to "separated" pieces of the root that "spread in all directions" recalls the diasporic nature of Agent Orange, whose diffusion through waterways and bloodlines marks the continuance of wartime violence, but also marks forms of kinship that emerge between disparate populations held together by a shared experience of chemical contamination. The spread further connotes refugee populations who fled because of war and who now make up the Vietnamese diaspora in other nations. Rhizophora thus marks a biological thread woven among historic, political, social, and economic circumstances.

In the scene that I describe at the start of this chapter, which is the first full section in the film's tripartite portrayal, a politics of play interrupts the utility of morning ritual. The two women knowingly perform the routine for the camera while recognizing the presence of a viewer. The inversion of axes, in which the horizontal becomes vertical, creates a sense of displacement while the motionless camera creates an immovable frame for the action. This playful representation mobilizes possibilities for the mundane. It also features aesthetic styling as a desirable and integral part of care. Notably, throughout the entire scene, the women never leave the plane of their shared bed. Unlike the previous documentary portrayals, in which a bed is figured as a place of entrapment to which a disabled body is "confined," this bed is a place of partnership, of care, of humor, of imagination. It is a bed like the ones that disability justice advocate Leah Lakshmi Piepzna-Samarasinha describes as entire "worlds" from which care, activism, and politics emerge.[24]

In a conversation with one of the artist-creators, Julia Metzger-Traber recalled to me the manner through which this representation emerged from the daily activities of the residents.[25] In particular, she mentioned that the two women portrayed in this section were, in fact, close friends and roommates who had developed this symbiotic partnership to help each other with daily activities. They consequently decided to express this relationship in dance. For in dance, the weight exchange between bodies molds force into something to be received and traded rather than unidirectionally imposed. Each body is responsible, and enabled to respond. Perhaps the threat of unpredictability looms; however, it is mediated by the premise that every action is always already being received by another, new, consequent action. This is how dance produces new sensory horizons.

The sensory approach proffered by *Rhizophora* indeed opens into what Petra Kuppers has poetically named a *rhizomatic model of disability*, which holds together the haptic space between disability representation and its lived experience. Kuppers articulates how this model produces frictions between the

FIGURE 5.2. A scene from *Rhizophora*. One woman is wearing green, dancing against a white sky. The blurry outline of trees in the background. Courtesy of Davide De Lillis and Julia Metzger-Traber.

signified meaning of words like *disability* and *pain* and the sensory-feeling of experiences, without singularly defining *one* experience of disability, but rather opening up multiplicity through an "abundance of meanings."[26] In describing how rhizomatic thinking refigures genealogies of kinship, Kuppers writes, "There is no necessary resemblance for disabled people, we mostly have to make our families ourselves, choose our community. Often, there is no patrilinear descent, no matriarch, no heteronormative narrative that duplicates itself into the future. To call for a ritual of non-essential, strategic disability community is a rhizomatic act: to put out feelers."[27] For Kuppers, the undoing of genealogies and heteronormative relations occurs through the extension of "feelers" that produce networks through sense. Against the tree-based genealogies that are central to Confucian-based notions of filial lineage that I describe at the start of the chapter, and the eugenic targeting of rhizomatic forms of foliage by chemical forms of imperial warfare, the experience of becoming with exposure extends outward in many directions at once to queer the forms of care that could result from exposure. The potential of kinship created through rhizomatic connections exists in their oscillation and vibrational spread, in which Kuppers observes what she terms a "dance."

Kuppers's sensory feeling of dance parallels Randy Martin's definition of dance as a site of action, an event in which politics are enacted. In Martin's seminal 1998 work *Critical Moves*, he defines dance as "the reflexive mobilization of the body—that is, as a social process that foregrounds the very means through which bodies gather. Through dance, the means and ends of mobilization are joined together and made available to performers and their publics. Dance, so conceived, does not name a fixed expression but a problem, a predicament, that bodies find themselves in the midst of, whose momentary solutions we call dancing."[28] This definition of dance foregrounds the meeting of bodies, and the relational fields created between them, as foundational to social processes. Martin suggests that dance is itself a form of processual inquiry, and also its own provisional response.

Similarly, performance studies scholar and longtime practitioner of Contact Improvisation (CI) Nita Little describes how dance encourages dancers to breach their attentional limit and engage differently with time.[29] She further articulates how CI facilitates the recognition that one's actions are coconstituted by the actions of others (human and nonhuman), which results in a process of actualization that is itself a manner of world-making. This attention to relation becomes a political way of engaging with others and expanding one's possibilities for being in, and with, the world. Little writes, "Actualizing is a political attentional action that is formative of our self-sensing. Being sense-able is to be of the world we are experiencing, as distinct from being 'in' it and thus separate from it. When we actualize as the world in this way, the possibilities for motion increase exponentially. . . . As our bases are enriched in their potentials by the actions of attention that begin in new imaginings of the self, they result in enhanced relational potentials."[30]

Sensing through CI, for Little, is therefore not a passive act of reception, but rather a practice of worlding. Though the movement in *Rhizophora* is not a formal performance of CI, as many of the dancers do not directly engage with one another's bodies through contact, the improvisational sensory movement among the foliage similarly expands attentional limits to create new sensory experiences of time for the viewer. Time does not exist in a linear teleology of cause and effect, problem and solution, as is so often inscribed in models of medical cure. Rather, sensory interaction is about being sensitive rather than sensible by other rational standards. This actualization of the world gives way to increased "relational potentials" for bodies usually depicted as objects of care rather than in a relational exchange of care. What is engaging, then, about the female duet in *Rhizophora* is how care of self and other are interwoven or, rather, inextricable. The women arrive at this relation of care as a result of their interaction with each other in the Vietnam Friendship Village. Their kinship, as portrayed in this short scene, attests to another model of care outside of nuclear family structures, which often carry with them a dutiful obligation to rehabilitate karmic pasts. The care exchanged through dance in this scene importantly redirects the moral presupposition, cited by Gammeltoft, about a disabled person's "inability" to care for their kin. The bed becomes a place from which care is cocreated. Both Martin and Little conceive of a type of collision event in which dance enacts a process of becoming between and within exposed bodies. In this manner, dance embodies what Karen Barad has termed the "intra-activity" of entities whose differentiation is in fact an act of connection and commitment rather than separation.[31]

Writing from the perspective of feminist science and technology studies, Astrid Schrader provides a parallel approach for expanding the frame of witnessing action and reaction to consider the "response-ability" of bodies intra-acting with one another. Schrader challenges how scientific experiments come to value certain observable characteristics as "ecologically and/or politically relevant" while limiting its reception to other potential modes of data collection. Through observing the dinoflagellate *Pfiesteria piscicida* and its intra-actions with fish, Schrader notes how the organisms' ontologies are defined by their interactions with and responses to their environments. Though Schrader employs the term *response-ability*, which could invoke a discourse that reifies an ableist hierarchy of responsiveness, I'm interested in how disability studies could crip her attention to the interactions and coconstitutions of changing environments. Part of Schrader's turn toward the term *response-ability* is also embedded in her call for more "responsible" scientific frameworks of causality—particularly in response to claims that the dinoflagellate *Pfiesteria piscicida* is a toxic entity. Her claim, therefore, is less about reifying an ontological ideal level of responsiveness as an "ability," and more about the suggestion that methods of witnessing and measuring change and adaption, and codifying levels of toxicity, are limited by linear models of cause and effect that fail to measure the intertwining of events over time. This call to witness a larger ecology of entwinement between bodies and environments that are deemed "toxic" is fundamental to understanding how systems for measuring toxicity become sedimented within observational methods, as in the case with Agent Orange. The history of confinement for racialized, lower-class, and disabled human bodies deemed "toxic" is inextricable from these practices; in Vietnam, following the wars in Southeast Asia in the 1970s, disability became codified as a toxic "social evil" to dispel.[32] Important to Schrader's formulation, therefore, is the expansive possibilities and indeterminacies of ontological intra-acting that acknowledge how organisms act and react in ways that may not be recognized by current systems of observation, but which are fundamental to processes of materialization.[33] This telos of becoming is fundamental to performance, particularly in improvisation, where the action unfolds as a sequence of reactions. To think dance, then, is to question the ontology of causation and a subsequent teleology aimed at resolving the separation between cause and effect. More specifically, dance provides a helpful methodology for sensing, in its particular attention to embodied exploration, adaptation, intra-action, and play.

The social and political meanings of play are vast and dependent on the cultural contexts in which play occurs. Play can be social, and an isolating retreat, figured within the imaginary, or believed to be a method of progressing the self. Play demonstrates power relations among those who play, and implements the social rules of the playing space. Play is accessible to some, while regarded as a scarce indulgence for others. Importantly, play is often figured as the opposite of work, though the relationship between play and productivity has certainly shifted culturally in the past few decades. The Vietnamese word most closely related to *play* is *chơi*, which references everything from a game or activity to a buoyant personality. Although the full range of play's meanings is beyond the scope of this particular chapter, I am particularly curious about two types of play that I witness in the videopoem. Play theorist Brian Sutton-Smith classifies these two versions of play as the *rhetoric of play as imaginary* and the *rhetoric of play as frivolous*. By Sutton-Smith's delineation, the first form of play describes improvisation, flexibility, and creativity in human and animal worlds, whereas the play of frivolity is usually ascribed to the "idle or the foolish" who "enact playful protest against the orders of the ordained world."[34] These two descriptions of play describe the speculative projection that play enables—a type of performative space that does not reenact prescribed circumstances of the social order, but works to expand and resist them. Play is also often restricted to the realm of childhood, so I also caution against the universal infantilization of those who engage in play, particularly within the context of neurodiverse populations, who are often socially treated like children in need of protective "care" and "development." As I mentioned, Agent Orange representation has relied heavily on the portrayal of children to foreground a narrative of rehabilitation through development. Thus, I do not aim to prescribe that play aids in the progressive development or rehabilitation of the self, as a psychological perspective may purport. Rather, I'm interested in how the haptic space created through dancing bodies, between the subjects of the film, and between them and the flora, opens up a playful space both for imagining as a political practice and for embodying those resistant spaces that upset normative orders of the world.

The third section in the film, titled *thời gian trà*, or teatime, was choreographically modeled after a ritual teatime that the residents shared daily, in which Đô, one of the residents featured in this section, would invite his friends to gather and have tea. However, again, it is not a literal portrayal of this communal activity. Instead, there is an immense sense of play in this scene whose animated and disjointed nature reorients the viewer's sensual and kinesthetic engagement with the subjects of the film. The camera moves, along with the residents, through enlarged flying UNO cards as two women emphatically throw brightly colored cards at each other in a game that takes place among equally brightly colored playground equipment and twisted neckties. Unlike the still frame of the Waking Up scene, the camera incorporates the viewer into the animation of bodies as it dips and weaves through the actors and surrounding foliage. One actor who has been hiding behind a palm tree emerges liltingly from behind its fronds with a teapot and teacup, animating the cup in a cyclical gesture as he sways toward another man seated in a wheelchair. The seated man, eyes closed, begins to respond to the teacup's initiations with his nose, following these olfactory impulses as if inhaling the smell of imaginary tea as the cup circles his torso. Throughout this duet, playing cards continue to cut across the frame, peppering the lilt of the men's dance with the gravitational fall of the cards. Then, a woman in red with a crown upon her head enters waltzing with a staff. The staff becomes her companion in this dance. She steps in and

FIGURE 5.3. Teatime scene from *Rhizophora*. One woman is wearing black and yellow, holding large playing cards. Courtesy of Davide De Lillis and Julia Metzger-Traber.

out of the camera's frame as the viewer is both invited into this waltz and simultaneously distanced from her experience. She does not dance for the camera, but rather among the interactions that surround her. Here, in the experience of play, within a community of residents who are often relegated to a realm of the outside "other," often selectively chosen against, I notice a shift in the sensible. The enactment of surreal excess in this scene does not reperform daily routine; it seems to suggest a parallel experience of disability often obscured by narratives of cure. In fact, what is sensible about the scene gives way to another affect altogether. Perhaps, even, a *sense* of companionship.

What differentiates *Rhizophora* from its documentary predecessors, then, is a rupture from the narrative of Agent Orange victimhood that requires repair by recuperation into heteronormative life. More specifically, dance in this context facilitates dissensus—a refiguring of the sensible through the redistribution of the senses articulated by Jacques Rancière. *Rhizophora* does not depict able-bodied others (parents or caretakers) who care for the residents; rather, they are portrayed through interactions with one another. Each of the scenes commingle functional activities with a choreographic interpretation of them. In doing so, the dance negates the very pragmatism inscribed by the activities. Alternatively, the dance becomes central to understanding the essence of each of these activities, even though the expenditures of energy far exceed what would be considered sensible for achieving the daily task. Dance consequently offers a sensory exposure to what otherwise would appear to be mundane activities. Unlike other documentary films that aim to narrate a "day in the life" of a disabled person in Vietnam by relying on realist portrayals of the person reenacting their lives for the film's audience, *Rhizophora* traffics in the possibilities of the absurd and fantastic that are facilitated by sensory experiences of the subjects' lives. It enacts Murphy's concept of *alterlife*, which she defines as a "becoming with exposure, [which] exists in the profoundly uneven and interdependent distribution of life chances."[35] Consequently, rather than a sense of empathy or "pity" for the subjects of the film, *Rhizophora* ignites a sense of joy and play as it incorporates viewers into an ongoing process of relation and exchange with the dancers. The stakes are shifted such that imagination and play become sensible responses to environmental harm.

Kinship Matters

Drawing from the works of those who insist on the mattering of matter, and the emergent relations among them, I propose that *Rhizophora* importantly refigures what is sensible and *dissensible* in relation to Agent Orange.[36] If the *sensible* is sedimented by regimes of observation that define normative boundaries of sense (limited to distinct delineations among sight, sound, smell, taste, and touch), and further reify rational standards for the use of these senses for meaning-making, then the *dissensible* redistributes these taxonomies of sense by entangling multimodal sensory-feelings without a predetermined purpose or end.

Throughout the film, small scenes interstitially weave the more choreographed representations of daily life. In these connective moments, the dancers wear brown and green clothing and move improvisationally in a landscape of foliage. The viewers are to presume that these trees represent (or are) the *Rhizophora* mangrove trees from which the film takes its name. In these scenes, the movers do not overtly perform a narrative arc that ends in the consummation of heterosexual coupling or pairing, nor do they replicate their own daily activities to be witnessed by outside others. Rather, they move sensorially within the space, subtly responding to the ecology of plant and human bodies that surround them.

A close-up of a hand emerges alongside a dense layer of vegetation. The image is accompanied by the sound of string instruments, likely cellos, creating short resonant strokes as if the cellos themselves are warming up their resonant hollows for sound. Like the tentative nature of the score, fingers emerge like tentacles probing the leafy frame created by the appendages of the tree. A dance materializes in the close-up between the hand and its environment, producing a sensory relation that stretches outward. The scale of this engagement further dissects the subjects of the film to feature what Erin Brannigan calls the "microchoreographies of organs" as flows of energy pass over and through the surfaces of porous bodies.[37] The close-up of the hand within the leafy environment draws attention to the liveliness of both the hand and the trees that frame it. Liveness is coconstituted by their haptic interaction. Dance, as epistemology, materializes the friction between these multiple scales of becoming with exposure.

In this final scene, in which the residents are engaged in their own, multiple, sensory worlds, they seem to dance just for themselves. The viewer is contingently invited into the dance as the camera moves about the scene, creating an affective kinesthesia; however, the dancers also choreographically actualize a world all their own, alone and together, at once. The videopoem returns to the scene of the forest where it began; however, now, there are many bodies among the trees. The dancers move with sense, eyes closed, gently articulating with fingers and toes. The camera cuts between close-ups of various bodies, to suture together the dirt in the toes of one mover to the blinking eyelids of another,

FIGURE 5.4. A scene from *Rhizophora*. Many people are wearing brown and green, dancing in a forest. Courtesy of Davide De Lillis and Julia Metzger-Traber.

from the fronds of a fern to a braid of hair. In the final shot, the camera zooms out to show each body moving to a separate rhythm in its own microworld, in proximity but not in explicit relation to the others. As the cello cuts out, the dance continues.

Ultimately, *Rhizophora* produces a different sense of being in the world by disrupting linear narratives to cut together different interactions between disabled bodies. The scenes are not portrayals of disability being recuperated into a narrative of normative life, but rather they are depictions of autonomous moving, sensing bodies actualizing communal worlds through their collective movement explorations. The film thus renders a politics and poetics of dance as an eco-phenomenology through which disability rhizomatically participates in world-making. Contamination is not rendered an object of shock to be analytically resolved. Instead, it becomes a moving entity that lives in and through moving bodies. As such, *Rhizophora* offers alternative sensibilities for engaging with disability, dance, and the changing environment that surrounds us.

Perhaps what is most inviting about *Rhizophora* is its appeal to sense *with* ecologies of human and plant bodies, attuning us to the intra-activity of bodies exposed to, living with, affected by, and composing the matter of an Agent Orange community. While these haptic encounters observed in *Rhizophora* occur through dance, on film, and in an institutionalized space, the videopoem playfully invites the viewers to consider how exposure entwines bodies in ways not yet recognized by normative perceptual systems—outside regimes of scopic observation and the institutions built to perpetuate them. These scenes invite us to reconsider how cellular, chemical, and extant bodies coexist and are woven together, not only by their communal targeting by the US military complex, but also as porous bodies in a process of becoming through their mutual exposure. The decimation of landscapes can be calculated in more than just its loss of profit for human-centered agriculture or its effects on a chain of food production that serves human bodies.

To consider, witness, and experience dance in an epoch of contamination and indeterminacy therefore is to attune to sensory modalities for navigating an exchange between bodies and, consequently, the matters that are created between them. Dance figures action and reaction in a coconstituting bind that destabilizes narratives of a sole initiator. Instead, an impulse generated in one body is transferred among bodies and alters the composition of those bodies in its transmission. So too, do the attentional limits of these bodies expand into multiple spatial and temporal frames at once. These sensory exchanges, at the cellular level, are bodies that open themselves to potential reexposure, acknowledging and inviting their porous boundaries to commingle with that of the foliage. As disability, especially in relation to Agent Orange, has been managed by the quarantining of contaminated landscapes with concrete barriers and fences, and, consequently, bodies exposed to Agent Orange continue to be kept separate, the possibility of mutual exposure between a trans-species ecology of bodies is ever more critical. Thus, to acknowledge the alterlives of sensing human and nonhuman bodies in their processes of becoming is not to ignore the uneven distribution of exposure's consequences. Rather, the friction created by these meetings of bodies offers multiple sensory entries into the debilitation of exposed ecologies, and also a network of care and kinship practices that emerges as alternative avenues for living with contamination.

NOTES

1   I have previously critiqued the rhetoric of diplomatic reparation put forth by the founders and funders of the Vietnam Friendship Village; however, I also acknowledge the gathering space that centers like the Vietnam Friendship Village offer. For more information, http://www.vietnamfriendship.org/.
2   Kafer, *Feminist, Queer, Crip*, 8.
3   Gammeltoft, *Haunting Images*, 142.
4   Nguyen, *Journey to Inclusion*, 25.
5   USAID, *Disability Rights Enforcement*.
6   Gammeltoft, *Haunting Images*, 75.
7   Gammeltoft, *Haunting Images*, 73.
8   Erevelles, *Disability and Difference*; Meekosha and Soldatic, "Human Rights"; Nguyen, *Journey to Inclusion*.
9   Nguyen, *Journey to Inclusion*, 34.
10 Murphy, "Alterlife and Decolonial Chemical Relations," 496.
11 Kim, *Curative Violence*, 14.
12 Kroløkke et al., *Critical Kinship Studies*, 8–11.
13 Tsing, *Mushroom*, 33.
14 Piepzna-Samarasinha, *Care Work*, 33.
15 Helen Meekosha and Karen Soldatic articulate the importance of acknowledging identifications of impairment within the Global South as an important site of political identification used to initiate the redistribution of resources. They write, "Recent international claims for retributive justice can be linked to a global politics of impairment, such as the Vietnamese Agent-Orange Movement against the US military complex. These political mobilisations around retributive justice for created impairment are rarely mentioned in the global disability rights movement. Impairment, positioned in this way, draws heavily on medical science to make claims for a global resource transfer from the North to the South, as a strategy for 'global payback' for crimes committed under the colonisers' project" (Meekosha and Soldatic, "Human Rights," 1392).
16 SWNS, "This Is the Legacy."

17 Fox, "Agent Orange: Coming to Terms," 234.

18 Kashi, *The Leaves Keep Falling*; Catherine Karnow, *Agent Orange: A Terrible Legacy*.

19 Reagan, "Representations and Reproductive Hazards," 58.

20 Peeples, "Imaging Toxins," 201.

21 Gammeltoft, *Haunting Images*, 57.

22 Schmitz, "Growing on the Edge."

23 *Rhizophora*, film directed by Davide De Lillis and Julia Metzger-Traber, 2015, https://vimeo.com/111310332.

24 Piepzna-Samarasinha, *Care Work*, 72.

25 Julia Metzger-Traber in discussion with the author, April 12, 2016.

26 Kuppers, "Toward a Rhizomatic Model," 226.

27 Kuppers, "Toward a Rhizomatic Model," 233.

28 Martin, *Critical Moves*, 6.

29 Contact Improvisation (CI) is a form of improvisatory movement based on the exchange of weight between bodies. It was formally developed in the 1970s in Europe and the United States and is primarily characterized by its use of physical touch and its emphasis on the process of responding to constantly changing physical realities rather than on producing a predictable result or product (Paxton, "A Definition," 26). The dancing in *Rhizophora* is not a formal practice of Contact Improvisation; however, I find that the principles of CI help to contextualize the improvisatory movement in the videopoem in ways that demonstrate how sense-based movement can expand attentional limits to changing environments.

30 Little, "Restructuring the Self-Sensing," 254.

31 Barad, "Nature's Queer Performativity," 125.

32 Nguyen, *Journey to Inclusion*, 37.

33 Schrader, "Responding to *Pfiesteria piscicida*," 297.

34 Sutton-Smith, *Ambiguity of Play*, 11.

35 Murphy, "What Can't a Body Do?"

36 For further discussion of the intersections of materialism and race, racial capital, settler colonialism, and disability, see the discussion among Kyla Wazana Thompkins, Michelle N. Huang, and Chad Shomura in issue 6.1 of *Lateral: A Journal of the Cultural Studies Association*, and Mel Chen's seminal work, *Animacies*.

37 Brannigan, *Dancefilm*, 45.

6. DISABILITY BEYOND HUMANS

Aurora Levins Morales and Inclusive Ontology

SUZANNE BOST

In my work on Latina feminisms and disability, I've found posthumanism to be an unexpected intellectual ally. I'm intrigued by what posthumanist theories have to show us about the different shades of agency attached to elements like trees, dogs, air, and plastic. Posthumanism has taught me to be wary of viewing agency, power, or embodiment as stable qualities that an individual either possesses or does not. I've learned from posthumanists like Karen Barad that agency occurs in "intra-actions" among human, nonhuman, material, and seemingly immaterial entities: "The space of agency is not restricted to the possibilities for human action. . . . What is at issue rather, are the possibilities for iterative reconfigurings of the materiality of human, nonhuman, cyborgian, and other such forms. Holding the category 'human' ('nonhuman') fixed (or at least presuming that one can) excludes an entire range of possibilities in advance, eliding important dimensions of the workings of agency."[1] Drawing from Judith Butler's writings on performativity and the quantum physics of Niels Bohr, Barad expands agency beyond humanist (and individualist) free will. Though this might seem like a dismantling of agency for some, being able to think about mobility and action without autonomy is useful for disability studies.

In *The Posthuman*, Rosi Braidotti outlines what she calls a "critical posthumanism," one that "opens up perspectives for affirmative transformations of both the structures of subjectivity and the production of theory and knowledge."[2] I find real affinity between my own view of ethics and "the new transversal alliance across species and among posthuman subjects" that Braidotti describes: an alliance that "opens up unexpected possibilities for the recomposition of communities, for the very idea of humanity and for ethical forms of belonging."[3] Braidotti traces a genealogy of critical posthumanism through its Western intellectual roots (including Marxism, existentialism, feminism, and poststructuralism, each of which "created other visions of the self" outside of humanism); she also points to the ways in which postcolonial thinkers "explicitly questioned the relevance of the Humanistic ideal" and its Eurocentric assumptions.[4] Yet Braidotti doesn't account for what non-Western epistemologies have to add to the critique of humanism. Of course, Braidotti is trained in continental philosophy; it is probably up to those of us whose training reaches outside this tradition to point out alternatives to humanism that are not necessarily defined in relation to humanism itself.

In an essay that critiques the intellectual Eurocentrism of posthumanist geography, Juanita Sundberg writes, "I am discomforted by the ways in which geographical engagements with posthumanism tend to reproduce colonial ways of knowing and being by enacting universalizing claims and, consequently, further subordinating other ontologies."[5] Zoe Todd likewise critiques posthumanism as a trendy "Euro-Western academic narrative" that essentially reinvents a wheel, developing ideas that resonate with existing Indigenous cosmologies without invoking Indigenous writers.[6] Sundberg and Todd are right to critique the "Euro-Western" bias that underlies discussions of posthumanism. Humanism and posthumanism are part of a culturally limited narrative that does not account for the variety of ways of being and knowing in our world. In her analysis of disability and transnationalism, Nirmala Erevelles characterizes posthumanism as reducing materiality to textuality and presenting "local, fragmented, and partial analyses that fail to foreground the global structures that produce differential effects on different populations."[7] While many posthumanist theories strive for a holistic and inclusive framework, the focus on relations beyond the level of the "the human" (like ecosystems, infection, interspecies survival, or Baradian intra-action) does tend to gloss over cultural difference and embodied inequality. In any case, why would we confine our thinking to frameworks that are rooted in masculinism, individualism, and colonialism? What I see in the work of feminist of color writers like Aurora Levins Morales, Gloria Anzaldúa, or Alexis Pauline Gumbs are alternative epistemologies that do not center "the human individual" or the positivist science of the Enlightenment. This is not an alternate genealogy for posthumanism: it is a parallel universe of ideas.

Here is where my work on Levins Morales comes in. Though she is best known for her contributions to 1980s feminist-of-color writing, Levins Morales's work has expanded in the last decade to reflect her experiences with epileptic seizures, stroke, and chemical sensitivity—experiences that highlight the ways in which individual being is permeated by the ecosystems it touches. This writing presents a weblike ontology—guanakán, Levins Morales calls it, borrowing from Taíno epistemology—in which human and nonhuman entities are materially intertwined. This framework shifts the locus of health and (dis)ability from the individual to multidirectional interactions among humans, plants, and toxins. These webs of connection are both "prehumanist" (drawn from precolonial Indigenous traditions) and post-, eschewing both the assumption of linear progress implied by the term "post-" and the Western philosophical tradition from which posthumanist theory derives. The posts of "high theory" have limited resonance for my focus on Latina/o/x studies, whose relationship to modernism, humanism, feminism, and many other -isms is complicated by conquest, mestizaje, forced migration, and contested legal status. Yet the need to make ethical claims about human actions relative to (dis)ability, health care, reproduction, climate change, and citizenship makes me reluctant to abandon the vocabularies of humanism altogether. So I propose an "other-than-humanist" approach to attend to the trans-corporeal, the ecological, and the otherworldly dimensions of Levins Morales's work.

Levins Morales is probably best known for her writings of the 1980s, including her contribution to Cherríe Moraga and Gloria Anzaldúa's groundbreaking collection, *This Bridge Called My Back: Writings by Radical Women of Color* (1981), as well as *Getting Home Alive* (1986), the mixed-genre collection she coauthored with her late mother, Rosario Morales. These essays and poems focus on the deterritorializations and cultural mixtures that underlie Levins Morales's identity as a Puerto Rican Jew who spent her childhood in rural Puerto Rico before moving to the United States. Chronic illness has oriented Levins Morales's more recent work in a different direction, focused on creating therapeutic histories and healing communities. *Remedios: Stories of Earth and Iron from the History of Puertorriqueñas* (1998), *Medicine Stories* (1998), and *Kindling: Writings on the Body* (2013) offer what she describes as "medicinal history": healing self and community by reimagining the oppressive stories in which we are embedded. These stories reflect not just the author's personal identities but also the wider agencies of global commerce and imperialism, from the first populations in Africa through the European conquest of the Americas. For *Remedios*, Levins Morales conducted extensive historical and botanical research, contextualizing her own story within a larger ecology of violence and adaptive response. In this broad history, the perseverance of humans, animals, and plants offers lessons for survival in conditions of abuse. Critics have seemed more hesitant to embrace the imaginative, interdisciplinary reach of Levins Morales's historical work.[8]

Kindling focuses more tightly on the author. When doctors and insurers refused to recognize her claims for integral health, Levins Morales turned to community-based therapies, like re-evaluation counseling (a group storytelling process that imagines new healing pathways via narrative) and the World Wide Web, including social media and her own interactive website (www.auroralevinsmorales.com). The website, which is promoted in the introduction to *Kindling*, extends the author's health and embodiment to networks real and virtual, sharing blogs, selling books, and offering her services as speaker or writing coach in trade for massage, air filters, or nontoxic products. Monthly payments can earn sponsors certificates of contribution to the author's works. As the website proclaims, "It takes a village to keep the blogs coming."

Cripping Genealogy

These diffuse approaches might not seem obviously connected to the framework of "crip," which derives from histories of "out-and-proud" disability activism that often focus on individual bodies and their nonnormative mobilities.[9] Though Levins Morales did use a wheelchair for a few years after experiencing a stroke, holistic treatment at the International Center for Neurological Restoration in Cuba restored her ability to walk unassisted. The majority of her writings about illness, disability, and medicine revolve around conditions that are generally invisible and, thus, often not regarded as disabilities: chronic fatigue immune dysfunction syndrome, multiple chemical sensitivity disorder, and epilepsy. Moreover, her orientation to ability and healing is environmental rather than identitarian. Yet, to the extent that *crip* disrupts convention and undermines social norms, the term works well here. I appreciate Robert McRuer's recent attention (in *Crip Times*) to the limits and possibilities of the term *crip*, which he regards as being "far stretchier" than its implied association with mobility impairment, stretching to encompass "non-normative or non-representative disabilities—disabilities, shall we say, that would never be legible beneath the universal access symbol for disability."[10] This illegibility resonates with the opaque body at the center of Levins Morales's work and her struggles for access and recognition. McRuer's definition of *crip*, however, differs from Levins Morales's approach: "*Crip* does, however, generally stand in opposition to both the medical model, which would reduce disability to the univocality of pathology, diagnosis, or treatment/elimination, and to some forms of the well-known social model, . . . which suggest that *disability* should be understood as located not in bodies per se but in inaccessible environments requiring adaptation."[11]

While Levins Morales clearly opposes corporate medicine as it is practiced in the United States, she does embrace what we might call homeopathic medicine (especially tinctures derived from plants) and the interdisciplinary brand of socialized medicine that she experienced in Cuba (documented in her Cuba journals, published in *Kindling*). Moreover, she explicitly focuses on environmental and social conditions as the source of her disabilities (especially the chemical toxins that inhibit her liver function and the social choices that make these toxins so prevalent in our air and water). Levins Morales's contributions to the performance project Sins Invalid resonate with the radical disability pride associated with the term crip, but she never embraces this term herself, so I avoid situating her work in a genealogy relative to crip theory in the same way that I pose her relationship to posthumanism as being one of resonance, not kinship.[12] Levins Morales overtly critiques jargon and theoretical fads as power trips designed to maintain hierarchies. These are linkages thick with friction.

Like most genealogies, this one begins with a human figure in the present. But this genealogy is not interested in the linear temporality of descent or the intellectual inheritance of human progenitors. The other-than-humanist ethics I find in Levins Morales operate like a web, with tentacles that reach across times, places, and cultures with productive epistemological intercourse. This web comes from Indigenous arachnid creatrixes as much as the internet connections formed in and through the author's website, complicating the distinctions associated with most categories of social thought.

Levins Morales is not just a poet/writer but also a historian, though an unconventional and self-proclaimed "radical" one. In *Remedios,* histories derived from her doctoral dissertation, she casts her historiographic net widely to tell the story of how she came to be the embodied being that she is. She describes this story as revolving around "intertwining histories":

> One is the vast web of women's stories spinning out in time and space from the small island of Puerto Rico and encompassing some of the worst disasters to befall humanity: the Crusades; the Inquisition; the African slave trade; the witch persecutions; the European invasions of America, Africa, Asia, and the Pacific; and the enclosure of common lands in Europe itself, that sent a land-starved and dispossessed peasantry out rampaging in the wake of greedy aristocrats, merchants, and generals across the world—and all the plagues, tortures, rapes, famines, and killings that accompanied these events.[13]

The "other story" in *Remedios* is about the ritual abuse of the author during her childhood in Puerto Rico, and she calls this story "exactly the same," though "smaller": "invasion, torture, rape, death, courage, solidarity, resistance."[14] In its focus on shared structures of abuse, *Remedios* incorporates not just "actual" historical figures but also imagined people (like the first mother of sub-Saharan Africa) as well as nonhuman animals and plants.

This history is not primarily a temporal one; Levins Morales links people and things in ways that defy time and space. This multi-perspectival approach is unwieldy, impossibly inclusive, and certainly more imaginative than empirical (since there are no written records for much of what Levins Morales wants to tell). *Remedios* winds through 186 fragments of (hi)story, spanning the globe with a cast of hundreds, including a deer mother, piñon, Saint Teresa of Avila, gingerbread, the "Wild West," Queen Nzinga, Nannytown, tuberculosis, Pura Belpré, needleworkers, the barrio, and milk thistle. In this context, ginger is a real agent and ally (stimulating digestion and pulling you out of bed) as much as the hurricanes of the Boriken goddess Guabancex (who "drags the birds of Africa out to sea and throws them on the beaches of Brazil") or the twentieth-century Puerto Rican librarian and writer Pura Belpré (whose stories lift children into the sun where they can "grow tall and strong").[15]

The histories in *Remedios* revolve around healing, and in some ways the text is a "crip genealogy," a history designed to shed light on the author's own disabling experiences. It also "crips" the idea of genealogy and history to prioritize therapy over lineage. "I started graduate school [at the Union Institute, in History] and therapy within two weeks of each other because at some level I understood that the two processes were intimately linked," Levins Morales explains.[16] She came to history in the same way that she came to her own body's sensitivity to chemicals and propensity for seizures. She was not just trying to make "sense" of unfortunate events; she was putting these experiences in the broader, holistic context in which they take shape, assume meaning, and might unfold or flourish otherwise. Her history is not just about the telling or the analysis. It is performative: "The history I gathered here is like the medicinal plants growing in a long-abandoned garden."[17] The preface to *Remedios* describes moving "back and forth between my own nightmares and revelations and the web of history," building history from lost stories, lost cures, dreams, and revelations.[18] This historical method sidesteps empiricism to fuel imaginations with worlds of possibility for ethical thriving. In an interview I conducted with her in 2015, she explained: "I was conscious that I wasn't trying to be comprehensive; I was trying to be medicinal. And so I was researching those stories; I was creating a support group for myself across time."[19] Yet *Remedios* is not therapeutic in any conventional way: rather than aiming to eliminate illness or pain, it constructs networks and highlights the ways in which we are intertwined with the world around us. The work, itself, flourishes.

Health beyond Humans

In "Mountain Moving Day," an essay she wrote (and delivered via Skype) for the Society for the Study of Gloria Anzaldúa conference in 2010 (a session I attended in the flesh in San Antonio, Texas), Levins Morales specifically identified the need for a "strong, vocal, politically sophisticated, disability justice movement led by queer working class and trans people of color," which might have made Anzaldúa willing to embrace the term "disabled" when she was diagnosed with diabetes in the 1990s. But "it wasn't there yet."[20] As with the broad histories in *Remedios*, and as with the disability justice movement (which Levins Morales characterizes as a "systemic" approach rather than an individual one), "Mountain Moving Day" describes illness and disability as environmental rather than individual conditions.

> Illness has been one long hurricane season for me, chunks of cement and metal roofing flying through the air, big trees made into heaps of splinters and shredded roots. What takes me to the core, to the place of new insight is listening with all my being to the voice of my own flesh, which is often an unbearable task. What lets me bear it is political, is a deep ecological sense of the web in which my flesh is caught, where the profound isolation of chronic illness forces me to extend awareness beyond individual suffering, . . . the mind-bending build up of toxins where nausea and nightmare meet, dragging me from my bed at three a.m. to lift cups of bitter tinctures [to] my lips with cramping hands, and leach the poison from my own liver.[21]

This language moves between core and ecosystem, between first-person possessives ("all my being" and "my own flesh") and a "mind-bending build up" of toxins, tinctures, and flying chunks of cement that physically intra-act with the body. Individual suffering occurs in the mind/body, "where nausea and nightmare meet," but is bigger than the human self. The ecological "web" in which the individual body is caught is a source of both poison and community. "Our bodies are in the mix of everything we call political," Levins Morales writes; in Puerto Rico, bodies are inseparable from US colonialism, "agricultural choices forced on people whose economic lives are ruled from afar," industrial pollutants and pesticides that create "unbreathable cities and abandoned coffee farms and tainted water." Since our bodies and the land share the effects of profit motives and pollutants, bodies and land share the same matter: "If I write about our bodies I am writing about the land and what has been done to it."[22] Throughout her work, Levins Morales seems to favor the organic over the inorganic (if such a distinction is possible, and sometimes it is not). She bemoans the advertising campaigns that tried to persuade Puerto Rican families that buying Tang is better than eating fruit from the trees. Yet, since the trees are presumably treated with pesticides, maybe Tang is more healthy (if one can make it without "tainted water").

Remedios presents an inclusive ontology of a Puerto Rican ecosystem. In this text that has a "Botánica" instead of a bibliography, yam and milk thistle are two of the plants whose animacies and agencies we see in close detail. Wild yam "makes what the body makes. Something golden and potent slipping into the bloodstream to ripen the eggs, preserve the skin, grow babies, erase pain."[23] This "body" is never assigned a species, but yam is its ally when "slipped" into the bloodstream. The section on yams ends with a direct address to an unknown partner in conversation: "Here, taste the starchy root dried to chalky slices, the medicine of trust."[24] Trust implies an edge of risk involved in taking the "starchy" roots of another into one's own body and allowing that other to perform its "medicine." Milk Thistle is a teacher whose lessons could apply across species: "Milk Thistle teaches guerilla warfare. Adaptogen milagrosa, Milk Thistle works with what is here, the yellow layers of toxins, the charcoal grit, the green bile slow as crude oil pooling in the liver's reservoirs, waiting to learn to flow. Milk Thistle says take what you are and use it."[25]

This passage focuses on adaptation to all that is "here" (elements organic and non—like bile, toxins, charcoal, and crude oil), resonating with Barad's theory of intra-action, the inclusive materialization of the heterogeneous stuff that comes together at any point in time/space. When Milk Thistle "says take what you are," it implies that "you" are the mixture of elements that come together, for better or worse, within the body's processing system. Milk Thistle does not need to be human in order to have agency, so there is no reason to assume that "Milk Thistle" is personified in these passages or that "you" that uses the plants is human. Plants are agents, too, especially as they commingle with surrounding matter. At the same time, the human body is just one ingredient of (present and future) compost.

A poem Levins Morales wrote after her stroke blends organic and inorganic in a more clearly affirmative way. In "Exoskeleton," she describes her wheelchair as an extension of her own body or, even, as a lover. When she slides into it, "suddenly I am uplifted and embraced. . . . / I am surrounded by the yellow ribs of this new body." This "new body" that embraces her has bones of "enameled-steel." It is also made up of social and political matter, a "statement to the world / that I can't walk another step." The chair, itself, performs disability, "speaks for me . . . ," and serves as the "shiny carapace / that lets the world know my species."[26] In a society in which illness or disability must be legitimated by medical professionals in order to be covered by insurance, the speaking wheelchair gives her access to both the medical benefits and the social stigmas attached to the "species" designation it signifies.[27]

Disability itself expands our understanding of species. Enlightenment humanism, the root of our "human sciences," has revolved around a false universal: a concept of the human that is implicitly white (not enslaved or colonized), male (not pregnant or menstruating or lactating), and able-bodied (physically and mentally self-reliant). Liberal humanists often seek to expand "the human" enough to let "others" in, but physical stability, individual capacity, and freedom still underlie this notion. Increasingly, feminists, antiracists, and disability scholars have sought to think of agency beyond this species boundary. In "Exoskeleton," Levins Morales describes the fatigue that immobilized her as "when the plugs in the arches of my feet / are pulled out," as if her body, itself, was a mechanized vehicle requiring energy routed to it through electrical cords. This intermingling of flesh, metal, rubber, and electricity produces mobility that is non-individual. It enables the speaker (when plugged in) "to fly down the sidewalk the way I fly in dreams," expanding capacity beyond material or empirical limits.[28]

I could call this intermingling a cyborg, with a nod toward Donna Haraway, but we don't need a term from Western postmodernism, posthumanism, military capitalism, and science fiction to describe this erotic expansion of movement. There is a resemblance between Levins Morales's "Exoskeleton" and the idea of the cyborg, but their genealogies, their politics, and their aesthetics are distinct.[29] Alison Kafer provides an extended "close crip reading" of the cyborg in Feminist, Queer, Crip, first providing a necessary critique of the ways in which Haraway romanticizes (as embodied utopias or provocative monsters) the technological intertwinements that are material realities for many people with disabilities. Yet Kafer finds Haraway's cyborg to be an ally in her search for a vision of "crip futurity"—a future not dependent on resolving corporeality into individual "wholeness."[30] Haraway's later turn to companion species helped her to decenter the cyborg (along with its kinship to monstrosity, the military industrial complex, and the racialized economics of Silicon Valley) and to turn to friendlier interminglings among species. In "Reconfiguring Kinship," Haraway explains, "cyborgs could no longer do the work of a proper herding dog to gather up the threads needed for serious critical inquiry. So I happily go to the dogs . . .

in order to help craft tools for science studies in the present time."[31] Balancing both cyborgs and companion animals in one's mind is helpful for imagining disability, especially that experienced by Levins Morales, which is based on the monstrous effects of colonialism and industrial agriculture as well as more nurturing couplings with wheelchairs and web donations.

It is in this vein that I find resonance between posthumanism and the work of Levins Morales. This is not a gesture that Levins Morales would necessarily embrace. In one of her best-known essays from the 1990s, "Certified Organic Intellectual," subtitled "On Not Being Postmodern," Levins Morales asserts that "the ideas I carry with me were grown on soil I know. . . . The intellectual traditions I come from create theory out of shared lives instead of sending away for it." "I know that the complexity of unrefined food is far more nourishing than the processed stuff," she concludes, rejecting the (generalized, reified) products at Safeway in favor of those at the farmers' market.[32] We do not need prepackaged thinking to explore the trans-species webs of relation that both Haraway and Levins Morales favor. These webs are not organized by theory; they are native plants that grow wild and are covered in soil. But "organic" is an elusive ideal these days, involving such impurities as government certification and Whole Foods stores in urban food deserts where no one can afford their inflated prices. The organic is mediated by inorganic management. So where do we go for accessible healthy produce?

Toxicity and Ethics

Levins Morales's website is, I would argue, a virtual farmers' market, a multidirectional genealogy, a place for trans-corporeal collectivity and exchange. It's not postmodern in the ways that the internet was assumed to be in the 1990s (the disembodied, hyperreal territory of the military industrial complex); auroralevinsmorales.com emerges from material needs and lives in the activities of embodied users. The networks the website forges in support of these lively matters use the tools of postmodernity in premodern or nonmodern fashion, with hyperlinks leading to anticapitalist barter and spiritual astrology. The various options to "Support Aurora" include contributing labor (like grant writing or web support), donating materials for the maintenance of her toxin-free "tiny house on wheels," and becoming a "*patreon*," or sustainer, which evokes both the premodern tradition of artistic patronage and the logic of an ecosystem that requires nurturance. Each of these means of support will feed a community with blogs, poems, and public events.

My understanding of ecosystems is influenced by the work of Stacy Alaimo, among others. Alaimo comes from a feminist, new materialist background, revolving around a critique of human behaviors that have damaged our ecosystem and poisoned our own bodies. But these concerns are not just human; they revolve around larger questions of environmental justice that include ocean animals and plants as participants. Since Levins Morales is sensitive to multiple chemicals in her environment—one of the conditions that motivates Alaimo's theory of "toxic bodies"—justice for her would entail broad environmental transformations.[33] (In a lecture she delivered at Loyola University Chicago in April 2017, Levins Morales critiqued my use of the label "chemical sensitivity" and claimed the term "environmental violence," instead. I want to keep the emphasis on "sensitivity," though—as a form of vulnerability, connectedness, and perhaps even agency.) Levins Morales writes, in *Kindling*, "What isolates me is not my illness, but the widespread distress that prevents people from choosing non-toxic products."[34] This "widespread distress" encompasses economic, cultural, and ethical matters, like the for-profit industry of "personal care" products and their advertisements that persuade humans that smelling like perfume is better than smelling like humans, the individualistic belief that one person's choices are his or her "own business" rather than the business of us all, and the natural and artificial chemicals in which we unthinkingly soak our bodies. For Alaimo, chemical sensitivities suggest an "ontological shift," "dissolv[ing] something so basic to the sense of what it is to be human—a sense of being a discrete entity, separate from one's environs."[35] Healing Levins Morales, then, must include not just a cultural shift (rethinking our shared participation in a toxic narrative), but also an ontological shift in our perceptions of what it means to be human. We need to replace our belief in the human individual with an understanding of our trans-corporeal relations within a collectivity.

In an essay also published in 2013, titled "Guanakán," Levins Morales borrows from indigenous Puerto Rican cosmology to describe the body as a radically permeable entity. Skin is not a wall or a barrier, she argues:

> It's a conversation, cells lined up in a smooth collaboration, a layered surface that is constantly exchanging molecules with everything else. What's more, a surface full of doors and windows, through which all kinds of wildlife passes. If skin is the wall of a house, that house is made of dried grass, is full of insects and small mammals and nesting birds, is its own habitat, constantly shedding stalks, or, to change the metaphor, is made of soft wood, growing mosses and mushrooms on its surface even as the shredded bark and wood fall away into the rich surrounding soil.[36]

That final sentence, like the body itself, is a lush compilation of materials joined loosely by commas in a shared habitat. Levins Morales uses the term "guanakán," drawn from the Taíno way of saying "our center," to reference "that cloudy gathering of denser particles and pulses in which our awareness exists"; guanakán is a less "bulky" way of saying "body-mind-nature-thing."[37] Guanakán is a nonmodern ontology, an organic alternative to the constraints of empirical science and individual autonomy manufactured by humanism. Life on the web holds every entity open to the fluctuations that come from relation; it is a continual process of coevolution.

From the perspective of contagious illnesses and environmental toxins, there are no individuals or boundaries; health is a state shared by all of us rather than the property of a few lucky individuals. Levins Morales's website performs this insight: making her individual thriving a public concern by soliciting resources from across the web. Digital health, however, is difficult to regulate. A website is a symbiotic network that links entities in sometimes healthful and sometimes unhealthful ways. The internet might seem like a "safe" environment for someone with chemical sensitivity: she can remain in the space of her own home (a space that she has constructed to minimize its toxicity toward her) while interacting with others. Indeed, in the interview I conducted with her, Levins Morales stressed the importance of being able to shop, to collaborate, and to conduct research online. There is reciprocal responsibility for members of an online community: sharing resources and advice, mobilizing local networks when someone is in trouble, and simply bearing witnesses. But there is also a great deal of shared vulnerability within such a web. Bad advice, anger, and judgment can circulate in unhealthful ways, just like credit card numbers that fall into the wrong "hands." There are toxicities in a digital environment, though they are different from those one might find in a physical house, forest, or ocean. Indeed, the internet has its own guanakán, which intersects with the guanakanes of everyone who goes there.

What is the difference between the Indigenous idea of guanakán and the web formed by contemporary toxicity? The language of toxicity implies a polluting agent threatening the integrity of a body (a body we like to imagine as pure). Toxicity, according to modern understanding, is perverse because it involves nonhuman agents (like the hyperbolic smog monsters and killer tomatoes of science fiction). Under Enlightenment humanism, only humans, with their dominating gift of reason, are proper agents. We are supposed to have lost our belief in magic, animism, and alchemy. Toxicity is like a resurgence of the primitive, a refusal of matter to abide by its supposed inanimate state. Yet

Levins Morales's idea of the guanakán, like new developments in critical post-humanism and ecocriticism, reminds us that humans never were apart from nature. Though we liked to think of ourselves as transcendent, we have always been subject to/with nonhuman cohabitants.

Contemporary toxic matters fall on both sides of the supposed organic/inorganic line: pollen, infectious microbes, lead paint on a child's toy, snake venom, cleansers meant to purify our bodies and homes, or emails "phishing" for personal data all take on agency in their chemical activities. With a linguist's delight for the changing meanings of words, Mel Chen, in *Animacies*, traces the shifting meaning of "toxic" from its association with poison in the 1600s to contemporary (metaphoric?) applications of the term to describe social atmospheres. The definition of toxin, then, "has always been the outcome of political negotiation."[38] Chen suggests that the "basic semantic schema for toxicity" is a real or assumed threat (of damage or alteration) posed to one body by another proximate body. It is important to bear in mind that neither of these bodies is static and that their shared relation intertwines them. Toxicity "meddles with" subject/object relations, which are at the heart of humanism.[39] This is true in two ways: first, supposed inanimate objects (like dioxin) are agentic in a way that objectifies the human recipient of their toxicity. Second, beyond this role reversal, the coherence of both "proximate bodies" is unstable as they infect and transform each other in a multidirectional manner: soap leaves residue on skin; skin leaves cells on soap.

What if we resituated toxicity as a neutral aspect of multispecies cohabitation, relational and communal rather than poisonous? In Nan Enstad's account, though it represents the triumph of global capitalism in insinuating itself into our very flesh, toxicity also leads us to recognize new subjectivities and new publics based on shared vulnerability and distributed agencies rather than the humanistic medical model of individuated subjects sealed off from each other and the outside world.[40] In an account of her (non)solitary suffering in *Kindling*, Levins Morales describes the ambivalent simultaneity of vulnerability and distributed agency that comes with toxicity:

> In the steepest pitch, the darkest hour, in the ring of deadly wind, the only salvation is to expand, to embrace every revelation of my struggling cells, to resist the impulse to flee, and hold in my awareness both things: the planetary web of life force of which I am part, and the cruel machinery that assaults us: how greed strips and poisons landscapes and immune systems with equal disregard, how contempt for women, and the vastly profitable medical-industrial complex conspire to write off as hysterical hundreds of thousands of us bearing witness through decades in bed.[41]

The same threads that carry contempt and poison and greed also link hundreds of thousands of people whose bodies dialogue with both illness and "life force." The difficult question is, can we prioritize the positive connections that flow with the toxicity? As Chen puts it,

> Although the body's interior could be described as becoming "damaged" by toxins, if we were willing to perform the radical act of releasing the definition of "organism" from its biological pinnings, we might from a more holistic perspective approach toxicity with a lens of mutualism. . . . Thinking of toxins as symbiotes—rather than, for instance, as parasites which seem only to feed off a generally integral being without fundamentally altering it (which would perhaps be our first guess)—not only captures some toxic affectivity but enables me to shift modes of approach.[42]

Following this call to "shift modes of approach," perhaps instead of seeking either the elimination of toxins from our environment or the harnessing of toxins for good (neither of which would be possible given the shifting meanings of and various reactions to toxic matters), we could ask, instead, "What outcomes emerge from our participation in webs of toxicity?" or even "What do our partners in symbiotic infection have to teach us about our communal responsibility?" These latter approaches would de-center human morality and human agency as the source of toxic exposure. This is not a matter of looking on the "bright side" of a problem but, rather, of taking responsibility for our participation in fluctuating ecosystems.

With this shift of approach, I'll return briefly to Levins Morales's website to examine potentially healthful relations of toxicity. Auroralevinsmorales.com brings together humans, money, and scattered physical spaces of speaking and witnessing. Though it is the author's page, it is also a communal space, "the village it takes" to sustain a writer. When a trail of linkages takes one outside the site, there is an option to "return to *our* website" (emphasis added), welcoming viewers to a space where they are at home. The first person plural "our" also makes viewers responsible for the connections and content of the site. The menu options at the top of the page divide the site into different neighborhoods that organize different sorts of webs of relation (my terms, not Levins Morales's). If I click on "What We Can Do Together," the focus is on collaborative efforts to bring the author's words to wider worlds. I can learn about how to bring the author to my hometown, what her needs would be in terms of hosting and sponsorship. Indeed, using these digital pathways is what enabled me to meet Aurora in the flesh.

It is thrilling and terrifying to have one's vitality dispersed in tension throughout a community weighted with unknown toxins. This is a political ecology wherein our every decision has implications that reverberate through like- and un-like-minded allies. (We are indeed all allies in our shared web, allies in a variety of possible projects and combinations, whether we like it or not.) As Barad writes, in her influential vision of posthumanist ethics, "Intra-acting responsibly as part of the world means taking account of the entangled phenomena that are intrinsic to the world's vitality and being responsible to the possibilities that might help us flourish."[43] Agency, in this sense, is not about individual responsibility or human morality; it is even more difficult. One does not simply rattle the web with their individual movements but actually participates—along with other human and other-than-human agencies—in the materialization of the web. Since we are co-making the world together, we must "[take] account of the entangled materializations of which we are a part, including new configurations and new subjectivities, new possibilities."[44] We should practice, like Milk Thistle, guerilla medicine. Of course, it might not always be good medicine, but we can (re)invent it as we go.

NOTES

1   Barad, *Meeting the Universe Halfway*, 178.

2   Braidotti, *The Posthuman*, 66.

3   Braidotti, *The Posthuman*, 103.

4   Braidotti, *The Posthuman*, 38, 24.

5   Sundberg, "Decolonizing Posthumanist Geographies," 34.

6   Todd, "Indigenous Feminist's Take," 7–9.

7   Erevelles' emphasis on textuality and fragmentation suggests that her view of posthumanism is more postmodern than the posthumanisms of scholars like Barad and Alaimo. Erevelles, *Disability and Difference*, 48.

8   In one of the only articles published about *Remedios*, Efraín Barradas is critical of the blurring of history and imagination in the text. According to Barradas, Levins Morales "deja de ser historiadora y se convierte en poeta y crea la realidad que busca y que no halla en los archivos ni en los libros de historia. . . . Quizás como escritora, pero no como historiadora, Aurora Levins Morales tiene todo el derecho a crearse su pasado. (Ella diría que la historiadora tiene el mismo derecho; no sé si esté de acuerdo) [stops being a historian and becomes a poet and creates the reality she searches for and does not find in archives or history books. . . . Maybe as a writer, but not as a historian, Aurora Levins Morales has every right to create her past for herself. (She would say that the historian has the same right; I'm not sure if I am in agreement)]." Barradas describes this construction of history as "dangerous" in his article's abstract. Barradas, "El recuerdo como remedio."

9   McRuer, *Crip Times*.

10 McRuer, *Crip Times*, 19.

11 McRuer, *Crip Times*, 19.

12 Levins Morales wrote a number of pieces for Sins Invalid, including *Stroke*, a dance performance-poem about her 2007 stroke. See www.sinsinvalid.org.

13 Levins Morales, *Remedios*, xxiv.

14 Levins Morales, *Remedios*, xxiv.

15 Levins Morales, *Remedios*, 107, 53, 183–84.

16 Levins Morales, *Medicine Stories*, 3.

17 Levins Morales, *Remedios*, xxv.

18 Levins Morales, *Remedios*, xxvii.

19 Levins Morales, "Shared Ecologies and Healing Justice," 191.

20 Levins Morales, *Kindling*, 5.

21 Levins Morales, *Kindling*, 6.

22 Levins Morales, *Kindling*, 7, 10.

23 Levins Morales, *Remedios*, 5.

24 Levins Morales, *Remedios*, 6.

25 Levins Morales, *Remedios*, 204.

26 Levins Morales, *Kindling*, 159–60.

27 Tobin Siebers writes about how, while traveling without his leg brace, he is mis-recognized as nondisabled by airline employees and denied early boarding. This experience resonates with Levins Morales's in its reliance on the visible for identity recognition and the assumption that one's identity must appear in a predictable way. Siebers, "Disability as Masquerade," 1.

28 Levins Morales, *Kindling*, 161–62.

29 When it comes to rethinking the boundaries of bodies, species, and agency, though, Donna Haraway's work is helpful since it emerges from an analysis of material conditions in which humans and other-than-humans mediate each other. Haraway's work helps to account for ethics in these trans-species relations by decentering "the human" as the sole author, agent, and (un)ethical actor in trans-species ecosystems. Her 1980s cyborg manifesto deconstructed the binaries at the heart of our flesh (male/female, subject/object, nature/culture, human/machine) and, specifically drawing from the model of women of color feminism, reconceived ethical action as a process of building networks between and among unlike people/beings. Rather than taking the individual human as the locus of responsibility, agency, for Haraway, occurs in "the profusion of spaces and identities and the permeability of boundaries in the personal body and in the body politic." Her career has focused on shared agencies through the conjoined relations of humans, nonhuman animals, parasites, and databases. Haraway, *Haraway Reader*, 30.

30 Kafer, *Feminist, Queer, Crip*, 105.

31 Haraway, *Haraway Reader*, 297.

32 Levins Morales, *Medicine Stories*, 67.

33 The National Institute of Environmental Sciences uses the term "idiopathic environmental intolerance" (IEI), a term that casts doubt on the origins of the illness and

poses the sufferer as one who is "intolerant." In opposition to this framing, the terms multiple chemical sensitivity (MCS) and environmental illness (EI) place the burden on chemical environments. Alaimo's *Bodily Natures* reveals how the medical industry has dismissed these disorders as psychosomatic. Yet "psychosomatic" (which is not the same thing as "imagined") might actually be the best way to understand the intersection of mind and body in our experience of illness as an assault on the self. Disorders like MCS/EI highlight the unruliness of individual matter and the diffuseness of health as an interspecies event.

34 Levins Morales, *Kindling*, 74.
35 Alaimo, *Bodily Natures*, 120.
36 Levins Morales, "Guanakán," 1.
37 Levins Morales, "Guanakán," 2.
38 Chen, *Animacies*, 191.
39 Chen, *Animacies*, 195.
40 Enstad, "Toxicity and the Consuming Subject," 62–64.
41 Levins Morales, *Kindling*, 6.
42 Chen, *Animacies*, 205–6.
43 Barad, *Meeting the Universe*, 394.
44 Barad, *Meeting the Universe*, 384.

7. "MY MOTHER, MY LONGEST LOVER"

Cripping South Texas in Noemi Martinez's South Texas Experience Zine Project *and* South Texas Experience: Love Letters

MAGDA GARCÍA

I think it's the heat that infest[s] us into this immobility. Unable to move, the tentacles of the valley vilified into an evil omnipresent character in the story that is my life.
—SOUTH TEXAS EXPERIENCE ZINE PROJECT (2005)

my mother, / my longest lover / imperfect lover / forked my border tongue / kept this wound alive / It's so hard to love you Texas
—SOUTH TEXAS EXPERIENCE: LOVE LETTERS (2015)

Situated in the Rio Grande Valley of South Texas (referred to colloquially as the Valley or South Texas), cultural worker and zinester Noemi Martinez has continually expanded on discussions of queerness, race, and disability and developed her own understandings of what it means, feels, and looks like to live as a self-identified queer crip Chicanx/Tejanx single mother through personal and collective zine projects over the course of nearly two decades. Writing within and from a region that continues to decrease community resources, such as access to reproductive services, Martinez's zines focus on the importance of writing for women of color, women of color feminisms, and crip life via reflections on mental and physical health. Usually unremarked upon within the national imaginary, which tends to homogenize the US-Mexico border, the Rio Grande Valley drew national attention in the summer of 2014 when it rapidly became the entryway for thousands of Central American women and child refugees. During the Trump administration, the region became embroiled within national politics as debates over the border wall and ecological destruction mounted because of the Trump administration's plan to further expand the border wall along the Rio Grande River. Currently, the Rio Grande

Valley has become emblematic of both increased support for the Republican Party and the heavy COVID-19 pandemic death toll in Latinx communities. Furthermore, environmental concerns continue to be at the foreground because of Elon Musk's SpaceX, which is located on Boca Chica Beach in the border city of Brownsville, Texas.

Martinez's cultural work extends to contributions to digital sources, such as *Bitch Media*, and a range of literary journals and magazines, including *TAYO Literary Magazine*, *Yellow Chair Review*, and *Hip Mama Zine*. Her poetry and prose address and reflect on her experiences as a poor single mother of color, the sexualization and racialization her daughter and son experience as they come of age in the Rio Grande Valley, chronic physical pain, and corresponding impacts on mental health. Furthermore, Martinez creates mixed media art comprising watercolors, screen print ink, paper, and wood—materials used to depict assemblages of landscapes, hearts, and cardinal directions to represent the disorientation that accompanies experiences of anxiety and depression within the broader context of space/place. Her work is influenced by Gloria Anzaldúa's foundational writings on the Rio Grande Valley as well as by more recent crip social media initiatives such as the Disability Visibility Project's #TheFutureIsDisabled. As a zinester, Martinez has been creating and circulating zines since 2000 under her micropress, Hermanx (formerly Hermana) Resist Press. Here, I specifically focus on Martinez's *South Texas Experience Zine Project* (2005) and *South Texas Experience: Love Letters* (2015) because they illustrate Martinez's queer crip of color experience in spatial and affective terms. The 2005 zine presents reflections on the Rio Grande Valley as a site capable of overwhelming the senses of the crip body, while the 2015 zine interweaves these experiences with a series of photographs of the Rio Grande Valley terrain and prose and poetry in remembrance of migrant lives and deaths.

Martinez's work offers a complex understanding of crip life that—similar to Alison Kafer's insistence on crip as political and mobile and Jasbir Puar's notion of debilitation as a way to focus on what disability identification often obscures—forgoes the notion of crip as an identity grounded in overcoming or, largely, even residing within the territory of the individual. Compounded by her focus on invisibilized disabilities and illness, specifically within the realm of the mental, emotional, and sensory, and without negating the material realities and physical effects of disability, Martinez offers her crip body as an affective lens through which the space/place that is the Rio Grande Valley is refashioned. The *South Texas Experience Zine Project* (2005) and *South Texas Experience: Love Letters* (2015) focus on rendering a sensual and affective encounter with the region that is South Texas and its colonial markings, which Martinez refers to as "ghosts." In this way, the zines illustrate an encounter of the queer crip brown body with a space/place marked by waves of colonization and conservatism, yielding often disorienting results. I focus on Martinez's representation of the Rio Grande Valley as home—that is, home as a complex, contradictory, and contested site—and the modes of psychic and physical survival along the US-Mexico border her zines illustrate. A poetic depiction of home, the zines starkly highlight the connection between affect and space/place—and the negotiations and tensions that live in this connection.

Through my focus on Martinez, I emphasize and engage crip of color work taking place at the sublocal level. In regard to Martinez's work, this means addressing and delving into an in-progress archive that spans two decades—a time frame that places Martinez within 9/11, the Bush administration's Secure Fence Act of 2006, the 2014 influx of Central American women and child refugees through the Rio Grande Valley, and the Trump administration. Within the context of queer/crip of color genealogies, Martinez's cultural production overlaps with Anzaldúa's 2004 passing—presenting a continuation and expansion of work focusing on illness, the queer of color body, and the Texas-Mexico border first established by Anzaldúa's 1987 *Borderlands/La Frontera: The New Mestiza*. Nevertheless, Martinez's deployment of the term *crip* signals toward a post-Anzaldúan engagement with disability enmeshed within a punk, emo, and goth ethos. In this way, Martinez exemplifies the continued existence and importance of subcultural queer Chicanx/Latinx independent publishing, as well as the starkly anticapitalist and nonproductive practice of zine-making documented by Michelle Comstock and Adela Licona, to the creation of crip of color genealogies.

"Eminent Danger, Eminent Domain": Contextualizing South Texas

The Rio Grande Valley of South Texas may not be familiar to readers located outside of Texas. Indeed, within Chicanx, Latinx, or feminist and queer studies, the area is most often encountered within Anzaldúa's *Borderlands/La Frontera: The New Mestiza*. Knowing the Rio Grande Valley exclusively through Anzaldúa both renders this area of the US-Mexico border static and neglects a significant trajectory of literary and cultural scholarship: Jovita González, Américo Paredes, Rolando Hinojosa, Sonia Saldívar-Hull, José David Saldívar, and Ramón Saldívar. While the 2014 arrival of Central American women and child refugees and the 2019 furor over expanding the border wall across large, therefore costly, areas has brought the region to national attention, being acquainted with only these images overlooks the enmeshment of colonial legacies of racial violences and the effects of 9/11 on this particular region. Within the realm of contemporary Chicanx, specifically Chicana, cultural production, Martinez joins writers, artists, and performers located in or emerging from the region such as Celeste De Luna, Nansi Guevara, Amalia Ortiz, ire'ne lara silva, and, within South Texas more broadly, Virginia Grise, Laurie Ann Guerrero, Isabel Ann Castro, and Natasha I. Hernandez (founders of the zine *St. Sucia*), Carmen Mendoza, Carmen Tafolla, and Norma Cantú. The Rio Grande Valley is, furthermore, historically significant because of the waves of colonization that come to shape US Chicanx and Latinx identity and establish the Mexican and US nation-states, as discussed by scholars such as Raúl Coronado. Legacies of conquest and continued iterations of coloniality starkly mark the economic and geopolitical landscape of this region, which possesses some of the poorest communities in the US. *Colonias*, or rural unincorporated areas, exemplify these markings, as undocumented Mexican migrants and Mexican Americans live alongside each other in areas formed through need. Although *colonias* allow Mexicans and Mexican Americans to become renters or even property owners, the institutional neglect of these areas results in substandard infrastructure, including inadequate cooling and heating and instances of flooding that damage the wooden, concrete, or mobile structures. Rural and lacking infrastructure, *colonias* are not ground for economic development. Rather, these areas are disregarded by modernity precisely because they bolster modernity itself by providing the labor necessary for commercial agriculture, factories, and warehouses located on both sides of the border.

Julie Avril Minich emphasizes the significance of the Rio Grande Valley as a site of extreme inequality, particularly in regard to health, and also an important site of Chicanx cultural production. In her article on Oscar Casares's short-story collection, *Brownsville*, Minich opens with Anzaldúa's deeply affective description of the US-Mexico border to foreground how the border shapes emotional and mental realms: "A borderland is a vague and undetermined place created by the emotional residue of an unnatural boundary.... Tension grips the inhabitants of the borderlands like a virus. Ambivalence and unrest reside there."[1] For Minich, "Casares, like Anzaldúa, treats the border not solely as a political institution but also as a collective, traumatic psychosomatic experience."[2] Minich turns to Casares's work to examine how literature serves as a site for understanding the inequalities surrounding mental health within a racial context. By doing so, she places mental health statistics, such as the fact that Mexican American and Black communities receive the least medical care for depression, and the cultural biases held by mental health practitioners in conversation with the realm of the imaginary. Literature, particularly fiction, comes to function as the antithesis to the medical establishment's notion of health, particularly mental health, as dehistoricized and ultimately residing within the individual—ignoring the "virus" that Anzaldúa identifies. Similar to Minich, I focus on Martinez's zines to highlight and examine how the border is affectively experienced and illustrated.

Zones of Haunting and Debilitation: The *South Texas Experience Zine Project* (2005)

Martinez's South Texas Experience zine series (re)envisions the Rio Grande Valley through a queer crip of color embodiment and consciousness. I echo Licona's understanding that "borderlands spaces can be considered material narratives; that is to say spaces have histories, contested histories, and they are continuously productive of new stories, stories in the making, that are contested and contingent."[3] The *South Texas Experience Zine Project* is the size of a standard sheet of paper folded into fourths and thirty-two pages in length. The cover includes a cropped image of a 1949 newspaper article on Reynosa, Tamaulipas, located across the border from McAllen, Texas. An image of what appears to be a cabaret dancer in a bikini top accompanies the newspaper story. The back cover features a flowering succulent and the words "Every time we meet it's just to say goodbye" at the bottom of the image. The zine is created in true do-it-yourself form, with grainy images of skies with clouds, small houses and wooden structures surrounded by dry landscapes, and photographs of Martinez serving as visual accompaniments to the zine's prose and poetry.

While the *South Texas Experience Zine Project* can be categorized as a personal zine, it nevertheless functions in a manner that avoids categorization of Martinez's queer crip body as the focal object or even subject of study. Rather, what we receive at the zine's opening is an invitation to experience the Rio Grande Valley alongside Martinez. The zine's focus on the experiential provides an entryway into, to borrow from Licona, an understanding of the space that is the Rio Grande Valley as a material narrative onto which a story in the making is outlined through Martinez's embodied experience as a queer crip Chicanx. While Martinez presents a refashioned vision of the Rio Grande Valley through her self-identified queer crip body and reflects on physical and psychic pain, she does not provide a listing of medical diagnoses. The result is an understanding, experience, and deployment of the crip body that refuses the boundaries between individual and collective often established through medicalized notions of disability and an insistence on blurring the boundaries between the queer crip body and the space/place within which it is located. Martinez's maneuvers instead render the Rio Grande Valley, and its overlying histories that serve to delineate particular populations in particular spaces for, to borrow from Puar, "debilitation," as the object and subject of study.

The zine invites us to experience the Rio Grande Valley through Martinez's senses: "I want to show you how it smells in the valley. Orange blossoms in the Spring. Making limonada every evening. How the days are short because we avoid the sunlight. Beautiful but I curse it all the time. How I run errands at night. Only at moments looking up to the sky."[4] She further focuses on the heat, referring to the sun as a "deadly calavera," and writes sensually about her bodily experience in this heat and brightness: "A staleness in this air that permeates. Humidity fills your nostrils. Staleness that makes you move a little slower, painstakingly slow while the sweat accumulated under your nose, under your bra, behind your knees."[5] Martinez's depiction of how the Rio Grande Valley climate feels and clings to the body, as well as her positioning of the reader as the one experiencing these sensations through the use of "your," further works toward destabilizing the notion that it is her queer crip body under analysis. The heat becomes yet another spatial element that is experienced through the lens that is Martinez's body, echoing the practice that Licona refers to as "reverso" in her discussion of zines' potentialities. According to Licona, "Practices of reverso emerge to return and, importantly, refract the normative gaze, produce critical inquiries into questions of (mental) health, madness, pathologies, morality, and pleasure, and to re-present embodied practices of healing, resistance, and activism. Through acts of contortion, distortion, aggression, confession, desire, and reconciliation, bodies and be-ings are being re-membered and re-configured in zines."[6] Martinez, I offer, engages in acts of distortion in her representation of the South Texas heat. Sunny skies and a hot climate may initially suggest relaxation and recreation, which holds true for particular segments of youth and seniors, namely the spring-breakers on South Padre Island and the winter vacationers who patronize local Rio Grande Valley businesses, but here the commingled effects of sun, heat, and humidity gain a haunting quality that must be escaped, thereby rendering the opposite effect—shortened days. The disorientation produced by Martinez's descriptions serves to illustrate shifts in mood and mental health, issues that she discusses in her poetry and *Hermanx Resist* blog posts. Further building on the sensual, Martinez creates a scene of the Rio Grande Valley through scent: "Right now, I smell burning mesquite. Not the wood chips to 'enhance' flavor but the real kind that's been hacked in someone's backyard, where passers [b]yers offer to buy some."[7] She continues, "South Texas orange blossoms in March. Nescafe. old spice. Ariel soap and Suavitel. [T]he sound of el paletero down the street. I suppose scent associations are not related to anything tangible, nothing in particular, only memory. But my brain and heart are often illogical."[8] Martinez further focuses on the Rio Grande Valley's ephemeral qualities through her linking of mood and climate: "Nothing ever matches my mood here, nothing reflects my current sentiments, weather wise . . . [a]ll bright happy sun, wet humid air, sticky armpit mood season."[9] An image of the top of a palm tree amid a wide sky dotted with fluffy clouds accompanies Martinez's words. At first glance, the image appears tropical, cheerful, and relaxing in its sunniness. However, within the context of Martinez's reflections on the climate, emotions, and mental health, the image gains a static, nearly artificial quality.

Martinez's emotions extend from what I understand as depressive, if not suicidal, feelings that she categorizes as "bad things" outward to the Rio Grande Valley as a region permeated by a sense of foreboding. Kafer's dismantling of disability's confines as medical diagnosis through examining the connection between emotions and how we experience temporality helps us understand how Martinez engages in an act of cripping the Rio Grande Valley by focusing on the space's affective qualities. For example, while Martinez's reference to mesquite may initially seem nostalgic, the second part of Martinez's reflection undercuts any such notion: "Burning mesquite coming in through the windows. It seeps and stays in everything. There is no way to rid yourself of that smell, you both hate it for its lingering presence, and welcome it for its associations."[10] Scent, then, becomes a source of haunting.

Temporalities further shift in Martinez's account of "bad things" as she describes being transported to a different time, albeit with a similar feeling: "I've been doing bad, bad things and that ain't good. / a little while ago I was driving to the post [sic] 24/hr post office. smoking. and it felt like 2002 all over again. Black lipstick, one headlight."[11] Martinez continues, "there's a playlist I've been listening to. I called it breaking the girl. [S]hit. [T]hat ain't good either. Reading the Bell Jar / some things circling in my head I should write down, but haven't wanted to commit them to paper. Writing it down makes it real."[12] Significantly, Martinez ascribes a similar mood as intrinsic to the Rio Grande Valley through an excerpt of William Burroughs's 1953 *Junky*, which functions as a memoir of Burroughs's travels and experiences with drug addiction. Quoting Burroughs, Martinez writes, "A premonition of doom hangs over the Valley. You have to make it now before something happens, before the black fly ruins the citrus, before support prices are taken off the cotton, before the flood, the hurricane, the freeze, the long dry spell when there is no water to irrigate. The threat of disaster is always there, persistent and disquieting as the afternoon wind. The Valley was desert and it will be again."[13] Anzaldúa's "virus," Burroughs's sense of doom, and Martinez's focus on bodily and mental discomfort each highlight the sense of unease on which the Rio Grande Valley rests. The excerpt further underscores the sense of disorientation that Martinez conveys throughout her 2005 zine through the trope of heat and the broader South Texas climate. By quoting Burroughs, Martinez shifts the depressive, anxious, and pensive moods she describes as experiencing through her choice of reading and music, in conjunction with the image of a smoking figure wearing black lipstick and traversing night, beyond her own experience to longer-standing histories. Placed alongside each other, Burroughs's sense of the Rio Grande Valley as a site of anxiety due to the day-to-day experience of awaiting calamity in the attempts to subdue the region's desert terrain; Anzaldúa's description of the US-Mexico border as a site where tension, ambivalence, and unrest gain a collective and contagious quality akin to a virus; and Martinez's physical discomfort and mental exhaustion illustrated in her description of making her way through the region she calls home, whether in her physical body during the day (moving "painstakingly slow") or in her car at night ("Black lipstick, one headlight"), serve to provide material and emotional dimensions to the unease and disorientation that undergirds the Rio Grande Valley's slippages among past, present, and future.

Through acts of disorientation, Martinez emphasizes the space/place that surrounds and gives meaning to her body. Martinez's invitation to experience the Rio Grande Valley through and alongside her body creates the possibility of rendering visible and felt a palimpsest laden with histories of racial violence, conquest and colonization, and conservatism via the trope of the Rio Grande Valley heat. Continuing the journey on which Martinez invites us, she writes, "I think it's the heat that infest[s] us into this immobility. Unable to move, the tentacles of the valley vilified into an evil omnipresent character in the story that is my life."[14] Martinez's personification of the Rio Grande Valley serves to, at least momentarily, materialize the abstract processes of conquest, colonization, and racial violence: "Always present like one of the main characters in a play you really don't want to see and certainly don't want to read. That's why I see the memories and ghosts of South Texas interchangeable."[15] Underscoring the affective quality of South Texas's history, Martinez personifies memory through the figure of the ghost, casting South Texas as a haunted and, in her iteration of the Rio Grande Valley as an "evil omnipresent character," contested space. Martinez turns to local folklore to further illustrate these notions of haunting, particularly as they relate to histories of racial violence along the US-Mexico border.[16]

Martinez excerpts US amateur travel writer and historian Kathy Weiser-Alexander's account of "El Muerto," published in Weiser-Alexander's online magazine, *Legends of America*. "El Muerto" tells of the killing of Vidal, a Mexican cattle thief, by two Texas Rangers, Creed Taylor and William Alexander

Anderson "Big Foot" Wallace: "In a dramatic example of frontier justice, Wallace beheaded Vidal then lashed him firmly into a saddle on the back of a wild mustang. Tying the outlaw's hands to the pommel and securing the torso to hold him upright, Big Foot then attached Vidal's head and sombrero to the saddle with a long strip of rawhide. He then turned the bucking horse loose to wander the Texas hills with its terrible burden on his back."[17] The headless rider is said to haunt rural South Texas areas. Martinez's incorporation of local folklore into a personal zine further speaks to the blurring of the boundaries between her body and South Texas. Rather than focus on how she navigates South Texas, Martinez describes the impacts and effects of South Texas on her body—thereby positing the narratives born of conquest, colonization, and conservatism that impose meaning on her body (deviant because of her cripness, queerness, and her status as a poor single mother of color) as her and our object of analysis.

While the folktale that Martinez excerpts into the zine directly addresses the (extra)legal killing of Mexicans by the infamous Texas Rangers, killings that scholars such as Nicholas Villanueva Jr. and John Morán Gonzalez document, she places this history of racial violence alongside reflections on the experience of living in the Rio Grande Valley in a body rendered vulnerable by a region marked by poverty, local corruption, environmental pollution, and militarization/surveillance. By placing the folktale alongside these contemporary issues, Martinez echoes Puar's concept of communities and bodies of color as marked for debilitation rather than death. Working through the distinct sites of Black Lives Matter, the Dakota Access Pipeline protests, and struggles to end Israeli occupation of Palestine, Puar contends that, "slated for death or slated for debilitation—both are forms of the racialization of individuals and populations that liberal (disability) rights frameworks, advocating for social accommodation, access, acceptance, pride, and empowerment, are unable to account for, much less disrupt."[18] For Puar, then, "the term 'debilitation' is distinct from the term 'disablement' because it foregrounds the slow wearing down of populations instead of the event of becoming disabled," signaling toward her understanding of "debility" as reflecting "injury and bodily exclusion that are endemic rather than epidemic or exceptional."[19]

Although I recognize the difference between my site of analysis and that of Puar, I also emphasize the ways in which histories of conquest, occupation, and colonization continue to manifest in Texas. South Texas may perhaps not necessarily be understood as fully under occupation in the same manner as Palestine because of the slippages between Latinx identity, indigeneity, and generational versus more recent migration that conversations regarding settler colonialism in the United States foreground but, as Martinez illustrates, South Texas is a space/place that has become intrinsically classed and racialized through multiple waves of colonization and occupation: the initial Spanish conquest of Indigenous peoples; colonization by US Anglo settlers fighting against Mexico in their defense of slavery, culminating in the 1835–36 Texas Revolution; the 1846–47 US expansionist Mexican-American War and the subsequent 1848 Treaty of Guadalupe Hidalgo; and lynching of Mexicans and Mexican Americans by the Texas Rangers in the early 1900s. These instances of conquest and occupation shape the contemporary racialized economic and environmental conditions under which the local population faces an increased likelihood of illness amid living in impoverished conditions without access to health services even as these populations provide the labor for commercial agriculture, factories, and warehouses alongside both sides of the US border. Consequently, readers can view Martinez as affectively introducing them to an area haunted by waves of colonization and occupation and the resulting state of debilitation. By foregrounding her crip body's experiences within the context of the Rio Grande Valley of South Texas, Martinez also invites us to experience the condition of debility within the US-Mexico borderlands.

"Heat and Hate": *South Texas Experience: Love Letters* (2015)

Created a decade later than the *South Texas Experience Zine Project*, *South Texas Experience: Love Letters* is a photozine printed in full color. The zine is the size of a trade paperback and thirty-six pages in length. The front cover features a rural landscape with a dirt road amid brush and a bright blue sky with white clouds. The back cover depicts green cacti with dark purple prickly pears amid tall grass and wildflowers. The photograph on the front cover, in addition to several photographs in the zine, is credited to Martinez's teenage son, Jonathan River Hernandez-Martinez. The zine is grounded in reflections on Martinez's relationship to the Rio Grande Valley, but the terrain is the focal point, as images such as La Sal del Rey, a local salt lake, and dirt roads amid mesquite trees, cacti, and open skies with clouds are accompanied by poems written in memory of the migrants who have perished while crossing into the United States and those whose remains were unidentified and buried in mass graves. The zine's dedication reads, "for the stars walking under our sky."[20] The image of stars is repeated in Martinez's untitled poem, discussed below, pleading for South Texas to accept the memories, lives, and significance of unidentified migrants. The shift to a photozine, in conjunction with the notion of a love letter, emphasizes the affective relationship between Martinez and the space/

place that is the Rio Grande Valley. Furthermore, the 2005 and 2015 zines are connected by a recurring focus on and deployment of the South Texas heat as a trope for, to borrow from Puar, living in a state of debility and debilitation.

South Texas Experience: Love Letters opens with a focus on the atmospheric in the zine's references to weather and moods: "No seasons / I am looking again / for cold / Make this home / Make this home."[21] Martinez exhibits a sustained focus on the South Texas heat in both zines, but in 2015 she demonstrates an acceptance and claiming of the Rio Grande Valley as home, even with all the tensions and conflicts about which she continues to write as she casts her role as historian and poet as *curandera* (healer).[22] With famed late Tejanx/ Latinx singer Selena Quintanilla-Pérez's "I Could Fall in Love" (1995) as the soundtrack to the zine's poems, Martinez refers to South Texas as "my mother, / my longest lover / imperfect lover" and states, "I grew out of you. I grew into you. I came home."[23] The notion of coming home is, nevertheless, not a nostalgic one, which is evident in Martinez's poem titled, "It's so hard to love you texas." The poem offers a reflection of how Texas is regarded by outsiders—a reflection currently further augmented by conversations in the national media that cast Texas communities as evenly or predominantly in support of anti-abortion legislation or against critical race theory: "they call you a prison / we can't get out / The Valley pulls us back / but how can home be a prison / when you hold my secrets in sanctuary / watched my monsters manifest / hold my ghosts in your dirt / how can I leave them / I keep them alive / they keep me alive."[24] Martinez refuses the idea that she, or others who have similarly chosen to remain in or return to the Rio Grande Valley, are, in a sense, simply stranded or fully constrained by space/place. Although the reference to "monsters" and "ghosts" invokes images of horror as a way to relay historical, contemporary, individual, and collective experiences of violences, there is an insistence that these experiences are buried in the South Texas soil not as an escape from them but as a way to keep them safe. Martinez's notion of home is therefore grounded in slippages among the spatial, the temporal, the sensual, and the collective, which she further elaborates on through her focus on migrant deaths.

The use of Quintanilla-Pérez's "I Could Fall in Love" signals toward a love comprising yearning and apprehension and, ultimately, left unexpressed for fear that it will be unrequited. Similar to the song, the zine pleads and desires certain things from Texas even as it recognizes the violences enacted against both generationally poor Tejanxs and recently arrived undocumented migrants. In "I could fall in love with you," a poem titled after Quintanilla-Pérez's song, Martinez reflects on the process of choosing to claim the Rio Grande Valley as home. The poem specifically mentions living in Oklahoma, a place

Martinez describes as alienating because of its whiteness, as well as time spent waiting to return from "cold sterile rooms of Houston" to the Rio Grande Valley.[25] In doing so, Martinez places the Rio Grande Valley in a role reminiscent of a lover to which other lovers cannot compare. Martinez further addresses the entanglement of space/place, love, and pain, writing, "Not a person, no. / You, border lands / You, home, you bloodied me, / swallowed me, made me."[26] The images of being bloodied and swallowed, which echo the images of buried experiences, memories, and bodies, create a visceral sense of space/place as well as provide a visual of the ways in which Martinez views her queer crip body as marked by space/place. The reference to "cold sterile rooms" also provides a glimpse into what is possibly an encounter with illness, medicalization, and/or hospitalization. The 2005 zine predominantly centers the Rio Grande Valley within the context of Martinez's experiences, while the 2015 zine centers the Rio Grande Valley within a diffused context of migrant journeys, migrant deaths, and Martinez's role as historian.

The 2015 zine transitions the 2005 zine's focus on heat as it impacts the crip body to an emphasis on how heat affects yet another type of body marked for debilitation or even death, specifically the undocumented migrant body. In "Forecast," one of the zine's poems, Martinez writes, "extremely hot and humid / conditions will lead to / heart constraints / oppressive conditions / continue to surround / the valley, blankets / of heat and hate / 110–117 degrees on Friday," and ends with "prolonged exposure / can lead to / desensitization / remain inside."[27] These stanzas directly refer to the dangers of heat exposure, but they also allude, through the reference to "hate" at a moment of heightened anti-immigrant rhetoric as a direct result of the Trump presidential campaign, to desensitization to migrant deaths caused by the heat and surrounding rural terrain. In "Home You Learn to Love," heat further becomes emblematic of the Rio Grande Valley: "this is home home home / this is a season you learn to love."[28] The poem's closing lines further emphasize Martinez's use of heat as a prominent trope throughout both zines' representations and negotiations of the Rio Grande Valley as home: "dry heat / humid heat / rainy heat / tropical heat / this is a season / home you learn to love."[29] Home, as such, becomes a seemingly static season.

"Whispering Revolution": Creating Community through Debilitation and Death

Images of the rural South Texas terrain and poems memorializing migrants who have died crossing such terrain comprise most of the zine. In, "It's so hard to love you texas," Martinez writes, "I dream of walls / the dead / bring me ofrendas to write about them,"[30] returning us to the image of historian and poet as *curan-*

dera. By casting herself as a healer, Martinez reminds us of the broader context of debilitation and death within which she resides. The 2015 zine, then, continues the outward expansion begun in the initial 2005 installment, which becomes further evident in Martinez's plea to South Texas: "Love them like they were / yours, South Texas / Spirits now rest with us / walking hand in hand / or whispering revolution / in the ears of the living."[31] The broader contexts of debilitation and death that surround Martinez's depictions of cripness become generative sites of extending collective memory and sense of community.

For Martinez, migrant deaths are not outside of the nation but, rather, form part of the US and Texas histories of racial violence. Following Puar, I offer that these migrant bodies exemplify "death's position"; that is, "embedded in a distribution of risk already factored into the calculus of debilitation."[32] Martinez's focus extends beyond the event of death to the unidentified bodily remains buried in South Texas soil and, as reported in 2013, susceptible to violence even in death: "Love them despite / how we discarded their bones / in trash bags / Layered and layered / inside kitchen bags / in makeshift burials / Femur bone touching someone / else's skull or fingers."[33] The image of soil is also present in the poem "our bodies in the dirt," which alludes to an ethereal sense of being made of dirt as well as to a sense of burial: "Roots intertwine with legs / dying specks of light / sometimes our bodies—the dirt / fills the morning."[34] The image of legs entangled with roots invites further consideration of the improper burial of migrant remains and their now permanent entanglement with the land itself. Although these remains have been stripped of their dignity through their disposal, the poem offers an image of dirt, roots, and remains as one with each other. That is, the repetition of roots and legs offers a concrete visual of how migrant bodies come to form a literal part of the space/place that is South Texas—organic material forever present in the region's soil. In "Records for the Dead," Martinez starkly assumes the role of historian in her listing of the possessions found on migrant bodies: "Tucked into one pocket of her shorts / A ring on the middle finger of her left hand / She wore a Gold's Gym t-shirt / A boy about age five."[35] By listing the clothing, possessions, and age, the poem focuses on the individual body, followed by a shift to the body as object, emphasized by "four other bags of remains / Other bags of remains," in a mirror image of how these bodies were mistreated.[36]

The zine repeats a quote from a 2015 *Texas Observer* article on the illegal mass graves in which rural Brooks County, Texas, buried the unidentified remains: "One corpse was wrapped in a burlap / bag; other remains were found / inside a milk crate. Skulls were / wedged between coffins."[37] While Martinez does not dismiss the undocumented status of these migrants or the economic conditions that led to their dangerous journey, she generatively casts them as becoming part of communities living at risk of histories of racial violence, environmental contamination, and poverty. In "Texas My Texas," Martinez alludes to this risk: "Texas air on our limbs / exposure to eminent danger / eminent domain / we / Do not belong here."[38] Working via slippages between the dangers of contamination and militarization, Martinez writes, "Texas, mother of heroes, / comes for our children, still," reiterating conquest's haunting and continued wearing down of life, if not outright death, of South Texas and Texas more broadly.[39] The spirits of these migrants join this space of multiple dangers, traversing it as they walk hand in hand with or whisper revolution to the living.[40] By claiming migrant bodies as forever part of her home, Martinez offers the possibility of creating community, and possibly even rebellion, across life and death.

The notion of creating and recognizing community through debilitation and death is juxtaposed with the zine's last poem, "For You Again," which, like the 2005 zine's back cover, invokes a sense of once again meeting even if only to leave. This last poem references a figure, presumably a man, who performs physical labor on ranches for little pay. Martinez writes, "What goes through your head now / living east of the valley / displaced home of ours / twenty sum years / the threads of our roots / spread out thinly."[41] The notion of both a shared home and time, in conjunction with shared roots, speaks to a possibly romantic or familial relationship with the unnamed subject of the poem. While the unnamed subject's story remains unknown to readers, the zine nevertheless provides historical and contemporary context as well as sense of space/place for his story. By doing so, the 2015 zine echoes the 2005 zine's focus on the personal beyond the borders of the individual body by maintaining an emphasis on the interwoven nature of community across images of cripness, debilitation, and death.

La Sal del Rey: Site of Indigenous, Spanish Colonial, and US Civil War Intersections

The 2015 zine ends with an image of La Sal del Rey, a salt lake, spread across two pages. The other images in the zine are also of this same location. La Sal del Rey is located in Hidalgo County and ten miles from Hargill, Texas, a small rural town that has become significant within Chicanx/Latinx cultural and literary milieu because of Anzaldúa's burial at the town's local cemetery. The last image of La Sal del Rey focuses on dry grasses in a muddy marsh with brush and native trees in the background. Seemingly calm and desolate in its ruralness and muted colors, the site does not easily betray its historical and biological significance.

Biologically, the site is part of an "extinct inland sea" and "one of the most biologically diverse in the nation" because of its function as home to "1,100 types of plants, 700 vertebrate species, and more than 300 kinds of butterflies."[42] However, the site also possesses historical and cultural importance within Indigenous, colonial, and US Civil War contexts. Citing local historian Tom Fort, of the Museum of South Texas History in Edinburg, Texas, the *Brownsville Herald* describes the Indigenous, specifically Aztec, significance of the site: "There are indications or suggestions that Aztec trading parties, or those who traded with them, were obtaining salt from the Sal del Rey, and that would be back around the 1400s, or even earlier, and taking it down to Mexico."[43] An 1885 article in *Scientific American* signals to Spanish colonization in its recounting of La Sal del Rey's history, which, according to the article, was "originally known as 'La Noria de San Salvador del Tule,' [and] claimed to have been granted by the government of Spain, about the year 1708, to one Juan Jose Balli."[44] The site's name, La Sal del Rey, translates to "the king's salt," directly referencing the Spanish empire's claiming of the salt lake—a claiming that has left visible markings. As the *Austin Chronicle* describes, "Spanish explorers claimed the salt deposit for the king. Tracks left by heavily laden wagons headed for Mexico City can still be seen around the lake. During the Civil War, camels were used to carry the salt to Confederate troops."[45] I close by providing historical and cultural context for La Sal del Rey because it returns readers to an emphasis on space/place through the visual and the multilayered contexts seemingly obfuscated by a national focus on border militarization and surveillance. Images of La Sal del Rey, then, become emblematic of how cripness, debilitation, and death intersect within the southernmost area of the US-Mexico border—an intersection that readers can witness by accepting Martinez's initial 2005 invitation to experience the Rio Grande Valley through her body and continuing across the span of a decade.

NOTES

1   Minich, "Emotional Residue," 123–42.
2   Minich, "Emotional Residue," 123–42.
3   Licona, *Zines in Third Space*, 13.
4   Martinez, *South Texas Experience Project*, 3.
5   Martinez, *South Texas Experience Project*, 3–4.
6   Licona, *Zines in Third Space*, 70.
7   Martinez, *South Texas Experience Project*, 12.
8   Martinez, *South Texas Experience Project*, 15.
9   Martinez, *South Texas Experience Project*, 17–18.
10 Martinez, *South Texas Experience Project*, 12.

11 Martinez, *South Texas Experience Project*, 23.

12 Martinez, *South Texas Experience Project*, 23.

13 Martinez, *South Texas Experience Project*, 27.

14 Martinez, *South Texas Experience Project*, 5.

15 Martinez, *South Texas Experience Project*, 7.

16 Martinez, *South Texas Experience Project*, 9. Martinez similarly deploys notions of haunting and the dystopian in her further assessment of the Rio Grande Valley in "The Five Scariest Places in South Texas" (2016), published on her site, *Hermana Resist*. In this piece, Martinez delves into border environmental, governmental, and militarization issues. The sites that Martinez identifies are a heavily polluted reservoir and canal in Donna, Texas; a closed pesticide processing plant in Mission, Texas, that has resulted in cancer and birth defect clusters; widespread local corruption throughout the Rio Grande Valley; the ongoing erosion of women's reproductive rights (Martinez names this site "Uterus, TX"); and the Trump administration's planned border wall (Martinez starkly names this site "The Wall").

17 Martinez, *South Texas Experience Project*, 9.

18 Puar, *Right to Maim*, x.

19 Puar, *Right to Maim*, xiii–xiv, xvii.

20 Martinez, *South Texas Experience: Love Letters*, np.

21 Martinez, *South Texas Experience: Love Letters*, 2.

22 Martinez, *South Texas Experience: Love Letters*, 3.

23 Martinez, *South Texas Experience: Love Letters*, 14, 6.

24 Martinez, *South Texas Experience: Love Letters*, 14.

25 Martinez, *South Texas Experience: Love Letters*, 5.

26 Martinez, *South Texas Experience: Love Letters*, 5.

27 Martinez, *South Texas Experience: Love Letters*, 21–22.

28 Martinez, *South Texas Experience: Love Letters*, 20.

29 Martinez, *South Texas Experience: Love Letters*, 20.

30 Martinez, *South Texas Experience: Love Letters*, 15.

31 Martinez, *South Texas Experience: Love Letters*, 12.

32 Puar, *Right to Maim*, xiv.

33 Martinez, *South Texas Experience: Love Letters*, 12.

34 Martinez, *South Texas Experience: Love Letters*, 25.

35 Martinez, *South Texas Experience: Love Letters*, 28.

36 Martinez, *South Texas Experience: Love Letters*, 28.

37 Martinez, *South Texas Experience: Love Letters*, 29.

38 Martinez, *South Texas Experience: Love Letters*, 30.

39 Martinez, *South Texas Experience: Love Letters*, 30.

40 Martinez, *South Texas Experience: Love Letters*, 12.

41 Martinez, *South Texas Experience: Love Letters*, 32.

42 McLeod, "Day Trips."

43 Kelley, "For Thousands of Years."

44 "Texas Salt Lake."

45 McLeod, "Day Trips."

Part III
GENEALOGIES

8. CAN I CALL MY KENYAN EDUCATION INCLUSIVE?

FAITH NJAHÎRA WANGARÎ

In writing this narrative of my life, I'm honoring all the experiences I have had, the people and the places that have carried me through life. Literally and otherwise. In writing my disability experiences, I acknowledge that my account of my life or the experiences of muscular dystrophy may resonate with those of others; however, my account is not representative of all the experiences of all the other individuals and should not be used as a blueprint to invalidate the experiences of other people regardless of their personal claim to disability. If anything, it should contribute to the bulk of options that disabled persons should have access to. The writing of this piece was informed by insights shared by Beth Ferri in her work on disability life writing.[1] Her paper explores the place of autobiographical disability writing and the place of lived experiences as sites of knowledge.

Early Education

Crying uncontrollably after my sibling had left for school marks one of my earliest memories in this life. Tracing back based on the knowledge that I now have, it is safe to conclude that I was two years old if not younger. Our family lived on a public secondary school compound at the staff quarters where my feminist-in-practice mother was stationed at the time. The nursery school, as they were all referred to then, shared a fence with the secondary school. One could say there wasn't really a commute, as one needed to only go past the natural fence and you're in school. My brother and neighbors' children would go to school next door, and that left me with my adult family members or the neighbors for what seemed like most of the day. The energetic play sounds from the nursery was an experience I felt I missed out on and cried to be part of. Aside from fractured memories of drinking a lot of soda during what might have been an event based on a photo of my brother and I holding onto snacks, I have no memory of being enrolled at the nursery. While still residing at the secondary school, I have memories of what I now know was a school students strike. Dark of the night sights of huge flames of fire, noise, and sneaking away to safety on an auntie's back is another of those memories I carry from that age. The mention of these experiences is to call to the importance of social life experiences and an honoring of these instances at the early age when conversations on formal education are initiated.

Because of transfers and upward mobility on the part of my mother in her profession over the years, I attended three learning institutions for my preprimary education over the span of two to three years. At the last location, where I got to transition into primary school, we also stayed at the staff quarters, which shared a fence with the primary school we were enrolled at. I have memories of racing to the shops with my brother, playing with my neighbors so much I looked like earth herself, attempting to ride an adult-size bicycle, climbing fruit trees at a teacher's home, typing my first letters on the secretary's typewriter with lessons from her and leaving the house when we heard the school bell, given there was no way to ever be late for school when it was steps away. This area still holds so many of my fondest memories. At this school, one of my classmates and friends would get seizures, and it had gotten to the point where we knew how to support him, with guidance from our class teacher. The language of instruction was in my mother tongue, gĩkũyũ, and we also had movie afternoons at school where they would do translations into mother tongue, complete with sound effects. My classmate at the time, who I later learned had epilepsy, only markedly stood out when he had a seizure, though we all quickly reverted to play or whatever else we were doing. This remains, in my child's mind, my earliest memory of what I could now refer to as interaction with disability.

While this detailed recount of my preprimary and early primary years may seem nostalgic, it bears information that may often be considered necessary when collecting background information during assessment. From a disability point of view, I had a perfectly delightful childhood with a well-rounded upbringing. Because I did not attach any emotions of pity onto my friend and classmate who had seizures, the experience of him being part of my life is one that I recognize was foundational in my own relationship with disability. Growing up in the village settings as I did, friendships extended beyond school interactions and allowed for human interactions away from whatever power dynamics may exist in the school settings. Years after we had moved away from the area, my class teacher shared with me photos of my classmates, and we as a family made occasional trips back to visit my friend's family. Later, when my own disability started manifesting, the idea of what was ordinary already included individuals with disabilities, decades before I could claim disability for myself. Up until seven years old, I could not have been identified as having a disability, based on the disability assessment tools that I have become familiar with in my professional training.

At the age of eight, our family relocated, and my new school commute was 3.9 kilometers each way. Reporting time at the new school was 6:30 a.m. There were vehicles plying the route, but they were quite unreliable in the morning, and this meant that the daily trek in what was often biting cold became the new reality for my sibling and me. Over the years, I became aware of how revolutionary my mother was for her times. She is among those few women who legally sought dissolution of marriage and got full custody of all children, raising us away from the unhealthy home environment that my biological father had created in the early 1990s. The women who made such moves were on the receiving end of brutal shaming at a time when religious commitment and the dogma of the "good Catholic woman," who stayed in marriage regardless, was commended. My grandparents—both of whom had not received formal education beyond the basics of adult education that my grandmother received, allowing her to calculate her milk sales—fully supported her in this move, a luxury in love that, I recognize in listening to other shared stories, some of my mother's age-mates did not have. For the most part of my life, well into my twenties, the dominant practice, which is still evident, is one that shames single-mother-led households.

About half a kilometer on the route to school was the home of one of the teachers at the school, a friend to my biological father who was not too pleased at the turn of events in his friend's marriage and who took it upon himself to exert whatever little power patriarchy gifted him by looking for opportunities to punish my siblings and I during the time we were at the school.

This teacher would break into a fast pace whenever he noticed us walking behind him, knowing full well that any amount of lateness to school was punished either by caning or cleaning up the school, experiences this adult teacher seemed to take much pleasure in putting an eight-year-old and a ten-year-old through. During the one school term we were at the school, I had learned to sing "Amazing Grace" in my mother tongue, a memory I cherish to date. I also landed face-first on protruding gravel while playing with my friends during lunch break, which led to my getting rushed to get stitches by my grandfather, who miraculously appeared as he plied the route during the pre-mobile-phone time. I also spent numerous nights at my grandparents, thanks to the dread of the morning commute, and this led too often to a panicked mother arriving home to a missing child. I could not possibly imagine the horrors playing out in my mother's mind the first time she arrived home to a missing child without having the convenience of technology to assure her that I was safe and no harm had befallen me.

Formal education in Kenya, having been introduced by the settler colonizer Christian missionaries, has for the most part seen the entrenchment of religious practices into the education curriculum. "Amazing Grace" seemed to prophesy a redemption that needed an acknowledgment of the need to be saved. However, no amount of grace could keep my face away from the gravel when my body lost balance while playing in the school compound, an occurrence that could be on record as the first clear instance of physical weakness.

This school term exposed me to a number of emotions and experiences. For one, I could not understand why an adult could be as mean as that teacher was, intentionally callous. To the point of projecting their patriarchal entitlement onto the lives of children and inflicting pain and hurt. The verbal and physical abuse inflicted by this teacher, aimed at our family without his friend, my biological father, in the equation, became my initial encounter as a child with abuse as a display of power. At this point in my life, the societal perceptions and projections about single-mother families overshadowed my daily challenges with the walk to and from school. They made me more aware of power dynamics and power imbalances. In a sense, they may have prepared me for the next phase of my life, where my physical capabilities would call unwarranted attention to my body.

At the next school, we had moved to a different town, with home this time being about 3 kilometers away. We had neighbors who also went to the same school, with whom we walked to school and back, including the occasional hunt for clay at the swamp we traversed. Our immediate neighbors at home were our age-mates, so my sibling and I had company for the endless play, Saturday homework sit-downs, and amazing friendships. Another family in the neighborhood had cool equipment that their father would let us all take turns playing with during the weekends and holidays. I later learned that he was an occupational therapist and came to recognize this equipment in therapy rooms I would occupy much later in life. Our new school was great for many things, but I quickly came to dread Tuesdays and Thursdays during my two years at the school. These were the school's game days, which meant mandatory running around the large school field, with each class taking turns. Every week. Whatever running or attempts at running I was doing to get to school and back home already felt enough. It didn't help that I was the last one, every single time. Soon, I was wishing for the embarrassment in the form of running to get over and done with so I could get to either hold the skipping rope or be one of the sides of the gate as the other kids rushed through the makeshift gate play-ing "In and out the bamboo forest." I had figured out by this point that running was not my strongest skill, given all the falling plus stitches thus far, and figured out how to continue playing with my friends, both at school and home. There is only so much shame from repeated failure that a child can take. As Brené Brown asserts, "You can't shame people into changing their behaviour." I asso-ciated the shame that I felt with the fact that my legs couldn't carry me as fast as those of the other children.[2] I also do not understand why no adult gave me the option to opt out of this repeated experience.

In saying this, I remain unaware of the intentions or the thoughts that may or may not have crossed my teachers' minds as they watched me fall on my face numerous times on the tracks and come in last in the biweekly races.

Other than the period I rode the bus to and from school when recovering from a running-related injury, no other markers of difference were apparent at school. Not from the school management or teachers at least. I had figured out how to wait till my classmates had rushed out of class, to avoid more of what were now frequent falls, and how to take the longer route around to avoid the route with stairs when getting around school. All this while still enjoying knitting lessons, tie and dye, molding with clay, and getting my share of pun-ishments for mother tongue speaking like the next learner. The practice of pun-ishments for speaking any language other than the colonial English has been widely practiced in Kenyan schools. Years later, many emotions later, I look back at my schooling up until that point and I remain grateful. Grateful that, aside from the endless conversations within myself, no other conversations highlighted the changes that I was experiencing at the time. It was easy to get lost in the experiences of school days and time at home.

This gratitude comes from the experiences that became my life once I moved to my final school for primary education at eleven years old. Besides having to figure out how to speak a totally new language, Sheng—the slang derived from Kiswahili and other languages—with my limited mastery of Kiswahili itself, which was not previously in my spoken vocabulary, I also started getting direct questions from teachers and other learners about my "walking style," as they re-ferred to it. My sibling had not joined me at the new school; this meant I was now the only one with this marked difference. This was the first instance this difference was of note to me, too, as it had otherwise always felt like an ordi-nary occurrence with my sibling sharing the same experience. With the classes being on the upper floor for the upper primary learners, I did not have the lux-ury of avoiding stairs at this new school. They were everywhere! I was glad that the outdoor field at this school was so much smaller, however; this meant that physical education lessons happened separately for all classes. Our class teacher, who also happened to be our physical education (PE) teacher, asked why I was out of breath and unable to keep up with the others. My initially unrehearsed answer to this teacher, that I had "chest problems," became my go-to answer for the rest of my basic education. My panting sounds after a brisk walk or attempts at running were quite helpful in making the narrative believable. This school was not so keen on running as a skill, which was a point of immense gratitude for my preteen self. I got to play goalkeeper during our class PE football games, though I have no memory of how that came about, whether it was on my suggestion or that of my classmates or teacher. I no longer dreaded PE at this new school; I could hold the skipping rope without explanation. At this school, I felt some allegiance to my classmates, one who had diabetes and had to get insulin shots and another who was a good friend and struggled to excel in classwork. When the teachers and schoolmates asked after my "walking style," it felt like an aspect of me that needed to be explained. My quips that I was tired or other variations seemed to suffice, as they stopped asking shortly after I'd settled into the school. The language barrier at the school was more of a constant mark of difference that just couldn't go away, no matter how much I tried to learn the language to blend in. My language proficiency in English and my mother tongue didn't seem to help with the blending in either, at least not with my schoolmates. The interactions with the school community at this school, while they called attention to my apparent difference, allowed and supported my existence within the community.

This school was the first place I had a name used to describe me: "weird" was what a schoolmate called me as they passed me when going up the stairs to the classes. To this day, the word doesn't fit well in my vocabulary. I'm more comfortable with "disabled," or any other terms that I may choose to refer to myself with. The power of naming as an internal move has for me been an empowering one, one that allows for meaning to be assigned to the terms regardless of the meanings that they may have among disabled or nondisabled persons in the world.

Two years before transitioning to secondary school, our then mathematics teacher learned that I had my heart set on being a Catholic nun when I grew older and saw this as a point of ridicule. As a twelve-year-old who admired what I now recognized as the contemplative lifestyles of the nuns I had encountered and my Jesuit priest pen pal, I was deeply hurt that this teacher chose to make fun of me. It was not clear to me then how I could communicate my discomfort and hurt to another adult at the time; hence I decided that making sure I scored dismally in the teacher's class would communicate my hurt by not excelling. All along, I had easily been a teacher's favorite at all the schools I had attended, and my mother, being a teacher too, had shown me the high praise that teachers enjoyed by extension from good performance in their classes.

All this while I continued to excel in the other subjects. I did not feel so powerless then. At the end of the year, when I passed in that subject, which was a requirement for transition to the final year, I made the point to disclose my original plan, which turned successful when the teacher summoned me to ask after my seeming miraculous turnaround. The teacher's verbal taunting upon hearing my explanation was so much that I decided to report them to one of the senior teachers; said taunting teacher did not report for duty in the new school year. I suspect my report may have had something to do with this.

In capturing all these events, I argue that within the everyday life of a student with a disability—diagnosed or undiagnosed—a host of sociocultural issues may be at play that may actively be contributing to their retention and success within the education system. The senior teacher to whom I reported was also the same teacher who had been our class teacher in the previous class, so I had safety in knowing that my disclosure of their colleague's behavior would not be met with doubt.

Active Inclusion

During the final year at the school, our class went for a field trip to Naivasha greater area, within the Rift Valley, and we were all excited for it! The first stop on the trip was Olkaria Gorge, situated at the floor of the Rift Valley. As we began our descent, it quickly became clear that I would not be able to balance on my feet like my classmates, and the teachers and members of management accompanying us on the trip worked seamlessly to physically support me till we were at the floor of the gorge. I remember that my legs were violently shaking, and I took time to recover as the others explored nearby. I vaguely remember a conversation before we were to head back up to where the vehicles were, yet I can certainly recall the feeling of safety and being cared for as the adults who had accompanied the group coordinated themselves to ensure that I was carried back to where the vehicles were. The trip to Olkaria left me feeling safe and accepted. It communicated that I had every right to participate in classroom learning as well as extracurricular activities and that there would be people to offer support whenever needed. As a learner who had thought that I would have to excel academically to cement my worth, to make society ready to support me, it had not been obvious at the time that this support could extend to physical support for what would in some instances be termed as "nonessential" activity. The same year, a teacher in training from the Department of Special Needs Education at Kenyatta University came to our school for a few sessions.

Despite being a family friend, I had not had close proximity to what her studies at university were focusing on. Her short stint at the school did to some extent reinforce my feelings of safety being at the school and the fact that all students got whatever extra attention they needed.

Transition into high school was one that I was excited about. I reported to Gatanga Girls Secondary School ready to take on whatever school had in store for me. I was aware that I'd have to figure out how to operate in a new environment, carve out a new system for myself as I had done at home over the years. Having changed schools more than a few times, I did not have any anxieties around being in a new environment. It also helped that a few of my former schoolmates from previous schools were either already at the school or would be reporting the same year.

The validation that I belonged in a regular school—even the chance of being the only one with a disability, which I had received in my last primary school—followed me to secondary school, and I was eager to go on school trips. I ended up going for my first one only weeks after reporting to school. I had noted how the steps into the school truck were; the name "truck" is specific, because it was indeed a lorry truck that had been converted into a passenger-carrying school bus. I have no recollection of when portable additional steps were fabricated to extend the steps of the bus to the ground. What I know for sure is that I was happy to not be physically carried onto the bus every single time. For my active outgoing self, my concerns in secondary school continued to shift. I was more aware of the increased difficulty of moving around the school compound, which is situated right on the hills, with very few alternatives to the stairs connecting the different levels of the school. Along with my continued participation in activities outside school came the increasing questions from curious age-mates. Most of them did not ask direct questions, and I'm grateful for this. Coming up with answers that I didn't have bothered me even more as I went through secondary school.

At some point after the first year of school, I approached our former class teacher, who also served as the school's guidance and counseling teacher. She had taught us for at least a year by then and had actively been making modifications to her Home Science lessons and instructions for my body. Some were subtle, like allocating a waist-level locker, while others were more direct, such as ensuring that I cooked on the waist-level cooking surfaces during practical lessons; cumulatively, they all made me feel more accepted within the school. This also supported my growing trust in her, to the point of approaching her for guidance and counseling sessions. From the point of our initial meeting onward, we met numerous times, often during night private study time. She became my sounding board as I explored my body's makeup, as it was apparent that something was amiss at this point, as well as other aspects of my teenage life that I was struggling to make sense of.

At the time, I had no concerns about her knowledge or expertise in my specific embodied state, and I found safety in her promise of confidentiality and nondisclosure. Even though I did not have answers in the form of a diagnosis by the time I had completed secondary school, she gets a lot of credit for supporting me to go through secondary school and complete it as successfully as I did, given all she did. Over the years there have been conversations about the place of therapists and counselors within schools, and questions about whether or not they should also be members of the teaching staff. As I acknowledged earlier the fact that my experiences may not be similar to the next person's, I also recognize that guidance and counseling departments in schools have been sites for discrimination and justification of discriminative actions by schools against learners who do not fit the normative expectations of the education system. As I write this, the situation of queer Kenyan students who are expelled from schools based on their real or perceived queerness—which is pathologized as a behavioral concern—comes to mind.

Is It a Curse?

The Kenyan education system at the time of my schooling was such that it was about a year after completing secondary school before one could join postsecondary learning institutions. Our family tradition had been that you get a job during this time, and I was no exception to this practice. In what looked like a good turn, an uncle had an opening at his shop, which was located in one of the towns we had lived in when I was in primary school.

Around this time, our search for a diagnosis had led to a few suggestions; for a time, I was given referral to occupational therapy for what was thought to be a prolapsed spinal disc. Three or four times a week for six months, I had therapy sessions at the local government hospital where our neighbor happened to be working as the lead therapist. Any missed sessions were reported to my mother, who was at the time less than pleased at my seeming lack of interest in getting better. She was clearly worried about how I would manage the daily commute to campus during my studies, which were fast approaching.

About the same time, my siblings and I firmly turned down my mother's suggestion to visit a known religious televangelist known for his healing of the sick. This was the first time that we had actually addressed the elephant in the room in a family conversation.

Much as I desired answers, all of me was tired, the hospital visits didn't seem to yield any answers, and the situation seemed more grim. The whole family had now focused on seeking the elusive answers, and turning to religion, which seemed to hold the promise of cure from any and all ailments, as was being promoted by the televangelists, was yet another of those options. I recognize how hard it was for us as a family to talk about an issue that could not be named.

The start of classes gave me a much-needed break from the painful therapy sessions that always left me fatigued for days, with no way out.

For the next four years, commuting to Kenyatta University from our home in Githurai, which took about an hour, was my ticket out of therapy sessions, but I still had to do annual review visits with the occupational therapist.

When I was twenty-three years old, two months away from my undergraduate graduation, after a lot of insistence from my lovely mother, we went for "review" with the occupational therapist. He had been our neighbor growing up and had always invited us over on Saturdays when he put his daughters through physical exercise for them to shed some of the weight he thought was too much for their preteenage bodies. During these sessions, back then, my brother and I were more than encouraged to work harder so our bodies would regain the abilities they once had. Looking back, I'm struck how much the cure trope has applied in my life. The further away I moved from the normative body, the more rigorous became the efforts to fix it.

Around the same time, it was revealed to me that it had always been thought that my paternal grandmother, after whom I'm named, had supposedly placed a curse on our family because I had been taken away from the home. This "curse" had brought on a blanket of silence over the whole family for years, and it was weighted with such fear that no one dared speak about it openly. Ironically though, my awareness of this line of thinking came to me without any feelings of dread and assured in the depths of me that it didn't hold any truth.

By this time, I had a defined "bounce"; this was the easiest way to define my mobility growing up, at the time when "bouncing" was part of pop culture. Many of my age-mates had taken up this style of walking—even though most of them were male, so it didn't seem to call for much extra attention. It was better to be thought to be taken with popular culture than to be asked questions whose answers I did not have. Nancy Mairs, who had multiple sclerosis, describes her movement as a "swagger" in her autobiographical book.[3] The first time reading her accounts of her disability, in all aspects, felt like home to me. To be seen, to be written about too. All through university life, despite actively taking a course that was specific to disability, I did not feel like I could claim disability. After doing rounds with top doctors that yielded no answers, it did not seem like I was justified in claiming disability. I went through university experiencing what Ellen Samuels describes as "the uneasy, often self-destroying tension between appearance and identity; the social scrutiny that refuses to accept statements of identity without 'proof.'"[4] These tensions on my part were made tougher by the fact that I did not bear any proof yet. If asked after my apparent difference, I had to go through life mentioning the most profound symptom at any point.

When, during that review a few months away from my graduation, the occupational therapist suggested that it might be muscular dystrophy, I was beside myself with joy. We still had to await confirmation from a neurologist, which came later the same month. The next few months were quick transitions, from a state of not knowing what is happening with my body, to then having a vague idea, to then getting a confirmation for a progressive chronic condition, all leading to the point where the gaps in narratives on lives with muscular dystrophy of people of African descent living on the continent became clear to me. I spent the better part of that year looking for other people outside of our family with muscular dystrophy, and meeting with medical and paramedical professionals who seemed to know less than what I had learned from my internet, learnings confirming what my body knew all along.

Without any luck, I launched a blog and created a space for myself to contribute to disability life writing as a Kenyan Black woman. I had a desire to allow others to see themselves in my blog posts. To not feel lost and isolated for as long as I had without a diagnosis. At the time, blogging was the most reachable place to situate my contributions after diagnosis and to initiate a knowledge base as well as possibly a support platform. Years later, the blog continues to fulfill this role and has connected more than fifty individuals who are affected by muscular dystrophy in Kenya. With my continued growth in my own disability identity, I honor the ancestors with disabilities, such as Audre Lorde, as cited by Beth Ferri, whose reflections on identity and visibility of disability rely on the second Kwanza principle of Kujichagulia, which asserts that "to define ourselves, name ourselves, speak for ourselves instead of being defined and spoken for by others."[5] Audre Lorde calls for the writing of disability narratives by individuals with disabilities, and her words continue to ring true decades later. Through her life, and even my own experiences so far, it can be argued that there is no neat line that separates those with disability and those without disability and, even less, between the binary of ability/disability.

The constant fluidity of my daily experiences, having a disability that can be termed as a chronic illness, coupled with the instability of daily capabilities dependent on a host of factors, make it that there cannot be a neat line. For on the days where I'm feeling an excess of energy, a full day of rigorous physical activity waddling on my feet may be possible, while equally valid days moving about the world in my wheelchair do not then mean that I can only claim disability on the days when I'm making use of mobility devices. In the words of Ellen Samuels, "Coming out, then, for disabled people, is a process of redefinition of one's personal identity through rejecting the tyranny of the normate, positive recognition of impairment and embracing disability as a valid social identity."[6] By claiming the term "disabled" as I do, I assert that I'm in full recognition of my impairments as well as proudly sharing space with individuals who are actively working to build community with other individuals with disabilities in their lives.

That said, it should not be lost on us that initial identification as having a disability, or even claiming to be disabled, doesn't spare one from the constant conversations, such as

"Is there another way to get there, other than the stairs?"

"Yes (or No)—But it's only on the first floor, it's not far. Who needs to use a lift?"

These seemingly regular conversations call for disclosure of one's disability or level of impairment beyond the presumptive conclusions that random strangers have based on outward appearance. While some of these questions can be ignored or shrugged away, disclosure of disability and level of impairment remains at the core of state-mandated disability services and access that requires those with disability to be engaged in constantly proving the legitimacy of said disability.

While being fully aware of these realities, those with disabilities may from time to time, when their individual situations allow them, choose to move through life without calling attention to their disabilities. It is with this awareness that I remain grateful for having gone through basic-level schooling without an official diagnosis, as I feel it allowed me to exist in the world where modifications were being made for me as a human being, not necessarily one with a disability. None of this is to say that I enjoyed the emotional turmoil that this limbo exposed myself or my loved ones to; absolutely not, it is to call attention to the various functions that diagnosis and identification play in a learner's life when the overarching aim is to support the learner to continue existing in their home environments—which include neighborhood schools—and planning for these situations, as it allows for the ease to transition through life. Moving through life without calling attention to one's disability may be considered as passing, whether intentional or unintentional. However, the trouble with passing is that it engages with power, the hierarchies that have been created around bodies and minds. In my experience over the years, individuals may or may not have recognized my disabilities, and moving through a world created by nondisabled persons primarily for nondisabled individuals means never-ending negotiations with disability and identity. "Thus, we see how passing can become a subversive practice and how the passing subject may be read not as an assimilationist victim but as a defiant figure who, by crossing the borders of identities, reveals their instability."[7] This further complicates the situations in which accusations on fraud or faking are leveled against those with disabilities, diagnosed or undiagnosed.

Family Support for Transition

This section, a blogpost I wrote to pay respects to my grandmother who has transitioned from this life, captures snippets of my life that show the dynamic ways in which families are key in the support of individuals with disabilities. That said, I also recognize that numerous individuals with disabilities across the world lose their lives from violence at the hands of families and caregivers every year. This continues to be recognized in the observation of the Disability Day of Mourning, remembering people with disabilities murdered by their families.[8] This serves as a reminder to recognize the narrative of my disability not as a blueprint for all others with disabilities in Kenya and beyond.

Disability Acceptance and Inclusion Lessons from My Cûcû
In loving memory, ûromama kwega kuuraga

It is going to be 3 years this 20th of August since you left us and I'm only just now being able to put this down. To write you into the world. To go back to writing on here.

We shared so many unspoken truths that made me feel so so safe around you

I have vague memories of carrying one litre water containers when my 6 year old age-mates were carrying ten litre and five litre ones
The small bundles of napier grass, handfuls probably when they carried bundles that weighed them down
You made sure I had a bundle to carry or a container of water
You made it feel okay for me to come early in the morning to get my mandatory 5 litres of water for washing the classrooms instead of having to carry them the estimated 4 kilometres walk to school at 7/8 years
In the age before mobile phones, I would be tired at the end of my school day and walk to your home less than 10 minutes away instead of the slightly more than 30 minutes brisk walk to our home in the next

town, this would leave my sibling making the walk home with friends often only to realise that I wasn't walking with my age-mates ahead or behind their group but I'd remained behind.

We celebrated the days when guka would meet us on the way in his Peugeot 504 KKC that he drove on the route and gave us rides home. It was blue, a beautiful blue. It is an easy colour to love when it represents such joy.

Oh, the times mum would get home and then have to make the extra trip after her commute from work to get me. I don't know how often this happened but I suspect it was quite often as mum eventually moved us to a school closer to home with a school transport option that was on the same route as her place of work then but I think we were only at the school for one school term.

I loved my shorts growing up, still do, the constant comments about my "skuembe" from people around me were often shushed by you

Just as you did anyone who attempted to pick on me for any "physical" reason. Little did we know all those years that for us these were signs of muscular dystrophy in me. Now I wear those shorts with pride.

You had me on dish duty as I could do this seated down, I can't quite remember when this started happening, but it went on well into my later years that's for sure.

Later I may have had other reasons for choosing Ikuma Secondary school for my teaching practice, perhaps those fond memories I had when I attended Ikuma primary school years back but cûcû's love and care must have been one of the leading ones.

In the three or so months of the school term, the longest I was away was a weekend, so we got to spend nearly all of it together.

The latrine and bathroom are located in a lower part of the compound, around this time it was a big gamble at whether or not I would be able to rise myself up and it would be an understatement to say that toileting around this time came with its levels of anxiety and fears. Over the years I'd lost count at the number of times I had miscalculated my moves and landed bare ass on a latrine floor and had to either call someone to help me up or struggled back to my feet somehow and felt like I had walked too many kilometres after.

At the school, there were also latrines so I couldn't perhaps, you know, hold it in till I got home like I'd made the habit all through later years of primary and university when I would commute from home or held it in till I got to that toilet with a toilet seat on the other side of campus.

For nights and early mornings if I wasn't half-squatting behind the house while you watched out for the dogs, I was peeing into the bucket that you had placed in my bedroom. I can't remember if we ever spoke about it and if we did what you might have said but this was one of those unspoken truths and beauties that made me feel so safe. I know for sure you didn't make a big deal out of it if my lack of memory of it is anything to go by.

I had less urinary tract infections in those three months than I'd had in my adult life that far.

My mornings with you were something else. I'd hear you wake up to milk the cows in the morning, you'd leave a sufuria with water heating up on the fire as you did this. This was my alert to wake up and take the time as you milked to boot, clear my head. I'd hear you come back into the house and turn on the radio and this would be my signal to get out of the bedroom as you would proceed to pour this water into a bucket and carry it down to the bathroom for me, adding some cold water from the tank that collected rain water outside.

There's this stool that was inside the bathroom, I'm not too certain if you only placed it there when I came to live with you so I wouldn't struggle to take a bath, but I have a feel this might have been it. Your daughter, my mother, might have had something to do with it too, I'm not sure.

I'd come back and get dressed and it wasn't up for debate with you that I should have breakfast before leaving. You made sure I did. You'd have my cup of tea or milk ready, you'd even cool for me given I still can't take hot drinks without burning my tongue, even now. There would be a fried egg on most days and slices of ugali from the previous night, ndûma, ngwacî or bread.

On most days I remember you walking me to the road, sending me off with warm loving words after making sure I didn't slide and land on my butt on the loose gravel that remained even after you swept ever so often to make sure there wasn't any at the gate.

I have been dropping plates and cups with anything in them or empty as far back as I can remember. If you're not offering me plastics, don't blame me when they break. If I'm balancing these and making sure not to fall on my face or on my back, you can bet that I'll drop them quickly for my rare chance to block the fall with my hands rather than my face or back or my head.

You always sent me off to sit down after having been in the kitchen catching up on the day's activities or some stories of things that happened so many years ago no one can quite tell anymore if they're just stories you made up to keep me entertained or they were facets of the stories of your life. You'd then carry whatever plate or cup for me as we continued talking into the night.

When in other parts of the world, away from that home, people would be busy philosophising all of this and calling it disability studies, taking it apart and analysing it with theories and debates on end, you, Cûcû, made me enjoy what Mia Mingus has come to call "Access Intimacy" in a way that I have only experienced with a handful of people all my life.

Forever on my mind and in my heart, I am better for having had you in my life.[9]

Own Your Truth

Growing into my disability and continuing to inhabit this body, my physical capabilities are progressively changing and often occupying spaces on the daily seems to require a disclosure of disability. I arrive at this point where I do not offer a neat answer to the query of whether my education was inclusive. Over the years I have met Kenyans who do not have access to disability as a label, neither is choosing it as a label an option. Disability defined as it has been—through the colonial British education and the Judaic/Abrahamic religions and existing interpretations meant to uphold hierarchical societies—makes it even more of a challenge to claim disability.

May this offering serve as a call to fellow individuals with disabilities to author their narratives, own their truths in all their diversity.

NOTES

1   Ferri, "Disability Life Writing."
2   "Brene Brown."
3   Mairs, *Waist-High in the World.*
4   Samuels, "My Body, My Closet," 233.
5   Ferri, "Disability Life Writing."
6   Samuels, "My Body, My Closet," 237.
7   Samuels, "My Body, My Closet," 243.
8   Disability Day of Mourning.
9   Njahîra, "Disability Acceptance and Inclusion Lessons."

9. CRIP GENEALOGIES FROM THE
POSTSOCIALIST EAST

KATEŘINA KOLÁŘOVÁ

Englishman: Do you know Caravaggio?

Marek: Cara-what?

Englishman: Sweet unconsciousness! The primitive! The brute!

You do not know it, but you are the true creator of the art in the world! If it were not for
   you, art would not happen . . . if your body did not exist . . .

Marek: My name is Marek

[. . .]

Englishman: So cruel . . . sweet innocence . . . Still asleep, we wake you up tonight!

—MANDRAGORA, directed by Wiktor Grodecki, 1997

Meet Marek—the main protagonist of Wiktor Grodecki's *Mandragora*—a
runaway adolescent boy striving and struggling to find his path to happiness
in the Czech Republic of the 1990s, the period of immense social, political,
economic, and cultural restructuring following the 1989 collapse of the socialist state regime. Bright-eyed with hopes for opportunities that the new times,
commonly dubbed as "transition" or "transformation," will surely bring, Marek
embodies the postsocialist subject. In the meantime, he engages in sex work
to pay for his drugs, gambling, and other "pleasures" of postsocialist freedom,
and also to give himself a provisional home in hotel rooms that he shares with
boys like him.

The Englishman, the other protagonist of the opening scene, and Marek's
customer, is likewise a representative of a kind; he is a prototype of the "sex-
hungry foreigner" imagined to cruise the streets of Prague (and other Eastern
European cities) in the 1990s looking for young boys and men who would provide him with exotism and new pleasures for a good price and who would fulfill

his colonial fantasies of bringing sexual awakening, emancipation, and education. Since the border opening in early 1990s, Eastern Europe has been a place of blooming transnational sex tourism. Supposedly, one of the main attractions of the region has been the professed sexual openness and flexibility of its population (and of men, in particular) and their eagerness to please.[1]

Mandragora (1997) by Wiktor Grodecki, a US-based Polish émigré, is the last sequence in a trilogy that maps "Europe in transition" onto the development of sex-work and pornographic businesses in postsocialist Eastern Europe.[2] *Not Angels but Angels*,[3] the first film of the series, is a documentary focused on male-to-male sex work and its exploitative transnational scale.[4] It features young men (most of them minors) talking about sex work, AIDS, and their visions of a future away from prostitution. *Body without Soul*, also shot as a documentary, shifts the perspective toward the porn-production networks operating from Prague that service foreign (mostly German) markets.[5] *Mandragora*, the only feature film in the series, symbolically closes the trilogy by retracing the motifs of the documentaries and tying them together through a narrative line that accentuates the cruelty of the promises of postsocialist rosy futures. In contrast, *Mandragora* reimagines post-1989 Prague as the dystopic hyper-urban site—the capital "Sin City" of the East European 1990s—overrun by its "underworld" of impromptu casinos and gambling stations, "homosexual" nightclubs, street prostitution and criminality, and drug addiction.

Mandragora's vision of postsocialist reality offers a harsh antidote to the overoptimistic fantasies of the revolution that, according to many Cold War pundits, was supposed to mark the end of history. Its thick moral panic attached to the homosexual transactional sexual economy at the same time clashes sharply with the imaginaries of the (homosocial and homoerotic) "togetherness" circulated most famously by the Pet Shop Boys' cover of "Go West" (released in 1993) that became a symbol for the fall of the "wall" separating the global East and West.[6]

> (Together) We will love the beach
> (Together) We will learn and teach
> (Together) Change our pace of life
> (Together) We will work and strive
> (I love you) I know you love me
> (I want you) How could I disagree?
> (So that's why) I make no protest
> (When you say) You will do the rest.[7]

Calling up images of the open air, blue skies, sunny wintertime, and a peaceful life, in their 1990s reinterpretation, the lyrics of "Go West" mirror the aesthetics of the postrevolution, and the hopefulness of the end of the Cold War. *Mandragora*'s visions of postsocialist futures are haunted by the incessant ghosts of death, mostly from overdose or AIDS. As one of the characters puts it, in response to a question of whether he is not scared of AIDS, "Why, we all got it anyway." And, indeed, just before we see Marek, the antihero of *Mandragora*, die of an intended overdose in a public toilet, we learn that his lover and partner in the sex business is dying of AIDS.

Helping to articulate and give concrete shape to affects of disenchantment with the postsocialist developments and social changes—perhaps we can call it "transformational pessimism"—Grodecki's films intriguingly capture the first cracks in the postsocialist consensus about the liberating and morally invigorating nature of postsocialist capitalism and the (neo)liberal versions of democracy. In their representations of (homosexual and) transnational sex work, the films offer a location through which we can interrogate the affective investment in, and the ultimate failure of, the promise of what I describe elsewhere as a "postsocialist rehabilitation" that depended to a great part on figurations of racialized, disabled, and queer subjects.[8]

Sexuality has been explored as one of the key vectors through which to study the reshaping of the politics in postsocialist Eastern Europe. For instance, Gail Kligman and Susan Gal have famously argued that gender and sexuality discourses were crucial to reestablishing and renegotiating the meanings and spheres of *the social* and *the political*. Kligman and Gal even argue that post-1989 political processes were themselves "shaped by control of reproduction." Věra Sokolová then foregrounds the ways in which the sexual and the economic intertwined, noting that the explorations of sexuality "tell us a lot about the ways economic transformation and openness to the 'West' have helped redefine cultural values and models."[9] In this text, I build off these feminist analyses of sexuality and go beyond them to look at how discourses of sexuality intersect with disability to articulate racialized differences and to set up differential economies of ability and vitality. I look at two films from two different moments of postsocialist transformation—early 1990s and mid-2010s—that both turn to intersectional complexities around sexuality to critique the post-1989 developments, and foreground the failures of the promised futures. I read *The Way Out* (*Cesta ven*, 2014)[10] and *Mandragora* (and the different affects they capture) against each other because their juxtaposition creates a version of crip genealogy that frustrates a straight, linear notion of progress. Such frustration is conditional, as feminist queer crip scholars argue, to reimagine disability outside the limits of (white- and nation-centered) identities of recognizability.[11]

Despite their focused exploration of the transnational homosexual sex work and porn industry, *Mandragora, Not Angels but Angels,* and *Body without Soul* are complicit in the epistemology of the homophobic panic, the stigmaphobic abjection of HIV/AIDS, addiction, and other forms of cripness/disability. Furthermore, they engage in racialized othering and uphold the symbolic regimes that pose whiteness as requisite to a life's value. For (rather than despite) these problems and failings, Grodecki's oeuvre and its public reception represent an important, conflictual addition to the archive of postsocialism—a feverish, ambivalently queer, troubled and troubling response to the forceful, indeed compulsory, optimism of the time—by articulating disillusionment of unfulfilled hopes and dystopic horizons where the future appears gloomy (perhaps even impossible) in the face of deaths from exhaustion, drugs, and/or AIDS. The rereading of Grodecki's films I offer here portrays the forgotten peripheries of male sex work, substance addiction, HIV/AIDS, and youth homelessness, realms where the positivity of the "transformation" did not reach and that thus bring evidence of the slow buildup of neglect.

Elsewhere, I have focused on the ways that Grodecki's films construe "Eastern Europe as alienated and objectified through the forceful entry of unregulated markets,"[12] and how projecting the "corruption of the soul"[13] as "the most threatening of the 'syndromes of postcommunism'" onto homosexual sex work utilizes the homophobic moral panic to displace any potential critical reflection of the exploitation of the Eastern Europe workers.[14] Here, I explore the dense ambivalences articulated by *Mandragora* as sites from which to destabilize the white "northern" canon of disability theory by pushing the ways in which disability has been recognized and made intelligible in postsocialist contexts.

The geopolitical and temporal location of postsocialist Eastern Europe is one of the sites that bears witness to the complex and complicated transnational translations of disability theory *and* to the ways in which its predominantly white and West-focused canon cannot take hold of the embodied effects of the postsocialist shock cure and its continuing reverberations. I propose to read the films as an archive that speaks to the material history of Eastern *postsocialist* Europe and an archive from which it is possible to start thinking (and draw part of *a* genealogy of) antiracist feminist queer disability/crip critique.

As the genealogies of disability epistemologies in postsocialist spaces are often mapped onto the canonized genealogy of postsocialist democracies, troubling the narratives of postsocialism and the genealogy of the victorious "after" becomes part and parcel of troubling and opening up disability epistemologies and reimagining crip genealogies. The genealogical outlines are about imagining the future as much as they are about tracing and recording the past. The futurity written into the genealogical imagination is mostly, Alison Kafer notes, the futurity of the compulsorily abled, flexible, and fit (for reproduction) whiteness.[15] Subverting the straight lines of genealogical projection (straight as in both heteronormative propriety and the abled embodiment and enmindedness) also means to attend, Eunjung Kim argues, to the ways in which straight lines are produced through "fold[ing] time," which folds past and future together in such a way that the present becomes impossible to inhabit.[16] *Mandragora* captures the sense of unlivable present while also subverting and disidentifying from the straight lines of futurity. I therefore approach the archive created around Grodecki's films as a queer/crip site from which to start mapping out the interweaving of race, disability, sexuality, and the nation, and to reconceptualize the lineage and genealogy of feminist queer antiracist crip theory; an archive fully revealing inner incoherencies and the ways that crip genealogies are troublesomely interconnected with the material movement of ideologies, economies, and bodies across transnational borders.

After a short discussion of genealogy as a critical project, I unpack the ambivalent ways *Mandragora* charts out the "interarticulations" of disability and race:[17] first, I attend to how race and sexuality come to matter, in forms of disabilities/cripness, to point out the limits in the disability epistemologies traveling across the borders. I then stay with the trouble of subjects and disabilities that do not change and get better. The geopolitical space of Eastern Europe has been ambivalently and chronically stuck between conflicting narratives— on the one hand, after the revolutions in 1989 and the collapse of the Soviet Union in 1991, the post-Soviet/Eastern Bloc was seen as a transition laboratory to prove the global success of (neo)liberal capitalism; on the other hand, more recently, Eastern Europe is seen as a laboratory of totalitarian tendencies on the rise. Or quite simply, Eastern Europe is seen as stuck in the past, stuck in the middle of its progress to "transform" into the historical present. In the last section, I finally explore *The Way Out* and the ways in which it reveals the racialized materialities of "being stuck" and racialized modes of chronicity.

Mixed Genealogies

Crip histories, as much as the ways in which we learn such histories, can hardly be straight, respectable, uncomplicated, rational, and straightforwardly sanitary. Sometimes, furthermore, as José Muñoz chronicled, ways of desire, laughter, and survival need to be carved out in proximity to mechanisms of oppression.[18] For all its traffic in homo- and AIDS-phobic fantasies of a white nation, and all its othering and negation gesturing, *Mandragora* also articulates forms of yearning, desire, and reaching out to the Other, to ways of knowledge and desire that the Other embodies. Afterall, othering is, Sara Ahmed notes, an ambivalent gesture of directionality/orientation. It is a form of "negation as well as a form of extension" of the self.[19] In a risky reading that I propose here, films chronicling sex work and homosexual desire register yearnings to disidentify (even if they inevitably fail to do so) from the dominant ideology of postsocialist rehabilitation. *Mandragora* creates a messy and problem-ridden part of the conflictual archive of postsocialism that can serve us in critical reading and understanding of the violence hidden in the scripts of postsocialist rehabilitative citizenship.

Postsocialist histories and genealogies of disability are hardly straightforward. The workings of genealogy itself, Ahmed proposed, "could be understood as a straightening device, which creates the illusion of descent as a line."[20] Moreover, the genealogical idea of a descent and "passing along" marries the familial with the racial: "Whiteness gets reproduced through acts of alignment, which are forgotten when we receive its line."[21] The "good genealogical straight lines" are lines re/producing whiteness.[22] This text builds off of Ahmed's work and explores how different forms of whiteness and different modalities of ethnicization and racialization are produced through specific alignments of sexuality and disability, alignments that bring together notions of illness and pathology, and the homosexual panic with idea of a nation. With all its troubles, *Mandragora* allows us to outline other/ed, twisted, and "knotted" genealogies from the point of homosexual, nonreproductive, non-straight, unwholesome, paid-for, virus-infected, across-the-borders sex acts that put the straight line of genealogy under pressure.[23]

In *Mad for Foucault,* Lynne Huffer emphasizes the ironic impossibility of clear and un/leaky divisions between epistemic paradigms and ruptures. Such questioning of forward orientations is helpful when thinking crip archives against the context of postsocialism and Eastern Europe. All these concepts are overdetermined by historical directionality caught up in the webs of binaries posing historical, cultural, and economic delay; lagging behind; and underdevelopment against progress, modernity, and development. While lagging behind and such are ascribed to disability, the East, and (post)socialism, progress represents the norm, the future, and West/Global North. *Mandragora* and *The Way Out* frustrate such binaries, and twist the straight line of progress/ion that connects development, ability, and liberty with the spread of the global market economy. They frustrate the aspirational process through and in which Eastern Europe was expected to emulate the West and effectively "beco[me] the same."[24]

The ideals of liberty and freedom have, as Lisa Lowe traces in *The Intimacies of Four Continents,* troubled histories. Lowe's newly drawn genealogy of liberalism reveals "intimate" relations with the colonial state. Lowe notes, "It is precisely by means of liberal principles that political philosophy provided for colonial settlement, slavery and indenture."[25] *Mandragora* and *The Way Out* draw out how Lowe's reminder of the intertwined archives of colonial exhaustion and liberalism hold true for the similarly and complexly intertwined histories of global neoliberal capitalist expansion and histories of spreading democracy—and, as I show here, histories of sexual and disability emancipation.

Taking a cue from Lowe, any discussion of notions of liberty and liberating epistemologies, thus also disability epistemologies, translated and imported into the postsocialist context need to be set against other forms of imports and especially against the "intimately connected" economic relations of in/equality. In other words, Lowe cautions us to pay attention to the interplay of liberal promises of individual rights, freedoms, and empowerment, on the one hand, and the dynamic and relations of the global markets and forms of exploitation through global economy, on the other. *Mandragora* and its documentary prequels bring this difficult intimacy home: the disability epistemologies introduced into the Czech Republic (and elsewhere in Eastern Europe), through transnational circuits alongside (and truly as an integral part of) the global markets, do not and cannot speak to (all) forms of cripness brought about by global capital and by the immense and groundbreaking reorganizations of postsocialist societies.

Disability epistemologies have been (and continue to be), of course, part of complex transnational translations. More recently, attention has been given to how disability and crip epistemologies can be and are reformulated and reconstituted through such translations. Yet, disability transnational dialogues happened earlier. Disability knowledges were circulated across the East-West divide and across the different regions of the East and within the sphere of Soviet influence long before the collapse of Cold War dichotomies and barriers.[26]

Since the early 1990s, disability activists have been finding inspiration in the Western disability emancipation movement; emerging journals reported on the independent living movement, access in the public space, and forms of self-advocacy.[27] More importantly, foreign initiatives were coming to Czechoslovakia/the Czech Republic and other postsocialist spaces with the aim of introducing disability knowledge and, through such translations, cultivating a (particular kind of) civic society. To follow these initiatives and map out what parts of the disability epistemological canon were introduced, how exactly they influenced the work of disability activists and scholars, and what were the "intimacies" of such initiatives calls for more research, the extent of which is beyond the scope of this text. However, I do want to contextualize my reading of *Mandragora* and *The Way Out* against the contemporary context of disability epistemologies within the Czech Republic. To that end, when, several years ago, I reached out to several disability activists who had founded key disability rights NGOs in the 1990s, it turned out several of them had met through intense courses organized by a US-Israeli foundation that offered a curriculum forwarding concepts of disability rights and emancipation for people with disabilities. The personal networks created in the courses, as well as the disability knowledge offered through the curriculum, were—as far as the understanding of these activists go—essential for setting up the respective NGOs working with people with disabilities.

Groundbreaking as such organizations and knowledge transfers have been and continue to be for the advocacy, community work, and recognition of people with disabilities, Lowe's argument about the usefulness of liberal ideology to the exploitative economy raises haunting questions about the effects and ideological role of the discourses of "normalisation [of disability]" and respectable citizenship that were prominent in 1990s disability knowledge transfers.[28] Furthermore, the focus on the intimacies between liberatory knowledges and exploitative economies also brings out the fact that the import of foreign—predominantly Western—ways of knowing and acknowledging disability disconnected, covered over, and largely served to discredit the already existing epistemologies developed in situ across Eastern European spaces.

Paradoxically, such translations of disability epistemologies effected a disconnect where an earlier—complex and troublesome—mixing happened: between race, ethnicity, sexuality, and disability. The Czechoslovak state socialist discourses of disability and race densely intertwined.[29] Admittedly, such interarticulations were primarily called up to legitimize pathologizations of Roma people and to enforce their compulsory "integration."[30] However, the white Western canon will not help to undo the haunting of the racialized and racist usages of disability introduced and cemented over the state socialist period. Rather, the individualized notions of disability rights and emancipation allow for new versions of racist invocations of disability. In this sense, my reading of *The Way Out* argues for crip genealogies that force us into acknowledgment and dealing with uncomfortable pasts.[31]

I want to come back to Ahmed once more to find inspiration in her concept of "mixed genealogy [which] attend[s] to how things do not stay apart from other things."[32] Similar to Huffer, Ahmed here troubles any notion of a clean historical break between the past and the present. As I discuss below, Grodecki's films bear testimony to the twisted lines of "capitalist" genealogies as well as to how the projections of transition construe its racialized failures. Furthermore, Ahmed's caution that "when genealogy straightens up, when it establishes its line, we have simply lost sight of this mix" speaks to the ways in which certain knowledges stick around (I address this briefly when discussing *The Way Out*). It also speaks to the ways in which grand narratives of the postsocialist transitioning into liberal democracy and market economy rely on presentations of socialism as an aberration and a detour in the natural history of development, in which socialism remains solely "the longest and most painful route from capitalism to capitalism."[33] As such representations echo with genealogies of racial/ized difference, thinking critical antiracist and crip theory needs to involve a critical perspective of postsocialism; or, more precisely, it needs to involve engagement with postsocialism as an analytic rather than simply a time period or thematic ascription.

Ahmed turns to "a mixed-race body" as a space from which to devise a new theory of "mixed genealogy" that would acknowledge and write into history racialized bodies and simultaneously foreground the ways that all matter and forms of corporeality are organized along racialized lines. It seems that Eastern Europe in the state of postsocialism provides a fitting space into which to translate Ahmed's interrogation of "mixing." It is a space wherein different temporalities, regimes of knowing, bodies, and goods cannot stay apart from each other.

Below, however, I look at different modes of "mixing up"—itself a metaphor of racialized cripness—the straight, pure lines of futurity. First, I turn to the ways the across-the-border sexual economies cannot stay away from racialized erotic attachments and mixing (both seductive and shunned) between the East and the West, and from various modes of racialized "becoming crip." Simultaneously, the concept of mixed genealogies, as I argue, makes visible the seams and contact points among various modes of racialization (some temporarily redirecting the "Orientalizing" gaze from the Eastern European bodies to across the Western borders, some yet (re)producing the otherness of the Roma) involved in construing the fantasies of the white nation rehabilitated from the socialist past into (moral and economic) health.

As such, mixed genealogies promise to reveal the modes of cripness mixed up in the discourses and ideological frameworks of postsocialism that remain inarticulate and unintelligible in the bounds of white disability liberal epistemology. And lastly, by embracing notions of ambivalence, impurity, and the stickiness of things that will not stay apart, mixed epistemologies promise to open space for thinking and staying with the affect of "being stuck," rather than adhere to the overcoming imperative of the rehabilitative morality of "going West."

Mixed Feelings

Spaces become racialized by how they are directed or orientated,
as a direction that follows a specific line of desire.
—AHMED, *Queer Phenomenology*

In one of the first reflections on the movements of desire across the borders between the Czech Republic (and Prague specifically) and the West, Matti Bunzl charts the ways that structures of "Orientalizing" of the "Eastern subject" materialized (in) a busy form of sex exchanges across the East and West borders. A careful ethnographer, he follows predominantly Austrian gay men traveling east for their weekend fun and explores what Joseph Boon termed the "imperialist economics of boys."[34] Bunzl's ethnography records how the preexisting racialized orientation toward Eastern Europe—orientation that uplifts the historical lineage that posits "the East" as a space of primitive backwardness (seen to reflect clearly in the totalitarian tendencies)—adapted to the new ideological and economic purposes of neoliberal capitalism. It is thus a surprising reversal of this established representation of Eastern Europe as an antidote to modern civilization and a region stuck between progress and backwardness, when, in unexpected contrast, Grodecki's films dramatize the "Orientalizing" nature of the Western gaze directed toward Eastern bodies.[35] The references to Slavic-ness are also a distinct form of racialization: both groups of geopolitically situated male bodies are being aligned with historically sedimented understanding of racialized difference; employing the highly potent discourses of sexuality, the usual hierarchy of these racialized categories becomes questioned and unstable.[36]

Now, I finally come back to where we left Marek and the Englishman, in the midst of a sexual/monetary/viral/power/epistemological transaction. This *Mandragora* scene captures the racialized scandal of (homosexual) sex work across East-West borders and, in search of a punchline, manages to parody itself. After the Englishman picked out Marek from the group of young men offering themselves to the cruising eyes of potential customers, Marek is led into a luxurious apartment in central Prague; the generous space of the room, the intricately carved solid wooden doorframe, wallpapers heavy with golden reliefs, the fireplace, and the overabundant adornments create the fantasy of past aristocratic greatness disrupted by the state socialist regime. Metaphorically, thus, the room returns Marek to a rehabilitated history line. After the initial exchange that established the Englishman as the cultured and Marek as the primitive, Marek is put onto his own pedestal—quite literally—and his naked body is arranged into the pose of Donatello's David. As the pedestal turns around to tunes of classical music and exposes Marek's youthful body to his host's gaze, the culturedness of the Englishman is re-signified as over-culturedness, incapacity, and impotence—to achieve sexual gratification. The Englishman needs to turn the flesh into a text, the corporeal into textual. To climax, he needs to wrap Marek's body into a highly stylized praise grounded in the canon of the Western art and culture and woven into a complicated syntax. To punctuate this contrast between the uncivilized and primitive, yet virile, young, able-bodied Marek and the depraved masculinity of the Englishman, and to dramatize the threat he represents, *Mandragora* has the Englishman attempt to castrate Marek, again quite literally.

Mandragora might be most explicit in pointing to the figure of the customer/Westerner as the queer homosexual vessel of pathology and *sick* menace threatening the future of the postsocialist society. Yet, all of Grodecki's films work with the binary logic of "Orientalism," reversing the significations of the East-West symbolism. The films and the public debate they initiated foreground the juxtaposition of the vulnerable postsocialist subjects and the morally depraved leery Westerners. Reviews of the film repeatedly use morally charged metaphors ("the loss of human dignity") and paint images of the cruel sexual practices demanded by the "foreign sex-hungry customers."[37] Thus, comparison of the dualities of civilization and culturedness, nature and primitiveness, to regress and progress, history and future, are utilized and turned to signify the West as the impotent—yet sexually leery—overcivilized, oversaturated with culture, luxurious and wealthy but also filled with pathology, viruses, and deadliness. Whereas the brute, primitive, uncivilized East stands here for (white) virile and abled masculinity. The homophobic sentiments about the moral decline and threat to the national body—"homosexuality, young boys' prostitution, drugs, increasing criminality, youth gambling, dismal family relations and the absence of positive values in the contemporary so-called civilised society"—mold and carry the mixed feelings about the future of the postsocialist societies and about the dominance of the West over it.[38]

The early postsocialist years were permeated by rampant sexism and pervasive sexualization and objectification of women, as well as by a desire for the

West. In fact it was mostly through women's bodies and through allusions to (heterosexual) sex that the new "sexy" goods coming from the West were advertised. Even more startling to note, then, that *Mandragora* is celebrated as a timely and urgent memento warning against the dangerous Western influences bringing social and sexual decay through practices of excess. The depictions of the sex business and porn industry become a provoking and morally reinvigorating commentary on the postsocialist transformations that came with opening the national borders and markets to foreign capital and goods.

Mandragora's narrative of young men's and boys' moral downfall, caused by their naïve desire for quick cash to enable them to become consumers and by the Westerners' "morbid" desire turning the young men into consumable goods, is read as a testimony of "the petrifying phenomenon" of the times. The public is urged to "not close your eyes!" from its message that reveals that "our times are sick."[39]

The intersection of queer sexuality, disability, and racialized notions of Eastern Europe and of the foreign Other was utilized to articulate and carry the collective affect of transformational disillusionment. One of *Mandragora*'s reviews captures this affect in its rawness: "AIDS was *the only thing the life in freedom* 'got' for the prostitute David."[40] Grodecki himself repeatedly lamented the moral collapse of Eastern Europe whose "soul" was arguably corrupted by the West's exports of excess.[41]

Through its morally charged narrative, the films reconstitute the West as a site of moral danger, sexual threat, and health risk to perhaps uncultured, yet innocent and healthy, East European body/ies and nations. Importantly, as is clear from the warning expressed by some feminist voices of the early 1990s, the spread of transnational sex work, trafficking, and the porn industry posed a health threat not only because it was "in the era of AIDS," but also because this is "a phenomenon associated in our minds with *the Third World*."[42] Becoming a site for the growing sex industry arguably threatened the health and moral growth of the nation, but perhaps most acutely it was seen as a threat to the success of the ideological/moral project of the transition into becoming the same with the West. It threatened to deepen the associations with the undeveloped Global South. These too were the racialized implications of the concerned discourses on the transnational sex work in Eastern Europe.

Even if we leave the explicit disability connection through HIV/AIDS out of the equation for now, and allow—as we must—space for the ambivalence of desire and erotic attachments, the sex labor performed by "flexible" Eastern bodies is a form of affective labor, reproducing, relaxing, and rejuvenating some bodies through using up others as they were situated in global economies that unevenly distribute capacity/disability as well as desire and erotic attachments. These circuits represent one of the ways in which disability (as a specific economy of capacity and vital powers) comes to matter through processes of racialization and "Orientalist" Othering. In this sense, *Mandragora* attempts to "elucidate the neocolonial Western project of charting and thereby inventing a new, post-transition Eastern Europe."[43]

The postsocialist public affects attached to the sexual exchanges across the borders are not racialized only through the ascription of categories of national/ethnic alterity, sexual immorality, and potential viral load, but also, and as importantly, through their juxtaposition and dynamic dialogue with other forms of postsocialist co-articulations of disability and race. The ideological work of racialization that Grodecki's films and their public debate do for the larger project of postsocialist national convalescence is more complex. For one, to be able to construe the appealing narrative of the nation in danger, the representation of the sex workers is whitewashed. Neither *Mandragora* nor the documentaries speak to the fact that many of the young boys and men (and women) involved in sex work were Roma or immigrants from countries farther east of the Czech Republic. In this, Grodecki's films fail to interrogate the structural impacts of the new globalized economy and the ways these impacts intersect specifically with the processes of racialization and "social death."[44]

Simultaneously, as the homosexual threat arriving from the West was called up, other cultural locations bringing together sexuality, disability, the (white) nation and its others (re)surfaced in the public realm: for instance, the formation of new topographies of race-motivated exclusions, the politics of remembering and commemorating *porajmos* (the holocaust of Czech Roma and Sinti communities) that also called up the special politics of race, and discussions about the past and ongoing sterilizations of Roma people that highlighted a different mode of using sexuality as a vector for producing racialized notions of disability.[45]

While these events are not directly dramatized in the discussed films, they do leave their mark, as an absence. The focus on the nation's body, and on the dangerous foreign elements that the discussions around *Mandragora* reinforced, externalizes other forms of racialized conflicts and thus serves as an effective whiteness-centering device. With this in mind, the task of mixed genealogies is to highlight how—despite all effort to prove otherwise—these cultural locations of intersections of race and disability cannot be unstuck from each other, how they cannot be kept apart. Thus, representation of prostitution, transnational sex work, and foreign bodies/viruses that arguably hurt the nation's body and endanger its able-bodiedness stick together to histories and presents of racial violence, specifically against Roma people.⁴⁶ Reconnected and mixed, they line out much more complicated visions of legacies of the postsocialist transformation.

Indeed, these different stories cannot be kept apart, literally. In *Mandragora*'s subplot line, Marek accompanies his partner in business and lover to Ústí nad Labem, the town where his parents live and that he ran away from. Only a few years later, in 1998, Ústí nad Labem became a site of an internationally observed racial conflict—a wall was to be built to divide the supposedly inadaptable Roma and the white "respectable citizens." Interestingly, here the arguments about the value of houses and comfortable lives were not seen as hurting the "soul of Eastern Europe."

After some back-and-forth, and state as well as international intervention, the wall was finally taken down and not rebuilt. Yet, the city district in which the wall was to be built remains a material chronicle to the postsocialist policies of abandonment toward the Roma communities; till the present, the district is marked as "socially excluded locality" and attempts to limit the movement of the Roma citizens. Many other physical and symbolic borders were raised on multiple locations across the whole Czech Republic to separate those who, arguably, live up to the demands of the postsocialist realities from those who fail in transforming themselves into the "rehabilitated citizens."

In sum, *Mandragora* dramatizes the pain of the aspiration and desire for new lives. At the same time, it reinforces the ideology of the white nation by emphasizing its vulnerability to foreign threat and by re-centering whiteness and its strategic amnesia. Yet, it also highlights the uneven distribution of labor and vitality. Moreover, the forms of cripness that I read into and through Grodecki's films about sex work—drug addiction, HIV, trauma from sexual violence and exploitation, stress and exhaustion from social abandonment, all of which link to across-the-border sex acts and their racialized nature—remain unrecognizable through the disability epistemology translated in these early transnational knowledge transfers. These forms of cripness transgress the disability knowledge married to liberal forms of recognition geared toward phantasms of the independent and respectable citizen of the postsocialist state.⁴⁷ But, perhaps more importantly, this ambivalent and troubling stick-togetherness of these discourses poses questions about what specific racialized omissions individual genealogies of disability produce. As I cautiously suggest above, in the case of postsocialist Czechoslovakia and Czech Republic, the turn to Western concepts with their particular genealogies does not help to undo certain forms of stickiness.

On Being Stuck

The affective politics of postsocialist "transformation" or "transition" foreground one-directional transience that achieves so-called rehabilitations from and overcoming of bad socialist pasts. The racialized figure of "the inadaptable" serves to decry those who are supposedly "stuck" and inveterate. The concept of *inadaptability* (*nepřizpůsobivost*)—defined in one of the popular encyclopedias as "the inability to adjust [to change, to new conditions of life, to new forms of responsibilities]"[48]—constitutes a very powerful intersection of disability, race, gender, and sexuality called upon both in articulating the negative foil to discourses of moral deservingness and belonging in the postsocialist nation.

Here, I therefore shift the focus from the bodies, affects, and knowledges that move across borders to bodies, affects, and cripness that do not seem to change and cannot move across space. Instead of the postrevolutionary "transition," I touch "the long-lasting and seemingly permanent situations of stasis [that constitute] the time afterwards."[49] In the remainder of this essay I turn to modes of stuckedness that irritate the genealogies built around change, progress, and modernity.

The figure of the chronic has been probed as a figure that disrupts the normative chronopolitics of "nation-state, capitalist and heteronormative structures."[50] I explore how focusing on the chronic, the stuck, and the lingering can serve us in carving out epistemologies of racialized disability that do not comply with compulsory improvement, personal initiative, and change on the way to a good life. Furthermore, I propose that staying or even embracing the state of being stuck might be necessary to reveal how affects of optimism and positivity, so powerful in the affective landscape of postsocialism, are constitutionally linked to racialized forms of chronic abandonment.

I now turn to a scene from *The Way Out*, another film that portrays how disability, gender, sexuality, and race stick together. *The Way Out* chronicles a struggle of a Roma woman and her family—in its cruel everydayness and ordinariness—to survive, imagine, and create a livable future. If *Mandragora* (and its documentary prequels) articulates a rather acute sense of disillusionment and the bursting of the postrevolution dreams, then *The Way Out* captures the long time afterward, in which abandonment turned chronic and racialized violence came to matter(s) in forms of unrecognized disabilities and inarticulable cripness.

A camera's eye takes us into a doctor's office. We listen in to a conversation between a young Roma woman, Žaneta, and her physician. She has come in with complaints of disturbed sleep, shortness of breath, chest pains, and a general feeling of discomfort and ill health. As a part of what seems a routine review of the patient's medical history, the doctor asks Žaneta to count how many abortions she has had. "I had one when I was 15, 17, 19. I wanted to finish school." While the camera focuses on Žaneta's face, we never see the doctor; he is allowed to remain a disembodied invisible presence of the rational mind, a voice of medical science that combines expert and moral authority. As with the abortions, with no immediate reference to her present complaints of ill health, the doctor notes Žaneta's father's drinking problem and her mother's early death, to finally dismiss Žaneta's problems as *nothing more than* the result of anxiety and stress. We never see Žaneta consult a doctor or address her health in any other way afterward.

In its understatedness, which nearly makes this scene look insignificant for the overall film narrative, the encounter between Žaneta and the representative of the medical/moral authority is a key scene that foregrounds the ways that exhaustion, anxiety, and stress condition Žaneta's life and yet remain inarticulate for what they also are: a material and bodily impression of a racialized social dynamic and social death.

The scene outlines how chronicity is located on the intersection of race and disability; or, more precisely, how it articulates racialized cripness. As the film narrative develops, Žaneta's lack of well-being and health is underwritten by the general precarity not only of her own family but also of the larger local Roma community. An enormous labor burden falls on her as she attempts to secure her family's survival and as she desperately tries to retain their fragile position within classed respectability. We witness the amount of affective labor she offers to support her partner, her sister, her daughter, even her father and his new family. We witness the family's gradual descent into debt, homelessness, and breakdown. On the way, the film narrative reframes Žaneta's anxiety and stress, the signs of her ill health previously dismissed by the medical authority, as part of her supposedly hereditary burden, as a result of the exhaustion brought about by the need to navigate the many forms of racialized violence and systemic racism.

The encounter in the doctor's office, however, reveals another layer and a different—chronic—temporality of how race becomes matter, and of how race and disability commingle. With his focus firmly located in theories of racialized heredity, the doctor goes beyond the checklist of Žaneta's pregnancies and terminations to preach to her about how "important [it is] to know your family burden," to know "[your] parents' and grandparents' mental health and medical history" in order to anticipate not only "what mistakes [you] will make" and what "[you] will most probably die of," but, most importantly, to be aware of what "*[you] will burden [your] surroundings* with." In this, the doctor's speech brings eerie echoes of eugenic rationalities, and of the continuing histories of sterilization of racialized and disabled people that challenge the notion of a clean cut between the two regimes—the state socialist totality from the post-socialist democracy. Officially legitimized and promoted by the socialist state, the sterilization of Roma women continued well into the 2000s, long past the fall of the regime.[51] Žaneta's own embodiment is always already marked with a past larger than herself/itself—her chronic mattering defined by the temporal loopings of the racialized im/possibilities of life and by the mixed genealogies of crip knowledge.

The Way Out captures modes of crip chronicity in its cruel banality, a racialized past rematerializes in the present in the form of impossible futures and inarticulate future horizons. The depiction of Žaneta's medical examination not only illustrates the concrete problems Roma people face accessing medical care, but it can also be theorized as laying out how forms of racialized chronicity overlap and underscore each other, and how their overlap renders racialized chronicity inarticulable. As the physician equipped with the archives of medical expert knowledge reaches into Žaneta's collective pasts, the racialized logics that mold the social require Žaneta to perform endurance as they leave material imprints on her body, exhaust her, depress her, make her anxious, and wear her down. Yet, all these effects are re-signified as the biological truth of her family, her race, and her biological collective fate—a fate that is excluded from the collective belonging within the (white and abled) body of the Czech nation.

The Way Out thus pictures a different form of crip chronicity that for many becomes terminal. Here, racialized past overdetermines the present and implodes the future. The racialized temporality ingrained in the idea of (Roma) "inadaptability" produces the chronic vulnerability and cripness that (because of the moral judgment underwriting the notion of mal/adjustment) remain inarticulable and beyond recognition. I juxtapose *Mandragora* and *The Way Out* here in a gesture of yearning for coalitions among communities living in the precarious conditions of the (morally) abject.

Thinking about the possibilities of antiracist disability epistemologies and politics, I started charting a "mixed genealogy" that would speak to the specific historic experience of postsocialism and that would frustrate straight, white, and abled future-bound prospects of genealogical projects.

Responding to Lowe's call to pay attention to troublesome intimacies and to ask about the intimacies intertwining across-the-border affirmative disability knowledges with exploitative mechanisms of transnational economies, I have started to think about the interarticulations of disability, sexuality, and race from an uncomfortable place of negativity. The dystopic visions we encounter in public debates opened by Grodecki's films foregrounded ugly feelings of racialized homosexual panic and the abjection of sex work, HIV, and drug addiction, revealing how cruel optimism cannot stay away from its aftermath: crip histories of abandonment and neglect, legacies that are only becoming intensified by the current wars, migrations, and other global developments.[52]

The ugly feelings that Grodecki made visible are material marks of crip epistemologies and their mixed genealogies. I do not argue for (re)claiming these negative affects, but have proposed to trace them as gestures of inarticulability that can reorient crip epistemologies. The mixed genealogies need to stay with the trouble, allowing us to be stuck with these affects in a move to imagine crip epistemologies.

Set against the context of the 1990s, Grodecki's films represent a rare archive of the queer, the *sick,* the perverted, the homosexual, the drag, the drug addicted—in other words, the films also create an archive *of the abjected* that throws into relief the epistemological frameworks based around identity and recognition that is conditioned by respectability and *proximity* to normalcy. Thus, I read *Mandragora* as *a* part of a complicated and uncomfortable queer-crip archive and an archive that speaks to mechanisms of "Orientalizing" as well as white ethnicization; it is an archive that speaks to processes of whitewashing, silencing, and mechanisms of displacement over racialized conflict *within* the national body. Despite its troubling and problematic features, or despite its final nod to the normative ideologies, *Mandragora* is a crucial commentary and a trace of desires unfulfilled. Thus Grodecki's films destabilize the narratives of "capitalist rehabilitation" and tentatively gesture to mixed genealogies.

The juxtaposition of *Mandragora* and *The Way Out* with which I close then brings forth what *Mandragora* attempts to override. Working with the cultural imaginations of chronicity as a temporal term referencing time failing to proceed in its expected course—as a form of disorder of time, temporality out of bounds—mixed genealogies can look to the chronic as an enlargement of time that conflates past, present, and future, where the chronic means constant looping between these forms of temporal referencing and mattering. Such frustrations are crucial for thinking about interarticulations of disability, race, sexuality, and postsocialism in the context of Eastern Europe.

Acknowledgments

I want to thank the editors of the volume for opening the discussion on what it means to imagine lineage of antiracist disability studies and for so caringly bringing us together to think with one another. I want to thank the other contributors for sharing their thoughts. I am very grateful to Eunjung Kim for comments on the earlier version of the essay.

NOTES

This work was supported by the Czech Science Foundation (grant number 20-09830S).

1   Cf. Hall, "Rent-Boys." The contemporary feminist authors were also worried about the Orientalizing perception of Eastern European bodies as sexually (permanently) available, flexible, and always encouraging a sexual interaction. For instance, Jiřina Vrábková names "forced prostitution" as one of the key problems of women's emancipation in the region. She quoted one of the foreign customers of sexual workers: "Czechoslovakian girls are pretty, snugly, educated, cultured, and, at the same time, cheap." Vrábková, "Women's Priorities and Visions," 74. There is a significant body of feminist work discussing transnational sex work against the broader context of the postsocialist Eastern Europe, and its transnational dimension. See, for instance, Davydova, "Criminal Networks"; Parvulescu, *Traffic in Women's Work*; Suchland, *Economies of Violence*; Kligman and Limoncelli, "Trafficking Women after Socialism." For a more detailed discussion of sex work in the context of the Czech Republic, see Havelková and Bellak-Hančilová, *Co s prostitucí?*

2   Wiktor Grodecki, on his website, https://www.barrandovfilmschool.com/about -founder/; accessed February 21, 2022.

3   Wiktor Grodecki, dir., *Andělé nejsou andělé*, 1994.

4   Kevin Moss terms Grodecki's films "pseudo-documentaries" to point out their highly stylized form and Grodecki's interventionist approach. Moss, "Who's Renting."

5   Wiktor Grodecki, dir., *Tělo bez duše*, 1996.

6   "Go West" was originally performed by the Village People, though it was the cover by Pet Shop Boys that became emblematic for the fantasies of a newly unified world after the "fall" of the socialist states.

7   "To go west" also means to die, and to "be destroyed; to disappear, vanish; to end in failure, come to grief" (*Oxford English Dictionary*). This is however not where the queer pun-play ends. Pet Shop Boys performed this song at the AIDS Charity event in 1992, https://web.archive.org/web/20120827184236/http://www.petshopboys .net/html/interviews/very012.shtml; accessed February 21, 2022.

8   Kolářová, *Rehabilitative Postsocialism*.

9   Gal and Kligman, *Politics of Gender*, 17; Sokolová, "Don't Get Pricked!," 253.

10 Petr Václav, dir., *Cesta ven*, 2014.

11 Cf. Kim, "Toward a Crip-of-Color Critique"; Minich, "Enabling Whom?"

12 Kolářová, "Mediating," 159.

13 Grodecki, "Chtěl," 45.

14 Havel quoted in Kolářová, "Mediating," 157. Grodecki proudly noted that the then Czech president Havel sent him a letter commending him for his films; https://www .barrandovfilmschool.com/about-founder/.

15 Kafer, *Feminist, Queer, Crip.*

16 Kim, *Curative Violence*, 18.

17 Chen, "'Stuff of Slow Constitution.'"

18 Muñoz, *Disidentifications.*

19 Ahmed, *Queer Phenomenology*, 115.

20 Ahmed, *Queer Phenomenology*, 122.

21 Ahmed, *Queer Phenomenology*, 121; cf. Povinelli, "Notes on Gridlock."

22 Ahmed, *Queer Phenomenology*, 121.

23 Kulpa and Mizielińska, *De-centering Western Sexualities.*

24 Gržinić, "Europe's Colonialism," 135.

25 Lowe, *Intimacies*, 9.

26 Shaw, *Deaf in the USSR*; Kolářová and Winkler, *Re/Imaginations of Disability*; Galmarini-Kabala, "Between Defectological Narratives."

27 These knowledge transfers in the Czechoslovakian context still wait for a comprehensive mapping and analysis. See also Phillips, *Disability and Mobile Citizenship*; Rasell and Iarskaia-Smirnova, *Disability in Eastern Europe.*

28 The in-depth analysis and discussion of these specific knowledge transfers and their embeddedness into economic and ideological circuits of exchange is beyond the space and scope of this essay. To offer a short example to substantiate my claims, the archive of one of the organizations working with people with intellectual disabilities contained materials from this course that I was allowed to go through. It featured a special "module" discussing "transition," that is, the efforts to bring people with intellectual disability from institutional to community living; other materials put emphasis on work and employment of people with intellectual disabilities. The here-quoted phrase is taken from a handwritten handout that included the following quotes and references: "Definitions of normalization: Nirje, Bengt, 1969; 'making available to the mentally retarded patterns and conditions of everyday life which are as close as possible to the norms and patterns of the mainstream of society.'" It also included several quotes from Wolf Wolfensberger (1972): "utilisazation of means which are as culturally normative as possible in order to establish and/or maintain personal behaviours and characteristics which are as culturally normative as possible"; Wolfensberger (1983): "the most explicit and highest goal of normalization must be the creation, support, and defence *of valued social roles* for people who are at risk of social devaluation" (emphasis original).

29 For more on this, see, e.g., Shmidt, *Child Welfare*; Shmidt, *Politics of Disability*; Henschel, "Embodiment of Deviance."

30 Kolářová and Herza, "Engineering Socialist Integration."

31 For a discussion of related conundrums, see Lezlie Frye's chapter in this volume.

32 Ahmed, *Queer Phenomenology*, 143.

33 Verdery, *What Was Socialism*, np.

34 Quoted in Bunzl, "Prague Experience," 78.

35 The notion of "backwardness" of the Eastern European region has a very long and influential history. Larry Wolff's *Inventing Eastern Europe* (1994) traces it back to the Enlightenment's narratives of progress, rationality, and science. The Cold War and the fall of the Soviet "bloc" have reinvigorated such ideological constructions of Eastern Europe. Chirot's *The Origins of Backwardness in Eastern Europe* (1991) can stand as one of the illustrative examples of this trend. The website promoting the book claims to "mak[e] a convincing case for very deep roots of current Eastern European backwardness" (https://jsis.washington.edu/publication/the-origins-of -backwardness-in-eastern-europe/; accessed July 22, 2022). Apart from the already quoted works that unravel the coloniality of such a claim, I would like to point out Dzenovska's *School of Europeanness* (2018), or the newest collection of feminist, queer, and antiracist work on dialogues between postcolonialism and postsocialism: Koobak, Tlostanova, and Thapar-Björkert, *Postcolonial and Postsocialist Dialogues* (2021).

36 For discussion of the racialized nature of the image of "un petit slavs," see, for instance, Melegh, *On the East-West Slope*.

37 Sádlík, "*Mandragora* varuje," 6.

38 Sádlík, "*Mandragora* varuje," 6.

39 Jeníková, "Šokující dokument," 5.

40 Lederer, "*Mandragora* šokuje," 7 (emphasis added).

41 Grodecki, "Kdo," 120–21.

42 Vrábková, "Women's Priorities and Visions," 74–75 (emphasis added).

43 Bunzl, "The Prague Experience," 78.

44 Cacho, *Social Death*.

45 The public discussion of the Czech Roma and Sinti holocaust concentrated around one specific location, the location of the war concentration camp close to the South-Bohemian village, Lety. The socialist state built a pig farm precisely on the location of the camp for Roma, Sinti, and people that lived "Gypsy life-style" (Pape, *A nikdo vám nebude věřit*). Since 1989, the Roma activists have been pushing for closing the farm and creating a respectable commemoration site. It took till 2017 to get the Czech government to support and finance this move. The public debates and the fact that it took nearly thirty years to move the pig farm from the place of former concentration camps where hundreds of Roma Czech citizens died is indicative of the respect, value, and recognition granted to Roma citizens; it is also indicative of the limits of collective belonging and identification and the whiteness of the imagined "national body" in the post-1989 Czech/oslovakia. The pig farm was finally being torn down in July 2022, as we were finalizing the work on this chapter.

46 It would be a misguided fantasy to believe that we can record all forms of race-motivated violence and aggression. It is, however, important to recall the names of at least some of the Roma people murdered during the 1990s: Emil Bendík (†23 February 1991), Tibor Berki (†13 May 1995), Helena Biháriová (†15 February 1998), Erika Gáborová (†20 September 1997), Milan Lacko (†17 May 1998).

47 Admittedly, they would also transgress the disability knowledges married to visions of socialist collective utopia and the socialist versions of respectable politics.

48 *Diderot* (*Všeobecná encyklopedie*).
49 Lorenz, "The Chronic," np.
50 Lorenz, "The Chronic," np.
51 The Roma women who suffered this procedure did not receive reparations until 2021.
52 Berlant, *Cruel Optimism*.

10. THE BLACK PANTHER PARTY'S 504 ACTIVISM AS A GENEALOGICAL PRECURSOR TO DISABILITY JUSTICE TODAY

SAMI SCHALK

On May 7, 1977, the cover story of the *Black Panther*, the weekly newspaper of the Black Panther Party (BPP), read "HANDICAPPED WIN DEMANDS—END H.E.W. OCCUPATION." The page included three images: the first photo features two Black men—a wheelchair user, Brad Lomax, and his fellow Panther member, Chuck Jackson, who stands behind Brad's chair; the second image is of a blind Black man named Dennis Billups, holding up a protest sign that says, "You don't have to see to know"; and the third picture is of a crowd of people of various races outside a building with a seemingly non-Black woman wheelchair user in the center of the frame.[1] Cover stories are reserved for the most important or pressing news of a particular moment. The choice to place a disability rights activist win on the cover of a Black activist newspaper is undeniably symbolic of the BPP's belief that the success of the Health, Education and Welfare (HEW) occupation, now more commonly referred to as the 504 sit-in or the 504 demonstration, was not merely important news, but news relevant and connected to the Panthers' own antiracist, anticapitalist, and antiimperialist work. The placement of the success of the 504 demonstration on the cover of the *Black Panther* is in many ways the height of disability politics within the Black Panther Party. It is the most explicit and symbolically significant moment of coalition and solidarity with disabled people in the entirety of the paper's publication between 1967 and 1980, and thus provides a launching point for this essay.

The Black Panther Party was a revolutionary, antiracist, anticapitalist, antiimperialist organization started in Oakland, California, in 1966. The Panthers originally focused their activities on armed self-defense and patrol of police within Black communities, rapidly obtaining national and international

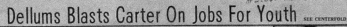

FIGURE 10.1. Cover of the *Black Panther* on May 7, 1977. Alexander Street Black Thought & Culture Digital Archive.

membership and influence. While the Panthers reached their membership height in the late 1960s, their political influence and activities continued until 1982.[2] In the 1970s, however, under intense scrutiny and suppression by the FBI as well as in response to changes in gun laws, the BPP shifted its focus away from armed resistance to community survival programs, such as their breakfast for children program and free health clinics. This shift was reflected in changes to their ten-point platform. The first version of the BPP's platform, drafted in October 1966, focused on freedom and the "power to determine the destiny of our Black Community" via calls for full employment, "land, bread, housing, education, clothing, justice and peace."[3] In March 1972, however, the platform was revised in two key ways that reflected changes in the priorities and investments of the BPP. First, point one was changed to call for freedom and the "power to determine the destiny of our Black *and oppressed communities*."[4] Second, the ten points were expanded to include a call for "completely free health care for all Black and oppressed people."[5] In this later era of the Black Panther Party, party members began to more explicitly articulate forms of disability politics as exhibited by their engagement with the 504 demonstration.

The 504 demonstration was a major milestone in the disability rights movement. It was a twenty-five-day occupation of the San Francisco regional office of the Department of Health, Education and Welfare, during which more than a hundred protesters refused to leave until the national HEW secretary, Joseph Califano, signed into effect regulations for Section 504 of the 1973 Rehabilitation Act. Section 504 was the first piece of federal legislation dictating civil rights for disabled people. It stated that programs receiving federal funds, such as public schools and universities, could not discriminate against or exclude qualified people on the basis of disability. Although the Rehabilitation Act was signed in 1973, Section 504 wouldn't go into effect until regulations that defined who was disabled and what constituted discrimination were drafted and approved. After years of delays, disability rights activists nationwide organized, warning that if the regulations were not signed by their deadline, they would stage sit-ins at HEW offices across the country on April 7, 1977. The protests in Washington, DC, and other locations lasted for a single day, but the protest in San Francisco continued for weeks, thanks to careful planning and organizing by disabled activists in the Bay Area. The occupation of the HEW building in San Francisco garnered extensive local and national news coverage, ending only when the regulations were finally signed. The 504 sit-in remains the longest nonviolent occupation of a federal building in US history.

In most scholarly accounts of the 504 demonstration, the role of the Panthers is relegated to a brief mention that the BPP provided food throughout the twenty-five-day occupation of the San Francisco Health, Education and Welfare regional office building.[6] Though several scholars of the Black Panther Party have written about the BPP's community survival programs and health activism in the 1970s, no Panther scholarship discusses their involvement in the 504 sit-in. Only Susan Schweik's "Lomax's Matrix: Disability, Solidarity, and the Black Power of 504" provides extensive scholarly engagement with this history, though recent publications by disability activists and the Longmore Institute's *Patient No More* exhibit on the 504 demonstration have added new details on the role of the BPP as well.[7] This chapter builds on this work to add additional details about the BPP's engagement with the sit-in and place this activism in conversation with contemporary articulations of disability justice.

Disability justice is a relatively new activist practice and framework developed in the mid-2000s by disabled people of color, disabled queer people, and disabled queer people of color, such as Patty Berne, Mia Mingus, Leroy Moore, Leah Lakshmi Piepzna-Samarasinha, and the group Sins Invalid. It builds on and extends the work of the early disability rights movement, which was often very white, middle-class, and single-issue-focused. Those involved with disability justice readily acknowledge that they appreciate and benefit from the advancements achieved by the early disability rights movement. However, not dissimilar from how the Black Panthers were responding to the fact that African Americans had achieved legal civil rights, yet were still socially and materially oppressed, disability justice practitioners seek a broader understanding of anti-ableism that is not limited to state-sanctioned civil rights, which often benefit primarily disabled people who are already relatively privileged by race, class, gender, sexuality, and citizenship status. Further, disability justice is an inherently intersectional approach. Patty Berne writes that disability justice understands white supremacy and ableism as "inextricably entwined, both forged in the crucible of colonial conquest and capitalist domination.... [Therefore, one] cannot comprehend ableism without grasping its interrelations with heteropatriarchy, white supremacy, colonialism and capitalism."[8] Disability justice values and centers leadership of those most affected (i.e., multiply marginalized disabled people), anticapitalism, cross-movement organizing, sustainability, cross-disability solidarity, interdependence, collective access, and collective liberation.[9] Practitioners of disability justice recognize that their work "already connects and overlaps with many movements and communities' work," especially work by feminist and queer people of color within reproductive justice, transformative justice, and healing justice groups.[10] Finally, disability justice challenges medical and legal definitions of who is and is not disabled, consciously and purposefully including those who are sick and chronically ill in their work.

In this chapter I argue that the Black Panther Party's material and ideological solidarity with 504 activists can be read as a genealogical precursor to disability justice today. The term *genealogical precursor* draws both from the work of Black feminist literary theorist Ann DuCille, who argues for an understanding of Black—especially Black women's—literary traditions that is "far less natural, absolute, linear, and homogeneous than" scholarly efforts at official canon building might suggest, and from the work of Michel Foucault, who uses the term *genealogy* to suggest a historical method that moves away from grand progressive narratives to instead emphasize the multiple origins of cultural changes.[11] I use *genealogical precursor*, therefore, to describe something of the past that has historical, ideological, and material connections to something of the present in ways that cannot be determined in a purely linear or causational way. One might trace genealogical precursors by charting how the work, scholarship, or activism of one individual or group was influenced by or benefited from the work of another individual or group through multiple layers of temporal or geographical remove. As such, I do not intend to present a progressive narrative in which the Black Panther Party represents a past Black engagement with disability that we replace with disability justice, even as their work contained ableist missteps. Instead, I use the term *genealogical precursor* to argue that concepts undergirding disability justice today were circulating in different, but related, ways within the activities of the Black Panther Party and that this circulation of similar ideas is important to understanding the history of disability politics within activism by Black people and other people of color, which is so often overlooked and erased in disability studies.

By connecting concepts in disability justice to the BPP's work in the 1970s, I argue that disability studies scholars and activists must expand our understanding not only of what constitutes disability politics today, as disability justice activists are doing, but also of what constituted disability politics in the past, especially within Black and other oppressed populations. Disability politics within marginalized communities have sometimes been overlooked by disability studies scholars because these groups oftentimes use different language, frameworks, and approaches than white mainstream disability rights groups. This chapter, therefore, seeks to partially correct this misrecognition by modeling analysis of the Black Panther Party as one illustrative example of how disability politics are articulated within groups who do not view themselves as exclusively or primarily disability rights groups. In doing so, I aim to encourage more nuanced readings of disability history that include people of color while still interrogating the whiteness and racism of the disability rights movement and disability studies more generally. Therefore, rather than approaching this history from the angle of *how did Black people participate in the disability rights movement?*, I instead ask, *how did issues of disability appear within Black activist movements and how can we understand this as part of disability activist history?* More specifically, as a literary and cultural theorist, I use the BPP's own explanation of their work, primarily via the *Black Panther* newspaper, to understand how they engaged disability politics as an integrative part of their revolutionary agenda. To do so, I undertake a detailed analysis of the multiple ways the BPP was involved with the demonstration and how they rhetorically positioned disability rights in relation to their larger activist goals and ideology. In closing, I briefly discuss other ways that the BPP was involved in issues of disability both before and after the 504 demonstration, in order to underscore that disability politics, while not often explicitly centered in the Panthers' work, was understood as integral to achieving radical liberation and justice for all in the United States.

"We've Always Been Involved": Black Panthers and the 504 Sit-In

The Black Panthers were involved with the 504 demonstration from start to finish, participating via the most commonly cited activity of providing daily food deliveries, as well as sending representatives to give speeches, putting out a press release endorsement, supporting two members of the BPP in their roles inside the protest, and publishing numerous articles in the *Black Panther*. I discuss each of these activities in turn.

Nearly all accounts of the sit-in note that a major part of its success was due to extensive coalitional support. This support came in the form of volunteers, donations, and endorsements from a variety of other activist groups and organizations focused on not only disability rights, but also gay rights, women's liberation, civil rights, and more.[12] Organizers of the 504 demonstration secured this support in the planning stages of the protest and expanded their reach throughout the duration of the sit-in. While the Black Panther Party was not listed as part of the "504 Emergency Coalition" in the first press release by protest organizers, according to HolLynn D'Lil, who acted as insider photographer and press for the protest, BPP member Ellis White spoke at a rally on the first day of the demonstration, April 5, 1977.[13] D'Lil quotes White as later saying: "We've always been involved. We've had reps here from the beginning. The issue is self-determination. More human rights. Whether handicapped people have a right to survive. Whatever they do to ensure survival, we support. Califano threw drug addicts and alcoholics out of the handicapped group. They belong too. The issue is money. It's in keeping with our principles—survival."[14]

Here White insists on not only the early involvement of the Panthers in the 504 demonstration, but also how their involvement was directly in line with the BPP's "principles," that is, the ten-point platform, which first and foremost called for freedom and self-determination for all oppressed communities. The Black Panther Party understood disabled people, along with other people of color, people in poverty, women, and gays and lesbians, to be fellow oppressed members of society who had to fight for survival in a racist and ableist capitalist system. This understanding of the need to fight for the survival of all oppressed people aligns with the cross-movement solidarity and collective liberation emphasized within disability justice.

The BPP's solidarity with disabled people in general and the 504 protesters specifically is further articulated in their April 8, 1977, press release, written and delivered by Michael Fultz, editor of the *Black Panther*.[15] The statement reads,

> Along with all fair and good-thinking people, The Black Panther Party gives its full support to Section 504 of the 1973 Rehabilitation Act and calls for President Carter and HEW Secretary Califano to sign guidelines for its implementation as negotiated and agreed to on January 21 of this year. The issue here is human rights—rights of meaningful employment, of education, of basic human survival—of an oppressed minority, the disabled and handicapped. Further, we deplore the treatment accorded to the occupants of the fourth floor and join with them in full solidarity.[16]

Like White's statement above, here the BPP's official public endorsement also emphasizes human rights, survival, and solidarity among oppressed groups. The BPP's role, however, was not limited to being a supporter in name alone; the Panthers also contributed in key material ways.

First, at least two members of the BPP, Brad Lomax and Chuck Jackson, the disabled and nondisabled Black men featured on the May 7 cover of the *Black Panther*, were on the inside, as part of the sit-in, and also acted as two of the representative delegates to Washington, DC, for the 504 Coalition. As a disabled member of the Black Panther Party, Lomax worked to incorporate disability politics into the efforts of the BPP. That said, as a rank-and-file member, Lomax's work had to align with the goals and ideology of the BPP. In an interview, former BPP leader Elaine Brown asserts that Lomax's participation in the 504 demonstration and his work at the Center for Independent Living (CIL) was considered part of his work for the Panthers. Lomax's work, therefore, is an example of the key role that multiply marginalized individuals play in acting as a bridge between groups and is also a reflection of disability justice's valuing of leadership by those most affected. Brown elaborates that while Brad Lomax and Ed Roberts, leader of the CIL, brought awareness of disability rights to the Panthers, the BPP's existing ideological position of focusing on systemic change for all marginalized groups meant that further transforming their thinking to include disability politics "wasn't hard."[17] Brown states that soon after being made aware of disability politics, the BPP ordered all of its buildings to install wheelchair access ramps. Brad Lomax was an essential figure, whose multiply marginalized identities fostered connection between the Panthers and disability rights. The BPP's investment in the sit-in and disability politics more generally, however, was rooted in the Panthers' broader coalitional and revolutionary thinking.

As most accounts of the Panthers' involvement in the demonstration state, the Panthers also contributed materially by donating food. More specifically, once it became clear that the sit-in was going to continue beyond a day or two, the BPP began bringing daily hot dinners, such as fried chicken or meatloaf.[18] The BPP also, according to Brown, brought in mobile showers for the protesters and supplied a form of security as well.[19] Although the exact form of this security is unclear, it is apparent that members of the BPP, familiar with the tactics of federal agencies and the police, ensured that supplies got through the door. For example, one *Black Panther* article stated that more than a week into the sit-in, "with all incoming telephone service abruptly cut-off, and all food denied entry—Party members saw to it that a sympathetic guard 'discreetly' allowed the breakfast foods they had brought upstairs to the demonstrators."[20] Similarly, in her memoir, Corbett O'Toole writes,

> I happened to be in the lobby the first night that the Black Panthers brought us dinner. The FBI blocked them and told them to leave. The Panthers, being extremely sophisticated about how to manage police interactions, merely informed the FBI that they would be bringing dinner every night of the occupation. They would bring the food, they would set it up, and they would leave. If the FBI prevented them from doing that they would go back to Oakland and bring more Black Panthers until the food got delivered to the protesters. The FBI soon backed down.[21]

The material support provided by the Panthers in the form of members on the inside, food, and supplies was essential to the longevity of the protest, but perhaps most importantly for the historical record is the extensive coverage of the demonstration the BPP provided in their newspaper.

For the majority of the BPP's existence, from 1967 to 1980, the *Black Panther* newspaper served as one of the BPP's main political tools, providing a way to inform members and raise money. The paper included a wide range of news stories about injustices done to Black people across the country as well as advertisements for Panther programs, political cartoons, educational and theoretical articles on social issues, and international news from other revolutionary anti-imperialist causes. In 1977, the *Black Panther* provided the most national coverage of the 504 protest—only one local paper, the *San Francisco Chronicle*, covered it more often. The BPP published ten articles and announcements of varying lengths about the demonstration between April 16 and July 7.[22] After the demonstration ended, the 504 sit-in was mentioned an additional eight times in the paper in related stories, such as "Protest Systematic Exclusion: Disabled Sue A.C. Transit" and "Disabled Score Victory over Supermarket Barriers: Blind Mother Fights Bias for Custody of Children."[23]

The *Black Panther* coverage of the demonstration is significant because it meant that thousands of Black people were being informed of disability rights in a way that framed disability politics as directly connected to Black community concerns—as part of a larger radical agenda for freedom for all oppressed communities.[24] The impact of a major Black activist organization directly supporting and increasing awareness of disability rights among Black Americans cannot be directly calculated. Nonetheless, the national distribution of the *Black Panther*'s coverage adds to my argument for reading the BPP's work as a genealogical precursor to disability justice because it is a moment in which, rather than distancing themselves from disability, as is so often the narrative about communities of color and disability, Black people embraced and understood disability politics as a necessary interrelated part of collective liberation overall.

The articles in the *Black Panther* portrayed the sit-in as an important and necessary act, calling it "a powerful and significant protest for human and civil rights of handicapped and disabled people."[25] The rhetoric in the paper makes clear the connections between the disability politics being enacted in the sit-in and the work the BPP had already been doing to increase the freedoms of oppressed people. In the first article on the demonstration, for example, the paper noted that, "despite stereotypes and stigmas, real and very much alive" protesters "have embarked upon a serious drive to control and transform the oppressive conditions of their lives."[26] The emphasis on oppression, stereotypes, stigma, and other sociopolitical concerns in the *Black Panther*'s representation of the 504 sit-in presented readers a social model of disability that paralleled the BPP's own understanding of race and class oppressions.[27] In an address at a victory rally after the end of the demonstration, leading member of the BPP, Erika Huggins, a former political prisoner with arthritis who was denied adequate medical care during her incarceration,[28] made the connection of oppressions explicit when she stated that "the United States has always had its niggers.... And they come in all sizes, shapes, colors, classes, and disabilities, ... The signing of 504, this demonstration, the sit-in, this beautiful thing that has happened these past weeks, is all to say that the niggers are going to be set free."[29] To the Black Panther Party, therefore, disability rights were an obvious part of their goal to obtain freedom and self-determination for all oppressed communities, here metaphorized into "niggers" as a generalized term for those excluded and exploited within the United States, not inherently tied to race alone.

Further, in line with the Black Panthers' critiques of the federal government, the newspaper also highlighted the Ford and Carter administrations' failures to follow through with implementing the 504 regulations. Unlike other nationally distributed papers, which often mentioned 504 regulation implementation costs and resistance rationales alongside coverage of the protest, the *Black Panther* focused on rights, access, and empowerment.[30] The one time the newspaper did discuss the costs of mandating accessibility, it was to critique a cost-benefit model of decision making. The editorial article sarcastically asks, "How much will it cost us for 'you people' to have your human rights?" before detailing the estimated costs alongside the profits "the newly-employed disabled people will add to the gross national product."[31] The article estimates that "to allow 35 million Americans to have an equal access/barrier-free environment necessary to live full and decent lives" will cost "a little over 8 ½ cents per disabled person. Not very much at all."[32] The editorial continues by stating, "How much? Well, from the human point of view, a great deal more than the racists and reactionaries are willing to give up without a fight. If the rednecks and the others don't have 'cripples' to hate and make fun of anymore; if 'niggers' and the rest of the oppressed in this society aren't the enemy anymore, then who will all that anger and frustration built up within the 'silent majority' be turned against?"[33] Here once again, the BPP makes direct connections between the operation of racism and ableism in ways that do not seek to compete or compare, but rather, connect.

One of the concerns when analyzing how marginalized groups discuss "other" forms of oppression is that those who are multiply marginalized are sometimes erased from the conversation. In the case of the *Black Panther*'s coverage of the 504 sit-in, however, Black disabled people and disabled people of color were prioritized. In addition to the direct involvement of Black disabled Panther Brad Lomax, the newspaper published an interview with Dennis Billups, the blind Black man pictured on the May 7 cover.[34] In the interview, Billups encouraged his "brothers and sisters that are Black and that are handicapped" to "Get out there, we need you. Come here, we need you. Wherever you are, we need you."[35] The interview with Billups was edited, so the choice of what to include is purposeful. It is particularly important that the editors included the following statement from Billups: "I'm not a member of the Black Panther Party. I'd like to join the Black Panther Party. I am a member of the Black Panther Party as far as my own initiative and soul is concerned. They have fed us. They have given us respect. They have treated us as human beings."[36] This quote not only reflects the BPP in a positive light, emphasizing their coalitional work, but also suggests that the BPP wanted to highlight the potential for (more) Black disabled involvement and inclusion within their work via Billups's statement.

Further, this interview with Billups and a later interview with Lomax together acknowledge the particularity of the lives of Black disabled people and other disabled people of color.[37] A decade before the coining of the term *intersectionality*, Lomax referred to being Black and disabled as "multi-disabilities," while, in another article on the congressional hearings at the San Francisco HEW office, the *Black Panther* made sure to include mention of a minority panel of four people, "all of whom eloquently expressed the 'double whammy' experienced by handicapped minorities."[38] The choice to include explicit representations of disabled people of color demonstrates the BPP's commitment to intersectional thinking, a key aspect of disability justice today. Throughout their coverage of the demonstration, the *Black Panther* interviewed, quoted, and named several other individual protesters, often protesters of color. Other papers almost exclusively interviewed and quoted the white disabled leaders of the protest, such as Judy Huemann, Kitty Cone, and Ed Roberts, as well as HEW officials and politicians. The inclusion of so many rank-and-file protesters in the newspaper's coverage of the sit-in reflects the BPP's emphasis on the "power of the people" and the role that every individual has to play in a revolutionary agenda.[39] Importantly, in an interview for the *Patient No More* exhibit, Dennis Billups said that he felt excluded at times during the protest and has been surprised to see how much he has been left out of the historical record of the 504 demonstration.[40] This further underscores the importance of the *Black Panther* to the intersectional history of the sit-in. Further, the Panthers' emphasis on the power of the people relates to disability justice principles like interdependence and collective liberation, which also rely on people contributing and participating in whatever ways they are able with the support of others who can contribute and participate in other ways.

All of this is not to say, of course, that there was no ableism within the BPP or within its representations of disabled people and disability rights. The *Black*

Panther's coverage of the 504 demonstration occasionally used ableist language, such as describing the protest as "inspiring" or "most poignant," while also repeatedly referring to Brad Lomax as being "victimized by multiple sclerosis."[41] This language, Schweik argues, reveals "a general lack of disability consciousness" within the BPP.[42] Schweik's choice of the term "disability consciousness" here is essential, because it highlights that the Panthers were generally not yet aware of how language was being used and transformed within disability rights communities even as they supported the work emerging from disabled activists. The use of this type of language does suggest that writers and editors for the *Black Panther* had not fully divested themselves of ableist thinking.

However, within the overall rhetoric used in articles about the sit-in, the language leans toward progressive for its time, such as using both handicapped and disabled as descriptors. Furthermore, the intent was still predominantly aligned with a disability rights approach rather than with a medical or charity model of disability that words like *inspiring* and *victim* might suggest. For example, the word *inspiring* was almost always used in conjunction with another adjective, such as "inspiring and powerful" protest, "tremendous, inspiring victory," or "spectacular and inspiring victory," which, while not negating the ableist implications of inspiration, suggest that what was inspiring was the protest's power, length, and success more than merely the fact that it was done by disabled people.[43] Importantly, the words inspiring and inspiration were never used to describe any disabled individual, but rather in reference to the protest, the victory, and once, to the fact that the Black civil rights song "We Shall Overcome" was used as "an unofficial theme song" and as a "source of hope and inspiration" by the protesters.[44] Taken as a whole then, while the BPP was perhaps imperfect in its execution, especially in regard to ableist language, the Black Panthers strongly supported the 504 demonstration in material and ideological ways because of their existing revolutionary agenda seeking freedom and self-determination for all oppressed people. The BPP's support of the demonstration, in the form of public endorsements, members participating in the sit-in, delivery of food and other supplies, and extensive coverage in their newspaper, is representative of how the Panthers' ideology included space for disability politics in a way that can be read as a genealogical precursor to disability justice today.

The BPP and Disability Politics beyond the 504

The success of the 504 sit-in depended on a number of factors: the planning, tenacity, and creativity of the protesters; the extensive media coverage, which put pressure on politicians; and even, ironically, the ableism of employees at the HEW office who deeply underestimated the resolve and capabilities of disabled people, notoriously patronizing protesters the first day by serving punch and cookies.[45] The occupation could not have lasted as long and safely as it did, however, without the extended network of supportive groups and organizations, such as the Black Panther Party. Schweik argues that this support is often framed as coming from "other" activist groups in a way that erases the connections and overlaps among social justice organizations and individual identities. To address this potential erasure of enactments of disability politics in non-disability-focused organizations and movements, Alison Kafer proposes an "expansive approach to disability politics" that centers coalition.[46] To take Kafer's proposal seriously, we ought to look beyond the singular, though important, moment of the Panthers' support of the 504 demonstration in the spring of 1977 to the BPP's additional engagements with disability-related issues to recognize the various ways disability politics were enacted within the antiracist activities of the BPP. We might look, for example, to the June 1977 educational community forum for people with disabilities titled "We Have a Right to Live," held at the Panthers' Oakland Community Learning Center and emceed by Lomax as a clear example of how the party followed up with their investment in disability rights after the conclusion of the 504 sit-in.[47] Extending even more widely, we might also explore the BPP's health activism via free clinics, their fight for improved medical care within prisons and jails, or their advocacy against the creation of a Center for the Study of Violence at UCLA that would participate in experimental psychosurgery research on populations deemed violent. Each of these issues represents a key area of radical Black activism that intersects with disability justice in ways not yet explored within disability studies or Black and African American studies.

While disability studies scholars may debate where the boundaries of the field might be, particularly in regard to issues of health, illness, and disease, disability justice activists and thinkers "are building an analysis that includes political and historical understandings of disability, bodies, ableism, pace, illness, care, cure, aging, the medical industrial complex and access."[48] Disability justice activists often include terms like sick and chronically ill to acknowledge and include people who may not identify as disabled, especially those who have been made sick or ill because of white supremacist and heteropatriarchal violence. To fully understand how the work of the Black Panther Party and other social justice groups primarily aligned with antiracism, antisexism, or antihomophobia serve as genealogical precursors to current articulations of disability justice, we must explore beyond their involvement with actions explicitly connected to disability rights to look at health and medical activism more broadly.

We must, as disability justice practitioners argue, move beyond a civil rights framework to a justice framework. When disability studies scholars expand our understanding of what constitutes disability politics, understanding that disability politics can be enacted by those who might never call their work disability activism or identify themselves as disabled, then we can begin to build a stronger understanding of how disability activism and anti-ableist thinking has occurred historically within a wide range of activist and community spaces, especially among racialized and other oppressed groups. This understanding of diverse enactments of disability politics within the activism of racial, gender, and sexuality minority groups can aid in building better coalitions. The work of the Black Panther Party therefore is merely one illustrative example of this kind of intersectional anti-ableist work, which values cross-movement solidarity and therefore serves as a useful genealogical precursor to disability justice activism today.

NOTES

1   The original image caption misidentified Dennis Billups as Dennis Phillips, but he is mentioned and quoted in other articles under his proper name.
2   For more extended histories of the BPP, see Bloom and Martin, *Black against Empire*; Nelson, *Body and Soul*; or Spencer, *The Revolution Has Come*.
3   "History of the Black Panther Party: Black Panther Party Platform and Program," The Black Panther Party Research Project, https://web.stanford.edu/group /blackpanthers/history.shtml, accessed May 20, 2017.
4   "History of the Black Panther Party" (emphasis added).
5   "History of the Black Panther Party."
6   For example, see Fleischer and Zames, *Disability Rights Movement*, 54; Shaw, *Activist's Handbook*, 240; Shapiro, *No Pity*, 67; Longmore, *Why I Burned My Book*, 107; Meade and Serlin, "Editors' Introduction," 2; and Scotch, *From Good Will to Civil Rights*, 115.
7   See D'Lil, *Becoming Real in 24 Days*; O'Toole, *Fading Scars*; Moore, "Black History of 504 Sit-In"; and Thompson "Black History Month 2017."
8   Berne, "Disability Justice," 11.
9   Berne and the Sins Invalid Family, "10 Principles of Disability Justice."
10 Mingus, "Reflection toward Practice," 108.
11 DuCille, *Coupling Convention*, 147; Foucault, *Discipline and Punish*, 185–86.
12 Groups who provided support for the 504 protesters "included the Butterfly Brigade, 'a group of gay men who patrolled city streets on the lookout for gay violence,' who smuggled walkie-talkies into the occupied building; Glide Church; local and national labor organizations; members of Delancey Street, the famous grassroots rehab program for substance abusers and former felons, who brought breakfast into the building each day; the Chicano group Mission Rebels, who also provided food; and the Black Panthers." Schweik, "Lomax's Matrix."

13   D'Lil, *Becoming Real in 24 Days*, 19, 57.

14   D'Lil, *Becoming Real in 24 Days*, 56. Based on the location of this quote in the book, it's unclear whether the quote comes from White's rally speech on April 5 or from later, most likely on April 8, the fourth day of the protest, which is the chapter in which this quote and White's photo (captioned as an image from his rally speech) both appear.

15   In a footnote, Schweik includes informal communication with Fultz in which he recalls organizing the Panthers' delivery of food and giving an "extemporaneous" speech at the protest because Elaine Brown, leader of the BPP at that time, was unable to attend. I have been unable to locate any transcript or date of Fultz's speech. D'Lil lists Brown as "outside support." D'Lil, *Becoming Real in 24 Days*, 58.

16   Quoted in D'Lil, *Becoming Real in 24 Days*, 58.

17   Brown, "Leader of the Black Panther Party."

18   "Rights for Disabled at Issue, B.P.P. Lends Support: Powerful Protest by Handicapped at H.E.W.," *Black Panther*, April 16, 1977, pp. 4, 20.

19   Brown, "Leader of the Black Panther Party."

20   "Rights for Disabled at Issue," 4.

21   O'Toole, *Fading Scars*, 60.

22   The *Black Panther* articles and announcements about the sit-in were "Rights for Disabled at Issue"; "Comment: The Harder You Look into the Light, the Brighter You Become," April 23, 1977, pp. 2, 12; "Bulletin," April 23, 1977, p. 2; "Delegation to Go to Washington, Demand H.E.W. Sign 504: Hearings, Support Rally Highlight Handicapped Protest," April 23, 1977, pp. 4, 12; "Carter, HEW Secretary Califano Snub Disabled Delegation: Handicapped Rally—Sign 504 Now," April 30, 1977, pp. 4, 10; "Pressure Forces Califano to Sign 504 Regulations: Handicapped Win Demands—End H.E.W. Occupation," May 7, 1977, pp. 1, 6; "Editorial: What Price Freedom," May 7, 1977, p. 2; "504: Civil Rights for the Disabled," May 7, 1977, p. 5; "BPP Members Interviewed on Handicapped Protest for Civil and Human Rights. Disabled Movement Born: 'We Have a Right to Rebel,'" May 14, 1977, pp. 5, 8; and Joan Tollifson, "Comment: Disabled: We Are No Longer Invisible," July 2, 1977, pp. 2, 12.

23   "Protest Systematic Exclusion: Disabled Sue A.C. Transit," *Black Panther*, July 2, 1977, p. 14; "Disabled Score Victory over Supermarket Barriers: Blind Mother Fights Bias for Custody of Children," *Black Panther*, August 13, 1977, p. 10.

24   The number of people who received or read the paper can only be estimated. In May 1978 the editor of the *Black Panther* estimated they printed approximately 5,500 copies of the paper per issue. Spencer, *The Revolution Has Come*, 192.

25   "Rights for Disabled at Issue," 4.

26   "Rights for Disabled at Issue," 20.

27   A version of the social model was explicitly included in a quote from a protester, who stated, "If they'd take away the handicaps (like stairs, and others barriers for wheelchair-confined and otherwise disabled people), then we wouldn't be handicapped." "Rights for Disabled at Issue," 20.

28   See "Medical Malpractice as Methods of Torture at Niantic State Farm for Women," *Black Panther*, November 21, 1970, p. 17.

29 Quoted in "Pressure Forces Califano," 6.

30 For examples of other articles in major national papers that focused much more on cost, see Hicks, "Equity for Disabled," 29, or Bill Peterson, "Schools Hit Cost of Ending Bias," A8.

31 "Editorial: What Price Freedom," 2.

32 "Editorial: What Price Freedom," 2.

33 "Editorial: What Price Freedom," 2.

34 The Paul K. Longmore Institute on Disability's exhibit, *Patient No More*, includes an important interview with Billups about his experience with the 504 sit-in. See Billups, "Disability Rights Activist Dennis Billups."

35 "Comment: The Harder You Look," 12.

36 "Comment: The Harder You Look," 2.

37 "BPP Members Interviewed," 5, 8.

38 "BPP Members Interviewed," 8; and "Delegation to Go to Washington," 12.

39 "BPP Members Interviewed," 5.

40 Billups, "Disability Rights Activist Dennis Billups."

41 "Carter, HEW Secretary Califano Snub," 10; "Delegation to Go to Washington," 4; and "Pressure Forces Califano," 6. Across the ten articles covering the 504 demonstration in the *Black Panther*, approximately ten thousand words total, the words *inspiring* or *inspiration* were used six times total, the word *poignant* was used twice, and the words *victimized* or *victim* were used four times (all four in reference to Lomax's multiple sclerosis).

42 Schweik, "Lomax's Matrix."

43 "Carter, HEW Secretary Califano Snub," 10; "Editorial: What Price Freedom," 2; and "BPP Members Interviewed," 5.

44 "Pressure Forces Califano," 1.

45 Shapiro, *No Pity*, 66.

46 Kafer, *Feminist, Queer, Crip*, 153.

47 "Disabled Persons Gather at O.C.L.C. Community Forum: We Have a Right to Live," *Black Panther*, June 25, 1977, pp. 4, 20.

48 Mingus, "Reflection toward Practice," 108.

Part IV

INSTITUTIONAL UNDOING

11. MODEL MINORITY LIFE, INTERRUPTED

Asian American Illness Memoirs

JAMES KYUNG-JIN LEE

"In the beginning is an interruption," writes medical sociologist Arthur Frank. "Disease interrupts a life, and illness then means living with perpetual interruption."[1] Frank's not-so-oblique reference to the creation myth in the Hebrew Bible, a kind of primal interpellation, recasts human subjectivity as anchored in a fundamental wounded embodiment. In this revised origin story, vulnerability and contingency precede forms of health and able-bodiedness. It is a narrative that is easily forgotten though, given that contemporary US social life is organized by an altogether different form of hailing, in which our full personhoods are recognized by whether we can conform to what Frank calls the restitution narrative: yesterday, I was healthy; today, I am sick; but tomorrow I'll get better. Hewing to restitution as your story demands subjection to biomedical authority, of becoming a patient in order that a physician might turn you back into a recognizable (healthy) human. But illness interrupts ableist ontology in the final instance, which explains in large part the explosion of illness memoirs in the last quarter century, as many Americans (and others whose ill or disabled embodiment put them in contact with a biomedical field for which they'll brook little love) feel moved to share their experiences of illness, injury, and disability.

Until recently, however, Asian Americans largely exempted themselves from exploring self stories of illness, disease, and finitude, except to narrate how to fix broken bodies. It's not that, contrary to mainstream news accounts, Asian Americans don't want to think or write about illness. To the contrary, they have willingly participated in building the prestige and popularity of the illness memoir's dance partner, the physician memoir, and have been quite successful at it. Asian Americans have been writing about illness for quite some time, but not from the vantage of being illness; rather, Asian Americans write about illness, and about treating illness, as physicians. The physician's story reinforces and distills the prevailing social narrative of Asian Americans as model minorities, a narrative far more durable and plastic than the people expected to live it. Indeed, this representation of Asian Americans as model minorities coincides with an ongoing passionate attachment to fantasies of indefinite health.[2] Asian American physician narratives buttress this connection, for which group is more poised to be a non-sick person than the professional existentially and socially produced to diagnose and cure what ails you? As normatively able-bodied people whose job it is to make other bodies normatively able-bodied again, Asian American physicians and their stories ostensibly affirm the success frame of model minority life for both somatic and social life: indefinite health mutually reinforces irrevocable economic mobility.

Draw a Venn diagram of these two modes of life writing—the (Asian American) physician writing his, the (non–Asian American, mostly white) ill or former patient composing hers—and you'll be hard-pressed to find an Asian American in the overlap. The sentence that you just read I first wrote in 2014; it would have been followed with my mention of less than a handful of memoirs written by Asian Americans about their experiences with illness. I would have mentioned 2011 as the first time a piece of life writing by an Asian American was published: Fred Ho's *Diary of a Radical Cancer Warrior*, by Skyhorse Publishing.[3] I would then have cited Brandy Liên Worrall's 2014 self-published memoir *What Doesn't Kill Us*, her story about her struggles with breast cancer.[4] And then I would have written this: "that's it"—and then spent the better part of this chapter reflecting on why the dearth of such writing about illness by Asian Americans.

But then something broke, in the latter half of this decade: 2016 saw the release of Kalanithi's viral memoir; this same year Ecco's (an imprint of HarperCollins) release of Padma Lakshmi's *Love, Loss, and What We Ate* featured her struggles with endometriosis, though secondary to the primary themes of her failed marriage with Salman Rushdie, her careers in modeling and food reality television, and her relationship with her mother and her child.[5] In 2017, Christine Hyung-Oak Lee published her memoir *Tell Me Everything You Don't Remember: The Stroke That Changed My Life* with Ecco, the first time in US history that a major trade press published a work of nonfiction by an Asian American whose narrative was primarily occupied by illness.[6] Then on February 5, 2019, two memoirs came on the market: Julie Yip-Williams, posthumously published by Random House, chronicled her story of both her colon cancer and treatment, and her struggles as a disabled Asian American woman;

and Esmé Weijun Wang's *The Collected Schizophrenias*, published by Graywolf, presented a series of essays that reflects on her schizoaffective disorder.[7] It was as if, in an instant, scales fell from the eyes of US publishers and readers alike: if, as a collective, Americans demanded of their Asian American colleagues lives of exceptional mobility and affirmation of the US cultural project, then perhaps, in this surge of readerly purchase in Asian Americans getting sick and dying before their eyes, Asian America could also provide a pedagogy for optimizing this narrative of inevitable declension. Asian Americans, can you teach us how to die well?

Herein lies a paradox within this genre of writing by Asian Americans, the illness memoir, emergent and perilously, precariously new. Who would want to read a story of a sick Asian American when the only Asian American story consistently valorized and rewarded is the model minority one?[8] And yet here model minorities lie, beset with pain and wounds that incarnate their inevitable finitude, and the narration of these failing bodies suggests a double movement in them. On the one hand, the reading public, as a microcosm of American attitudes toward their Asian American neighbors, needs to read in the authors something redemptive in their illnesses, so that even death might be as good and valuable as Asian American lives are supposed to be—the social power of the model minority narrative and the success frame that governs Asian American (and others') desire to live into it, even unto sickness and death. On the other hand, the illness memoir genre evidences a relatively new structure of feeling in watching model minorities get sick and sometimes die. The perforce challenge in this narrative possibility is of the Asian American person trying to craft a narrative from the body that doesn't do or actually refuses to do what it is supposed to do—to labor to extract capital from herself and her network. The pressure is real, especially for Asian Americans: revaluing their bodies from the stigma of unproductivity into something else requires a cultivation of narrative from which Asian America has had until very recently no sui generis resources, and even fewer ways of imagining illness and death as vehicles to reaffirm the success frame. To signify illness differently, a pivot away from this insistence and imperative of productive redemption would thus gesture to a perilous and—at least for me, maybe for you?—utopian differential ontology.

What follows are thick descriptions of three Asian American authors who write into this paradox. In so doing, they map out idiosyncratic attempts at forging a renewed uptake of the self whose connection to the model minority narrative is shredded but still tethered. In trying to establish for themselves a post-diagnosis ethos, they turn to the memoir as means to return to themselves a self initially shattered and surprised by their no longer healthy body. Witness then in these readings of these self stories attempts to enact in a public forum—first through blogs, then through published memoir—an insistence in writing and (readers) reading acts of "commitments to self and others."[9] You may not like how they journey or where they arrive, but in trying to write in the afterlife of the (healthy) model minority, these Asian Americans narrate whether they are up to the task of what new identity illness brings them. At the least, they deserve our coming up beside them and honoring their labor by following where they go even if we don't have to or want to go there just yet.

Cancer and Leftist Ableism: Fred Ho

Fred Ho's trademark bombast is evident in the prologue of *Diary of a Radical Cancer Warrior*, as he figures himself a warrior instead of a mere survivor/victim of cancer.[10] A characteristically long-winded sentence illuminates the stakes that Ho lays out for a narrative that chronicles his experiences and struggles with colorectal cancer and its treatment, stakes distilled in the subtitle of the book: *Fighting Cancer and Capitalism at the Cellular Level*. The lines read as such: "Make no mistake: this is a war to the end, an end to which success or failure depends on how much we make ourselves to be the principled warriors in seeking solutions and not compromises to our personal health, wellness, transformation, and to curing the planet once and for all of the greatest threat to life itself."[11] Ho returns again and again throughout his memoir to this extended metaphor of warfare, and of himself as a cancer warrior, even as the modalities of war-making against his disease shift dramatically about two-thirds of the way into the book: after his cancer returns a fourth time, Ho rejects all medical treatment and turns exclusively to naturopathic modes of therapy; by the book's end, he proclaims that he "completely reject[s] the notion of a complementary medicine."[12] Thus, by the end of the book and, presumably, of his life (he died in 2014), Ho's stance as a principled warrior figures his enemy to be not only the cancer that afflicts him but also the biomedical regime that he'd earlier marshaled for his war against cancer, but that he views as no longer a solution but instead another problem in the deep imbrication of cancer and capitalism.

Ho's narrative filtering of his experience of cancer and medical treatment as a form of warfare is both mundane and significant. It's mundane in part because this discourse around cancer and warfare has had a fairly long if recent history. Although he mentions it nowhere in his book, the idea that cancer be fought as a war had its origins in the United States during the mid- to late 1960s, when medical practitioners began to develop new protocols of chemotherapy to treat what had been, until then, the fatal and heartbreaking diagnoses of childhood leukemia.[13] In the wake of some therapeutic successes, leading cancer researchers and wealthy elites hoped to mobilize the resources and scale of the federal government to move expeditiously in finding a "cure" for cancer. On December 9, 1969, a group called the Citizens Committee for the Conquest of Cancer put out a full-page ad in the *New York Times* that read, "Mr. Nixon, you can cure cancer."[14] A bill passed overwhelmingly in Congress, and on December 23, 1971, President Nixon signed the National Cancer Act, which allocated $1.5 billion over three years (almost $10 billion in 2017 dollars), a passage that journalists quickly dubbed the "president's personal war on cancer."[15] The use of warfare rhetoric to enact social policy is a hallmark of twentieth-century marshaling of national resources that speaks to the ways that actual warfare was one of the few ways that national policy and, more importantly, transformations in state structures and resources took place; warfare turns policy into patriotic practice. But as Susan Sontag points out in her classic essay "Illness as Metaphor" (1978), if warfare has been a controlling metaphor in descriptions of cancer and its treatments, its variety of distortions by way of military language gives its depiction a speculative dimension: "Cancer is being magnified and projected into a metaphor for the biggest enemy, the furthest goal. Thus, Nixon's bid to match Kennedy's promise to put Americans on the moon was, appropriately enough, the promise to 'conquer' cancer. Both were science-fiction ventures."[16] Its scope and scale perhaps help us understand also how much such language suffuses micro, individuated relations and experiences that turn phrases such as "died after a long battle with cancer" or "we will fight this cancer together" as common parlance.

Ho's usage is made significant by the sheer fact that, mundane as the metaphor is, his book remains the first published account of cancer written by an Asian American, a milestone made possible by his notoriety within leftist circles.[17] He began writing about his experience with cancer, shortly after his diagnosis, on several online sites, including his Myspace page, but in 2011 he agreed to curate his cancer diaries into book form in hopes that he might reach a wider audience. If there is a conceptual anchor to the diary, it is Ho's attempt to map a political reading onto the horrors of his experience as a cancer warrior, one who first fights cancer and later fights both the disease and allopathic medicine. Throughout the book, passages such as this early one frame the more mundane descriptions of daily life: "I am daily convinced that fighting cancer is a war. It is a war fought on the medical/cellular level, it is a war fought on the social-economic-political level against the U.S. HMO system of profiteering off healthcare, and it is a war fought on the spiritual-physical-mental-manual level of yin-yang."[18] Later, Ho returns again to the deep connection between his fight against cancer as his personal mode of resistance against the malignant forces of capitalism: "The war will continue for a long time, not only for me personally to make sure no cancer cells ever grow again inside of me, but to support the ongoing greater war to remove the cancer of capitalism from this world."[19] Such passages typify Ho's recursive strategy to wrest political meaning out of his suffering, which augment each time the cancer returns until, after it returns the fourth time following a brief year of remission, Ho turns on the biomedical regime on which he had relied, albeit with some measure of ambivalence for its profit motive. "Mainstream medicine is the succubus," Ho opines late in the book. "While you are in repose, believing it to be there for your best interests, it is in reality functioning according to its own logic, which inevitably is to facilitate the interests of capitalism (profits), all the while convincing you, along with its practitioners (many of whom are well intentioned), that it is healing you when indeed it is not and, often, making you sicker."[20] Thus his personal struggle with cancer and later his decision to reject allopathic medical technologies constitute nothing less than his contribution to this war, a form of activism that demonstrates that autonomy from what he calls the "teratogenic-carcinogenic-iatrogenic matrix" will facilitate well-being and healing, which includes, tentatively, a hoped-for but never realized cure.

But this hoped-for yet never realized cure, like his insistence in cultivating his warrior's style—both a commitment to healing as an operation against the degradations of cancer, medicine, and capitalism—relies on ableist assumptions of activism that presume health, wholeness, and the restored body as the marker of transcendence over the evils of capitalism and cancer. Throughout the book, Ho insists that a new treatment or regime will be the one to help him "beat cancer," one that he increasingly pins on his desire to assume complete control of his health care. When he breaks with allopathic treatment, Ho insists, again recursively, on what he calls a "no compromise manifesto," which includes the top priority of leading his own treatment; later, in a letter to his sister, who also experienced cancer twice, Ho recounts that "I am for the first time in the cancer war, truly free and feel great because I'm in charge."[21] To this assertion of freedom, Ho notes his restoration to health, the lowering of his blood pressure, the alleviation of his neuropathy, the partial return of his sexual function, and his considerable loss of weight.[22] His assertion of freedom as individuation, made manifest by his daily individual actions of naturopathic self-improvement, depends largely on an attachment to what Tobin Siebers calls an ideology of ability, which at its core is a barely acknowledged faith in the restorability and perfectibility of the body.[23] To this extent, warrior activism rests on a fundamental belief in bodily and narrative restitution, an ethos with which Ho closes his narrative, when asked how to receive a cancer diagnosis: you can think of it as a horrific curse or, Ho concludes, "you can take it as a gift, an opportunity to change yourself *forever*, to never go back to the carcinogenic matrix of the life you once lived, and to build a new person and new life that is truly better!"[24] Ho's exclamatory tone, as if yelling at himself as well as you, enlists the rhetoric of cure that is built into those that populate cancer center brochures and hospital billboards: my institution, for example, dubs itself simply as the "Anti-Cancer"; a recent TV advertisement for Dana Farber has it rescuing people from certain death: they are still "here" thanks to the hospital's work.[25]

This notion of cancer as a gift is not unique to cancer memoirs but, given Ho's particular iteration of cancer as a bodily signifier of global capitalism, and his way forward in treating and fighting one's cancer—to assert control over one's treatment, to cultivate the body by optimizing its intakes—creates a strange and ironic correlation between Ho's leftist ableism and contemporary neoliberal notions of the care of the self.[26] Ho's final call to change yourself "forever," this never-ending cultivation of the self precisely at the moment one is no longer reliant on something that might approximate institutional or civic life, imagines warrior life as one that demands a commitment to the utopian as perfectible, and to the autonomous, which, to return to the significance of this text as a first by an Asian American, welcomes back the specter of the model minority that continues to haunt contemporary Asian American stories.

What is strangely but perhaps not surprisingly missing from this extended meditation on a struggle with cancer as warfare is a well-trodden genealogy offered by Audre Lorde in *The Cancer Journals*, written less than a decade after Nixon's war on cancer. Lorde's insistence that the silence that she encountered within breast cancer circles was a systemically shared suffering and vulnerability, one that demanded a rhetorical and identitarian transformation, from cancer victim to cancer warrior. In inveighing against the assumption that women who had received mastectomies should wear breast prosthetics so as not to make others uncomfortable, Lorde reminds her readers that the then prime minister of Israel, Moishe Dayan, wears an eyepatch for a lost eye, and recounts, "The world sees him as a warrior with an honorable wound, and a loss of a piece of himself which he has marked, and mourned, and moved beyond."[27] To which Lorde then extends this metaphor of the wounded, vulnerable warrior to herself and other women: "Well, women with breast cancer are warriors, also. I have been to war, and still am. . . . For me, my scars are an honorable reminder that I may be a casualty in the cosmic war against radiation, animal fat, air pollution, McDonald's hamburgers and Red Dye No. 2, but the fight is still going on, and I am still a part of it."[28] Lorde calls attention to her wounded body not as perfectible, but as a vulnerable, contingent body that is still meaningful, and meaningful precisely in its shared vulnerability with others similarly afflicted. The question of why Ho seems not to have read Lorde's vision of warrior identity remains open and curious, given his repeated public commitments to what he calls "matriarchal socialism" as a corrective to patriarchal capitalism.[29] (This is not to mention what is at stake in this shared investment in imagining cancer as warfare as opposed to, say, coexistence.)[30] But something tells me that his possessive attachments to control, autonomy, and ableism that undergird his activism prevent Ho from imagining the possibility that simply bearing witness to his fellow cancer survivors—including those who die—might offer a far more radical, dare I say, utopian vision of sociality that may decide that simply being a community of wounded storytellers may be just fine.

Illness and Intersubjectivity: Brandy Liên Worrall

While not anywhere near a place resembling utopia, Brandy Liên Worrall's memoir chronicles an assemblage born of her bodily woundedness. At first glance, there seems little room for Worrall to listen to what her body tells, buffeted as she is by an array of familial and work expectations. Her narrative hurtles through time and space as she reveals her travails as the rebellious daughter of a Vietnamese immigrant mother and Vietnam War (American) veteran father; as the long-suffering wife of an Asian American studies professor, from whom she'll get divorced; as the devoted but harrowed mother of two children and later a third child; and, perhaps most importantly for our purposes, a formerly healthy turned ill person, and throughout much of the book a patient suffering from breast cancer and its attendant therapies. There are certainly vestiges of fantasies of familial bliss peppered throughout the memoir, of her youthful crush on a young, charismatic professor that results in marriage and children, of her jet-setting brother-in-law delivering lectures on cutting-edge architecture while playing in amateur hockey leagues. But Worrall's narrative opens abruptly: "Things are not fun right now. In fact, they kinda suck."[31] And with that, we are invited to journey with her into her maelstrom of familial and somatic chaos. By the end of the first chapter, we already have foreshadowing of a marriage in shambles, her brother-in-law dead from lung cancer. In the immediate moments after her cancer diagnosis, Worrall offers a glimpse of what Ronald Dworkin calls a "narrative wreck," an unmooring of narrative stability in which sensory processes are both overloaded and unable to register.[32] Standing with Charles, her husband, on a corner in Vancouver, and finding it impossible to figure out where to go—literally and figuratively—Worrall recounts, "The atmosphere suddenly became so foreign, everything with its vitality, unaware of or unconcerned with my diagnosis."[33] Here, Worrall's sense of complete discombobulation echoes Arthur Frank's observation that illness disrupts a fundamental component of how persons tell their stories, which is a capacity for temporality. "The conventional expectation of any narrative," Frank writes, "held alike by listeners and storytellers, is for a past that leads into a present that sets in place a foreseeable future."[34] By contrast, Frank continues, "the illness story is [narratively] wrecked because its present is not what the past was supposed to lead up to, and the future is scarcely thinkable."[35] For Worrall, the scarcely thinkable future is exacerbated by the divergent temporalities that she and Charles live, increasingly so when she begins her chemotherapy. "My life," she writes, "has come to a sudden halt. . . . But Charles just keeps on going. My cancer is shitty timing for him. He's got this huge blockbuster conference in a couple of weeks, so he's at meetings and press conferences nonstop. . . . No, life hasn't come to a halt. Rather, it's being lived out in spite of me."[36] Of course, it is neither that Worrall's life has halted nor that life is being lived out in spite of her, but instead that her life, now suffused with illness, operates on a differential temporality and geography than her still abled-bodied, healthy husband. Ill time is "shitty" for Charles; ill time is time lived out of spite for the healthy body. Likewise, while Charles shuttles across Vancouver, from home to school, moves transnationally and globally as he builds his professional reputation, Worrall's circuit is demonstrably more constrained, between home and clinic. Indeed, it is the divergent physical journeys between the two—Worrall's clinic becoming more home than their shared house, Charles reluctantly co-traveling with her for chemotherapy when not tethered to his work obligations—that further highlight how "unhomely" the home life has become. Worrall's vulnerable condition makes intolerable the capacity for Charles to live his ambitious futurity. Later, Charles will have an affair that will break up the marriage for good, but throughout the narrative the signs are apparent that the two are in different geographies, different temporalities, and are increasingly speaking different languages that deepen their mutual alienation well before the actual infidelity takes place.

But to the extent that her cancer wrecks whatever fantasy for a life she may have held with Charles, Worrall's illness also opens her to wholly unexpected and heretofore unimagined ways of connection, particularly with her parents. Temporalities and geographies of vulnerability open channels of communicability heretofore unknown to Worrall. While the squabbling between, particularly, daughter and mother persist throughout the memoir, the narrative also makes clear that new capacities for relation emerge, a kind of shared suffering. For example, in the aforementioned passage, in which she describes the atmosphere as foreign, figuratively a different country, shortly after her diagnosis, Worrall immediately recalls her mother's illness upon her arrival to the United States, both the result of experiencing a Pennsylvania winter for the first time and the loss and isolation born of displacement from Vietnam. "[My mother] told me of how she struggled," Worrall reflects, "how she almost died the first few months there, how she wanted badly to go home. She crossed the divide, and it was the hardest thing she'd ever done. That's when her new normal began. I understand now, Mom, the divide. The harsh precipice between there and here, then and now."[37] Later, as she awaits reconstructive surgery following her mastectomy, Worrall recounts her father's struggles with drug and alcohol addiction, his going in and out of rehab programs at the local VA hospital, and his lingering PTSD that she now relates to as someone "who's been through the shit."[38] Worrall even reconnects to her former child self, as a young girl who suffered epileptic grand mal seizures. Her ill and wounded body, the somatic site of her distance from Charles, also becomes the mode through which she enlivens the stories of her parents, whom she regards at the beginning of the memoir as, respectively, a "Crazy Asian Mother" and a "handful" of a father. Her narrative of illness slides into their stories, so that, structurally, chapters become recursive narrative occasions: a moment at a doctor's office, a procedure, or a particularly bad evening triggers an episode of her mother's struggles in Vietnam, or her father's recounting of war horror. Her parents' stories help fill in hers.

Indeed, early on in her memoir she recounts a recurring sequence of dreams, what she calls her "Vietnam War dreams," even as she also notes that her parents seldom talked of their experiences of the war. Yet in her "chemo haze," Worrall can no longer discern whether she has awoken from the dream of being hued by an "orange-red aura" with the smell of "singed skin": "The chemical smell and taste biting the insides of my nose, mouth, and throat make me wonder if Mom and Dad had the same assault on their senses when they breathed in the Agent Orange that was so casually dropped from planes flying overhead."[39] Of course, the extent to which the US military has been and continues to be dismissive of those exposed to the slow violence of its chemical warfare program is well documented.[40] But here Worrall suggests that not only does she receive a traumatic post-memory but that she is the recipient of an intergenerational poison. "See those bright trees suddenly dropping dead?" Worrall muses sardonically, "Nothing to worry about. Later: see those babies being born without limbs? Nothing to worry about. See those vets dying of prostate cancer in alarming numbers? Nothing to worry about. Stuff happens. See me getting poisoned so I can get rid of this inexplicable cancer? Nothing to worry about."[41] Agent Orange is passed from parent to child and, perhaps most ironically, both as the disease and as the cure, insofar as the cancer is an expression of the herbicide and as the chemotherapy constitutes a related animacy: chemical agents that may have caused her cancer are now being called on to cure her of her illness. And Worrall thus sees in her parents a shared toxicity. Even as cancer is an unqualified horror that speaks to shared trauma, illness becomes a mode through which a differential Asian Americanness might emerge, one determined by legacies of warfare and militarized poison that is somatically lived rather than intellectually imagined. In this way, the more legibly political identity—Charles, the studious Asian American studies professor—is less aware of its complicity in the institutions that damaged Worrall and her parents.

Worrall enacts what is possible when illness is neither avoided nor romanticized but fully engaged, the experience put to use toward relational means and ends. This gesture of reaching toward others, desire born of distinctive but mutual bodily contingencies, makes the memoir then not only the story of Brandy Liên Worrall's struggle with cancer but also an intersubjective familial narrative that frames the Asian American and her family far from the capitalist enterprise of model minority fantasy. Indeed, Worrall's narrative suggests that that familial fantasy—one that was barely available to her, in which she was expected to live out the life of the debt-bound daughter to her multiracial parents—would have been not only not helpful in her illness but may very well have destroyed her utterly had she been wedded to that fantasy. Instead, it is her deeply flawed, troubled, and broken family, out of whose wounds new modes of sociality are made possible, that should remind us of what Mel Chen has written regarding an animated relationship to toxicity, one that "propels queer loves, especially once we release it from exclusively human hosts, disproportionately inviting dis/ability, industrial labor, biological targets, and military vaccine recipients—inviting loss and its 'losers' and trespassing containers of animacy."[42] Perhaps less utopian than Chen's vision, Worrall's reimagined relationality is still an opening that guarantees nothing but binds her across space and time, reaching toward a desire shared even by those who are now dead.[43]

Christine Hyung-Oak Lee's Reassemblage

Unlike Ho and Worrall, who created their respective blogs in order to write out and through their experience with cancer and subsequent treatment, Christine Hyung-Oak Lee began hers not as an illness blog but as a medium through which she could journal while composing a novel and completing an MFA at

Mills College. On December 31, 2006, however, Lee wrote the following: "I am feeling strange. My brain is in a weird state right now—a combination of short brain games and lack of memory. While taking on the concept of a brain game earlier today, I suffered a memory overhaul. Now I can't say what I want to say or remember what I want to remember. It's just a weird situation."[44] She wished her readers a happy new year the following day, and then, on January 2, 2007, Lee composed a 472-word blog post titled "swimming ideas." Uncharacteristically, Lee doesn't use capital letters in this entry, and then describes her brain's actions as gustatory: "something in my brain burped. most of what i want to do is just out of my grasp. i feel like i know how to do them, but then when i go to do them, i just . . . CAN'T. day by day, i'm regaining my abilities, so i hope this is just temporary."[45] Later that day, she tried to craft a whimsical post about herself, and then her blog went silent for four days. On January 6, 2007, Lee gave her brain burp a name, a diagnosis: "Well. I totally had a stroke (seriously). The doctors are trying to figure out exactly why a 33 year old non-smoking woman would have a full blown stroke. I'll be back online when I can gather my thoughts, regain memories (I've lost some), etc. (I'm not talking about my initial attempts at gaining equilibrium, either). See you in a bit."[46]

Over the course of the next few weeks, months, and years, Lee and her readers watched her blog, *Writing Under a Pseudonym*, turn from a platform for cataloging her writing process into an illness blog, one that would resemble Worrall's and Jennifer Ho's (and to a certain extent, Fred Ho's Myspace entries, even Broyard's and Lorde's journal notes). And yet it became, unwittingly, a blog not so much about writing about illness as about writing through illness. The blog would become an online version of what she would later call her "memory book," a journal that she kept after her stroke, during her convalescence. This journal and the blog culminated on February 14, 2017, in the release of her memoir *Tell Me Everything You Don't Remember: The Stroke That Changed My Life*. The most immediate change to her life was the loss of short-term memory: severely damaged by a blood clot that prevented oxygen from reaching it, the dead tissue of her left thalamus left Lee unable to remember anything beyond fifteen-minute increments. Or, as she put it, "without my thalamus, my brain went offline. It retained nothing,"[47] which gives both her journal and her blog a primary, primal significance, a narrative surrogate for her lost memory: "My journal would act as my short-term memory bank, it turned out, for a long while to come."[48] Her journal and blog recorded in real time the manner in which her stroke interrupted the trajectory of her life narrative on December 31, 2006, and in the ensuing days profoundly and inexorably *disrupted* the ways that she had told her story, one that she could no longer resume. The blog became a testament to the narrative wreckage that Lee's illness wrought, which she later sought to reassemble through the act of writing her memoir.

The event of the stroke is a signal crisis for Lee, which in turn prompts her to look anew at the story she had told herself and lived into until that event. In the ensuing days of chaos, which she describes as both uncontrollable anger and grief, Lee tills this material to coax metaphor out of her bodily and, later, existential crisis. The proximal cause of her stroke was patent foramen ovale (PFO), a gap between the left and right atria of the heart that fails to close after birth, which allowed a blood clot to bypass the lungs and work its way to Lee's brain. "For thirty-three years I had hole in my heart, and I did not know it," Lee opens her memoir: "There was an actual hole in my heart, an undiagnosed birth defect, with which I lived."[49] Yet this is not simply a colloquial description of her PFO but a figuration both of the narrative that she lived and also of what caused this narrative to end by way of her stroke: "And then there was the hole in my heart that I tried to dam up with other people's needs and then filled with resentment."[50] The narrative that Lee so painstakingly constructed before her stroke, she discovers, had at its core this "hole," a symptomatic lack from which emerges, she learns, an accretion of dysfunction whose exposure is made possible by the stroke caused by the self-same hole. "There was a hole in my heart that made it impossible for me to be whole," she writes, "and then I had a stroke."[51] The stroke that changes Lee's life augurs the wisp of a form of wellness that her prior semblance of health made impossible.

The memoir slowly unpeels the toxicity of such values imposed on her, which in turn would become the precondition to her loss of voice and "wholeness." The literal hole in her heart, her PFO, makes it terrifically difficult for Lee to breathe normally, a congenital condition that plagues her throughout her life and that she learns, Foucault-like, to endure and turn into a value of fortitude. It is, of course, a value reinforced by her immigrant parents, who raised her "to be tough and impervious to pain."[52] Lee recalls that her father "valued stoicism in the face of pain and strength at all costs," and refused medical care for a perforated small intestine even though the ensuing sepsis sent him into extreme pain and life-threatening illness that resulted in doctors removing two feet of damaged intestinal tract. "He still brags about toughing it out," quips Lee.[53] From this she develops what Arthur Frank calls a dominating relation to her body, to the point of trying to suppress her body's needs, depriving it of food, cutting it physically to mitigate deeper psychic wounds, manifesting an overall revulsion to the body, a kind of hyper-Cartesian dualism: "The brain will excel in school. The brain will be the star. The mind will make up stories for the body's deficits. The mind will say her body is a failure. The mind will favor the brain."[54] Thus coterminous with the denigration of her body is Lee's favoring of the mind of her brain, that which Asian Americans, at the insistence of their parents, utilize to secure their futures of model minority success. While it is her parents, and in particular her father, who erect the scaffold of this dysfunctional dualism, it is Lee who lives her life to perfect this narrative of success, spurred on by the simultaneous elevation of her brain's mind and disavowal of her ostensibly uncontrollable body.

Lee's obsession with discipline and domination—of her mind and its regime over her body—informs the story that she tells of herself and the story she uses to live her life until her stroke. It is, in fact, this desire for discipline that Lee later realizes constituted the very structures that allowed her to believe that this was her desire rather than that of others around her. In a discussion about the distinction between semantic and episodic memory, Lee offers a litany of examples of past experiences that shaped the inertia of her life's momentum: "Episodic memory is about the Sundays my family spent hiking the San Gabriel Mountains, how I kept gasping for air, and how no matter how often we went, I never found it easier."[55] This remembrance of signs of her PFO, which as her younger self she ascribed to pain endurance, her father's grit, then triggers other episodes of her voice made lost: "That I crumpled under my parents' wishes for me to become a doctor. That they thought a writing career was too daring."[56] Likewise, Lee's marriage to Adam, which she initially regarded as an assertion of agency and revolt against her Korean immigrant parents by eloping with a Jewish man, becomes yet another instance of the loss of her "voice": after recounting that he would not assent to a DNR were she incapacitated, insisting that such was his decision, Lee reflects on living indefinitely on life support as a "kind of death": "In a sense, I was already not living my own life. I thought I was, because I had a career and I paid my own bills. But I was living Adam's life, cheerleading him and not myself."[57] The irony of her obsession for discipline then is that it only served to deepen her subjection to social narrative frames that circumscribed the desires of others as her own, a relegation of duty as her sole form of desire: "The thing is, I'd lost my voice in so many ways already, before the stroke even occurred. I had been unable to say, I am trapped in my life. That my obligations were interfering with my personal dreams. I made up rules and stuck to them because that was safe. It was, however, not brave."[58]

You'll notice in the previous paragraph that the passages from the memoir work themselves backward, Lee's acknowledgment of her lost voice taking place early on in her memoir. The day of her stroke represents not so much a critical event in her life but rather a critical and radical reordering of narrative, a story in which linear form will no longer hold. The days and months that followed brought about what is so often the case in illness, a crisis of identity when restitution is no longer available, a self bereft of a progressive narrative of restoration, a self thrown into chaos. All that she valued of herself, which included a photographic memory that allowed her to quote passages from books or recall credit card numbers of men who bought her drinks, is inaccessible to Lee, the damage to her brain disordering the very architecture of her life: "The stroke pushed on the weakest and most untested seams of my psyche. Where before I could never feel vulnerable—I wouldn't let myself—I was now vulnerable all the time. Where before I could not ask for help, I needed to ask for assistance to get through the day. Where before I could not allow myself to feel sad, I lost the ability to dam up my emotions. Where before I always planned in the interest of being in control, it was now impossible to do so. A part of myself really had died."[59] The stroke has Lee peer into a looking glass from which she discovers a self that is the converse of her formerly able-bodied version. And the death of this former self, which she will discern is truly gone, even after she "recovers" from her stroke, sends her into a deeper chaos from which she almost doesn't emerge: "Later in my recovery, when I was well enough to understand what had happened to me, to realize my deficits and become depressed about my stalled progress, when I wondered if my old life would ever return in any familiar form, I pondered taking a big dose of warfarin and then slicing my wrists."[60] The discovery of a new self as a former one dies, together with a desire to end this self by suicide, highlights the peril of the crisis born of the chaos that arrives in the wake of Lee's stroke, the double-edgedness of chaos that can never be mitigated or qualified: "Chaos stories show how quickly the props that other stories depend on can be kicked away. The limitation is that chaos is no way to live."[61] Gone are fantasies of progress, of linearity itself. For a time, Lee recalls, she can exist only in an interregnum.

Lee began her blog to document the undertaking of her novel, and was interrupted inexorably by the stroke. The blog and, in turn, the memoir then turns writing into an altogether different vocation, less an index to her ambition to match the economic or cultural capital of Adam, and more a mode of reenchanting her life altogether, writing as a movement for and beyond survival and toward a flourishing with and through her trauma. "Writing saved my life," she writes definitely: "I did not write that down [in my memory book]. But of that I am certain."[62] The soteriology of writing, however, is not recovery, but reconstruction. Lee never returns to a semblance of her pre-stroke self, but must build in the aftermath of chaos and trauma, an illness-born afterlife. "It took me years to be ready to write about my stroke," Lee recalls late in her memoir. "I did try to write about it. I wanted to write about it. I attempted to write an essay about my stroke no fewer than eleven times—there was no narrative, there was no structure to it. I wasn't ready. All in all, it took eight years to write it down. It took that long because I tried for eight years to put the stroke behind me. It wasn't until I had a baby and I had postpartum depression and my husband of fifteen years left me that I could look at the stroke."[63] Lee's stroke is so disruptive that it leaves next to nothing of her former life from which she can build her post-stroke story, the elements of her pre-stroke life a rubble that precipitates deeper crisis, a depression, and a loss of her familial and conjugal structures. She has, as she puts it, "no narrative, no structure" to the stroke and no narrative or structure to what follows, at least initially. So writing becomes a means to reconstruct a new syntax of her life, a reordering of her neurology and of what constitutes what Lee might consider her good.

Arthur Frank notes this recursive journey, that illness stories, shorn of the illusion of restitution and struggling to emerge out of chaos, mandate this different oblique relation to how the body remembers itself: "This self is not so newly discovered as newly connected to its own memory."[64] And in deep contrast to how she related to herself prior to the stroke, this new connection that Lee forges with her memory is not simply a return of her mind, but a renewed partnership with her body, still wounded, that she had long disavowed because she believed it failed to live up to the model minority expectation that she demanded of it and her mind: "But my mind and body, long at war with each other, would come to a great peace beyond my imagination. . . . My mind realized it needed my body, needed to recognize its new and strange strength."[65] Indeed, she commits to end the long tyranny of her mind over her body, one that plagued her with eating disorders, self-mutilation, and, at times, sex with others "to run away from my pain." "Now it was my body's turn to lead," Lee resolves: "I began to listen to my body, instead of ignoring its needs."[66] This too is the vocation of writing her stroke, writing as a material effect of the self as it narrates her trauma not as escape but as reckoning, a witness to the body that broke and must be seen in order for Lee's new narrative to emerge. Or, as Frank might put it, "the witness of suffering must be seen as a whole body, because embodiment is the essence of witness."[67]

So too then are we, the readers of our sick Asian Americans, witnesses to the suffering of their whole bodies—even Ho's, despite his disavowals. And one measure of the extent to which their writings were up to the task as acts of commitment to themselves and others—you and me—is to limn the contours of our own embodiment in our experience of reading stories through, not just about, illness. Do their accounts of their wounded bodies open, even if just halfway, a portal through which your and my body can account for our woundedness and bodily failures without recourse to excuse, shame, or calls for self-improvement? Does reading the story of someone now dead or something whose life is made contingent by deadly disease or condition make us, rather, feel immortal? The inclination to run away from these wounded storytellers or at least pity their lot may be understandable, but it is also an index of the extent to which we inadvertently hitch our fortunes to model minority ableism, our scholarly and political protests notwithstanding. But maybe, just maybe, our reading of such accounts can invite you and me into differential dispositions of our embodied trajectories, where our inevitable brokenness may half-open into something that looks like resonance or even recognition, in which stories of woundedness testify to an Asian American condition that champions of "grit" don't get. Ivy League schools may not call you or me, and you'll not be set up for a promotion, but you and I might find ourselves in a really unkempt space that we may realize is actually worth living in.

NOTES

Material in this chapter is adapted from "Styles of Asian American Illness" from *Pedagogies of Woundedness: Illness, Memoir, and the Ends of the Model Minority*, by James Kyung-Jin Lee, pages 95–98, 105–124. Used by permission of Temple University Press. © 2022 by Temple University. All Rights Reserved.

1   Frank, *Wounded Storyteller*, 56.
2   Lee, "Elegies of Social Life," 1–21.
3   Ho, *Diary*.
4   Worrall, *What Doesn't Kill Us*.
5   Lakshmi, *Love, Loss*.
6   Lee, *Tell Me Everything*.
7   Wang, *Collected Schizophrenias*.
8   In a phone call shortly after the publication of her book, Worrall relayed to me that she decided to self-publish after receiving rejection letters from publishers, with editors telling her that readers didn't want to read "another" breast cancer narrative. This, despite the many lists of breast cancer memoirs that demonstrate the unrelenting demands for such writing, like this one: https://www.sheknows.com/entertainment /articles/973507/breast-cancer-awareness-month-a-list-of-memoirs/. Worrall believes editors didn't think readers would be interested in an Asian American breast cancer story; I agree with her and, like her, think that editors deeply miscalculated what readers needed to learn from Asian Americans about illness and death.
9   Danielewicz, *Contemporary Memoirs in Action*, 1.
10 I need to say here that stories of Ho's sexually assaulting, harassing, and stalking women exist and that I believe them. This does not change my reading of his memoir; rather, it informs it.
11 Ho, *Diary*, xl.

12 Ho, *Diary*, 259.

13 Mukherjee, *Emperor of All Maladies*, 167–70.

14 Mukherjee, *Emperor of All Maladies*, 180.

15 Mukherjee, *Emperor of All Maladies*, 188.

16 Sontag, *Illness as Metaphor*, 69.

17 Ho's memoir was followed closely by Worrall's in 2014, which, to remind, was self-published because of the lack of trade interest.

18 Ho, *Diary*, 15.

19 Ho, *Diary*, 77.

20 Ho, *Diary*, 240.

21 Ho, *Diary*, 206, 224.

22 Ho, *Diary*, 218.

23 Siebers, *Disability Theory*, 8.

24 Ho, *Diary*, 260.

25 UCI Anti-Cancer Challenge, "Join the Anti Cancer Challenge"; Dana-Farber Cancer Institute, "'I Am Here' TV Commercial."

26 This term, "care of the self," of course, derives from the third volume of Michel Foucault's *History of Sexuality*, a work that marks a shift in Foucault's thinking from that of biopolitical governmentality to what one might call a bioethics. See also Dilts, "From 'Entrepreneur of the Self,'" 130–46.

27 Lorde, *Cancer Journals: Special Edition*, 60.

28 Lorde, *Cancer Journals: Special Edition*, 60.

29 Fred Ho, "Beyond Asian American Jazz: My Musical and Political Changes in the Asian American Movement," in Fujino, *Wicked Theory, Naked Practice*, 58.

30 S. Lochlann Jain challenges the implied masculinity in the warrior metaphor, even in Lorde, and wonders whether there are other forms of "resistance" to stultifying cultural expectations in living with cancer. Jain, *Malignant*, 82.

31 Worrall, *What Doesn't Kill Us*, 2.

32 Frank, *Wounded Storyteller*, 54.

33 Worrall, *What Doesn't Kill Us*, 29.

34 Frank, *Wounded Storyteller*, 55.

35 Frank, *Wounded Storyteller*, 55.

36 Worrall, *What Doesn't Kill Us*, 57–58.

37 Worrall, *What Doesn't Kill Us*, 30.

38 Worrall, *What Doesn't Kill Us*, 212.

39 Worrall, *What Doesn't Kill Us*, 64.

40 Nixon, *Slow Violence*; Sills, *Toxic War*.

41 Worrall, *What Doesn't Kill Us*, 64–65.

42 Chen, *Animacies*, 210–11.

43 Worrall's father died in 2015.

44 Christine Hyung-Oak Lee, "Brain Brain," *Writing Under a Pseudonym* (blog), December 31, 2006, https://jadepark.wordpress.com/2006/12/31/brain-brain/.

45 Christine Hyung-Oak Lee, "Swimming Ideas," *Writing Under a Pseudonym* (blog), January 2, 2007, https://jadepark.wordpress.com/2007/01/02/swimming-ideas/.

46 Christine Hyung-Oak Lee, "I Stroked Out," *Writing Under a Pseudonym* (blog), January 6, 2007, https://jadepark.wordpress.com/2007/01/06/i-stroked-out/.

47 Lee, *Tell Me Everything*, 55.

48 Lee, *Tell Me Everything*, 38.

49 Lee, *Tell Me Everything*, 1.

50 Lee, *Tell Me Everything*, 1.

51 Lee, *Tell Me Everything*, 2.

52 Lee, *Tell Me Everything*, 159.

53 Lee, *Tell Me Everything*, 160.

54 Lee, *Tell Me Everything*, 73.

55 Lee, *Tell Me Everything*, 67.

56 Lee, *Tell Me Everything*, 73.

57 Lee, *Tell Me Everything*, 102.

58 Lee, *Tell Me Everything*, 5.

59 Lee, *Tell Me Everything*, 11.

60 Lee, *Tell Me Everything*, 84.

61 Frank, *Wounded Storyteller*, 114.

62 Lee, *Tell Me Everything*, 46.

63 Lee, *Tell Me Everything*, 236.

64 Frank, *Wounded Storyteller*, 129.

65 Lee, *Tell Me Everything*, 199.

66 Lee, *Tell Me Everything*, 202.

67 Frank, *Wounded Storyteller*, 142.

12. FILIPINA SUPERCRIP

On the Crip Poetics of Colonial Ablenationalism

SONY CORÁÑEZ BOLTON

The Postcolonial Supercrip

We are in a US-constructed hospital in Manila in the US-occupied Philippines in the early twentieth century. Our clinical eye appraises a young Filipina woman with an interminable cough and labored breathing. Despite being ineluctably wedged within the space of institutionalized Western medicine, surprisingly it is "American tropical" Spanish that delineates how a literary genre engages in romanticized diagnosis of a brown and crip Filipina body.[1] In mestizo Filipino José Reyes's *Novela de la Vida Real* (1930), we have the representation of an unlikely figure engaged in crip medical poetry naturalizing and protracting Filipino Spanish well into the US colonial period (1899–1946). Spanish becomes the motor proliferating a literary and scientific diagnostic genre centered, in Reyes's case, on a crippled and debilitated Filipina Indigenous body.[2] Indeed, this Filipina is referred to as "trigueña," with an unambiguously dark complexion, an important representational choice given the identity of Reyes as a mixed-race elite Filipino. *Trigueña* is sometimes interchangeable with the Spanish word *mulata* and connotes a stronger tie to autochthonous or indigenized racial embodiment that is not captured consistently with *mestizo*. The "Doctor," the improbable medical master of Spanish poetics, enters the room to offer his final diagnosis of our disabled heroine, Rosarito:

EL DOCTOR.—¡Siempre escribiendo!

ROSARITO.—(Levanta los ojos, ruborosa y tímida.) ¿Qué quiere usted que haga? Es mi ocupación favorita. Además, escribiendo, llego a olvidarme de que realmente estoy enferma . . .

EL DOCTOR.—Pero si usted ya no está enferma. Lo que usted tiene
ahora es . . .

ROSARITO.—¿Qué es?

EL DOCTOR.—"Mielitis."

ANISIA [MADRE DE ROSARITO].—¿Y qué es mielitis?

EL DOCTOR.—(Con acento solemne y picaresco.)—Romanticismo,
señora.

Todos sonríen.[3]

Rosarito is a young poet, confined to bed, who cultivates Spanish letters in
the Philippines during the advent of US imperialism in Asia. Despite the tuberculosis debilitating her body, she resuscitates a minor tradition of Spanish
Filipino writing, thus rehabilitating the Filipino nation. We know this because
of the way the novel is framed for the reader, not only with a preface by the
author but also through a prologue penned by Teodoro Kalaw, one of Reyes's
contemporaries. Kalaw was from a prominent family and worked in Philippine politics for nearly the entire span of US colonial rule.[4] Kalaw writes, "He
leído esta novela con interés y la recomiendo a los que en Filipinas leen el cas-
tellano o quieren aprenderlo, que son desgraciadamente pocos en número cada
día."[5] The learning of Spanish is coupled with a moral imperative for the nation. Kalaw addresses this rehabilitation thus: "Ahora que abundan libros que
aunque brillantemente escritos son de tendencias y valor moral discutibles para
nuestra juventud, la lectura que nos proporcionan las obras del Sr. Reyes con-
stituye una excepción muy saludable."[6] The representation of Rosarito as an
unlikely Spanish poet constitutes the "healthy exception" for the youth of the
fledgling nation. Yet it should strike us as odd that the author would represent her stricken with tuberculosis and that the "room of her own" is located
in a hospital ward. Additionally, the fact that she would be read by Kalaw as a
healthy exception for a nation exposed to questionable morals serves to show
the rehabilitative function of Spanish. It is hard to imagine another reading
for this figure, given that Kalaw's own reading of the novel is so tethered to the
social functions of the reading of Spanish and the maintenance of this enlightened language in one of Spain's former colonies. What should we make not
only of the Filipina's mind that produces Spanish poetry but also of her body,
represented through the lens of illness?

Rosarito is the Filipina supercrip, allegorizing the plight of a nation ener-
vated by multiple and sequential colonial projects under Spain (1565–1898)
and the United States (1899–1946). Her appearance in a text produced in the
late US colonial period but articulated in (and articulating) Spanish demon-

strates that she occupies the intersection of Spanish and US colonialism. Spanish cultural production in the Philippines is historically seen as the vanguard literary and political work of a Filipino mestizo male elite. However, in Reyes's novel, a young Filipina poet is represented as the guardian of such a tradition. That she must be represented with debilitated health alludes to a supercrip function of Spanish as a language of diagnosis tied to the political health and capacity of the Philippines. Rosarito supercrips Spanish, showing that by elevating the most marginal of Filipino society she elevates the collective national project. Additionally, it is the Filipina body that shoulders the burden of illness and, by being represented in this way, becomes the object of rehabilitative uplift. The supercrip has been theorized by disability theorists as a rhetorical device describing disabled people that demonstrate ability that overcompensates the imagined limitations of their impairment, indeed, in many cases *exceeding* the capacities of the able-bodied or able-minded.[7] This narrative of the excellent crip person has been criticized as being a harmful inspirational narrative that has the effect of localizing disability as an individual issue rather than a widespread societal problem of accommodation.[8]

I offer a postcolonial reading of the supercrip in order to suggest that this framework can be used to describe the rise of what Franz Fanon calls "cultured intellectuals" during and in the aftermath of revolutionary moments of revolt against a colonial power.[9] The supercrip discourse is a valuable postcolonial lens through which to read the ways that colonized intellectuals, on the one hand, adapted enlightenment discourses for the purpose of redefining sovereignty under a colonial system that debilitated them and excluded them from liberal self-determination. On the other hand, the rhetorical device of the supercrip retrenches disability as the product of racialized feminization. That is to say, the "cultured intellectuals" to which Fanon referred are part of a vanguard of political thinkers in colonized societies for whom social protest and anticolonial thought are the provinces of the not-disabled. In short, if you can represent disability and rehabilitate it, you access ability articulated against the grain of colonial rule.

The racialized feminization of impairment and the cultivated capacity to represent it as an object of charity are pivotal ways that ableism becomes inherent to the project of Spanish letters in the Philippines. Through a framework I delineate as "colonial ablenationalism," I capture the ways that the racialized feminization of disability is instrumentalized by nation-building literary representation in the Philippines, such that the feminized body shoulders the burdens of disablement. This colonial form of ableism describes the ways that certain privileged colonized subjects refashion themselves as able-bodied and able-minded. They may indeed challenge colonialism but leave ableism intact in their political remonstrances.

Thus, it is unsurprising to see the colonial trope of impairment, which speaks not only to the violence of colonialism but also to the problematic promise of rehabilitation as a product of the solidification of racial hierarchy (mestizo versus *trigueña*). Colonial racial hierarchy is produced through a dialectic of rehabilitation and disability. This essay is an effort to crip postcolonialism in a fashion similar to arguments by theorists Clare Barker and Stuart Murray.[10] The engagement with the possible colonial meanings of the supercrip makes this "minor" tradition of Asian Spanish writing during US colonial rule a significant peripheral archive for a more global disability studies.

The tradition of Filipino writing in Spanish has two periods whose interaction is significant for the disability framework of this essay. The first is what is typically understood as the epoch of national consciousness produced, in no small part, by Spanish writing. During roughly the period between 1872 and 1896, the historical record observes an efflorescence of Spanish cultural production produced by mestizo bourgeois Filipinos writing in Europe and the Philippines. It should be noted that a major theme in critical Filipino studies and Philippine historiography has taken to task the extent to which this period has been overdetermined as defining the Filipino nation. Instead, scholars like Reynaldo Ileto, Deirdre de la Cruz, and Vicente Rafael have engaged in more subalternist reading practices that tell Philippine history from the bottom up—typically from the perspectives of the non-mestizo peasant classes.[11] I follow a similar path of reading from the margins but, unintuitively, through Spanish, the high-prestige language of the Philippine Enlightenment. The historical development and meanings of US imperialism shape the ways that disability as a framework can participate in postcolonial critique.

I situate my reading within the second period of major Spanish writing, sometimes called the "golden age" of Hispanic modernity in the Philippines, roughly between the years of the Spanish-American War and World War II (1898–1946).[12] Ironically, this golden age protracts into US colonial rule and rapid Anglophonization of the population.[13] Japanese bombardment of Intramuros, the Spanish colonial fortifications of Manila, is sometimes viewed as the period when Hispanism violently ends, returning the Philippines to "Asia" or an "Asia for Asians" as Japanese colonial propaganda enforced. Focusing on a little-known text like *Novela* during an understudied twentieth-century Spanish writing archive illustrates how meanings of mestizaje changed through disability. In the late nineteenth century, intellectualism and independence movements converged through the bourgeois articulation of a mestizo as the clear intellectual class of anticolonial struggle. This class of landed elite is typically distant from the concerns of the peasant, lumpenproletarian class.

In order to understand the crip Rosarito's significance to studies of Filipino Spanish and US empire, it is important to understand that Hispanic letters in the archipelago are historically and racially tied to a late nineteenth-century mestizo nationalism known as the Propaganda Movement.[14] Mestizo Filipino cultural producers like author José Rizal, painter Juan Luna, and folklorist Isabelo de los Reyes, just to name a few, effloresced Hispanic Filipino cultural critique spanning the political range from revolutionary to reformist. These "Hispanistas" worked across Europe in Spain, Germany, England, and France, propelling a diverse array of cultural production in many academic and literary genres: periodicals, journals, painting, novels, and poetry. They are hagiographically remembered as the mestizo "brains of the nation," a turn of phrase taken from "the First Filipino" José Rizal's famous essay "Las Filipinas dentro de cien años" ("The Philippines a Century's Hence," 1891), in which he stated that the Filipino mestizo intellectual formed the "cerebro de la nación" and demonstrates a clear medicalized corporeality for the Philippines.[15] This is unsurprising as Rizal, the Filipino national hero, was a medical doctor. During this late nineteenth-century "nationalist period," Filipino mestizo thinkers agitated for more sovereignty and rights from Spain via the production of a textual nucleus in Spanish.[16] Spanish was an enlightenment language in the Philippines that attested to a robust intellectual culture deserving of more independence.[17] The "brains of the nation" were coconstituted with the mestizo Filipino body. Contemporary discourses celebrate mestizaje and the Spanish that was produced by its cultured intellectuals. Similar reifications of mestizo intellectualism can be found in other former Spanish colonies (Mexico, Puerto Rico, and Cuba, for example). If the mestizo is the "cerebro" or cerebrum of the nation, who is the "cuerpo" or corpus?

Colonial Ablenationalism and the Disability Culture of US Empire

This essay shifts the conversation on this "minor tradition" of Spanish writing by Filipino mestizos by prioritizing the US colonial period rather than the epoch of Spanish colonialism. Mestizaje and the bodymind that it connotes appear to shift in meaning significantly during this historical period. This is where Rosarito, scripted as the Filipina supercrip, provides us with a vista through which to understand how race, intellectual capacity, and colonialism alter understandings of racial embodiment. Twentieth-century Hispanic modernity, Spanish literature, and the fluctuating meanings around mestizo racial embodiment demonstrate anxieties around independence, sovereignty, and capacity. These anxieties are rehearsed on a debilitated Filipina Indigenous supercrip.[18]

The supercrip is not mestiza but "morena," or brown. Her dark complexion does not connote or intuitively cite the bourgeois intellectual heritage of the late nineteenth-century Propagandists. And yet, in 1930, we can observe her rendering during the late US colonial period, supercripping Spanish through the production of romantic poetry from her hospital bed. Spanish literatures in the Philippines indicate genealogies of intellectual and robust cognitive ability, which have been measured as part and parcel of nationalist discourse. Because Spanish was normally associated with Chinese and Spanish mestizos, it is rarely represented as a language of non-mestizo Filipinos. Spanish itself ushers in a "criollo" (colony-born peninsular Spaniards) class, who later take on and transmute local Indigenous identity through mestizaje.[19] We see a modification from the mestizo nationalism of the late nineteenth century to José Reyes's interwar novel, wherein the heroine that is cast as the "bella cultivadora de las letras hispánicas" (beautiful cultivator of the Hispanic letters) is an indigenized morena Filipina rather than the mestiza.[20]

However, the ways in which more Indigenous articulations of Philippine Hispanic identity are represented is through the allegory of disability. The mestizo, a metonymy for transparent intellectual thought and cognitive capacity, rehabilitates the Filipina thus supercripping Spanish through an enminded feminine body that is visibly impaired. That is to say, Reyes rehabilitates the Filipina, making her reproduce a Hispanic patrimony that does not intuitively belong to her and that does not accurately describe Philippine indigeneity. However, I suggest that this representation does not represent a more egalitarian redistribution of capacity to non-mestiza Filipinas. Rather than expressing ownership of Hispanic Enlightenment, her constitution through disability demonstrates the mestizo author's proprietary relationship to her. He debilitates her body as an object lesson, demonstrating the rehabilitative function of a Spanish, which elevates her mind.

To wit, *Novela*'s most telling vignette, titled "La convaleciente" or "the (Filipina) convalescent," challenges the conventional genealogy of mestizo intellectual history in the Philippines. Rosarito allows us to trace a different transnational genealogy of disability. As I alluded to above, Rosarito, rather than being described as a mixed beauty, is represented as a *trigueña*. The term *trigueña* connotes dark-complexioned skin, citing a more Indigenous appearance in Filipino racial taxonomies. Unmistakable connotations of "indio," "swarthy," even "tawny" are also apt translations of the term in a Philippine context—a racial darkness that connotes a nativeness at odds with enlightened "cerebral" mestizaje. "La trigueña" Rosarito, taking after her mother (who I elaborate on more below), embodies the Indigenous characteristics through which "authentic" Filipina identity is staged. In the above interaction with the "Doctor," Rosarito represents a rehabilitation not only of the body but also of the mind—and thus the Filipina supercrip is fabricated with a whimsical and fanciful diagnosis of "mielitis" or "honey-itis."[21] She supercrips Spanish, demonstrating its rehabilitative powers to cure the pathological savagery of the Filipino native. The novel becomes the genre of her representation, while poetry is the subgenre that attests to her Hispanic mastery. Rather than the mestizo male national social scientist or novelist ushering in an enlightened modern Hispanic Philippines, as was the case in late nineteenth-century independence movements, a shift in mestizaje can be detected during US colonial rule—the edifying powers of mestizaje uplifts a Filipina poet as the conservator of Spanish letters through an unusual and even preternatural poetic dexterity not associated with "savage" subjects, much less women. *Spanish itself* becomes a diagnostic tool that uplifts the Filipino native, and the Spanish novel becomes the diagnostic genre navigating the debilitations of US imperialism. I suggest that this structure of representation is evocative of a structure of power I call "colonial ablenationalism."

Novela's deployment of the supercrip figure illuminates how ableism articulates with colonial nationalism in disabled representations in the early twentieth-century US-occupied Philippines—"colonial ablenationalism." Borrowing from the illuminating work of David T. Mitchell and Sharon L. Snyder, I argue that ableism emerges as a technology in the US colonial Philippines, articulating anthropological distinctions between a cognitive upper class and a perverse intellectually deficient underclass.[22] This perversity marks disability through a subject's deviation from national norms of racialized and gendered embodiment that renders the mestizo as the center of respectable, enlightened, and able-minded national politics. This separation transpires, as it has been extensively argued in Philippine and Filipino American studies, between white US Americans and the Filipinos who would become their custodial populations following the Spanish-American (1898) and Filipino-American Wars (1899–1902), which resulted in the US acquisition of the territories of Cuba, Puerto Rico, Guam, and the Philippines.[23] However, this also transpires among Filipinos themselves through an intracolonialism that historian Paul Kramer has called "imperial indigenisms." Kramer describes this as the process by which more elite Filipinos, generally Chinese and Hispanic mestizos, replicated US colonial dynamics within the Philippines. I suggest that the replication of these dynamics was partly focalized through ideologies of intellectual ability that shape notions of self-government, self-authorship, and sovereignty.

Mitchell and Snyder situate "ablenationalism" in a neoliberal era of late capitalism, in which they index the ways that certain disabled bodies can be integrated into flexible market categories, thus making even impaired bodies sites for the extraction of surplus value. This productively amends other work in disability studies in which the disabled body is theorized as so perverse precisely because it presents a difficulty for capitalist systems to exploit its labor power.[24] Perversity here connotes the risk of a particular maligned subject to become a ward of the state. To avoid such a fate, medical institutions, political bureaucracies, and cultural productions converge to rehabilitate such subjects into a vaunted if inappropriate and discriminatory version of autonomy.[25] In more contemporary strands of disability theory, scholars who attempt to transnationalize disability studies similarly situate their critiques within the strictures of late capital.[26] However, I situate the "biopolitics of disability" within a longer genealogy of colonial history that considers how US empire, and those rehabilitated by empire, historically depended on disabling discourses to rationalize the expansion of territory, influence, and capitalist extraction.[27]

Race organizes the bodymind in a hierarchical fashion, wherein colonial projects, their compromise of political sovereignty, and the emergence and domestication of a "native" colonial subject are justified based on a presumed cognitive and intellectual inferiority of Brown and Black bodies. The correction of their "perversity" is articulated through a colonial ethos of rehabilitation whose end goal is to approximate the self-determining and sovereign colonizer. Colonialism itself can be said to represent the systematized imposition of disability on native people.[28] Oftentimes those victimized by colonial processes respond to their imposition by positioning themselves as *not* disabled. Through a historical and discursive presumption of cognitive deficiency (and thus the inability to self-govern), we can identify racialized, imperial, and colonial genealogies of disability framed within an ideology of "colonial ablenationalism." I define this paradigm as the discursive, narrative, and generic mechanisms through which certain colonized subjects refashion themselves as enminded through a colonial and nationalist ideology of ability. This responds to the systematic dispossession of capacity from the native subject by retrenching similar techniques of disability representation that solidify the very racial hierarchies endemic to colonialism. These able-minded, yet racialized, enlightenment subjects identify more "native" subjects in need of reform, thus amending the debilities of the colonial not by challenging ableism but by positioning themselves as rehabilitators. In the US colonial Philippines, Filipinos themselves were invested in articulating alternative modes of "capacity" to navigate the uncertainties of multiple imperialisms.[29] In a way, such bourgeois colonized intellectuals fashion themselves as supercrips fluent in the language of colonial domination by identifying native subjects in need or uplift, rehabilitation, and intervention.

Despite their own "native past" ethnologically entrapping them, they learn an enlightened language borrowed from Euramerican knowledge paradigms overcoming their colonial "handicaps."[30] In the intersection of US colonial politics and Filipino mestizo cultures, the debilities of imperialism are diverted, cured, or rehabilitated via representations of feminized indigeneity.

The figure of Rosarito, the Filipina supercrip, underscores the ways that Filipino cultural production located at the historical intersection of US and Spanish colonialities falls in the trap of proliferating genres of diagnoses. These diagnostic genres rehabilitate the colonial language of Spanish, reanimating it under US colonialism, to identify feminized figures in need of reform. They are subject to the discourses of colonial rehab and diagnosis, thus propelling mestizo Filipinos into a nationalist rehabilitative class. The argument of this essay becomes deceptively simple then: you are not disabled if you can rehabilitate a colonial other. This may be an abiding and recurring logic in masculinist anticolonialism. By locating the political and racial subject of the Filipina supercrip, disciplined and normed by bourgeois gender and sexual regimes, I explore how we can interrupt this discursive architecture of colonial ablenationalism.[31] Reyes's *Novela* captures a flashpoint in the shifting meanings of indigeneity, mestizaje, and femininity near the end of official US colonial control marked by the Tydings-McDuffie Act of 1934. Cripping US and Spanish colonialism in the Philippines must align postcolonial disability studies, as an intervention into what Chris Bell has called "white disability studies," as a feminist and queer project.[32] That is, we must understand the ways that colonial disability rests on the management of bodies under and through regimes of bourgeois sexual respectability. The analysis of the institution of motherhood and the ways that Filipinas are disciplined by heteroreproductive futurity are of paramount importance toward the goal of mounting a queer postcolonial disability studies that explores diverse crip genealogies in a transnational encounter. Enfranchisement into the national body politic through the normative cultural institutions of motherhood, heterosexuality, and reproductive futurity marks an avenue through which literary genres of diagnosis obtain their power to regulate the Filipina body, through what theorist Victor Román Mendoza has called modes of racial-sexual governance.[33] In the following section I explore the confluence of motherhood and its imbrication with disability.

The "Atrophied Organism" of Model Motherhood

In this section I return to José Reyes's novel and how it postulates a foundational juxtaposition of Filipina womanhood and racial identity.[34] *Novela* represents two idealized forms of Filipina femininity whose representations are the structuring motif of Reyes's eighteen vignettes. Protagonizing what the fore-word to the novel calls the "vicios [and] inclinaciones malas" and the "virtudes humanas" of Philippine society are the Filipinas Anisia and Ángela.[35] Anisia's appearance is described as that of "una belleza típicamente filipina."[36] Reyes's narrative is invested in the construction of "a typical Filipina beauty" who pos-sesses a "cuerpo esbelto y rostro ovalado de tez morena . . . [con] cabellera larga, ondulante y negra como el ébano."[37] Reyes goes to great lengths indigenizing Anisia vis-à-vis her foil, Ángela: "Ángela era una beldad medio amestizada."[38] The shift that the reader can note is that the mestiza characteristics of Ángela are rendered as "menos atractiva que la otra" or less attractive than those of Anisia.[39] This rearticulates previous racialized gendered tropes of mestiza Filipinas as ideal, particularly during the nineteenth century.[40] Reyes's representation may indicate the ways that mestizo politics in this moment of US rule shifts to a na-tive feminine subject to romanticize and consolidate bourgeois gender and sex-ual norms in a native "authentic" past. We observe a shift in racial values through this novel in which the reader is temporally invited to return to a past indigene-ity, before the compromise of Spanish whiteness. Nevertheless, it is a mestizo male author that masterminds the romanticization of the "india" Filipina.

Through these Filipinas, Reyes elaborates two distinct trajectories for the Philippine nation, represented in the heteroproductive nuclear family and written through the pathologies and virtues of Filipina femininity. Anisia, the normative embodiment of Filipina virtue, shores up the Philippine nation through the gendered labor of motherhood within the context of a hetero-nuclear and respectable Filipino family. She is, indeed, the embodiment of the titular vignette "una madre modelo" or "a model mother."[41] She is the romantic and ideal wife for the protagonist and idealized Filipino, Mario—both models for the Philippine nation. However, the romanticism of this mother figure ob-tains by imperiling and debilitating her body.

So ideal is Mario and Anisia's life together, "en posesión de todo cuanto el hombre puede apetecer en el mundo,"[42] that colonial disability is narrativized as inevitable destiny: "La ley de compensación, sin embargo . . . hizo que un día cayese enfermo el menor de sus hijos," which, naturally, "llenaba de pesadumbre el corazón de la madre."[43] Anisia's "instinto maternal" is rendered almost pre-ternatural, given that she is charged with the sickly child's care. So, of course, the "foundational romance," to borrow from Doris Sommer,[44] sees the idealized heterosexual pair composed of the industrious Mario and the model of moth-erhood, Anisia, diverting resources to the treatment of an illness "[que] seguía su curso alamante, agravándose cada vez más."[45] Indeed, so dedicated and all-encompassing was Anisia's care that it imperils her own health:

Tantas noches pasadas de vela, junto al lecho del hijo enfermo, acabaron por quebrantar la salud de Anisia, cayéndo [*sic*] enferma a su vez. Pero enferma y todo, y no obstante contar con nodrizas y enfermeras, y con el cariño paternal y no menos solícito de su marido y de sus padres, que, en vano la advertían del peligro que corría su salud, convenciéndola de la necesidad de evitar aquellos desvelos que *atrofiaban su organismo*, no quiso apartarse jamás ni un momento del hijo idolatrado. Al fin, quiso el cielo escuchar los ruegos y premiar la dulce abnegación y sacrificio heróico de la madre, devolviendo la salud al hijo querido.[46]

Model motherhood is a complete surrender of health and well-being for the future of the nation embodied by the ailing health of the son. Filipinas are certainly represented as the more debilitated sex; however, the acute impairments render sacrificial motherhood a strength to be leveraged by the masculinist nation. Feminine sentimentality, emotionality, tenderness, and the labor of care are configured as important forms of bodily work whose physical realities debilitate the Filipina body; indeed, they "*atrophy* her organism." So profound is Anisia's maternal illness that despite her "constitución fuerte y vigorosa... llegó a padecer de clorosis, con insomnios... que degeneró después en consunción."[47] Tuberculosis is the final diagnosis for which "las eminencias médicas... las inyecciones y tónicos" were in vain.[48] Anisia's idealized "typically Filipina" body goes through a drastic change to the point where "estaba completamente desconocida."[49] No longer was she "la esbelta y encantadora mujer de antes."[50] She was no longer the slim and enchanting womanly figure that the reader comes to know just a few pages prior. The draining and debilitating labor of maternity is quickly narrativized via disability tropes of inspirational and all-encompassing care that even threatens the potential erotic appeal of the Filipina. Anisia becomes a pitiable sight "[que] daba lástima contemplar... su perfil macilento y sombrío, su figura melancólica y triste."[51]

Both Anisia and Ángela's exposition, whether as boon or perfidy to the nation, hinges on their identification with motherhood: "dios castiga a la mujer que ahoga en su seno el gérmen de la futura generación. Y nada hay ciertamente, más valeroso, más bello, más romántico en el mundo, que la maternidad."[52] Motherhood then stands as the principal institution through which Filipinas are integrated into the national imaginary. Their integration, however, is as diminished figures. Deviation from the ideal of Filipina motherhood marks a danger to be managed for the overall stability of the heteroproductive nation. Dedication to model motherhood means living within a debilitated state through which the sacrifice of care can be understood as meaningful and adjudicated as "authentic"—it is no accident, I wager, that Anisia is "típicamente Filipina" and thus is predisposed to such deleterious sacrifice. Disability becomes the very metric by which we can gauge the Filipina's dedication to the national labor of mothering. Filipina motherhood becomes tubercular in Reyes's novel in that the presence of sickness in the Filipina body demonstrates that her sacrifice of bodily wellness becomes a barometer measuring her worthiness as a mother and proper citizen. The disability of her body, once more, ensures that the future male progeny of the nation persists. It seems that the health of the Filipino nuclear family and its ability to be reproduced into and as national futurity hinges on the sickness of the Filipina body—her "organismo" atrophies into a future temporality that is national time. National time is a kind of crip time.[53] This "model mother" of the Philippines, in her debilitated state, establishes a heteroproductive nuclear logic within a framework of colonial disability. Nevertheless, while the son cared for by Anisia is the figure that the reader is asked to hope for full recuperation, Mario and Anisia's daughter, Rosarito, is represented simultaneously as a figure of diminished physical and enhanced mental capacities.

As I've elaborated above, Rosarito, the crip poet, appears in a vignette titled "La convaleciente" or "the convalescent," which brings the reader into the space of institutionalized medicine: "Era [*sic*] en la sala cuatro del Hospital General, en una de esas celdas donde la soledad es oprimente, y profundo el silencio en las horas nocturnales. Rosarito, una bella hija de Anisia, paciente de la institución, linda joven trigueña de dieciocho abriles, rasgaba nerviosa con la pluma-fuente sobre la nítida blancura de unas cuartillas impolutas."[54] Rosarito's illness restricts her to the bed of her "celda." The oppressiveness (oprimente) of her solitude, the writer instructs us, inspires a nervous scribbling (rasgaba) of her pluma-fuente (feather fountain pen). Represented for us is a compelling portrait of sickly femininity dedicated to the craft of the writing *of* or, perhaps, *on* "unas cuartillas impolutas." The portrayal of the "pluma-fuente" as the device of choice represents the young sick poet in a particularly romantic register. Imagine if in your convalescence with what we later come to find is "consumption," an illness whose virality spreads throughout Reyes's vignettes imperiling the novella's heroines, you are struck by a wave of inspiration more acute than the symptoms of your sickness.

What might be more striking than the intersection of bodily illness, acute impairment, and metered prose is the romanticization that is advanced not solely through the disablement of inspiration (or the inspiration of disablement) but also through the racialization of gender. The impairment and youthful mastery of the joven trigueña (brown young woman) possess a rehabilitative protocol. The above lines furnish a powerful racial corrective to the masculinist teleologies of Philippine Enlightenment, which have sacralized the mestizo ilustrado as the progenitor of the Hispanic letters. It should therefore surprise and intrigue that it is a "trigueña" and therefore indigenized Filipina who wields the pen of Philippine Spanish letters. Reyes sets into relief the feminized racial type of the Filipina trigueña on the "nítida blancura" (clear whiteness) of her prose. Figuratively, the "cuartillas" on which Rosarito composes her poems are literally white: "la nítida blancura de unas cuartillas impolutas."[55] I should note that *cuartilla* (quatrain) could have two possible meanings. In this context both make sense. *Cuartilla* is a term for "hoja de papel" or a sheet of paper. However, in a more ancient meaning, according to *Diccionario de la Real Academia Española*, *cuartilla* can refer to "una estrofa de cuatro versos" or more deliberately "una combinación métrica que consta de cuatro versos octosílabos, de los cuales asonantan el segundo y el último."[56] Given the hispanophilia that suffuses the romantic portrait of the dark-skinned (trigueña) poetisa, we shouldn't underestimate the portrayal of antique rhyming verse in the style of "redondilla." And lest the anticipation overwhelm, part of the Doctor's prescription for Rosarito's "mielitis" is more poetry!

From her bed, surrounded by a bevy of nurses, her doctor, and Anisia, Rosarito, "con labios enjoyados de sonrisa,"[57] recites

> Es la vida un perfume
> En la edad de las pasiones
> Dulce edad bella y florida
> En que triunfa la esperanza . . .
>
> Life is a perfume
> In the age of passion
> A tender, florid, and beautiful age
> In which hope triumphs

A poem to which "El Doctor" responds "entusiasmado" or excitedly: "Perfectísimamente. Si usted continúa cultivando las letras, llegará a ser una notabilidad algún día."[58] Note that it is a medical doctor who remarks that the "trigueña" poet will become a renowned writer. It is curious that it is a symbolization of the medical sciences, the masculinist figure that is meant to cure the body of Rosarito, who is endowed with the authority to legitimate her literary contributions in Spanish. There is an intriguing union of Spanish coloniality and medicalized disability wherein crip poetics enable this dark-skinned poetess to produce and reproduce the nation. While she has inherited this erstwhile

Hispanic heritage, it is within the context of colonial medicine that she emerges as a supercrip that professes uncommon literary acumen. And in perhaps the most saccharine discovery in Philippine letters is the overwrought and, frankly, idiotic poetry that is to follow, showing the reader the error of their ways. It is not actually Rosarito that is the star that we are meant to center, even in a half-baked proto-feminist liberalism that gives impetus to her poetic exploits in *Novela*. The Doctor is also a poet. The intersection of a colonial medical model and crip poetics also manifests in the Doctor's own intertextual poetic ode to those feminine careworkers that aid in Rosarito's convalescence—"la nurse":

> Sencilla y humilde, como esa tímida flor que oculta su perfume entre el silencio de los altos muros, cuando el deber la llama y la coloca junto al lecho de dolor de los que sufren, prodigándoles el bálsamo espiritual de su ternura y solicitud, la nurse, con su albo traje y nívea toca graciosamente prendida sobre su cabecita, cual blanca y enorme mariposa, es dulcemente seductora. Pero también, en los paréntesis de ensueño a que tan bella y discretamente sabe ella entregarse de cuando en cuando, es ferviente de-vota de lo bello y lo sublime, y su alma, sedienta de luz, se abre como un capullo a la expansión. . . . fué [*sic*] para nosotros una revelación del alma delicada y paradójica de estas modernas hijas del presente, que llenan hu-mildemente una necesidad social, con su noble y humanitaria misión.[59]

Catherine Ceniza Choy argues in her book *Empire of Care* that the Filipina nurse is a pivotal form of racial and gendered labor that demonstrates the ar-ticulation of US imperialism as a form of benevolent assimilation and care.[60] Amazingly, we see this figure here in Spanish letters. Although Choy's study focuses on post-1948 US-Philippine relations, which saw the proliferation of American-trained Philippine nurses to the United States, the Doctor's ode to "la nurse" presages this feminization of medical care work. Indeed, it is in the invocation of the anglicized "la nurse" rather than the consistent use of "en-fermera" or "nodriza" that is curious. This demonstrates the extent to which Reyes's writing on "local" forms of Filipino subjectivity and culture in the Span-ish language still bear the mark of US colonialism. In this sense, such local, au-thentic portraits of Philippine life, while having the effect of localizing Spanish as a Philippine language, also represent one permutation of Filipino-American literature. This might be this essay's most controversial claim: this Spanish lan-guage novel written during and in response to US colonialism should be read as a part of Filipino American letters and literature. This inclusion demon-strates the extent to which Spanish literatures were in conversation with US imperial policy, which literally affects the poetical and thematic structure and representation of care and impairment in Philippine writing. This shows the ways that Spanish writing responded, integrated, and managed the influences of US empire. What might it mean to center Rosarito as a Filipina American figure? Rosarito is the colonial supercrip who in her convalescence undertakes the noble mission of cultivating the "Hispanic letters," rehabilitating the cultural deficit of the enlightened language in the Philippines. Stunningly, Rosarito, the "trigueña" brown supercrip, "la gentil convaleciente," continues a legacy of mestizo enlightenment enshrined in Spanish letters that was not initially meant for her. But here she is, "Rosarito[,] la bella cultivadora de las letras hispanas" for "aquellos amantes del sonoro idioma cervantino."[61]

Literary scholar Sami Schalk has interrogated the critical uptake and takedown of the term "supercrip" in disability studies literature. Schalk contends that we must "trace the intellectual and linguistic" origins of the supercrip. A likely origin of the supercrip discourse is early twentieth-century representations of the blind, whose apparent ability to be productive citizens changed perceptions around their capabilities to contribute to society. Indeed, the fact that they could do "normal" activities like hold a job, go to school, and the like is rendered superhuman and awe-inspiring. To wit, Schalk references Garland-Thomson's well-known analyses on discourses of freakery and enfreakment in the late nineteenth century.[62] In the context of the Euramerican diffusion of eugenics and racial science, Spanish Filipino writing produces an inspirational figure of a brown poet that cultivates Hispanic letters in Asia. Moreover, her literary ability is adjudicated by a medical professional whose diagnosis of Rosarito's "romantic" ailment allegorizes a diagnosis for the Philippines. At the same time, this analysis of the confluence of disability, medicine, and crip poetry demonstrates how race, gender, and sexuality shift under US imperialism from universally elegizing the mestizo to the feminization of Philippine indigeneity—a racial purity that is not at odds with Hispanic culture but rather is enhanced by it. What is connoted as Indigenous, autochthonous, and native in this text is tactically aligned with illness and impairment. In a form of generic and representational power I suggest we call the "colonial ablenational," we can observe how this alignment of the Indigenous with the disabled problematically shows us who needs to be rehabilitated and who does the rehabilitation. In *Novela*, the twinning of dutiful indigenized maternal care and its progeny results in a very different kind of Hispanic heroine: the convalescent trigueña in Asia. This recasts feminine debility as an inspirational trope that at once shows how Hispanism is an endangered species but also dramatizes its maintenance through the poetical acumen displayed by a body that one would not initially signify as possessing or having a stake in enlightenment modernity.

Genre as Diagnosis

Colonial ablenationalism describes the alignment of colonial subjects' representational strategies with ableism. Rather than challenge the ableism of colonialism, anticolonialism reproduces it. In the case of Reyes's *Novela*, this reproduction of colonial ableism involves the tactical racialization and feminization of disability anchored in the Filipina body. The ablenational, through diagnostic literary genres, works to uphold a racial nationalist form of able-bodied and enminded embodiment. I suggest that a Filipino subject's perceived evolutionary and political distance from a native subject attested to one's cognitive capacity to self-govern. In this essay, I have explored how the discursive field of mestizaje shapes a division of capacities in Filipino cultural politics in the early twentieth century and how such divisions are navigated through gendered debilitated representations of impairment and deficiency. The Philippines, a former Spanish colony, has its own genealogy of mestizo nationalism that goes underremarked in Latin American studies, and is undertheorized in Latinx studies, whose own discourses of mestizx diasporic and immigrant politics are shaped by antecedent histories of Latin American independence—narratives that excise transpacific understandings of Spanish coloniality. It is my belief that staging a transpacific understanding of mestizaje can bring seemingly ancillary genealogies of racial politics to the center, thus articulating frameworks between Asian American and Latinx studies via case studies of US empire in the Hispanic Philippines. From my vantage, the representational matrix of racialized disability makes these conversations productive and imminently possible.

In this genealogy of ablenationalist nation-building, one of the effects of the ideology of ability is that of effacing imperialism in favor of an abstracted intellectual subject (however reformed), disarticulated from the architectures of empire that argued for that subject's cognitive deficiencies in the first place. We can see in this crip genealogy that one of the effects of rehabilitation is the omission of a revolutionary past in favor of a reformed patient. Rehabilitative regimes gain their power through their discursive ability to silence the realities of the colonial, repackaging them as abstract freedoms. The stakes of using the framework of colonial ablenationalism have to do with globalizing Euramerican frameworks pertaining to corporeal and cognitive variation within historical genealogies of imperialism. Disability is a pivotal aspect that goes underremarked in histories of imperialism. What might it mean to look at histories of empire as themselves ruptures in global disability histories? In other work, I have pondered what it might mean for disability studies to be articulated as an activist and intellectual discourse in dialectical relation to a state formation that is embedded in a colonial past.[63] For this reason, "mestizo" literature can shed light on colonial genealogies of ableist ideology and nationalism, offering not only a crip genealogy of US imperialism in the Philippines, but also an alternative "global context" by which we can understand how ideologies of embodiment, disability, and capacity obtain differently.[64] More pointedly: What does it mean to ask the state for accommodation in the present while obviating the colonial past? What disabilities are propounded in such a compulsive omission of coloniality?

NOTES

1 Isaac, *American Tropics*.
2 What I mean by *indigeneity* and *Indigenous* in this essay are those representations of "pure" racial, non-mestizo types and literary figures attesting to a romantic return to an uncompromised "native" subject.
3 Reyes, *Novela de la Vida Real*.

> THE DOCTOR.—[You're] always writing!
>
> ROSARIO.—(raising her eyes, blushing and shy.) What would you have me do? It's my favorite pastime. Besides, writing I begin to forget that I'm actually sick . . .
>
> DOCTOR.—But if you have become better suddenly. What you have now is . . .
>
> ROSARIO.—What is it?
>
> DOCTOR.—"Mielitis."
>
> ANISSA.—And what is mielitis?
>
> DOCTOR.—(With a solemn and mischievous accent.)—Romanticism, madam.
>
> Everyone smiles.

I furnish text from Reyes's novel in the original Spanish. I place the Spanish in the body of the essay to preserve, center, and prioritize the original language of the text. All translations are my own.
4 Bolton, "Cripping the Philippine Enlightenment," 138–62.
5 "I have read this novel with interest and I recommend it to those in the Philippines that read Spanish or wish to learn it, which are unfortunately very few in number with each passing day." Reyes, *Novela de la Vida Real*, 1.
6 "These days books abound that although are brilliantly written have questionable moral value for our youth, the reading that Mr. Reyes's works provide us constitutes a very healthy exception." Reyes, *Novela de la Vida Real*, 1.
7 Clare, *Exile and Pride*.
8 Oliver, "The Social Model of Disability."
9 Fanon et al., *Wretched of the Earth*.
10 Barker and Murray, "Disabling Postcolonialism," 219–36.

11   See Ileto, *Pasyon and Revolution*; Cruz, *Mother Figured*; Rafael, *Contracting Colonialism*. For more on critical Filipino studies I recommend the anthology, Manalansan and Espiritu, *Filipino Studies*.

12   García Castellón, *Estampas y Cuentos*.

13   Cruz, *Transpacific Femininities*.

14   Thomas, *Orientalists, Propagandists, and Ilustrados*.

15   Mojares, *Brains of the Nation*.

16   For a rundown and takedown of the segmentation of Philippine historiography, see Ileto, "Outlines of a Non-Linear Emplotment of Philippine History," 130–59.

17   Reyes, *Love, Passion and Patriotism*.

18   Schalk, "Reevaluating the Supercrip," 71–87.

19   Quijano and Ennis, "Coloniality of Power," 533–81.

20   Vasconcelos, *La Raza Cosmica*.

21   The term *mielitis* can translate to *myelitis*, which is a neurological condition that manifests as an inflammation of the spinal cord. However, in the romantic context of Reyes's novel, it is unlikely that the "Doctor" gives a proper unwhimsical diagnosis. Oddly enough, myelitis can result in an inhibited communication between the brain and the rest of the body.

22   Mitchell and Snyder, *Biopolitics of Disability*.

23   Some of the most influential works in Filipino American studies that I draw on include Kramer, *Blood of Government*; Rafael, *White Love and Other Events*; see also Echavez, *The Decolonized Eye*; Anderson, *Colonial Pathologies*.

24   Ko, *Cinderella's Sisters*.

25   See Baynton, *Defectives in the Land*; Canaday, *Straight State*.

26   See Johnson and McRuer, "Cripistemologies," 127–47; Erevelles, *Disability and Difference*.

27   Mitchell and Snyder, *Biopolitics of Disability*.

28   Barker and Murray, "Disabling Postcolonialism."

29   Puar, "Prognosis Time," 161–72.

30   Trinh, *Woman, Native, Other*.

31   This is a type of racialized sexual power that Victor Román Mendoza has helpfully termed "racial-sexual governance" in his book *Metroimperial Intimacies*.

32   Bell, "Introducing White Disability Studies," 275–82.

33   Mendoza, *Metroimperial Intimacies*.

34   Resonant with Reyes's project is the specter of José Rizal's iconic María Clara, whose pure monastic mestiza femininity continues to inform even contemporary constructions of the Filipina. *Novela* precedes Rizal's *Noli Me Tangere* (1887) by more than forty years. Readers can thus observe a racial shift in understandings of gender relations that diverges from and also aligns with Rizal.

35   Translation: "vices and bad inclinations" and "human virtues." Reyes, *Novela de la Vida Real*, 1.

36   "a typically Filipina beauty." Reyes, *Novela de la Vida Real*, 1.

37   "a slender body and an oval face of brown complexion . . . with long wavy hair black as ebony." Reyes, *Novela de la Vida Real*, 1.

38 "Ángela was a beauty, somewhat mixed or mestiza." Reyes, *Novela de la Vida Real*, 1.

39 Reyes, *Novela de la Vida Real*, 1.

40 Such tropes of mestiza Filipinas were, perhaps, most famously invented by Filipino nationalist José Rizal (1861–96). Rizal is considered the Filipino national hero. He authored two Spanish novels, *Noli Me Tangere* (1887) and *El Filibusterismo* (1891), which are considered national classics. These examples of Filipino nationalist literature are foundational in consolidating gender and sexual norms for and within Filipino racial politics. For Filipina women, this is clear with Rizal's idealized mestiza character, María Clara. Denise Cruz penned a powerful study demonstrating how María Clara's whiteness continues to shape Filipina racialized gender and sexuality in the contemporary moment even though this character was invented in the late nineteenth century. See Cruz, *Transpacific Femininities*.

41 Cruz, *Transpacific Femininities*, 4–5.

42 "in possession of everything that a man could ever want in the world." Cruz, *Transpacific Femininities*, 5.

43 "The law of compensation, nevertheless . . . made it so their youngest son fell ill," which naturally "filled the mother with nightmares." Cruz, *Transpacific Femininities*, 5.

44 Sommer, *Foundational Fictions*.

45 "continued on her alarming course, the sickness worsening with each passing day." Reyes, *Novela de la Vida Real*, 5.

46 "The many sleepless nights spent at the sick child's bedside resulted in the diminishment of Anisia's health, falling ill herself. Despite her illness, and with the help of nursemaids and nurses, and with the paternal care and even the solicitous affection of her husband and parents, who, in vain warned her of how her health was jeopardized, convincing her of the necessity to avoid those sleepless nights that *decayed her body [atrophied her organism]*, she absolutely refused to be parted even a moment from her beloved son. Finally, she entreated the heavens to hear her cries and to reward the sweet abnegation and heroic sacrifice of the mother, returning health to her beloved child." Reyes, *Novela de la Vida Real*, 6 (emphasis added).

47 "Her strong and vigorous constitution . . . she began to suffer from chlorosis, with insomnia . . . which then degenerated into consumption (tuberculosis)." Reyes, *Novela de la Vida Real*, 4.

48 "Medical resources, injections, and tonics were in vain." Reyes, *Novela de la Vida Real*, 4.

49 "She was, suddenly, completely unrecognizable." Reyes, *Novela de la Vida Real*, 4.

50 "She was no longer the thin and enchanting woman as before." Reyes, *Novela de la Vida Real*, 4.

51 "She inspired pity to even contemplate her . . . her malnourished and somber profile, her melancholic and sad figure." Reyes, *Novela de la Vida Real*, 4. I have translated *pena* here to *pity* but it might very well be translated to *shame*. Anisia's debilitated and diminished figure might, indeed, inspire shame.

52 "God punishes the woman who drowns within her womb the seed of future generations. And there is nothing, certainly, more courageous, more beautiful, more romantic in the world than motherhood." Reyes, *Novela de la Vida Real*, 4.

53   Kafer, *Feminist, Queer, Crip.*

54   "She was in room four of the General Hospital, in one of those cells where the solitude is oppressive, and the silence is profound during the witching hours of the night. Rosarito, Anisia's beautiful daughter, patient of the institution, a young brown woman of eighteen Aprils, nervously scratched with her fountain-pen on the neat whiteness of clean sheets of paper." Reyes, *Novela de la Vida Real*, 54.

55   "the clear whiteness of several flawless quatrains." Reyes, *Novela de la Vida Real*, 54.

56   ASALE, RAE, *Diccionario de la lengua española*, Edición del Tricentenario, accessed April 2, 2019, http://dle.rae.es/. A *cuartilla* can refer to a "stanza of four verses" or, more deliberately, "a metric combination that contains four octosyllabic verses, of which the second and the last assonantly rhyme."

57   "With lips embellished with a smile." Reyes, *Novela de la Vida Real*, 58.

58   "Sublimely perfect. If you continue cultivating the word, you will become renowned one day." Reyes, *Novela de la Vida Real*, 59.

59   "Modest and humble, like the shy flower that hides her scent within the silence of these tall walls, when duty calls her and places her at the bedside of those who suffer in pain, bestowing upon them the spiritual succor of her tenderness and solicitude, the nurse, with her white uniform and snow-white headdress graciously placed upon her little head, she, a white enormous butterfly, is sweetly seductive. But also, within the parentheses of daydream where she so beautifully and discreetly ventures from time to time, she is a fervent devotee of the beautiful and the sublime, and her soul, thirsty for light, opens up like an expanding cocoon. . . . For us it was a revelation of the delicate and paradoxical soul of these modern girls of the moment, who humbly fulfill a social need, with their noble and humanitarian mission." Reyes, *Novela de la Vida Real*, 59–60.

60   Choy, *Empire of Care.*

61   "Rosarito, the beautiful cultivator of Hispanic letters" for "those lovers of the sonorous Cervantine language." Reyes, *Novela de la Vida Real*, 60.

62   Garland-Thomson, *Extraordinary Bodies.*

63   Bolton, "Cripping the Philippine Enlightenment."

64   Erevelles, *Disability and Difference.*

13. DIFFERENTIAL BEING AND EMERGENT AGITATION

MEL Y. CHEN

This chapter schematically addresses—first by focally considering, then by turning askew—the relationship between what I call "differential being" and the environment at large (virtual, social, physical) of the contemporary university that must be navigated as a part of the normative educational process. In asking questions about the collective entity of the university, its institutionality, and the bodies—human, nonhuman, and inhuman—within it, I have been concerned with the ways in which fluency or its interruption become marked, as well as ways in which the systemic maintenances of difference are adjudicated.[1] In so doing, I am grateful for studies of institutional difference and diversity, resistance, chemicality, illness, and disability that have given this current piece an appreciable orientation.

In writing this chapter, I wanted to respond to Julietta Singh and Nathan Snaza's call to attend to "undergrowth," which they define in relation to "myriad encounters, relations, and affective shuttlings that enable 'education' even if they happen at a scale . . . that is outside of traditional humanist ways of viewing education," as well as "fugitive ungovernability."[2] Inspired by considerations of undercommons, as well as meditations on those subdetectible regions below the marking thresholds of being that congeal around identity, I'm particularly interested in the forms of undergrowth that, in denying, challenging, or circuiting cogitation, summon the risk of disability or incapacity, such as questions of development or more broadly the narrative progression by which a learning body must undergo ordered changes.[3] Underdevelopment, by strict definitions, marks a "failure" of the encounter between body and institution, and that failure is too easily cast on an individuated human/inhuman body rather than, say, the neoliberally configured institution itself. Here I draw on my newer work on what I understand broadly as "agitation," which takes account of—to use their superficial categorizations—self-evidently "political" as well as physiologically emergent agitations. These include the incitements to movement of mind and body—"intolerances"—brought about by pharma drugs or insupportable levels of pollutants; ocean water in a strong wind; the unruliness of children already subject to securitizing impulses in early education; and the collectively choreographed gestures of street protest. The attribution of "agitation" travels through all of these, and keeps intention, and therefore agency, at bay. Indeed that is the trick of the use of agitation: in helping to allege the machinic, or forms of mental incapacity, in agitators it can be used to assist in processes of inhumanization. Instead of accepting the common discursive segregation of these examples, I actively consider their agglutination, or at least a remapping at larger scales, as well as why etymology might suggest a meaningful way to relate them. I write at a time when it feels important both to continue to expand what is meant by disability, albeit with an awareness of the capitalization of medicalized or securitized categories (that is, ones taken up in regimes of security), as well as do the work of translation for various long-standing forms of material oppression and the contemporary novelties of becoming. At the same time, disability can confer a selective entitlement, or reveal an interior hierarchization, because as a social and administrative category it tends toward the recognizable (iconic disabilities are taken as more legitimate or valid, particularly in a system that attributes properties to recognizable subjects). Taking honestly the reflexive impulse of disability studies, "disability" can and should be itself examined, disaggregated, in the interest of understanding its own fluent traffic in relation to the *racialized* workings and accountabilities of institutions like the university, in terms of diversity mandates and attributions, as well as the deployment of broad notions of "deficit" to race-, gender-, and class-marked categories while an idealized form of imperial whiteness goes unmarked. In all of these discussions, I believe that considering materiality and affect, in ways that do not start from the fantasy of this unmarked figure, can make palpable some cherished forms of undergrowth.

"Differential being," in this chapter, refers to ways of being in space, time, and sociality that allow for variabilities that in themselves are not cognizant of social difference, and yet manage to interpellate those differences. The categories called "race" and "disability" are notions that sum—into labile, responsive form—massive distributions of being, sensation, and matter, distributions with interested histories. Affect studies suggests that if the calculus of race and disability often seem simple or formulaic in terms of legislation, labor practices, or public policy, what they reveal under examination, even within these domains, are deeply contingent, highly specific formulations that only come to *seem* entrenched and repetitive. It is true not only of race, but of disability, that the scopes of their deployment are endlessly flexible and appropriative. I have thus felt compelled to think in relation to both notions ever since sensing the vastness of their complicity with the mechanisms of capitalism and, by association, education, which inevitably articulates (even if complexly) into majoritarian society and its embroilments. Differential being allows for cuts like "slowness," which, on the one hand, do not attach securely to either race or disability but engage in traffic with both and, on the other, still expose bodies to the management and discipline of the university.

Undergrowth, undercommons. Undergrowth (one take, anyway): the apparent relative slowness of the universe that nevertheless makes good on what it suggests.[4] Undercommons: what can be found in and around the university, in spite of the canceling tendencies of the settler state found within it. That is, by pointing to the universe before the university, I celebrate an undergrowth that defies value judgments or quantificatively shriveled takes on its beneathness and rather owns a promise of subtension, a vastness of potential that remains in spite of everything. As those studying the university's dependency on diversity have pointed out, the tyranny of names includes those of race and disability put (along with a few other exclusives) to the work of co-optational diversification. Undergrowth and undercommons recognize that, as much as these tyrannical imaginations may lay claim to something of what's there, there is always a supplement or a fundament that escapes their reach.

But, lest undergrowth yield too easily to a metaphor of soil, for all its decolonial promise, and the uses of fundament, I also wonder about air—the ether, the stuff of material question. There is a strange, I think undeservedly stark opposition between substance and air, let's say, the serious, grounded, rational masculine subject and the ditzy airhead that continues to circulate, which still crystallizes and values intellectual work as well as restages environment itself. I am thinking here of the work of anthropologists Timothy Choy and Jerry Zee, who build on Choy's meditations on the failed substantiations of Hong Kong air because of the failure of social theory to take air as "anything but solidity's lack."[5] Rather, they attend to the state or thing called "suspension," which is a way to allow for the viscous and the airy to be at peace rather than the categorially segregating divide that yields descriptions like "materials in air." Dissatisfied by the stubborn exclusivities attributed to human embodied-minded being (e.g., skin boundaries, apex of sentience), as well as the easy promulgations of presumed exteriorities (e.g., "air" that is not of "body") across a swath of educational domains and lay pedagogies, I take "suspension" to offer, for the purposes of this essay, that the very materiality of human being—as well as the presumed externality of the stuff with which it engages—must remain in suspense, casting continued doubt on, for instance, the facial phenotypes of race and the visible prosthetic determinants of disability, as well as the forms of becoming involved in, for instance, *breathing things*. Finally, my respect for the ample mysteries of suspension that escape contemporary epistemological closure is tied in some way to my having been influenced by discussions on the right to opacity and wiliness: the project of exhaustive knowledge for its own sake mimics the rapaciousness of colonial desire, and one response to it is to reject the obligation to be known or knowable.[6] These are anticolonial discussions that wax and wane in the literature, but remain necessary because of the sticky coloniality of what has been established as scholarly.

There is nothing mechanistic about the grace and the magic of this indeterminate (as far as the nominalist is concerned) place of undergrowth, as I see it. But it is certainly a place that has, in addition to structures, mechanics, pathways, emergences. I return here to agitations. As suggested above, agitations cross the realms of the human, inhuman, and nonhuman and capture some form of un-rest. That un-rest can be naturalized as political activity, but traditionally only in certain predictable senses attuned to favored definition. And when un-rest is either indicted or dismissed, accusers can borrow precisely on discourses on materiality or mechanicity to allege mental loss: agitators may be doing, but they can't grasp what they are doing.[7] Affect theories have opened questions of politics back into matter, bringing, for instance, materiality studies to consider long-standing lessons about race's materialities that were/are brought about by a vast colonial imagination. I have turned to the workings of intoxication, considered as a kind of material being, sometimes temporary, sometimes durative, that assists in yielding affordances to certain bodies and cancellations of others, intensified by extant framings of security, criminality, and medicality.

In the university, agitated gesture—whether in the form of politically legible protest, aggressive physicality, or movement (including stillness or slowness) inopportune to favored class habitus—has no proper home, save perhaps in the possibilities of dance training or intramural sport. And on the choreographically imagined stage of political demonstration, disabled gesture is too often removed from the possibility of the political. With the exception of nonnormative movements domesticated for the purpose of representing the value of minoritized disability in the university—for instance, the rolling of a wheelchair—illegitimated expression, as wrong or slow cognition, or as nondeliberative or ill-classed gesture, co-conspires to begin or complete one's removal from the university or to guarantee that joining the community is not possible.

And yet agitations of all kinds, as I have argued elsewhere, "deserve" the mark of the political insofar as their evacuation from the political has delegitimated them and insofar as they may exist precisely as a response to the oppressive environment of the extended university or to a history of institutional violence.[8] What I describe as emergent agitations, then, are those that reside in or emerge from regions of undergrowth.

I constantly try, within the spaces of the university, to invite forms of movement or stillness—anything but what we have been trained. When I deliver talks, I have developed the practice of opening them with an invitation to be otherwise, while speaking to the disciplining of bodies in a place that would seem to care only for their complement, the mind; the raciality of that disciplining; and the removal of bodies defined as improper or insurgent. The more outright militarization of the university's spaces and bodies—the panoply of campus police actions—is complemented by a securitization of movement falsely sensitized to class, race, and disability, such that measures of identity difference alone could signal a danger to "the community" (which is presumed thus to exclude race-marked, class-marked, and disability-marked people). Within the university it remains all too easy to be a Black student taken to be in the "wrong" place, such as a dorm; a non-national taking "too long" to answer a question at an exam; a student whose physical twitches and adventurous intellectual jumps, as if they were of a piece, serve together to discredit. If all of these scenarios have happened (they have), the structuring of security suggests that most such incidences go unreported.

While there are so many incidences within the university I have witnessed in my years there, I want to turn to think especially about the undergrowth that *isn't* considered to be housed inside a neatly boundaried university or active only within its particular, teleologizing terms. I'm interested in thinking about spaces perhaps kin to the university (not just its "satellite campuses") and carrying some of its mandates, invested in productions of knowledge, but not believed to operate by its fullest norms. After all, if so many spaces of higher education have become almost caricatures of what they once threatened, undergrowths and their pedagogies can still—perhaps especially now—be found everywhere.[9] My commitment to the potentials found in even the most thoroughly "institutional" university must be complemented—first and foremost for myself—by a pedagogy of spaciousness and a memory that most knowledges have *not* come of it; rather, the learning in this place is but one version, full of "tools" and precise vocabulary, lexical and bodily, that could be repurposed, yet is woven into mandates of capital and hierarchy, and implicated both historically and in the present with unambiguously eugenic and colonial exertions of dominance. (Those precise lexical vocabularies mentioned above preview the latter portion of this chapter, whereby language is pitted against other modalities of reference, of knowledge.) That reflexive pedagogy is there to remind me why there should be no surprise when an Asian nonbinary student performs an absolutely unusual (again, for the university) dance at the conclusion of my What Is Queer Cultural Production class and another student who has in our classroom rarely ventured beyond convention is the first, not the last, to pronounce it "amazing"; there should be no surprise when one of the first two nonverbal students at Berkeley is randomly assigned a presentation about Temple Grandin's work scientifically likening the prevalent anxiety characteristics of agricultural animals to the anxieties of autistic people (she problematically adheres to dismissing the potential of so-called low-functioning autistic people, a cline linking autism and "function" to which many autistic people object), and pronounces that the only thing that makes him anxious is Temple Grandin. In a space where it takes courage not only to be a racialized isolate, but also to rock, to twitch, to stand when others are not standing or to sit when others are standing, to laugh out of sync, to lie down, to have any kind of a discernible smell other than racialized, classed, gender-appropriate scents, to make intellectual connections between circumscribed domains and across accepted genres that "sound mad," undergrowth must remind that it is not only there, it constitutes a ground by which the "there" of the university may be defined.

So here I deliberately turn, not to a canonical scene within the nominal space of the university, but rather to a place closely associated with its elements of legitimated knowledge, inheritance, enlightenment, and archive—the state library—a kind of institutional and knowledge-legitimating proxy (though in some instances libraries continue to adhere to the commons of "public" in ways that many public research universities have seen fit to abandon); and I will wonder about intoxications working within it, for reasons that I hope will become clear.

The Queensland State Library sits in the heart of downtown Brisbane, Australia, and is located near several universities, among them the University of Queensland and Griffith University. Some elite universities in Australia are dubbed the "sandstone universities," a reference to the local stone found in prominent display in buildings in campuses such as the University of Queensland and the University of Sydney—an architecture conferring dignity, solidity, permanence (through settlement), tying land's resources to the nature-transforming trick of masterful human knowledge. The history of education for Aboriginal and Torres Strait Islanders is one of many stories of exclusion from the sandstone universities, stories of the combination of occupation of land and denial of entry, and is far from being remedied.

In this context, the Queensland State Library appears as a stage for commissioned art in a permanent installation by artist Fiona Foley called *Black Opium* (2006, ongoing).[10] A lifelong, multidisciplinary artist, Foley is of the Badtjala Aboriginal people who are based on Fraser Island; currently she is also a senior lecturer at Griffith University. Her attention to the legacies of a massively consequential Queensland law, which includes many independent works, has an insistently pedagogical thrust in the sense that she is, across the diversity of forms and implications of her artwork, also invested in getting Queenslanders—especially white Queenslanders—to understand the impact of the law on the history *and* present of the state.

Black Opium's central historical material, leveraged for the present, comes from more than a century ago: Queensland's 1897 Aboriginals Protection and Restrictions of the Sale of Opium Act.[11] This law ostensibly addressed a perceived shift in economic and race relations, casting as a scene of danger the trafficking of a poor form of opium from Chinese to Aboriginal and Torres Strait Islander hands. Its administration profoundly affected Aboriginal and Torres Strait Islander life in Australia; it rewrote not only the uses of drugs, but the very terms of governance, the handling of Aboriginal and Torres Strait Islander, as well as Chinese, capital; the management of space, and interracial sex and kinship (noting here the racialization of Indigenous people). Previously, white Queensland employers would pay Aboriginal and Torres Strait Island workers in the form of opium ash, in ways that were tied to the keeping of a chemically *docile*—noninsurgent and indeed nonagitating—labor force. They became aware, however, that the workers were turning to Chinese sellers of opium ash, insistently, as I saw in the state archives, dealing only with Chinese sellers, not white suppliers. It's unclear whether this shift actually coincided with the explicit danger of death that Aboriginal and Torres Strait Islander people faced with the addiction of some to this poor and harsher form of ash, but the government perceived that the Chinese were part of the intensification.

While I have important questions to answer about Chinese accountability for a circumstance that yielded vastly different economic lives and freedoms, an undergrowth account requires that one simultaneously note that Chinese communities and individuals were managing to form independent relationships—of trade, collaborative work, and intimate lives—with Aboriginal and Torres Strait Islander people and also threatening a form of commercial exchange that deprived white traders of their stronghold on opium. Opium ash, also called black opium, was a post-use product, the actual ash of smoked opium, that normally had been imported from China by a web of traders. But the protection law turned into a radical form of abuse that was then copied across Australia:

the establishment of Aboriginal reservations, the breaking up of families and communities, the control of sexual activity and movement particularly of Aboriginal and Torres Strait Islander young women, the expropriation of Aboriginal wealth by so-called police protectors, and the forbidding of interracial union (harboring) between Chinese and Aboriginal and Torres Strait Islander people, notably in the form of control of the residence of Aboriginal and Torres Strait Island girls and young women.

Foley's work has a diversity of forms, and much of it has focused on the form of the poppy. Both the poppy and the act feature prominently in her Queensland State Library installation. The installation, titled *Black Opium*, dated 2006 (but also marked as "in progress"), deploys large-scale dimensions, working below, across, and overhead, and much of it is thus visually accessible from a fair part of the library—particularly an infinity symbol of aluminum poppy buds cast from molds and directly over the courtyard, uniting all four floors; there is almost no way to avoid it if you visit any part of the library. Black opium, as I mentioned, was one name for the ash; but "Black" also was a moniker for Aboriginal and Torres Strait Island people. Because this installation is located in the library, in some fairly obvious way it stages the politics of knowledge or knowledge production. But there is something clearly embodied, too, about this knowledge—as one could say is true of any university setting.

Down a third-floor hallway skirting the courtyard, small squares of different heights the size of doorways open to shallow individual cubbies, most of which have some kind of seating inside. Each cubby names a material player in the entanglements of the law: "Mangrove," "String," "Silver," "Shrine," "Gold," "Slow Burn," "Bliss." When I went to photograph those rooms, there were students busy at work in almost all of those cubbies. Interestingly, there are two separate rooms, one with documentary, as-if ethnographic photographs of Aboriginal people around that time, and the other with documentary, as-if ethnographic photographs of Chinese people around that time. I return to this below.

Each student or pair of students seemed to be enjoying the privacy and perhaps, just perhaps, maybe unwittingly too, a certain sensorium, an aura of environment. I think there may well be an invitation here to embrace a change in institutional space. And if these modulations are perceptual, I think we can rethink the distinction between "real" and "metaphorical" intoxication, which, I have found in my work on toxicity, isn't very stable. In my meditations on cognitive disability and elsewhere I've been exploring something called "intoxicated method"—which is at once a kind of acknowledgment of the chemical present of intellectual engagement but also a set of questions about chosen ways

FIGURE 13.1. Partial shot of Fiona Foley's permanent installation at the Queensland State Library, *Black Opium* (2006). A long hallway opens to small rooms facing the atrium.

FIGURE 13.2. A room from *Black Opium*, partially showing a study table, a bench, and adjacent walls showing Chinese photographs and an 1884 letter pertaining to the lead-up to the 1897 law.

FIGURE 13.3. An interior wall of photographs depicting Chinese communities from one of Foley's small rooms in the *Black Opium* installation.

of doing research and coming to knowledge. Ways that could involve something like the academic unthinkable of "categorial blurring," which is normally marked as incapacity or intellectual slowness—or a sincere attempt to embrace sensorium, embrace one's intoxication in such a way that it is not a form of temporary, voluntaristic pleasure—a blurring that in the usual sense would be only a point of arrival, a precise achievement for the creator, rather than perhaps a retreat from incessant taxonomy in one's own ways of reading and naming, a disabled loss. It is automatically ironic to raise this question of blurring in research venues (elite universities or ranked peer-reviewed journals), where the business of precision and analysis tends not to be questioned, and where moves away from them are read as anticognitive and thus somehow failing.

The most vivid and obvious example of a sensorium is the room set off at the end titled "Bliss," a markedly darkened space in which one seat faces a video screen playing a loop that shows short, phrasal excerpts of the 1897 act as well as other commentary, including an explicit nod to modes of sexuality and contagion, the "red plague" as a white venereal disease. The video loop has continuous shots of swaying poppies, mostly from a low angle, sometimes with a focus on one or a few poppies in a shallow depth of field, suggesting a kind of blurred intimacy and locality rather than mastery of the entirety of the visual space such as in a god's-eye view (and here my choice of god's eye is intentional, because I'm thinking of the mapping projects of colonial imaginaries that had to do with religion, resources, conquest). Instead, there is a relationship to the ground, and perhaps to land and the question of landedness.

In that way that visits are never strictly archival, but lively, during my personal visit with Foley, the artist mentioned that her mother, who was a Badtjala activist engaged in multiple projects of land care and sovereignty and who wrote a dictionary of Badtjala-English, and was engaged for decades in a struggle to establish environmental stewardship classes on Fraser Island, a struggle against the ecological management system of Queensland, the park service, which presides over the island even as the Badtjala people have fought a form of sovereign recognition that deeply restricts their care for the land. I have begun to feel the ways Foley's attention to the 1897 law and its effects on the present day involve a kind of trans-temporal reminding that feels more complex than the unidirectional form of historical agency of a legacy event: that thing "happened," and it "happens" "again"—in engaging intoxicated temporalities, Foley directly engages the experience and politics of memory as well as event. In June 2019, Fraser Island came into the news: a father wrested his child back from the jaws of a dingo (they were visiting the island, which is partly billed as

FIGURE 13.4. A still from the video in the "Bliss" cubby by Fiona Foley, depicting poppies waving in the breeze.

an ecotourism destination) and the authorities consulted on the issue were precisely the Queensland Park Service. An online parks page on dingoes refers to three conservation management factors of *education, engineering, and enforcement*,[12] rather than to the Badtjala authorities, who said that they had been kept at "arm's length" from the management of dingo species on the island.[13] The world-making of settlement tied knots between questions of race (including the designation of racial groupings such as whites and the racialization of Indigenous people), species (how species mattered and its exclusions from personhood), ecology (knowledges about taxonomy and relation, and what was alienable), capacity, and kinship (ancestral genealogies and their governance in different forms of state and Indigenous law) in ways that bring together animal studies, critical race, and Indigenous, disability, and sexuality studies in complicated ways. That omnipresent sense of legacy is one that not only has come to preoccupy my own work in ways I am still working out, but also haunts organizations that point to this law's originary scale and historical burden on the breaking up of Aboriginal and Torres Strait Islander families, numbers that are outdone even today by modern child welfare and child removal laws such as Link-Up Queensland (www.link-upqld.org.au). Their pedagogies greatly impact how that knowledge carries forward.

Returning to "Bliss": Ultimately I think there is a kind of *intoxicatory* sensorium at play here, an agitation that works "underfoot," that in that dim room pointedly refuses any kind of programmatic textual study a student might intend with their books. Keeping in mind Foley's nod to pedagogy, this is a form of different "study" (perhaps, thinking here, of Moten and Harney's "black study") that allows for a textual apprehension of the law, flashing over the screen, but always in combination with the swaying intoxication of the poppy buds from below at the level of the ground. Notably, that explicit language inevitably fades as the poppies come into focus, suggesting a giving-way of law and of anointed forms of knowledge, and a giving-back to opacity. It is a "study" that is also a way of breathing the black opium, alchemizing the ash, ash that has been breathed in and out by Chinese bodyminds before its journey to Queensland. Foley is known for her particular combination of beautiful aesthetics and challenging provocation. If, as I suspect, "Bliss" works as the final, rather than first, room in the sequence along the hall, a place where a "blotting or indeed blacking out" of the norms of "literary, visual, or rationalized enlightenment" might be imagined to take place, the materialities, visualities, and sheer arrangements of the other, previous rooms come in to sit with you: a kind of agitative un-learning. Is this also Black study? Moten refers to a transnational diversification of Blackness, but there is much more to consider in the politics of racialized knowledge, the intents of Black criticism, and the history of relations between blackness and Indigeneity that in the Australian context includes connections between activist Aboriginal Australians and the Black Power movement.

The video's effects blur the strict edges of what one has seen before. Mangrove, String, Silver, Shrine, Gold, Slow Burn, Bliss. There is an argument there about, for instance, whether the idea that the segregation between the Chinese and the Aboriginal–Torres Strait Islander rooms, or Chinese being and Aboriginal being (and note I do not mean here a denotative "identity," whether or not the documentary segregations of photos could be collated among themselves to suggest that), could ever actually be as perfect or permanent as the installation rooms seem to set up (such a questioning of constitutional segregation shows up in her other work, particularly in a photographic series I am considering elsewhere), and of course the "queered" families that resulted from their nonsegregation bear such witness. More broadly, the communities joined together commercially, carnally, in friendship, and otherwise. There is perhaps also an argument about what it means to be both grounded and engaged in an avowedly political intoxicatory witnessing—that is, neither canceled as a form of disablement, nor frivolously entertained as a form of luxurious voluntarism or consumption. Opium is one of those drugs that, under certain conditions, had as much to do with creative European cultures of nineteenth-century self-induced literary making as with racialized debility, survival, self-care, and chemical incarceration.[14]

The slowness of the opium here has a trace in both race and disability. I mentioned above that the opium was used in part to ensure a "docile" working population, one not subject to political agitation. Additionally, the Slow Worker's Act from the mid-twentieth century was one of the first Queensland laws to take on what I would call the integration of disabled bodies into the architecture of the economy, a bureaucratizing of disability. The Slow Worker's Act was meant to allow disabled people to be employed, albeit at wages lower than nondisabled people; in order to hire a disabled worker, the employer had to mark, for instance, how many fingers were "missing"; this calculation thereby determined the reduced wage rate, since the assumption was that productivity would be reduced in comparison to nondisabled laborers. Disabled workers' labor was thus worth less, even if recompensable. In 1968, within negotiations about taming competition (essentially making sure Aboriginal workers got paid enough not to undercut white workers), employers managed to reclassify Aboriginal workers as *all* falling under the Slow Worker's Act. This went on systematically until at least the 1980s. Note that I am not here alleging causality between, say, sedentary opium ash use and slow worker categorization. Rather, I point to a kind of conceptual and affective soup of policy marking racial and disability status, mediating among rights, perceived competitive populations of workers, codes of labor value, and materialities of time. It is appropriate here to reflect back on the valuation of slowness in the university. Certainly, being marked as slow renders some mindbodies unsuitable for the university—this seems increasingly true for humans and inhumans with any form of disability, whether marked or unmarked, visible or invisible—since the university's rushed temporalities create ever larger zones of exclusion marked as "incapacity." Beyond any intelligible interpretation of disability, slowness is an experience of some kinds of thinkers who might be invested in the meditative, or require time to live within modalities of undergrowth. It has also become a style of resistance to neoliberal regimentations of time, which the book *The Slow Professor* attempts to articulate, albeit with a fairly conservative scope.[15]

In my view, *Black Opium* not only captures a precise mode of slow agitation, slowness and agitation together, but also a provocation that insists one understand the *present* moment in altered temporal terms that go all the way back to 1897, and beyond to its own shaping. If redaction is the removal of information for official purposes of confidentiality, I think of *Black Opium* as enacting an epistemology (or arguably a cripistemology, to cite Johnson and McRuer's formulation) that in my view "redacts" secular or paranoid facticity, *as well as perhaps even precision*, in favor of a novel account of the scene, allowing the queer sexualities of Chinese-Aboriginal-Torres Strait Islander opium trading and bodily transgression to soothe, retort, and shine.[16] Against the languor of the poppies in the wind, the words of the act would seem to have no chance. "Traditional," "normative" forms of knowledge-making: It is not an irony here, to me, that Foley was inspired to do this work after reading a scholarly work by Rosalind Kidd on the history of opium legislation for Aboriginal and Torres Strait Islander people, which Kidd leveraged in her own attempt to remedy continued failure to return moneys taken by police protectors through the institution of the law. The opposition between scholarly apolitical work and nonscholarly resistance has in so many ways been a false one, even if there remains a significant relationship between elitism and what counts as legitimated knowledge. Instead, Foley's project demonstrates the fertility of exchange of forms of knowing, and indeed of scholarship, across ostensible divides of institution, pointing directly to the potency of undergrowth.

Foley's work might even be seen as suggesting a complex Indigenous-Asian epistemology, based not necessarily on a shared objective analysis so much as a kind of being together out of nonintegrity or paraintegrity. A being together rather than identitarian collapse; undergrowth does not claim nondifference. I say this in a non-utopian way, since in the context of this research I am also thinking about accountability. And this brings me back to meditate on the underside of the blurring intoxications of "Bliss" and the interest in an undergrowth free of sheer collapse, even as it enriches less-regulated knowledges of differences. The Australian scholarship on this period does not seem to deal directly with the kinds of questions I have about forms of Asian settler colonialism. A parallel discussion about mutually impacting capitalizations of "racial" difference in the university is due, particularly in light of the racialized groups at hand in Foley's work.

Molecular life has in it a kind of ordinary storm. Sometimes things crash and separate; sometimes they crash and gently coagulate; sometimes they generate new collectivities, if but for an instant. I am thinking here of actual molecules and their physics, and the agitations they undergo in the course of ordinary existence, but also of the behaviors of particulates that play a role in intoxication. In my previous work on animacy, molecularity was linked to sometimes spatially microcosmic and yet massively effective agencies such as toxicities, and represented one of many ironic potencies from the lower end of hierarchical orders of being. (It might be useful to contrast this use of *molecular* and the kinds of constitutional shifts it allows with the imagination of what Deleuze and Guattari called the *molar*, which would be most aligned with the positive categories and actors of the university, including the unmarked human package itself, who is white, nondisabled, masculine, "functionally" social, and creditable.) If I were to draw on what this offers, I might want to think about the ways in which agitation is not equivalent to the exertion of long life, even if it points to the right to one. In a queer kind of way, agitation may not last. It may be poorly resourced, but it is vigorous in its own way. Agitation as collectivity, no matter the durability of everybody within it, manages a form of political expression not dependent on individualistic virtuosity and promise of longevity; here I'm referring to the evanescence of queer liveliness, and the political agility that is neither dependent on permanence nor even, arguably, agility itself. And indeed that may be its key. Considering how such agitations are staged in the university raises questions about accumulation (and its partner, extraction), permanence, progressive development, and the durability requirements of difference (race and disability being either permanent, as a favored appearance of the university's self-image, or short-term, at the limits of its tolerability, administered as opportunities for nonpermanent labor or as a requirement that disability cannot last beyond a semester else it renders the person permanently inefficient and the university permanently and thus intolerably generous). Agitation is valuable, in some sense, precisely because it refuses identity, exists more comfortably as its undergrowth.

Witnessing Foley's *Black Opium*, in a welcome and rare sense, puts me in a kind of suspension, to call back the conception of Choy and Zee, which is a suspension for disciplinary work—how to do justice in the work and also what does justice mean here—as well as a rendering of materialities whose relations are unclear, blurred, but also contingent, in the sense not of causality, but of touch. Intoxication's plant-human-aerial-bloodborne materialities inhabit suspension. Whether or not such materialities align with "human" should also be relegated to suspension, insofar as their analysis in human terms (much less Wynter's "Man") constitutes a loss of sensitivity to undergrowth, including the slanting potencies, both resistive and oppressive, of intoxication. The undergrowth of education can be felt, immersively, in the stage of the Queensland State Library, and is made both real and inescapably contingent at the hands of the students who populate *Black Opium*'s rooms. Reflecting on the uses of difference, it is also worth asking whose agitations then "become" whose, in the perceptive/immersive encounter. These are agitations—whether or not by the visual or by poetry or the sensory and experiential timespaces of ingested substance—that may never be cognized as such, and yet remind a bodymind of its fundaments of being, ones that may have their own history of environmental injustice as the implantation of substance-borne rhythms, impingements of attention and thought, ulterior (as versus majoritarian calculation) cognitions, forgettings, re-memberings. Taking agitations in their informative breadth and their urgency—while bracketing exclusory accounts of the human, of agency, or of politics—allows transversal forms of differential being to "breathe" in an analysis, or in the stories we tell. And accounting for differential being allows attunement to emergent agitations that bear the marks of, and seek to act against, the exhaustive projections of colonial histories and presents.

Returning to Snaza and Singh's phrasing of undergrowth: "myriad encounters, relations, and affective shuttlings that enable 'education' even if they happen at a scale . . . that is outside of traditional humanist ways of viewing education," and "fugitive ungovernability," we have seen a canonical site of knowledge production that was not *the* university but bore its students; that engaged in essentially ungovernable affective shuttlings in direct (if complex) relationship to the university's knowledge mandates; that served up an intoxicated archive. There is no reason not to think of these as gifts, or in fact the ordinary unmarked turns of "education" at large, that perhaps includes unlearning, even as one agitates against the violence of the doubling of indictment, criminality, and medicalization of multiplied difference. If this is true, however, then new questions enter the fold of deliberation regarding what constitutes desirable education, the relation of difference to its multiplication *and* narrowing in the contemporary university, and even what constitutes the favored developmental narrative for a student's individual progress, whatever the political program. No less, the stapling of securitization and medicalization to the ostensibly "core" runnings of the university's educational processes requires that those of us who live with it must also find how to be with agitative being.

Acknowledgments

These are early thoughts that are greatly developed in my book; I thank Julietta Singh and Nathan Snaza for generous feedback, though I remain responsible for any errors. I also thank Fiona Foley for her generosity and for her work, *Black Opium*. The work represented here has benefited additionally from feedback from multiple audiences at talks as well as ongoing conversation with, and/or reading of drafts, by Julia Bryan-Wilson, Alison Kafer, Eunjung Kim, and Julie Avril Minich.

NOTES

1 With Dana Luciano I discuss "inhuman" in relation to a wide map of previous critical work engaging the human, in Luciano and Chen, "Has the Queer Ever Been Human?," 182–207. The discussion is extensive, but in the interest of affect I quote here: "The slash through non/human, then, attempts to recollect and foreground the very histories of dehumanization too often overlooked in celebratory posthumanisms. 'Inhumanisms,' in our view, performs a similar kind of work through its homonymic echo. Resonating against 'inhumane,' inhuman points to the violence that the category of the human contains within itself. Yet it also carries a sense of generativity— inhuman not simply as category, as a spatial designator or the name of a 'kind' of being, but as a process, an unfolding."

2 Snaza and Singh, "Introduction," 8.

3 Moten and Harney, *The Undercommons*.

4 My forthcoming book, *Intoxicated: Race, Disability and Chemical Intimacy across Empire*, examines the elusive promise of slowness and agitation and their induction into forms of inhumanization, as played out in two nineteenth-century cases of the congealing of race, disability, and chemical imagination.

5   Choy and Zee, "Condition—Suspension," 210–23.

6   Glissant, *Poetics of Relation*, 189–94. I thank Alanna Thain and Megan Fernandes, the organizers of Thresholdings: Intimacies, Opacities, Embodiments, and all the interlocutors at McGill University on March 25, 2019, for a stunning collective consideration of Glissant's notion of opacity throughout our day together. See also the performance of obscurity and the objectification of the possessive desire of Western knowledge in Silviano Santiago, "The Wily Homosexual." I think here too of Kadji Amin, Amber Jamilla Musser, and Roy Perez's description of "queer form," "a name for the range of formal, aesthetic, and sensuous strategies that make difference a little less knowable, visible, and digestible." Amin, Musser, and Perez, "Queer Form," 235.

7   There are innumerable examples of the criminalization or dismissal of unrest, as well as the defanging of dangerous subjects by alleging that they are not capable subjects. I am thinking here of Colin Dayan's argument about the law and its ability to hold slaves criminally *liable*, while at the same moment considering them mentally *incapable*. Dayan, *The Law Is a White Dog*, 138–76.

8   Chen, "Agitation," 551–66.

9   For neoliberal devisings tuned to extreme measures, the fictional TV series *WIA* does an excellent job of panning the cultures that result from the mandate of "doing more with less" (BBC, dir. John Morton).

10 Foley, *Black Opium*.

11 I have been studying this act and its ramifications since approximately 2014, with visits to the Queensland State Archives in Runcorn outside of Brisbane and the Queensland State Library; I have also benefited from a number of written works, including Rosalind Kidd, *The Way We Civilise*, which also has been named by Fiona Foley as an influence.. This is my first article on the act. I committed to not publishing anything on this work until it was far more than an object of scholarship, or an "archive," but something living today that deserves consideration under a more informed commitment to Aboriginal sovereignty. The legacy of the act is found in the articulations of race and indigeneity in Queensland and Australia, the profound alteration of Aboriginal life in Australia, Chinese economic and racial being in Australia (as well as forms of diasporic accountability), and the transhistorical urgencies of Link-Up (an organization that reunites Aboriginal and Torres Strait Island people with their families from whom they may have been separated eight or nine decades ago through the law's enactment), for which the 1897 law foundationally began a massive series of child removals that they say is even worse today. Most importantly, I wish to credit Fiona Foley with bringing so many of these elements home for me—for literally allowing me into her home and engaging with me in significant conversation about her work, which was very meaningful to me as well as deeply informative. In the midst of my research, seeing the *Black Opium* installation, as I told her, changed everything. The opportunity has been for me to rethink study; art; archive; and knowledge.

12 State of Queensland Department of Environment and Science, "About Fraser Island Dingoes."

13 "Aboriginal Elders Say Fraser Island Dingo Attacks 'Could Have Been Avoided,'" NITV, April 22, 2019, https://www.sbs.com.au/nitv/nitv-news/article/2019/04/22 /aboriginal-elders-say-fraser-island-dingo-attacks-could-have-been-avoided.

14 I attribute the phrase "chemical incarceration" to disability and mad studies scholar Erick Fabris. Fabris refers to the forms of obligatory (often opiate) sedative use imposed on formerly institutionalized psychiatric patients in *Tranquil Prisons*.

15 Berg, Seeber, and Collini, *The Slow Professor*.

16 Johnson and McRuer, "Cripistemologies," 127–47.

As part of the writing process for the introduction of this book, Alison and Eun-jung offered this prompt to the four of us, as individual writers and theorists:

> Write 800 words on a word, concept, text, image, framework, experi-ence, sound, sensation, movement, intervention, collective, figure, elder, imaginary, movement, tradition, or worlding that is key to your under-standing and practice of disability studies. We are most interested in items (or persons) that are idiosyncratic to your own orientations and solidarities; what constitutes your disability studies (DS) (or its archive or crip genealogy) and why?

We now share it with you, your students, your comrades and colleagues and co-conspirators. And if you write your 800 words, multiple 800 words, we would love to read them.

Toad

MEL Y. CHEN

My own orientations to the field of disability studies are an accumulation of a history of side-sallies, side-eyes, coming in at angles and that was not a wrong way to come. What was most important to me in DS was having a sense of welcome, welcome that came from the right people—thank you for taking me in—and with whom mindbody sparks flew. Many anointed canons of DS, bril-liant as the work is, have not felt very much central to my concerns. I mean that my orientations feel a little idiosyncratic for the field's self-fictions, or its pedagogical norms of inheritance. But attached to *disability studies*? Yes, I am—certainly I am—to the kind that makes possible cultures of embodied allowance, where crips I know better and learn how to love can, from within the grip of colonial grief and the rejection of white masterly posturing and possession as well as the joyous sendup of imperial erectness, still and very much rest, love, cry, love, dance. Perhaps appropriately to my orientation, then, the image that "articulates" crip genealogy is—please don't ask me whether this is serious, but whether it is a commitment, and it is—a toad gesture. When I think of crip genealogy, I think of world-making. It's not always clear what it means, but one thing I think is proper to it is the possibility to reimagine time and kinship (and then whether we even want inheritance to achieve any kind of solidity as a concept—I say probably not). The senses are here, and we haven't cripped them nearly enough in the scholarship, I think. I am attached to a gestural world, including words as gestures, that isn't centrally dependent on human meaning or being and spiritually and emotionally concentrates my disability "study" as much as it is a cross-species/trans-species encounter: it is something about honoring and remembering what is here and has been here and most easily bears the field's novel categories but for the norms of practice, diagnosis, imperial positioning, including here and now versus then and there. My transspecies starts with recognizing the violence of a faux but consequential speciation discourse applied to Indigenous, enslaved, and colonized persons, and rejects the idea that nonhuman beings have no place in our thought or consideration. My own tendentious humanity, living at a particularly unrecognizable racial juncture, has always felt the diagnostic province of others, and now I think mine is not worth claiming anyway, though I will affirm it for others who desire it. I believe crip genealogies can and should defer not only to the before of the colonial and recolonizing split between "man" and "animal"; they can and should also witness maps of unusual and yet true affinity. What does it mean to say that toads have been my greatest love, and that their movements hearten, plump, my crip genealogies? The toad wipes, the toad blinks, the toad hunches, cringes and wrenches, the toad scrapes and gapes, the toad pushes off, the toad sloughs and squints and steps through and the toad emerges toad, leaving skin puddle. What in there I might call gesture is, on some level, my fancy, though I don't think it's about imposing a template of symbolic rigor on the toad. Rather, it *becomes* a gesture to me, in part because I remain ignorant before many, but not all, rich potentials of its signaling and yet confident of our tentative equaling and also my humility. Inside me as I face this toad, I feel the same movements. In the cinema, I tend to fill with whatever or whomever has my attention, and I emerge with embodiments unimaginable before I entered the theater—Neo, Tom Cruise, etc. If this becoming-filled is (involuntary) consumption as much as observation, or if observation collapses into becoming, then I believe this becoming can sometimes be—in that queerly inconsistent way—a world-making. In this "transmission," which was not a transmission, the gesture has been a gesture after all: an arc traced in my being, given weight as a response-ability that might sit before thought and language, and when it becomes thought it presents as a high made low and a low made high, a primordial temporality of the present, slowness and squatness, wrongashuman, human's ugly, orthogonal to erectness. It is in some world minor, but it is also world.

Impostor Syndrome

JULIE AVRIL MINICH

This project represents my first time writing with other people. I expected collective writing to be hard, but I didn't know precisely *how* it would be hard.

Early in the process, when we decided we would each write an 800-word essay for this volume, I was excited about the assignment. And yet it was the day *after* we began to compile the full manuscript to submit to the press for copyediting that I finally sat down to start this piece. Note: I had drafted other versions of an 800-word reflection previously, but had deleted each draft. Each time, I was overwhelmed by the nakedness of my own words. *This* piece of writing, I was certain, would reveal to all that I am unqualified to be involved in this effort.

"Do you know what keeps you from writing your eight hundred words?" Mel asked me one day, on one of our coeditor Zoom sessions, and without hesitation I responded that it was my impostor syndrome. I didn't know what it was that was keeping me from writing until I verbalized it, but once the words were out of my mouth I realized something else: *Key to my understanding and practice of disability studies, key to my understanding and practice of scholarly knowledge in general, is the sense that I don't really belong.* (This sense of nonbelonging is not, of course, uniquely mine; the first time I heard the phrase *impostor syndrome* was also when I realized that I'm very much not alone.)

I remember the first SDS I attended. ASL interpreters and CART captioning at every single session! Margaret Price, seated two rows ahead of me, a pair of socks on her knitting needles! Access copies! For the first few sessions I didn't ask for an access copy, because those were for "people who really needed them," not for me. But then, at one session, there were copies left over and a second call went out, and I tentatively raised my hand. Until that first SDS, I thought my difficulty focusing at conferences was my fault. If I were a "real" academic, I too would be able to sit still for an entire panel, listening to paper after paper without fidgeting or losing focus. At that first SDS, I learned that if I brought my knitting into the conference room and gave my hands something to do or occupied my brain by reading along with the access copy or the CART transcription, I too could sit through a panel and retain most of the content.

I still did not know, after that first SDS, that I was not neurotypical, but it was nonetheless a revelation. At first, the main result was to shift my academic impostor syndrome into disability impostor syndrome: Was I "disabled enough" to ask for the things I need to moderate my attention inconsistencies? But even that shift did something important for me, prompting the hope that I wasn't an inherently bad scholar or lazy person, that alterations to my physical surroundings could increase my ability to engage with people and ideas around me.

(Parenthetical note regarding my use of the word *lazy* in the above paragraph: I do not believe there is anything wrong with being lazy! But for much of my life the word *lazy* has been a weapon that I wielded against myself, punishing myself for the gap between my own "productivity" and that of my peers.)

This is not to say that my academic impostor syndrome went away. Indeed, working on *Crip Genealogies* frequently stoked it. Over the years, as the four of us worked together, we all confessed feelings of inadequacy to each other. We all dropped out of the project for periods of time, and we talked often about what it meant to be crip writers writing criply together, which often meant intense bursts of activity followed by long periods of inactivity. But I could not lose the feeling that as soon as I put words to the page that were just mine, words that my coauthors would not come back to polish and refine later in the process, everyone would realize my incompetence.

It wasn't until Mel asked why I hadn't written my 800 words that I started to think criply about impostor syndrome. Specifically, I started to think about how the feelings of nonbelonging and unworthiness that get called *impostor syndrome* have accrued such medicalized language. What does calling these feelings a syndrome do for us? For one, it teaches us that the problem is within us, within our bodyminds, not with the norms of academic comportment and productivity. It also turns these feelings into something to vanquish instead of something to coexist with. What if I could listen to my impostor syndrome and let it ask me important questions about the arguments I make in my scholarship and my positionality in relation to those arguments without sliding immediately into nonbelonging/unworthiness?

I know I am not the only disability scholar to feel, constantly and simultaneously, both not academic enough and not crip enough. In some ways, disability studies alleviated my impostor syndrome, but in other ways triggered it. In particular, it has not only nurtured suspicions about my relationship to disability but also prompted me to ask whether the artists and writers I study portray disability in the "right" ways or enact the "right" kind of disability politics. And this latter concern, I came to realize most fully in the process of working on this book with my crip comrades, has had a limited and limiting effect on the kind of knowledge that is possible to place within recognizable crip genealogies. It has, I am certain, had a limiting effect on some of my own work. But even if my work has been limited by impostor syndrome, I also don't want to reject, pathologize, or overcome it. Maybe impostor syndrome is something to understand, to acknowledge, to work with—an occasion for making knowledge differently. Maybe sometimes it's good to make knowledge with an acute awareness of everything I still don't know. Maybe impostor syndrome can enable as well as impair: prompting difficult questions about moments of misfitting between myself and the intellectual genealogy/ies I claim, between the texts I love and the theories I use to read and teach them, between the knowledges I want to make and the institutions (both universities and fields of study) in which I make those knowledges.

Immigration Bags

EUNJUNG KIM

It was just one month before 9/11 in 2001. I had stopped by the emergency room in Seoul before I left on the plane to Chicago. Still dizzy with medication, I got off the plane at O'Hare Airport, and went through immigration. At the baggage claim, I dragged two unwieldy bags off the moving belt one by one. These bags are named as *immigration bags*. The bag is collapsible and expandable in three tiers. The fully expanded bags were lumpy and could not stand up on their own or move via the attached wheels. Perhaps the purpose of the bag is not mobility but a one-way trip. I wrestled with them one by one to stack them on the cart. It was my first time leaving my country, so I had packed so many things, afraid that I was not going to find things I needed in a foreign city. In one of the bags were four issues of the magazine *Gonggam*, published by the disabled women's group I have been part of. Each issue of the magazine came to existence out of many weekend meetings in the home shared by four disabled women. In the bag also were the xeroxed copies of *The Rejected Body*, *Sister Outsider*, *Inessential Woman*, *Loud Proud and Passionate* from the 1995 Beijing Women's Conference, and a collection of lesbian feminist writings. I don't remember the weight limit of each bag, and how I could bring all those books and more.

When I faced prejudiced and uncritical engagements with disability in women's studies classrooms in South Korea, disability studies (DS) was a place I dreamed of. I left what was familiar to me, what was too painful, too fast-moving for me to be part of, something I cared for too much. A degree program in DS was a sign of a space created to reveal the operations of society that exacts violence, oppresses, and segregates human and nonhuman beings according to their values and functions. DS meant a connection with others, a place where I could explore the questions I had, temporarily away from the demands of fast activism. But the institutional legitimacy in US academia came with a price, as it valued certain kinds of writing and thinking over others. With the alienation and exoticization of culture and ethnicity that I seemingly embodied, my exposure to DS was assumed to be a source of enlightenment. In one of the first courses I took, two professors conducted research on students about how our perceptions of disability would transform after learning about DS. We were asked regularly to answer the questions, "What is disability?" and "What is disability studies?" We were asked to keep journals monitoring our own thoughts, so that the changes in our thoughts before and after reading the canonical DS texts could be tracked. All of us knew what was expected, even though we didn't know everything. In this "education as intervention" model, there seemed no room for what students have brought into the classroom and what those could do with existing texts in DS. One other "international" student left the program after the first semester. I stayed. And I started reading all the "foundational texts" in the list given to us, written by mostly white scholars, if not all, in the United States, Canada, and the United Kingdom.

I was recently asked the same questions: How would you define disability and disability studies? The repeated exercise still lingers after twenty years. But this time, as I tried to come up with my own answers, I ended up with more questions: How do I recognize, acknowledge, and reckon with the white and Western legacy of DS and my participation in it? What part of my northeastern Asianness carries ethnic privilege in the United States and in the world? How can I fully investigate my complicity in South Korean capitalist crimes of industrial disasters and environmental harms that disable us? How do we work with scholars who challenge racism, capitalism, imperialism, and heteropatriarchy but consider disability as largely a white concern or who view DS as a manifestation of white supremacy? Next time I travel, what will I take and bring with me in my immigration bags whose six wheels refuse to roll? As I drag them, I sense my general reluctance to freeze disability and to courier knowledge out of its places and contexts for application. But maybe dragging back and forth is a way to weaken the borders and to erase the fantasy of single origin and instead to reveal coincidental geneses of ideas in multiple places and their connections. Maybe next time when someone asks me to define disability and DS, I'd say, "I would prefer not to" and pose different questions. Maybe we can start noticing what crossings do rather than selecting what is deemed worthwhile to be carried over.

May we feel the freedom to fill our bags with experiences, feelings, baggage, words, useless objects, what we know, and what we don't know, and drag them along the colonial borders until they disappear.

Faith, or Hope, or Desire: On Loving People, Not Institutions

ALISON KAFER

Eunjung and I wrote this prompt when we were feeling low, or so I remember. Neither of us were feeling like we had much to offer, and we procrastinated by thinking about how wonderful it would be to read the insights of everyone else. I don't think either one of us imagined we would eventually have to answer it ourselves. Reading it now, the very last day I can add my response to the volume, the cascade of terms itself feels like an answer. Not only is there no single "word, concept, text, image . . ." that rises to the surface as *the* thing, there isn't even a single category of thing. My thinking about disability studies has been shaped as much by the sound of her breathing as by the pace of his gait, as much by the sting of that encounter as by the embrace of that theory, as much by my failure of imagination on this issue as by their fierce solidarity on that one.

I never took a single disability studies course as a student. I found my first references to the field in the library at UC-Boulder, while taking a "continuing education" class to see if I could hold a pen, sit up long enough to take a class, navigate a hilly campus alone. It took ages for me to tune in to the content and stop worrying about what was going to happen if I dropped my book or where I was supposed to park my chair. I took a comparative religions course called Religion and the Body and I cried myself through every essay, turning in tear-stained papers that an open-hearted professor marked up with care. I don't really know what you're talking about, he wrote, but it reminds me of *this*, and *this*, and *this*, and I think you might have work to do *here*. His belief that there was something to be done saved me.

During my dissertation defense, one of my professors asked me what my project had to do with religion (I was getting a PhD in "women's studies and religion," after all), and I think I said something about ethics, or right relations, or justice. I'm certain we talked about how, if I'd known anything about the academy before applying to graduate school, I would have gone into a very different program. This is primarily how I've narrated my degree to others: a mistake, an idiosyncratic degree plan that skirted the edges of the requirements, a solo journey. All those interpretations are true. But perhaps my early immersion in feminist and womanist ethics, and my classmates' readings of Anzaldúa and hooks and Haraway via feminist theologies, shaped my thinking in ways I'm only now learning to untangle. I have spent most of my scholarly and teacherly life theorizing futures and imagining worlds for sick, mad, autistic, deaf, and disabled people. How much of that thinking was made possible by my exposure to those with deep faith that things can change for the better, that hope is not necessarily naïve, that one can simultaneously oppose ongoing histories of harm and believe deeply in the love of others? Don't get me wrong: I have not a single shred of religious faith. But I cannot stop imagining otherwise.

What does it mean to be saved by the words of others? I have often described myself as being saved by the vibrant and messy, complex and contradictory, infuriating and erotic field of disability studies, but that's not really true. I found the field through you, and you, and you, and you. You are the ones who saved me. And by that "you" I am not only thinking of specific artists and activists and scholars but also imagining people I don't yet know, people who I know are out there, percolating and testifying and scheming and dreaming. That knowing—call it faith, or hope, or desire; name it dream or speculative fiction or spell—is perhaps the one constant to my "orientations, solidarities, archives, and genealogies."

If you've read your way through this book, then you know that all of us have found ourselves at odds with disability studies, and yet here we are, hoping for otherwise. Karma Chávez sat across from me at a small table a few years ago, coffee and kolaches between us, and reminded me that we owe our loyalties to people, not to institutions. We were talking about our respective university jobs, and how to engage in feminist praxis within (and against) the academy. I think of her now, at the end of this long book grappling with the institution of disability studies, and I wonder what such radical loyalties might mean. I know they can't mean holding on to disability studies, or even disability, recognizing both as context-bound constructs, inevitably full of exclusions and gaps. But I believe, I have faith, that that letting go, can and must coexist with yearnings toward crip and disability justice futures and the people who inhabit them. I fail, and I fail, and I fail, but I'm still here, yearning for you, and them, and us.

Abolition and Disability Justice Collective. "Statement of Solidarity with Palestine."
May 20, 2021. https://abolitionanddisabilityjustice.com/2021/05/20/statement-of
-solidarity-with-palestine-from-the-adjc/.

Abourahme, Nassar. "'Nothing to Lose but Our Tents': The Camp, the Revolution, the
Novel." *Journal of Palestine Studies* 48, no. 1 (2018): 33–52.

Abu-Sitta, Ghassan. "There Is No International Community." Interview by Perla Issa.
Journal of Palestine Studies 47, no. 4 (2018): 46–56.

Aciksoz, Salih Can. *Sacrificial Limbs: Masculinity, Disability, and Political Violence in
Turkey*. Oakland: University of California Press, 2020.

Agard-Jones, Vanessa. "Bodies in the System." *Small Axe: A Caribbean Journal of Criticism* 17, no. 3 (2013): 182–92.

Agard-Jones, Vanessa. "Chemical Kin/Esthesia." Paper presented at the Human/Non-Human Colloquia Series, Berkeley, California, February 24, 2016.

Ahmed, Sara. *Queer Phenomenology*. Durham, NC: Duke University Press, 2006.

Alaimo, Stacy. *Bodily Natures: Science, Environment, and the Material Self*. Bloomington:
Indiana University Press, 2010.

Alexander, M. Jacqui. *Pedagogies of Crossing: Meditations on Feminism, Sexual Politics,
Memory, and the Sacred*. Durham, NC: Duke University Press, 2006.

Al-Mohamed, Day. Black #Disability History: Brad Lomax, Black Panther—
Revolutionary Black Nationalism and Disability Power. February 9, 2016. https://
leadonnetwork.org/wordpress/2016/02/09/black-disability-history-brad-lomax-black
-panther-revolutionary-black-nationalism-and-disability-power/.

Amin, Kadji, Amber Jamilla Musser, and Roy Pérez. "Queer Form: Aesthetics, Race, and
the Violences of the Social." *ASAP/Journal* 2, no. 2 (2017): 227–39.

Anaïs, Seantel. *Disarming Intervention: A Critical History of Non-Lethality*. Vancouver:
University of British Columbia Press, 2015.

Anderson, Warwick. *Colonial Pathologies: American Tropical Medicine, Race, and Hygiene
in the Philippines*. Durham, NC: Duke University Press, 2006.

Anzaldúa, Gloria. *Borderlands/La Frontera: The New Mestiza*. San Francisco: Aunt Lute, 2014.

Bailey, Moya. "Race and Disability in the Academy." *Sociological Review*, November 9, 2017. https://thesociologicalreview.org/collections/chronic-academics/race-and-disability-in-the-academy/.

Bailey, Moya. "The Ethics of Pace." *South Atlantic Quarterly* 120, no. 2 (2021): 285–99.

Bailey, Moya, and Izeta Autumn Mobley. "Work in the Intersections: A Black Feminist Disability Framework." *Gender and Society* 33, no. 1 (2019): 19–40.

Barad, Karen. *Meeting the Universe Halfway: Quantum Physics and the Entanglement of Matter and Meaning*. Durham, NC: Duke University Press, 2007.

Barad, Karen. "Nature's Queer Performativity." *Qui Parle: Critical Humanities and Social Sciences* 19, no. 2 (2011): 121–58.

Barker, Clare, and Stuart Murray. "Disabling Postcolonialism: Global Disability Cultures and Democratic Criticism." *Journal of Literary and Cultural Disability Studies* 4, no. 3 (Special Issue 2010): 219–36. https://doi.org/10.3828/jlcds.2010.20.

Barnartt, Sharon, and Richard Scotch. *Disability Protests: Contentious Politics 1970–1999*. Washington, DC: Gallaudet University Press, 2001.

Barradas, Efraín. "El recuerdo como remedio: historia y memoria en Aurora Levins Morales." *La Nueva Literatura Hispánica* 15 (2011): np. http://www.nuevaliteratura.com/index.php/nlit.

Baynton, Douglas C. *Defectives in the Land: Disability and Immigration in the Age of Eugenics*. Chicago: University of Chicago Press, 2016.

Bell, Christopher. *Blackness and Disability: Critical Examinations and Cultural Interventions*. East Lansing: Michigan State University Press, 2011.

Bell, Christopher. "Introducing White Disability Studies: A Modest Proposal." In *The Disability Studies Reader*, 2nd ed., edited by Lennard J. Davis, 275–82. New York: Routledge, 2006.

Ben-Moshe, Liat. *Decarcerating Disability: Deinstitutionalization and Prison Abolition*. Minneapolis: University of Minnesota Press, 2020.

Berg, Maggie, Barbara Karolina Seeber, and Stefan Collini. *The Slow Professor: Challenging the Culture of Speed in the Academy*. Toronto: University of Toronto Press, 2017.

Berlant, Lauren. *Cruel Optimism*. Durham, NC: Duke University Press, 2011.

Berne, Patty. "Disability Justice—A Working Draft." In *Skin, Tooth, and Bone: The Basis of Movement Is Our People: A Disability Justice Primer*, edited by Sins Invalid, 8–15. Berkeley, CA: Sins Invalid, 2016.

Berne, Patty. "What Is Disability Justice?" Adapted from Patty Berne's "Disability Justice: A Working Draft," June 6, 2020. In *Skin, Tooth, and Bone: The Basis of Movement Is Our People: A Disability Justice Primer*, 2nd ed., edited by Sins Invalid, 10–20. Berkeley, CA: Sins Invalid, 2020.

Berne, Patty, and the Sins Invalid Family. "10 Principles of Disability Justice." In *Skin, Tooth, and Bone: The Basis of Movement Is Our People: A Disability Justice Primer*, edited by Sins Invalid, 16–20. Berkeley, CA: Sins Invalid, 2016.

Bhandar, Brenna. *Colonial Lives of Property: Law, Land, and Racial Regimes of Ownership*. Durham, NC: Duke University Press, 2018.

Bhattacharya, Tithi. "Three Ways a Green New Deal Can Promote Life over Capital." *Jacobin*, June 10, 2019. https://jacobinmag.com/2019/06/green-new-deal-social-care -work.

Billups, Dennis. "Disability Rights Activist Dennis Billups on the 1977 Section 504 Occupation." Video oral history. Paul K. Longmore Institute on Disability Collection, 2014. https://diva.sfsu.edu/collections/longmoreinstitute/bundles/230642.

Bishara, Amahl, et al. "The Multifaceted Outcomes of Community-Engaged Water Quality Management in a Palestinian Refugee Camp." *EPE: Nature and Space* 4, no. 1 (2021): 65–84.

Black Panther Party Research Project. "History of the Black Panther Party: Black Panther Party Platform and Program." Accessed May 20, 2017. https://web.stanford.edu /group/blackpanthers/history.shtml.

Bleibleh, Sahera, Michael Vicente Perez, and Thaira Bleibleh. "Palestinian Refugee Women and the Jenin Refugee Camp: Reflections on Urbicide and the Dilemmas of Home in Exile." *Urban Studies* 56, no. 14 (2019): 2897–916.

Bloom, Joshua, and Waldo E. Martin. *Black against Empire: The History and Politics of the Black Panther Party*. Berkeley: University of California Press, 2013.

Bolton, Sony Coráñez. "Cripping the Philippine Enlightenment: Ilustrado Travel Literature, Postcolonial Disability, and the 'Normate Imperial Eye/I.'" *Verge: Studies in Global Asias* 2, no. 2 (2016): 138–62. https://doi.org/10.5749/vergstudglobasia.2.2 .0138.

Braidotti, Rosi. *The Posthuman*. Cambridge, UK: Polity Press, 2013.

Branch, Enobong. *Opportunity Denied: Limiting Black Women to Devalued Work*. New Brunswick, NJ: Rutgers University Press, 2011.

Brannigan, Erin. *Dancefilm: Choreography and the Moving Image*. New York: Oxford University Press, 2011.

"Brene Brown: The Courage to Be Vulnerable." *On Being* with Krista Tippett. January 11, 2015. https://onbeing.org/programs/brene-brown-the-courage-to-be-vulnerable -jan2015/.

Brothers Home Oral History Project, ed. *People Who Have Become Numbers*. Paju, South Korea: May Book, 2015.

Brown, Elaine. "Leader of the Black Panther Party Elaine Brown Talks about the Party's Involvement and Support of the 1977 Section 504 Occupation." Video oral history. Paul K. Longmore Institute on Disability Collection, 2014. https://diva.sfsu.edu /collections/longmoreinstitute/bundles/230640?searchOffset=0.

Brown, Lydia X. Z. "A Note on Process." In *All the Weight of Our Dreams: On Living Racialized Autism*, edited by Lydia X. Z. Brown, E. Ashkenazy, and Morénike Giwa Onaiwu, viii–ix. Lincoln, NE: DragonBee Press, 2017.

Bunzl, Matti. "The Prague Experience: Gay Male Sex Tourism and the Neocolonial Invention of an Embodied Border." In *Altering States: Ethnographies of Transition in Eastern Europe and the Former Soviet Union*, edited by Daphne Berdahl, Matti Bunzl, and Martha Lampland, 70–96. Ann Arbor: University of Michigan Press. 2000.

Burch, Susan. *Committed: Remembering Native Kinship in and beyond Institutions*. Chapel Hill: University of North Carolina Press, 2021.

Burch, Susan, and Hannah Joyner. "The Disremembered Past." In *Civil Disabilities: Citizenship, Membership, and Belonging,* edited by Nancy Hirschmann and Beth Linker, 65–82. Philadelphia: University of Pennsylvania Press, 2015.

Cacho, Lisa M. *Social Death: Racialized Rightlessness and the Criminalization of the Unprotected.* New York: New York University Press, 2012.

Campbell, Fiona Kumari. "Indian Contributions to Thinking about Studies in Ableism: Challenges, Dangers and Possibilities." *Indian Journal of Critical Disability Studies* 1, no. 1 (2020): 22–40.

Canaday, Margot. *The Straight State: Sexuality and Citizenship in Twentieth-Century America.* Politics and Society in Twentieth-Century America. Princeton, NJ: Princeton University Press, 2009.

Chakravartty, Paula, and Denise Ferreira da Silva. "Accumulation, Dispossession, and Debt: The Racial Logic of Global Capitalism—An Introduction." *American Quarterly* 64, no. 3 (2012): 361–85.

Chappell, Paul, and Marlene de Beer, eds. *Diverse Voices of Disabled Sexualities in the Global South.* Rochester, NY: University of Rochester Press, 2018.

Charlton, James L. *Nothing about Us without Us: Disability Oppression and Empowerment.* Berkeley: University of California Press, 1998; 우리 없이 우리에 대한 것은 없다. 전지혜 옮김. 서울: 울력, 2009.

¿Che.Ne.So? Composed by Barnaby Tree. In *Rhizophora.* Directed by Davide De Lillis and Julia Metzger-Traber. Edited by Katelyn Stiles. 2015. https://vimeo.com /111310332.

Chen, Mel Y. "Agitation." *South Atlantic Quarterly* 117, no. 3 (2018): 551–66.

Chen, Mel Y. *Animacies: Biopolitics, Racial Mattering, and Queer Affect.* Durham, NC: Duke University Press, 2012.

Chen, Mel Y. "'The Stuff of Slow Constitution': Reading Down Syndrome for Race, Disability, and the Timing That Makes Them So." *Somatechnics* 6, no. 2 (2016): 235–48.

Chirot, Daniel, ed. *The Origins of Backwardness in Eastern Europe.* Berkeley: University of California Press. 1991.

Choi, Lee Hyun. "South Korean Activists Urge Better Treatment of Asylum Seekers." *voa*, January 2, 2022. https://www.voanews.com/a/south-korean-activists-urge-better -treatment-of-asylum-seekers/6378557.html.

Choy, Catherine Ceniza. *Empire of Care: Nursing and Migration in Filipino American History.* American Encounters/Global Interactions. Durham, NC: Duke University Press, 2003.

Choy, Timothy, and Jerry Zee. "Condition—Suspension." *Cultural Anthropology* 30, no. 2 (2017): 210–23.

Chuh, Kandice. "It's Not about Anything." *Social Text* 32, no. 4 (2014): 125–34.

Clare, Eli. *Brilliant Imperfection: Grappling with Cure.* Durham, NC: Duke University Press, 2017.

Clare, Eli. *Exile and Pride: Disability, Queerness, and Liberation.* Durham, NC: Duke University Press, 2015.

Cohen, Cathy J. "Punks, Bulldaggers, and Welfare Queens: The Radical Potential of Queer Politics?" *GLQ* 3, no. 4 (1997): 437–65.

Comstock, Michelle. "Grrrl Zine Networks: Re-Composing Spaces of Authority, Gender, and Culture." *JAC* 21, no. 2 (2001): 383–409.

Cooper, Melinda. *Life as Surplus*. Seattle: University of Washington Press, 2009; 잉여로 서의 생명. 안성우 옮김. 서울:갈무리, 2016.

Coronado, Raúl. *A World Not to Come: A History of Latino Writing and Print Culture*. Cambridge, MA: Harvard University Press, 2013.

Crenshaw, Kimberlé. "Demarginalizing the Intersection of Race and Sex: A Black Feminist Critique of Antidiscrimination Doctrine, Feminist Theory and Antiracist Politics." *University of Chicago Legal Forum* 1989, no. 1 (1989): 139–67.

Cruz, Deirdre de la. *Mother Figured: Marian Apparitions and the Making of a Filipino Universal*. Chicago: University of Chicago Press, 2015.

Cruz, Denise. *Transpacific Femininities: The Making of the Modern Filipina*. Durham, NC: Duke University Press, 2012.

Cvetkovich, Ann. *Depression: A Public Feeling*. Durham, NC: Duke University Press, 2012.

Dana-Farber Cancer Institute. "'I Am Here' TV Commercial | Dana-Farber Cancer Institute." YouTube video, January 14, 2022. https://www.youtube.com/watch?v=RjesJt7VojA.

Danielewicz, Jane. *Contemporary Memoirs in Action: How to Do Things with Memoir*. New York: Palgrave Macmillan, 2018.

da Silva, Denise Ferreira. "The Banalization of Racial Events." *Theory and Event* 20, no. 1 (2017): 61–65.

Davis, Angela. "Dr. Martin Luther King Jr. Lecture in Social Justice." University of Pennsylvania, January 15, 2020. https://penntoday.upenn.edu/news/2020-mlk-keynote.

Davis, Angela. *Freedom Is a Constant Struggle*. Chicago: Haymarket Books, 2016.

Davydova, Darja. "Criminal Networks, Unfortunate Circumstances, or Migratory Projects? Researching Sex Trafficking from Eastern Europe." *Cultural Dynamics* 25, no. 2 (2013): 229–43.

Dayan, Colin. *The Law Is a White Dog: How Legal Rituals Make and Unmake Persons*. Princeton, NJ: Princeton University Press, 2011.

Dilts, Andrew. "From 'Entrepreneur of the Self' to 'Care of the Self': Neo-liberal Governmentality and Foucault's Ethics." *Foucault Studies* 12 (2011): 130–46.

Disability Day of Mourning: Remembering People with Disabilities Murdered by Their Families. Accessed March 13, 2020. https://disability-memorial.org/.

D'Lil, HolLynn. *Becoming Real in 24 Days: One Participant's Story of the 1977 Section 504 Demonstrations for Disability Rights*. Hallevaland Productions, 2015.

DuCille, Ann. *The Coupling Convention: Sex, Text, and Tradition in Black Women's Fiction*. New York: Oxford University Press, 1993.

Dunhamn, Jane, Jerome Harris, Shancia Jarrett, Leroy Moore, Akemi Nishida, Margaret Price, Britney Robinson, and Sami Schalk. "Developing and Reflecting on a Black Disability Studies Pedagogy: Work from the National Black Disability Coalition." *Disability Studies Quarterly* 35, no. 2 (2015).

Dzenovska, Dace. *School of Europeanness: Tolerance and Other Lessons in Political Liberalism in Latvia*. Oxford: Oxford University Press, 2018.

Echavez, Sarita. *The Decolonized Eye: Filipino American Art and Performance*. Minneapolis: University of Minnesota Press, 2009.

Enstad, Nan. "Toxicity and the Consuming Subject." In *States of Emergency: The Object of American Studies*, edited by Russ Castronovo and Susan Gillman, 55–68. Chapel Hill: University of North Carolina Press, 2009.

Erevelles, Nirmala. "Crippin' Jim Crow: Disability, Dis-Location, and the School-to-Prison Pipeline." In *Disability Incarcerated*, edited by Liat Ben-Moshe, Chris Chapman, and Allison C. Carey, 81–99. New York: Palgrave Macmillan, 2014.

Erevelles, Nirmala. *Disability and Difference in Global Contexts: Enabling a Transformative Body Politic*. New York: Palgrave Macmillan, 2011.

Fabris, Erick. *Tranquil Prisons: Chemical Incarceration under Community Treatment Orders*. Toronto: University of Toronto Press, 2011.

Falola, Toyin, and Nic Hamel, eds. *Disability in Africa: Inclusion, Care, and the Ethics of Humanity*. New York: Palgrave Macmillan, 2021.

Fanon, Frantz, Richard Philcox, Jean-Paul Sartre, and Homi K. Bhabha. *The Wretched of the Earth*. New York: Grove Press, 2004.

Fasfous, Ahmed F., et al. "Differences in Neuropsychological Performance between Refugee and Non-Refugee Children in Palestine." *International Journal of Environmental Research and Public Health* 18, no. 11 (2021): 5750.

Fassin, Didier, and Richard Rechtman. *The Empire of Trauma: An Inquiry into the Condition of Victimhood*. Princeton, NJ: Princeton University Press, 2009.

Ferri, Beth. "Disability Life Writing and the Politics of Knowing." *Teachers College Record* 113, no. 10 (2011). http://www.tcrecord.org ID Number 16433.

Ferry, Nicole. "Rethinking the Mainstream Gay and Lesbian Movement beyond the Classroom." *Journal of Curriculum Theorizing* 28, no. 2 (2012): 104–17.

Fleischer, Doris, and Frieda Zames. *The Disability Rights Movement: From Charity to Confrontation*. Philadelphia: Temple University Press, 2011.

Foley, Fiona. *Black Opium*. Queensland State Library, Brisbane, Australia. Permanent installation, 2006.

Foucault, Michel. *Discipline and Punish: The Birth of the Prison*. 2nd Vintage Books ed. New York: Vintage Books, 1995.

Fox, Diane Niblack. "Agent Orange: Coming to Terms with a Transnational Legacy." In *Four Decades On: Vietnam, the United States, and the Legacies of the Second Indochina War*, edited by Scott Laderman and Edwin A. Martini, 207–41. Durham, NC: Duke University Press, 2013.

Fox, Diane Niblack. "Agent Orange: Toxic Chemical, Narrative of Suffering, Metaphor for War." In *Looking Back on the Vietnam War: Twenty-First-Century Perspectives*, edited by Brenda M. Boyle and Jeehyun Lim, 140–55. New Brunswick, NJ: Rutgers University Press, 2016.

Fox, Diane Niblack. "One Significant Ghost: Agent Orange Narratives of Trauma, Survival, and Responsibility." PhD diss., University of Washington, Seattle, 2007.

Frank, Arthur. *The Wounded Storyteller: Body, Illness, and Ethics*. Chicago: University of Chicago Press, 1995.

Frey, John Carlos. "Graves of Shame." *Texas Observer*, July 6, 2015.

Fujino, Diane C., ed. *Wicked Theory, Naked Practice: The Fred Ho Reader*. Minneapolis: University of Minnesota Press, 2009.

Funk, Robert. "Disability Rights: From Caste to Class in the Context of Civil Rights." In *Images of the Disabled, Disabling Images*, edited by Alan Gartner and Tom Joe, 7–30. New York: Praeger, 1987.

Gal, Susan, and Gail Kligman. *The Politics of Gender after Socialism: A Comparative-Historical Essay*. Princeton, NJ: Princeton University Press, 2000.

Galmarini-Kabala, Maria Cristina. "Between Defectological Narratives and Institutional Realities: The 'Mentally Retarded' Child in the Soviet Union of the 1930s." *Bulletin of the History of Medicine* 93, no. 2 (2019): 180–206.

Gammeltoft, Tine M. *Haunting Images: A Cultural Account of Selective Reproduction in Vietnam*. Berkeley: University of California Press, 2014.

García Castellón, Manuel. *Estampas y Cuentos de La Filipinas Hispánica*. Cuentos de Clan. Ultramar: 3. Madrid: Clan Editorial, 2001.

Garland-Thomson, Rosemarie. *Extraordinary Bodies: Figuring Physical Disability in American Culture and Literature*. New York: Columbia University Press, 2017.

Ghai, Anita. *Rethinking Disability in India*. London: Routledge, 2015.

Giacaman, Rita. "Conceptual Frameworks of Disability in the Occupied Palestinian Territory with a Focus on the Palestinian Legal and Health Systems: Literature Review." The Disability Under Siege Network, 2021. https://disabilityundersiege.org/wp -content/uploads/2021/03/Conceptual-Frameworks-of-Disability-in-OPT-Literature -Review-FINAL.pdf.

Giacaman, Rita. "Reframing Public Health in Wartime: From the Biomedical Model to the 'Wounds Inside.'" *Journal of Palestine Studies* 47, no. 2 (2018): 9–27.

Glenn, Evelyn Nakano. *Unequal Freedom: How Race and Gender Shaped American Citizenship and Labor*. Cambridge, MA: Harvard University Press, 2002.

Glissant, Edouard. *Poetics of Relation*. Translated by Betsy Wing. Ann Arbor: University of Michigan Press, 1997.

González, John Morán. *Border Renaissance: The Texas Centennial and the Emergence of Mexican American Literature*. Austin: University of Texas Press, 2009.

Gorman, Rachel. "Disablement in and for Itself: Toward a 'Global' Idea of Disability." *Somatechnics* 6, no. 2 (2016): 249–61.

Grech, Shaun, and Karen Soldatic, eds. *Disability in the Global South: The Critical Handbook*. New York: Springer, 2016.

Grodecki, Wiktor, dir. *Anděle nejsou anděle*. Feature film. 1994.

Grodecki, Wiktor. "Chtěl jsem ukázat duši člověka." *Reflex* 7, no. 46 (1996): 44–46.

Grodecki, Wiktor. "Kdo prošel peklem." *Týden* 44, no. 4 (1997): 120–21.

Grodecki, Wiktor, dir. *Mandragora*. Feature film. 1997.

Grodecki, Wiktor, dir. *Tělo bez duše*. Feature film. 1996.

Gržinić, Marina. "Europe's Colonialism, Decoloniality, and Racism." In *Postcoloniality-Decoloniality-Black Critique: Joints and Fissures*, edited by Sabine Broeck and Carsten Junker, 129–44. New York: Campus Verlag, 2014.

Haddad, Toufic. *Palestine Ltd.: Neoliberalism and Nationalism in the Occupied Territory*. London: Bloomsbury Publishing, 2016.

Hall, Timothy M. "Rent-Boys, Barflies, and Kept Men: Men Involved in Sex with Men for Compensation in Prague." *Sexualities* 10, no. 4 (2007): 457–72.

Hammami, Rema. "On (Not) Suffering at the Checkpoint: Palestinian Narrative Strategies of Surviving Israel's Carceral Geography." *Borderlands* 14, no. 1 (2015): 1–17.

Hamraie, Aimi. *Building Access: Universal Design and the Politics of Disability*. Minneapolis: University of Minnesota Press, 2017.

Hamraie, Aimi. "Mapping Access: Digital Humanities, Disability Justice, and Sociospatial Practice." *American Quarterly* 70, no. 3 (2018): 455–82.

Haraway, Donna. *The Haraway Reader*. New York: Routledge, 2004.

Harker, Christopher. *Spacing Debt: Obligations, Violence, and Endurance in Ramallah, Palestine*. Durham, NC: Duke University Press, 2020.

Harris, Cheryl I. "Whiteness as Property." *Harvard Law Review* 106, no. 8 (1993): 1707–91.

Harsha, Nouh, Luay Ziq, and Rita Giacaman. "Disability among Palestinian Elderly in the Occupied Palestinian Territory (OPT): Prevalence and Associated Factors." *BMC Public Health* 19, no. 432 (2019).

Havelková, Barbara, and Blanka Bellak-Hančilová. *Co s prostitucí?: veřejné politiky a práva osob v prostituci*. Prague: Sociologické nakladatelství, 2014.

Henschel, Frank. "Embodiment of Deviance: The Biopolitics of the 'Difficult Child' in Socialist Czechoslovakia." *East European Politics and Societies* 34, no. 4 (2020): 837–57.

Hershey, Laura. "Wade Blank's Liberated Community." In *The Ragged Edge: The Disability Experience from the Pages of the First Fifteen Years of the Disability Rag*, edited by Barrett Shaw, 149–55. Louisville, KY: Avocado Press, 1994.

Hicks, Nancy. "Equity for Disabled Likely to be Costly." *New York Times*, May 1, 1977, p. 29.

Hill-Collins, Patricia. *Black Feminist Thought: Knowledge, Consciousness, and the Politics of Empowerment*. New York: Routledge, 2000.

Hinton, Anna. "On Fits, Starts, and Entry Points: The Rise of Black Disability Studies." *CLA Journal* 64, no. 1 (2021): 11–29.

Hix, Lisa. "Interview with Leroy Moore, Founder of Krip Hop Nation." KQED, February 14, 2011. https://www.kqed.org/arts/43903/interview_with_leroy_moore _founder_of_krip_hop_nation.

Ho, Fred. *Diary of a Radical Cancer Warrior: Fighting Cancer and Capitalism at the Cellular Level*. New York: Skyhorse Publishing, 2011.

Hoang Van Minh, Kim Bao Giang, Nguyen Thanh Liem, Michael E. Palmer, Nguyen Phuong Thao, and Le Bach Duong. "Estimating the Extra Cost of Living with Disability in Vietnam." *Global Public Health* 10, no. S1 (2015): S70–S79. https://doi.org/10.1 080/17441692.2014.971332.

Huffer, Lynne. *Mad for Foucault: Rethinking the Foundations of Queer Theory*. New York: Columbia University Press, 2010.

Hunter, Tera W. *To 'Joy My Freedom: Southern Black Women's Lives and Labors after the Civil War*. Cambridge, MA: Harvard University Press, 2004.

Ileto, Reynaldo C. "Outlines of a Non-Linear Emplotment of Philippine History." In *Reflections on Development in Southeast Asia*, edited by Lim Teck Ghee, 130–59. Singapore: Institute of Southeast Asian Studies, 1988.

Ileto, Reynaldo Clemena. *Pasyon and Revolution: Popular Movements in the Philippines, 1840–1910*. Quezon City: Ateneo de Manila Press, 1979.

Imada, Adria L. "A Decolonial Disability Studies?" *Disability Studies Quarterly* 37, no. 3 (2017): np. https://dsq-sds.org/article/view/5984.

INCITE! Women of Color against Violence. *The Revolution Will Not Be Funded: Beyond the Non-Profit Industrial Complex*. Durham, NC: Duke University Press, 2017.

Isaac, Allan Punzalan. *American Tropics: Articulating Filipino America*. Critical American Studies Series. Minneapolis: University of Minnesota Press, 2006.

Jaffee, Laura. "Access Washing at the Imperial University: Militarism, Occupation, and Struggles toward Disability Justice." PhD diss., Syracuse University, New York, May 2020.

Jaffee, Laura. "Student Movements against the Imperial University: Toward a Genealogy of Disability Justice in U.S. Higher Education." *Berkeley Review of Education* 10, no. 2 (2021).

Jaffee, Laura, and Kelsey John. "Disabling Bodies of/and Land: Reframing Disability Justice in Conversation with Indigenous Theory and Activism." *Disability and the Global South* 5, no. 2 (2018): 1407–29.

Jain, S. Lochlann. *Malignant: How Cancer Becomes Us*. Berkeley: University of California Press, 2013.

Jamal, Amal. "Conflict Theory, Temporality, and Transformative Temporariness: Lessons from Israel and Palestine." *Constellations* 23, no. 5 (2016): 365–77.

Jeníková, Eva. "Šokující dokument Tělo bez duše odhaluje podsvětí dětské pornografie." *Svobodné slovo* 88, no. 16 (1996): 5.

Jesook Song. *South Koreans in the Debt Crisis: The Creation of a Neoliberal Welfare Society*. Durham, NC: Duke University Press, 2009; 복지의 배신. 추선영 옮김. 서울 이후북스, 2016.

Johnson, Mary. "The Power of One Person." In *The Ragged Edge: The Disability Experience from the Pages of the First Fifteen Years of the Disability Rag*, edited by Barrett Shaw, 156–64. Louisville, KY: Avocado Press, 1994.

Johnson, Mary. "Rosa Parks and Access to Buses: A Little-Known Piece of the Story." *Ragged Edge* magazine, October 25, 2005. http://www.raggededgemagazine.com/blogs/edgecentric/archives//000566.html.

Johnson, Merri Lisa, and Robert McRuer. "Cripistemologies: Introduction." *Journal of Literary and Cultural Disability Studies* 8, no. 2 (2014): 127–47.

Joronen, Mikko, Helga Tawil-Souri, Merav Amir, and Mark Griffiths, eds. "Palestinian Futures: Anticipation, Imagination, Embodiments." *Geografiska Annaler: Series B, Human Geography* 103, no. 4 (2021 Special Issue).

Kafer, Alison. "After Crip, Crip Afters." *South Atlantic Quarterly* 120, no. 2 (2021): 415–34.

Kafer, Alison. *Feminist, Queer, Crip*. Bloomington: Indiana University Press, 2013.

Karnow, Catherine. *Agent Orange: A Terrible Legacy*. Vietnam Reporting Project, 2011. https://vietnamreportingproject.org/2011/05/a-terrible-legacy-2/.

Kashi, Ed, dir. Catherine Karnow, photographer. *The Leaves Keep Falling*. Vietnam Reporting Project and Talking Eyes Media, 2011. https://vietnamreportingproject.org/2011/05/the-leaves-keep-falling/.

Katz, Irit. "Mobile Colonial Architecture: Facilitating Settler Colonialism's Expansions, Expulsions, Resistance, and Decolonisation." *Mobilities* 17, no. 2 (2022): 213–37.

Kelley, Rick. "For Thousands of Years, El Sal del Rey Was Lure for Natives and Armies." *Brownsville Herald*, November 12, 2016.

Khúc, Mimi, ed. "Open in Emergency: A Special Issue on Asian American Mental Health." *Asian American Literary Review* 7, no. 2 (2016).

Kidd, Rosalind. *The Way We Civilise: Aboriginal Affairs—The Untold Story*. Queensland: University of Queensland Press, 1997.

Kim, Eunjung. *Curative Violence: Rehabilitating Disability, Gender, and Sexuality in Modern Korea*. Durham, NC: Duke University Press, 2017.

Kim, Eunjung. "The Specter of Vulnerability and Bodies in Protest." In *Disability, Human Rights and Limits of Humanitarianism*, edited by Michael Gill and Cathy Schlund-Vials, 137–54. Surrey, UK: Ashgate, 2014.

Kim, Jina B. "Anatomy of the City: Race, Infrastructure, and U.S. Fictions of Dependency." PhD diss., University of Michigan, Ann Arbor, 2016. https://deepblue.lib.umich.edu/bitstream/handle/2027.42/133499/jinabkim_1.pdf?sequence=1.

Kim, Jina B. "Disability in an Age of Fascism." *American Quarterly* 72, no. 1 (2020): 265–76.

Kim, Jina B. "Toward a Crip-of-Color Critique: Thinking with Minich's 'Enabling Whom?'" *Lateral: Journal of the Cultural Studies Association* 6, no. 1 (2017).

Kim, Jina B., and Sami Schalk. "Reclaiming the Radical Politics of Self-Care: A Crip-of-Color Critique." *South Atlantic Quarterly* 120, no. 2 (2021): 325–42.

Kligman, Gail, and Stephanie Limoncelli. "Trafficking Women after Socialism: To, through, and from Eastern Europe." *Social Politics: International Studies in Gender, State and Society* 12, no. 1 (2005): 118–40.

Ko, Dorothy. *Cinderella's Sisters: A Revisionist History of Footbinding*. Philip A. Lilienthal Asian Studies Imprint. Berkeley: University of California Press, 2005.

Kolářová, Kateřina. "Mediating Syndromes of Postcommunism: Disability, Sex, Race, and Labor." *JCMS: Journal of Cinema and Media Studies* 58, no. 4 (2019): 156–62.

Kolářová, Kateřina. *Rehabilitative Postsocialism: Gender, Sexuality, Disability, Race and the Limits of National Belonging*. Ann Arbor: University of Michigan Press. Forthcoming.

Kolářová, Kateřina, and Filip Herza. "Engineering Socialist Integration in the Age of Normalisation: Roma and People with Disabilities as Objects of Care in Socialist Czechoslovakia." In *Re/imaginations of Disability in State Socialism: Visions, Promises, Frustrations,* edited by Kateřina Kolářová and Martina Winkler, 167–215. Frankfurt am Main: Campus Verlag, 2021.

Kolářová, Kateřina, and Martina Winkler. *Re/Imaginations of Disability in State Socialism: Visions, Promises, Frustrations*. Frankfurt am Main: Campus Verlag, 2021.

Kołodziejczyk, Dorota, and Cristina Sandru. "Introduction: On Colonialism, Communism and East-Central Europe—Some Reflections." *Journal of Postcolonial Writing* 48, no. 2 (2012): 113–16.

Koobak, Redi, Madina Tlostanova, and Suruchi Thapar-Björkert, eds. *Postcolonial and Postsocialist Dialogues: Intersections, Opacities, Challenges in Feminist Theorizing and Practice*. London: Routledge, 2021.

Kotef, Hagar. *Movement and the Ordering of Freedom: On Liberal Governances of Mobility*. Durham, NC: Duke University Press, 2015.

Kramer, Paul A. *The Blood of Government: Race, Empire, the United States, and the Philippines*. Chapel Hill: University of North Carolina Press, 2006.

Kriegel, Leonard. "Uncle Tom and Tiny Tim: Some Reflections on the Cripple as Negro." *American Scholar* 38, no. 3 (1969): 412–30.

Kroløkke, Charlotte, L. Myong, S. W. Adrian, and T. Tjørnhøj-Thomsen. *Critical Kinship Studies*. London: Rowman and Littlefield, 2016.

Kulpa, Robert, and Joanna Mizielińska. *De-centering Western Sexualities: Central and Eastern European Perspectives*. Burlington, VT: Ashgate, 2011.

Kuppers, Petra. "Toward a Rhizomatic Model of Disability: Poetry, Performance, and Touch." *Journal of Literary and Cultural Disability Studies* 3, no. 3 (2009): 221–40.

Kuus, Merje. "Europe's Eastern Expansion and the Reinscription of Otherness in East-Central Europe." *Progress in Human Geography* 28, no. 4 (2004): 472–89.

Lakshmi, Padma. *Love, Loss, and What We Ate: A Memoir*. New York: Ecco, 2016.

Lambert, Léopold. "They Have Clocks, We Have Time: Introduction." *The Funambulist* 36 (June 21, 2021).

Lamper, Ivan. "Minulý týden." *Respekt* 8, no. 9 (1997): 52.

Langan, Celeste. "Mobility Disability." *Public Culture* 13, no. 3 (2001): 459–84.

Larkin-Gilmore, Juliet, Ella Callow, and Susan Burch, eds. "Indigeneity and Disability: Kinship, Place, and Knowledge-Making." *Disability Studies Quarterly* 41, no. 4 (2021 Special Issue).

Lederer, Jakub. "*Mandragora* šokuje otevřeností, nahotou však neuráží." *Zemské Noviny* 7, no. 243 (1997): 7.

Lee, Christine Hyung-Oak. *Tell Me Everything You Don't Remember: The Stroke That Changed My Life*. New York: Ecco, 2017.

Lee, Christine Hyung-Oak. *Writing Under a Pseudonym* (blog). https://jadepark.wordpress.com.

Lee, James Kyung-Jin. "Elegies of Social Life: The Wounded Asian American." *Journal of Race, Ethnicity, and Religion* 3, no. 2.7 (2012): 1–21.

Lee, James Kyung-Jin. *Pedagogies of Woundedness: Illness, Memoir, and the Ends of the Model Minority*. Philadelphia: Temple University Press, 2021.

Lee, James Kyung-Jin, ed. "The State of Illness and Disability in Asian America." *Amerasia* 39, no. 1 (2013 Special Issue).

Levins Morales, Aurora. *Aurora Levins Morales: Writing That Other World That Is Possible*. Accessed November 10, 2016. http://www.auroralevinsmorales.com.

Levins Morales, Aurora. "Guanakán." *Nineteen Sixty Nine: An Ethnic Studies Journal* 2, no. 1 (2013): 1–3.

Levins Morales, Aurora. *Kindling: Writings on the Body*. Cambridge, MA: Palabera Press, 2013.

Levins Morales, Aurora. *Medicine Stories: History, Culture and the Politics of Integrity*. Cambridge, MA: South End Press, 1998.

Levins Morales, Aurora. *Remedios: Stories of Earth and Iron from the History of Puertor-riqueñas*. Cambridge, MA: South End Press, 1998.

Levins Morales, Aurora. "Shared Ecologies and Healing Justice in the Work of Aurora Levins Morales: An Interview" (with Suzanne Bost). *MELUS* 42, no. 1 (2017): 186–203.

Licona, Adela C. *Zines in Third Space: Radical Cooperation and Borderlands Rhetoric*. Albany: SUNY Press, 2013.

Little, Nita. "Restructuring the Self-Sensing: Attention Training in Contact Improvisation." *Journal of Dance and Somatic Practices* 6, no. 2 (2014): 247–60.

Liu, Petrus. *Queer Marxism in Two Chinas*. Durham, NC: Duke University Press, 2015.

Longmore, Paul K. *Why I Burned My Book and Other Essays on Disability*. American Subjects. Philadelphia: Temple University Press, 2003.

Longmore, Paul, and Lauri Umansky. *The New Disability History: American Perspectives*. New York: New York University Press, 2001.

Lorde, Audre. *Cancer Journals*. San Francisco: Aunt Lute Books, 2006.

Lorde, Audre. *The Cancer Journals: Special Edition*. San Francisco: Aunt Lute Books, 1997.

Lorde, Audre. *Sister Outsider: Essays and Speeches*. Freedom, CA: Crossing Press, 1984.

Lorenz, Renate. "The Chronic: Renate Lorenz in Conversation with Mathias Danbolt and Elizabeth Freeman." *Springerin* 1 (Winter 2014): 17–23; in English at http://www.f-r-a-n-k.org/conversations/01/pdfs/150608_FRANK_conversations_Chronic.pdf.

Lowe, Lisa. *The Intimacies of Four Continents*. Durham, NC: Duke University Press, 2015.

Luciano, Dana, and Mel Y. Chen. "Has the Queer Ever Been Human?" *GLQ* 21, no. 2/3 (2015): 182–207.

Macharia, Keguro. "On Being Area-Studied: A Litany of Complaint." *GLQ* 22, no. 2 (2016): 183–89.

MacKenzie, Alison, et al. "Barriers to Effective, Equitable and Quality Education: A Rights-Based, Participatory Research Assessment of Inclusion of Children with Disabilities in Palestine." *International Journal of Children's Rights* 28, no. 4 (2020): 805–32.

Mahamid, Fayez Azez. "Collective Trauma, Quality of Life and Resilience in Narratives of Third Generation Palestinian Refugee Children." *Child Indicators Research* 13 (2020): 2181–204.

Mairs, Nancy. *Waist-High in the World: A Life among the Nondisabled*. Boston: Beacon Press, 1996.

Manalansan, Martin F., and Augusto Fauni Espiritu. *Filipino Studies: Palimpsests of Nation and Diaspora*. New York: New York University Press, 2016.

Maqusi, Samar. "Acts of Spatial Violation: The Politics of Space-Making Inside the Palestinian Refugee Camp." *ARENA Journal of Architectural Research* 6, no. 1 (2021): article 8.

Marable, Manning. "Blackness beyond Boundaries: Navigating the Political Economies of Global Inequality." In *Transnational Blackness: Navigating the Global Color Line*, edited by Manning Marable and Vanessa Agard-Jones, 1–8. New York: Palgrave Macmillan, 2008.

Marie, Mohammad, et al. 2020. "Anxiety Disorders and PTSD in Palestine: A Literature Review." *BMC Psychiatry* 20, no. 509 (2020).

Martin, Randy. *Critical Moves: Dance Studies in Theory and Politics*. Durham, NC: Duke University Press, 1998.

Martinez, Noemi. "The Five Scariest Places in South Texas." *Hermana Resist*, October 30, 2016. http://www.hermanaresist.com/the-five-scariest-places-in-south-texas/.

Martinez, Noemi. *South Texas Experience: Love Letters*. Weslaco, TX: Hermana Resist, 2015.

Martinez, Noemi. *The South Texas Experience Project*. Weslaco, TX: Hermana Resist, 2005.

McLeod, Gerald E. "Day Trips: The Salt Lake La Sal del Rey in Central Hidalgo County Is as Inhospitable as It Is Beautiful." *Austin Chronicle*, February 20, 2009.

McRuer, Robert. *Crip Theory: Cultural Signs of Queerness and Disability*. New York: New York University Press, 2006.

McRuer, Robert. *Crip Times: Disability, Globalization, and Resistance.* New York: New York University Press, 2018.

Meade, Teresa, and David Serlin. "Editors' Introduction." *Radical History Review* 94 (2006): 1–8.

Meekosha, Helen. "Decolonising Disability: Thinking and Acting Globally." *Disability and Society* 26, no. 6 (2011): 667–82.

Meekosha, Helen, and Karen Soldatic. "Human Rights and the Global South: The Case of Disability." *Third World Quarterly* 32, no. 8 (2011): 1383–97. https://doi.org/10.1080/01436597.2011.614800.

Melamed, Jodi. "Racial Capitalism." *Critical Ethnic Studies* 1, no. 1 (2015): 76–85.

Melegh, Attila. *On the East-West Slope: Globalization, Nationalism, Racism and Discourses on Eastern Europe*. New York: Central European University Press, 2006.

Mendoza, Victor Román. *Metroimperial Intimacies: Fantasy, Racial-Sexual Governance, and the Philippines in U.S. Imperialism, 1899–1913*. Perverse Modernities. Durham, NC: Duke University Press, 2015.

Metzger-Traber, Julia. Interview by Natalia Duong. April 12, 2016.

Mi-Hae Won. "Between Invisible Boundaries: Focusing on the Migrant Experience of Middle- and Older-Aged Women of Yongsan Red-Light District." *Trans-Humanities* 7, no. 2 (2014).

Milbern, Stacey Park. "Notes on 'Access Washing.'" Disability Justice Network of Ontario, April 25, 2019. https://www.djno.ca/post/notes-on-access-washing.

Miles, Angel L., Akemi Nishida, and Anjali J. Forber-Pratt. "An Open Letter to White Disability Studies and Ableist Institutions of Higher Education." *Disability Studies Quarterly* 37, no. 3 (2017).

Million, Dian. *Therapeutic Nations: Healing in an Age of Indigenous Human Rights*. Tucson: University of Arizona Press, 2013.

Mingus, Mia. *Leaving Evidence* (blog). https://leavingevidence.wordpress.com/.

Mingus, Mia. "Reflection toward Practice: Some Questions on Disability Justice." In *Criptiques*, edited by Caitlin Wood, 107–14. Self-published, 2014.

Minich, Julie Avril. *Accessible Citizenships: Disability, Nation, and the Cultural Politics of Greater Mexico.* Philadelphia: Temple University Press, 2013.

Minich, Julie Avril. "'The Emotional Residue of an Unnatural Boundary': *Brownsville* and the Borders of Mental Health." In *Symbolism 17: Latina/o Literature: The Trans-Atlantic and the Trans-American in Dialogue,* edited by Rüdiger Ahrens, Florian Kläger, and Klaus Stierstorfer, 123–42. Berlin: De Gruyter, 2017.

Minich, Julie Avril. "Enabling Whom? Critical Disability Studies Now." *Lateral: Journal of the Cultural Studies Association* 5, no. 1 (2016).

Mitchell, David T., and Sharon L. Snyder. *The Biopolitics of Disability: Neoliberalism, Ablenationalism, and Peripheral Embodiment.* Ann Arbor: University of Michigan Press, 2015.

Mojares, Resil B. *Brains of the Nation: Pedro Paterno, T. H. Pardo de Tavera, Isabelo de Los Reyes, and the Production of Modern Knowledge.* Manila: Ateneo de Manila University Press, 2006.

Moore, Leroy Franklin, Jr. "Black History of 504 Sit-In for Disability Rights: More Than Serving Food—When Will the Healing Begin?" *San Francisco Bay View,* February 11, 2014. http://sfbayview.com/2014/02/black-history-of-504-sit-in-for-disability-rights-more-than-serving-food-when-will-the-healing-begin.

Moraga, Cherríe, and Gloria Anzaldúa. *This Bridge Called My Back: Writings by Radical Women of Color.* 4th ed. Albany: SUNY Press, 2015.

Morgan, Jennifer L. *Laboring Women: Reproduction and Gender in New World Slavery.* Philadelphia: University of Pennsylvania Press, 2004.

Mosleh, Marwan, Koustuv Dalal, Yousef Aljeesh, and Leif Svanström. "The Burden of War-Injury in the Palestinian Health Care Sector in Gaza Strip." *BMC International Health and Human Rights* 18, no. 1 (2018): article 28.

Moss, Kevin. "Who's Renting These Boys? Wiktor Grodecki's Czech Hustler Documentaries." *InterAlia: An Online Journal of Queer Studies* 1 (2006). http://www. interalia .org.pl/en/artykuly/homepage/05_whos_renting_these_boys.htm.

Moten, Fred. "blackpalestinian breath" *SocialText Online,* October 25, 2018. https:// socialtextjournal.org/periscope_article/blackpalestinian-breath/.

Moten, Fred, and Stefano Harney. *The Undercommons: Fugitive Planning and Black Study.* London: Minor Compositions, 2013.

Mukherjee, Siddhartha. *The Emperor of All Maladies: A Biography of Cancer.* New York: Scribner, 2010.

Mukherjee, Siddhartha. *The Gene: An Intimate History.* New York: Scribner, 2016.

Muñoz, José Esteban. *Disidentifications: Queers of Color and the Performance of Politics.* Minneapolis: University of Minnesota Press, 1999.

Muñoz, José Esteban. "Feeling Brown, Feeling Down: Latina Affect, the Performativity of Race, and the Depressive Position." *Signs* 31, no. 3 (2006): 675–88.

Murphy, Michelle. "Alterlife and Decolonial Chemical Relations." *Cultural Anthropology* 32, no. 4 (2017): 494–503.

Murphy, Michelle. "What Can't a Body Do?" *Catalyst: Feminism, Theory, Technoscience* 3, no. 1 (2017): 1–15. https://doi.org/10.28968/cftt.v3i1.28791.

Na, Tari Young-Jung. Translated by Ju Hui Judy Han and Se-Woong Koo. "The South Korean Gender System: LGBTI in the Contexts of Family, Legal Identity, and the Military." *Journal of Korean Studies* 19, no. 2 (2014): 357–77.

Nahal, Maha Sudki, et al. "Palestinian Children's Narratives about Living with Spina Bifida: Stigma, Vulnerability, and Social Exclusion." *Child Care Health Development* 45 (2019): 54–62.

Nash, Jennifer C. *Black Feminism Reimagined: After Intersectionality*. Durham, NC: Duke University Press, 2019.

Nash, Jennifer C. "Slow Loss: Black Feminism and Endurance." *Social Text* 40, no. 2 (2022): 1–20.

Nelson, Alondra. *Body and Soul: The Black Panther Party and the Fight against Medical Discrimination*. Minneapolis: University of Minnesota Press, 2011.

Nguyen, Trien T. "Environmental Consequences of Dioxin from the War in Vietnam: What Has Been Done and What Else Could Be Done?" *International Journal of Environmental Studies* 66, no. 1 (2009): 9–26. https://doi.org/10.1080/00207230902757321.

Nguyen, Xuan Thuy. "Critical Disability Studies at the Edge of Global Development: Why Do We Need to Engage with Southern Theory?" *Canadian Journal of Disability Studies* 7, no. 1 (2018): 2–25.

Nguyen, Xuan Thuy. "Genealogies of Disability in Global Governance: A Foucauldian Critique of Disability and Development." *Foucault Studies* 19 (2015): 67–83.

Nguyen, Xuan Thuy. *The Journey to Inclusion*. Rotterdam: Sense Publishers, 2015.

Nielsen, Kim. *Disability History of the United States*. Boston: Beacon Press, 2012.

Nixon, Rob. *Slow Violence and the Environmentalism of the Poor*. Cambridge, MA: Harvard University Press, 2011.

Njahîra, Faith. "Disability Acceptance and Inclusion Lessons from My Cucu." *Muscular Dystrophy Society Kenya* (blog), August 10, 2019. www.mdskenya.blogspot.com.

Oliver, Mike. "The Social Model of Disability: Thirty Years On." *Disability and Society* 28, no. 7 (2013): 1024–26. https://doi.org/10.1080/09687599.2013.818773.

Orlansky, Michael D. *Voices: Interviews with Handicapped People*. Columbus: Ohio State University Press, 1981.

Orsak, Sarah. "How Disability Became White: Blackness and White Disability from Hollywood to Academia." PhD diss., Rutgers University, 2022.

O'Toole, Corbett. *Fading Scars: My Queer Disability History*. Fort Worth, TX: Autonomous Press, 2015.

Pape, Markus. *A nikdo vám nebude věřit*. Prague: GplusG, 1997.

Parekh, Pushpa Naidu, ed. "Intersecting Gender and Disability Perspectives in Rethinking Postcolonial Identities." *Wagadu: A Journal of Transnational Women's and Gender Studies* 4 (2007 Special Issue).

Parker, Ally Karen. "Ally Karen Parker on the 1977 Section 504 Occupation." Video oral history. Paul K. Longmore Institute on Disability Collection, 2014. https://diva.sfsu.edu/collections/longmoreinstitute/bundles/231040.

Parvulescu, Anca. *The Traffic in Women's Work: East European Migration and the Making of Europe*. Chicago: University of Chicago Press, 2014.

Paxton, Steve. "A Definition." *Contact Quarterly* 4, no. 2 (1979): 26.

Peckruhn, Heike. "Tracing Debility and Webbing Resistance to State Violence through Crip Epistemologies." *Political Theology Network*, June 4, 2021. https://politicaltheology.com/tracing-debility-and-webbing-resistance-to-state-violence-through-crip-epistemologies/.

Peeples, Jennifer. "Imaging Toxins." *Environmental Communication* 7, no. 2 (2013): 191–210. https://doi.org/10.1080/17524032.2013.775172.

Pelka, Fred. *What We Have Done: An Oral History of the Disability Rights Movement.* Amherst: University of Massachusetts Press, 2012.

Percy, Stephen L. *Disability, Civil Rights, and Public Policy: The Politics of Implementation.* Tuscaloosa: University of Alabama Press, 1992.

Peterson, Bill. "Schools Hit Cost of Ending Bias against Disabled." *Washington Post*, July 5, 1977, A8.

Pham, Diem T., Hang M. Nguyen, Thomas G. Boivin, Anna Zajacova, Snehalata V. Huzurbazar, and Harold L. Bergman. "Predictors for Dioxin Accumulation in Residents Living in Da Nang and Bien Hoa, Vietnam, Many Years after Agent Orange Use." *Chemosphere* 118 (2015): 277–83. https://doi.org/10.1016/j.chemosphere.2014.09.064.

Phillips, Sarah D. *Disability and Mobile Citizenship in Postsocialist Ukraine.* Bloomington: Indiana University Press, 2010.

Pickens, Therí Alyce. *Black Madness :: Mad Blackness.* Durham, NC: Duke University Press, 2019.

Pickens, Therí Alyce. "Blackness and Disability." *African American Review* 50, no. 2 (2017 Special Issue).

Pickens, Therí Alyce, ed. "Blackness and Disability: This. Is. The. Remix. or I Thought I Told You That We Won't Stop." *CLA Journal* 64, no. 1 (2021 Special Issue).

Pickens, Therí A. "Blue Blackness, Black Blueness: Making Sense of Blackness and Disability." *African American Review* 50, no. 2 (2017): 93–103.

Piepzna-Samarasinha, Leah Lakshmi. *Care Work: Dreaming Disability Justice.* Vancouver: Arsenal Pulp Press, 2018.

Povinelli, Elisabeth. "Notes on Gridlock: Genealogy, Intimacy, Sexuality." *Public Culture* 14, no. 1 (2002): 215–38.

Prashad, Vijay. *The Darker Nations: A People's History of the Third World.* New York: New Press, 2007.

Puar, Jasbir K. "Prognosis Time: Towards a Geopolitics of Affect, Debility and Capacity." *Women and Performance* 19, no. 2 (2009): 161–72. https://doi.org/10.1080/07407700903034147.

Puar, Jasbir K. *The Right to Maim: Debility, Capacity, Disability.* Durham, NC: Duke University Press, 2017.

Puar, Jasbir K. "Spatial Debilities: Slow Life and Carceral Capitalism in Palestine." *South Atlantic Quarterly* 120, no. 2 (2021): 393–414.

Puar, Jasbir, and Ghassan Abu-Sitta. "Israel Is Trying to Maim Gaza Palestinians into Silence." *Al Jazeera*, March 31, 2019. https://www.aljazeera.com/opinions/2019/3/31/israel-is-trying-to-maim-gaza-palestinians-into-silence.

Puar, Jasbir, Ghassan Abu-Sittah, Nadera Shaloub-Kevorkian, Dina Kiwan, and Shatha Abu Srour. "Disability Under Siege: Palestine." Roundtable, May 6, 2022. Pozen Family Center for Human Rights, University of Chicago.

Qato, Danya M. "Introduction: Public Health and the Promise of Palestine." *Journal of Palestine Studies* 49, no. 4 (2020 Special Issue): 8–26.

Quijano, Anibal, and Michael Ennis. "Coloniality of Power, Eurocentrism, and Latin America." *Nepantla: Views from South* 1, no. 3 (2000): 533–81.

Qutami, Loubna. "'The Camp Is My Nationality': Palestinian Situated Knowledge in the Global Refugee Crisis." *Critical Ethnic Studies* 6, no. 2 (2020). https://doi.org/10.5749/CES.0602.qutami.

Qzeih, Shahd Adnan M., and Rafooneh Mokhtarshahi Sani. "Sensory Perceptual Experience in Balata Refugee Camp." *Open House International* 44, no. 2 (2019): 36–44.

Rabaia, Yoke, Mahasin F. Saleh, and Rita Giacaman. "Sick or Sad? Supporting Palestinian Children Living in Conditions of Chronic Political Violence." *Children and Society* 28, no. 3 (2014): 172–81.

Rabie, Kareem. *Palestine Is Throwing a Party and the Whole World Is Invited: Capital and State Building in the West Bank.* Durham, NC: Duke University Press, 2021.

Rafael, Vicente L. *Contracting Colonialism: Translation and Christian Conversion in Tagalog Society under Early Spanish Rule.* ACLS Humanities E-Book. Ithaca, NY: Cornell University Press, 1988.

Rafael, Vicente L. *White Love and Other Events in Filipino History.* American Encounters / Global Interactions. Durham, NC: Duke University Press, 2000.

Rancière, Jacques. *Dissensus: On Politics and Aesthetics.* Edited and translated by Steven Corcoran. London: Continuum, 2010.

Rasell, Michael, and Elena Iarskaia-Smirnova. *Disability in Eastern Europe and the Former Soviet Union: History, Policy and Everyday Life.* London: Routledge, 2014.

Reagan, Leslie J. "Representations and Reproductive Hazards of Agent Orange." *Journal of Law, Medicine and Ethics* 39, no. 1 (2011): 54–61.

Regina, Bonnie. "Disability Rights Activist Bonnie Regina on the 1977 Section 504 Occupation and Her Experience as a Student with Disabilities at San Francisco State University." Video oral history. Paul K. Longmore Institute on Disability Collection, 2014. https://diva.sfsu.edu/collections/longmoreinstitute/bundles/230645.

Reyes, José G., with a prologue by Teodoro M. Kalaw. *Novela de la Vida Real.* Manila: Self-published, 1930. https://catalog.hathitrust.org/Record/000480508.

Reyes, Raquel A. G. *Love, Passion and Patriotism: Sexuality and the Philippine Propaganda Movement, 1882–1892.* Critical Dialogues in Southeast Asian Studies. Singapore: NUS Press/Seattle: University of Washington Press, 2008.

Rizal, José. *Noli Me Tángere:(Novela Tagala).* 2nd ed. Barcelona, 1909. http://hdl.handle.net/2027/inu.32000004766327.

Robinson, Cedric J. *Black Marxism: The Making of the Black Radical Tradition.* Chapel Hill: University of North Carolina Press, 2000.

Rocher, Paul. "Shooting Rubber Bullets at Demonstrators Is, in Fact, Lethal." Interview by Pascual Cortés and Gonzalo García-Campo. *Jacobin*, June 16, 2021. https://jacobin

.com/2021/06/police-brutality-protests-demonstrations-crowd-control-nonlethal-less
-lethal-weapons-tear-gas-rubber-bullets-rocher-interview.

Rowley, Michelle V. "The Idea of Ancestry: Of Feminist Genealogies and Many Other Things." In *The Feminist Theory Reader: Local and Global Perspectives*, 4th ed., edited by Carole McCann and Seung-kyung Kim, 77–82. New York: Routledge, 2016.

Rubin, Gayle. "Thinking Sex: Notes for a Radical Theory of the Politics of Sexuality." In *Pleasure and Danger: Exploring Female Sexuality*, edited by Carole S. Vance, 267–93. London: Pandora, 1992.

Russell, Marta. "Malcolm Teaches Us, Too." In *The Ragged Edge: The Disability Experience from the Pages of the First Fifteen Years of the Disability Rag*, edited by Barrett Shaw, 11–14. Louisville, KY: Avocado Press, 1994.

Sa'di-Ibraheem, Yara. "Jaffa's Times: Temporalities of Dispossession and the Advent of Natives' Reclaimed Time." *Time and Society* 29, no. 2 (2020): 340–61.

Sádlík, Jan. "*Mandragora* varuje před zlem v člověku." *Plzeňský kulturní přehled. Kultura* 5 (1998): 6.

Said, Edward W. *The Question of Palestine*. New York: Vintage, 1979.

Saldaña-Portillo, María Josefina. "The Violence of Citizenship in the Making of Refugees: The United States and Central America." *Social Text* 37, no. 4(2019): 1–21.

Salesses, Matthew. *Craft in the Real World: Rethinking Fiction Writing and Workshopping*. New York: Catapult, 2021.

Salih, Ruba, Elena Zambelli, and Lynn Welchman. "'From Standing Rock to Palestine We Are United': Diaspora Politics, Decolonization and the Intersectionality of Struggles." *Ethnic and Racial Studies* 44, no. 7 (2021): 1135–53.

Samuels, Ellen. "Critical Divides: Judith Butler's Body Theory and the Question of Disability." *NWSA Journal* 14, no. 3 (2002): 58–76.

Samuels, Ellen. "My Body, My Closet: Invisible Disability and the Limits of Coming-Out Discourse." *GLQ: A Journal of Lesbian and Gay Studies* 9, no. 1/2 (2003): 233–55. https://doi.org/10.1215/10642684-9-1-2-233.

Sandahl, Carrie. "Queering the Crip or Cripping the Queer?: Intersections of Queer and Crip Identities in Solo Autobiographical Performance." *GLQ: A Journal of Lesbian and Gay Studies* 9, no. 1/2 (2003): 25–56.

Santiago, Silviano. "The Wily Homosexual (First—and Necessarily Hasty—Notes)." In *Queer Globalizations: Citizenship and the Afterlife of Colonialism*, edited by Arnaldo Cruz-Malave and Martin Manalansan, 13–19. New York: New York University Press, 2002.

Schalk, Sami. *Black Disability Politics*. Durham, NC: Duke University Press, 2022.

Schalk, Sami. "Coming to Claim Crip: Disidentification with/in Disability Studies." *Disability Studies Quarterly* 33, no. 2 (2013). https://dsq-sds.org/article/view/3705/3240.

Schalk, Sami. "Critical Disability Studies as Methodology." *Lateral: Journal of the Cultural Studies Association* 6, no. 1 (2017).

Schalk, Sami. "Reevaluating the Supercrip." *Journal of Literary and Cultural Disability Studies* 10, no. 1 (2016): 71–87.

Schmitz, Nele. "Growing on the Edge: Hydraulic Architecture of Mangroves: Ecological Plasticity and Functional Significance of Water Conducting Tissue in *Rhizophora mucronata* and *Avicenni marina*." PhD diss., Vrije Universiteit Brussel, 2008.

Schrader, Astrid. "Responding to *Pfiesteria piscicida* (the Fish Killer): Phantomatic Ontologies, Indeterminacy, and Responsibility in Toxic Microbiology." *Social Studies of Science* 40, no. 2 (2010): 275–306.

Schweik, Susan. "Lomax's Matrix: Disability, Solidarity, and the Black Power of 504." *Disability Studies Quarterly* 31, no. 1 (2011).

Scotch, Richard. *From Good Will to Civil Rights: Transforming Federal Disability Policy.* Philadelphia: Temple University Press, 2001.

See, Sarita Echavez. *The Decolonized Eye: Filipino American Art and Performance.* Minneapolis: University of Minnesota Press, 2009.

Seikaly, Sherene. "The Matter of Time." *American Historical Review* 124, no. 5 (2019): 1681–88.

Shapiro, Joseph P. "In Search of a Word for (Shhh!) Disabled." *Washington Post*, August 25, 1991. https://www.washingtonpost.com/archive/opinions/1991/08/25/in-search-of-a-word-for-shhh-disabled/79874961-bef6-447a-b18e-2ed52aa4eb66/.

Shapiro, Joseph P. *No Pity: People with Disabilities Forging a New Civil Rights Movement.* New York: Three Rivers Press, 1993.

Shaw, Barrett. *The Ragged Edge: The Disability Experience from the Pages of the First Fifteen Years of the Disability Rag.* Louisville, KY: Avocado Press, 1994.

Shaw, Claire. *Deaf in the USSR: Marginality, Community, and Soviet Identity, 1917–1991.* Ithaca, NY: Cornell University Press, 2017.

Shaw, Randy. *The Activist's Handbook: A Primer for the 1990s and Beyond.* Berkeley: University of California Press, 1996.

Sheehi, Lara, and Stephen Sheehi. *Psychoanalysis under Occupation: Practicing Resistance in Palestine.* New York: Routledge, 2022.

Shmidt, Victoria. *Child Welfare Discourses and Practices in the Czech Lands: The Segregation of Roma and Disabled Children during the Nineteenth and Twentieth Centuries.* Brno: Brno University Press, 2015.

Shmidt, Victoria, ed. *The Politics of Disability in Interwar and Socialist Czechoslovakia: Segregating in the Name of the Nation.* Amsterdam: Amsterdam University Press, 2019.

Sibara, Jay. *Imperial Injuries: Race, Disease, and Disability in Narratives of Resistance to US Empire.* Forthcoming.

Siebers, Tobin. "Disability as Masquerade." *Literature and Medicine* 23, no. 1 (2004): 1–22.

Siebers, Tobin. *Disability Theory.* Ann Arbor: University of Michigan Press, 2008.

Sills, Peter. *Toxic War: The Story of Agent Orange.* Nashville, TN: Vanderbilt University Press, 2014.

Silverman, Max, Jeff Wallace, and John Whale. *Frantz Fanon's "Black Skin, White Masks": New Interdisciplinary Essays.* Manchester, UK: Manchester University Press, 2005.

Simpson, Audra. "On Ethnographic Refusal: Indigeneity, 'Voice,' and Colonial Citizenship." *Junctures: The Journal of Thematic Dialogue* 9 (2007): 67–80.

Sins Invalid. "Disability Justice for Palestine." YouTube video, August 2, 2014. https://www.youtube.com/watch?v=w_jre3409jA.

Sins Invalid. "La justicia de lenguaje es justicia para personas con discapacidades/Language Justice Is Disability Justice." June 8, 2021. https://www.sinsinvalid

.org/news-1/2021/6/8/la-justicia-de-lenguaje-es-justicia-para-personas-con
-discapacidadeslanguage-justice-is-disability-justice.

Sins Invalid. *Skin, Tooth, and Bone: The Basis of Movement Is Our People*. 2nd ed. Berkeley, CA: Sins Invalid, 2019.

Sins Invalid: An Unshamed Claim to Beauty in the Face of Invisibility. Home page. Accessed January 23, 2022. http://www.sinsinvalid.org.

Smallwood, Stephanie. *Saltwater Slavery: A Middle Passage from Africa to American Diaspora*. Cambridge, MA: Harvard University Press, 2007.

Snaza, Nathan, and Julietta Singh. "Introduction: Dehumanist Education and the Colonial University." *Social Text* 39, no. 1 (2021): 1–19.

Snounu, Yasmin. "A Critical Ethnographical Exploration of Disability under Apartheid Conditions: The Promising Potential of Palestinian Higher Education Institutions." PhD diss., Eastern Michigan University, Ypsilanti, 2019.

Snounu, Yasmin, Phil Smith, and Joe Bishop. "Disability, the Politics of Maiming, and Higher Education in Palestine." *Disability Studies Quarterly* 39, no. 2 (2019).

Sokolová, Věra. "Don't Get Pricked! Representation and the Politics of Sexuality in the Czech Republic." In *Over the Wall/After the Fall: Postcommunist Cultures through an East-West Gaze*, edited by Sibelan Forrester, Magdalena J. Zaborowska, and Elena Gapova, 251–67. Bloomington: Indiana University Press, 2004.

Soldatic, Karen, and Kelley Johnson, eds. *Global Perspectives on Disability Activism and Advocacy: Our Way*. New York: Routledge, 2019.

Sommer, Doris. *Foundational Fictions: The National Romances of Latin America*. Latin American Literature and Culture, vol. 8. Berkeley: University of California Press, 1991.

Song, Jesook. *South Koreans in the Debt Crisis: The Creation of a Neoliberal Welfare Society*. Durham, NC: Duke University Press, 2009; 추선영 옮김. 복지의 배신. 서울: 이후, 2016.

Sontag, Susan. *Illness as Metaphor and AIDS and Its Metaphors*. New York: Picador, 2001.

Spencer, Robyn C. *The Revolution Has Come: Black Power, Gender, and the Black Panther Party in Oakland*. Durham, NC: Duke University Press, 2016.

Springer, Kimberly. "Third Wave Black Feminism?" *Signs* 27, no. 4 (2002): 1059–82.

Srour, Shatha Abu. "Social Action to Achieve a Dignified Life for People with Disabilities in the Occupied Palestinian Territory." *The Lancet*, March 6, 2021.

Stamatopoulou-Robbins, Sophia. "Failure to Build: Sewage and the Choppy Temporality of Infrastructure in Palestine." *Environment and Planning E: Nature and Space* 4, no. 1 (2021): 28–42.

State of Queensland Department of Environment and Science. "About Fraser Island Dingoes." https://parks.des.qld.gov.au/parks/fraser/fraser-island-dingoes.html.

Stryker, Rachael. "Young People, Emotional Suspicion and the Emergence of Paediatric Selfhood in Palestine." *Children and Society* 34 (2020): 305–19.

Suchland, Jennifer. *Economies of Violence: Transnational Feminism, Postsocialism, and the Politics of Sex Trafficking*. Durham, NC: Duke University Press, 2015.

Sundberg, Juanita. "Decolonizing Posthumanist Geographies." *Cultural Geographies* 21, no. 1 (2014): 33–47.

Sutton-Smith, Brian. *The Ambiguity of Play*. Cambridge, MA: Harvard University Press, 2001.

SWNS. "This Is the Legacy of Agent Orange in Vietnam." *New York Post*, September 28, 2017. https://nypost.com/2017/09/28/agent-orange-is-still-causing-deformities-in -vietnams-babies/.

Tam, Louise. "Agitation and Sudden Death: Containing Black Detainee Affect." *American Quarterly* 69, no. 2 (2017): 339–45.

Tari Young-Jung Na, trans. Ju Hui Judy Han and Se-Woong Koo. "The South Korean Gender System: LGBTI in the Contexts of Family, Legal Identity, and the Military." *Journal of Korean Studies* 19, no. 2 (2014).

Tawil-Souri, Helga. "Checkpoint Time." *Qui Parle: Critical Humanities and Social Sciences* 26, no. 2 (2017): 383–422.

"The Texas Salt Lake, La Sal Del Rey." *Scientific American* (1845–1908) 52, no. 11 (1885): 165.

Thomas, Megan C. *Orientalists, Propagandists, and Ilustrados: Filipino Scholarship and the End of Spanish Colonialism*. Minneapolis: University of Minnesota Press, 2012.

Thompson, Villissa. "Black History Month 2017: Brad Lomax, Disabled Black Panther." *Ramp Your Voice*, February 17, 2017. http://rampyourvoice.com/2017/02/17/black -history-month-2017-brad-lomax-disabled-black-panther/.

Todd, Zoe. "An Indigenous Feminist's Take on the Ontological Turn: 'Ontology' Is Just Another Word for Colonialism." *Journal of Historical Sociology* 29, no. 1 (2016): 4–22.

Tompkins, Kyla Wazana. "On the Limits and Promise of New Materialist Philosophy." *Lateral* 5, no. 1 (2016). https://doi.org/10.25158/l5.1.8.

Trinh, T. Minh-Ha. *Woman, Native, Other: Writing Postcoloniality and Feminism*. Bloomington: Indiana University Press, 1989.

Troeung, Y-Dang. *Refugee Lifeworlds: The Afterlife of the Cold War in Cambodia*. Philadelphia: Temple University Press, 2022.

Tsing, Anna. *The Mushroom at the End of the World: On the Possibility of Life in Capitalist Ruins*. Princeton, NJ: Princeton University Press, 2015.

UCI Anti-Cancer Challenge. "Join the Anti Cancer Challenge." YouTube video, September 6, 2018. https://www.youtube.com/watch?v=rdet4-y6Xmg.

USAID. *Disability Rights Enforcement, Coordination, and Therapies*. July 2020. https:// www.usaid.gov/sites/default/files/documents/1861/FS_DisabiltyRightsEnforcement CoordinationTherapies_July2020_Eng.pdf.

UTRGV. "Rio Grande Valley Civil War Trail: La Sal Del Rey." Accessed March 7, 2019. www.utrgv.edu/civilwar-trail/civil-war-trail/hidalgo-county/la-sal-del-rey/index.htm.

Václav, Petr, dir. *Cesta ven*. Moloko Films, 2014.

Vargas, João H. Costa. *The Denial of Antiblackness: Multiracial Redemption and Black Suffering*. Minneapolis: University of Minnesota Press, 2018.

Vasconcelos, José. *La Raza Cosmica; Misión de La Raza Iberoamericana, Argentina y Brasil*. Colección Austral, 802. México: Espasa-Calpe Mexicana, 1948.

Verdery, Katherine. *What Was Socialism, and What Comes Next?* Princeton, NJ: Princeton University Press, 1996.

Veronese, Guido, and Federica Cavazzoni. 2020. "'I Hope I Will Be Able to Go Back to My Home City': Narratives of Suffering and Survival of Children in Palestine." *Psychological Studies* 65 (2020): 51–63.

Veronese, Guido, et al. "Spatial Agency as a Source of Resistance and Resilience among Palestinian Children Living in Dheisheh Refugee Camp, Palestine." *Health and Place* 62 (2020): 102304.

Villanueva, Nicholas, Jr. *The Lynching of Mexicans in the Texas Borderlands.* Albuquerque: University of New Mexico Press, 2018.

Vrábková, Jiřina. "Women's Priorities and Visions." In *Ana's Land: Sisterhood in Eastern Europe*, edited by Tanya Renne, 72–75. Boulder, CO: Westview Press, 1997.

Wacquant, Loïc. *Les Prisons de la Misère.* Raisons d'agir Editions, 1999;가난을 엄벌하다. 류재화 옮김, 서울:시사IN북, 2010.

Wade, Cheryl Marie. "Disability Culture Rap." In *The Ragged Edge: The Disability Experience from the Pages of the First Fifteen Years of the Disability Rag*, edited by Barrett Shaw, 15–18. Louisville, KY: Avocado Press, 1994.

Wade, Cheryl Marie. "It Ain't Exactly Sexy." In *The Ragged Edge: The Disability Experience from the Pages of the First Fifteen Years of the Disability Rag*, edited by Barrett Shaw, 88–90. Louisville, KY: Avocado Press, 1994.

Wang, Esmé Weijun. *The Collected Schizophrenias: Essays.* Minneapolis, MN: Graywolf Press, 2019.

Weima, Yolanda, and Claudio Minca. "Closing Camps." *Progress in Human Geography* 46, no. 2 (2022): 261–81.

Weizman, Eyal. *Hollow Land: Israel's Architecture of Occupation.* London: Verso, 2007.

Wolff, Larry. *Inventing Eastern Europe: The Map of Civilization on the Mind of the Enlightenment.* Stanford, CA: Stanford University Press, 1994.

Woroniecka-Krzyzanowska, Dorota. "Multilocality and the Politics of Space in Protracted Exile: The Case of a Palestinian Refugee Camp in the West Bank." *Transfers* 11, no. 1 (2021): 92–107.

Worrall, Brandy Liên. *Brandy's Cancer Bash.* https://cancerfuckingsucks.blogspot.com/.

Worrall, Brandy Liên. *What Doesn't Kill Us.* Vancouver: Rabbit Fool Press, 2014.

Wynter, Sylvia. "'No Humans Involved': An Open Letter to My Colleagues." *Forum N.H.I. Knowledge for the 21st Century* 1, no. 1 (1994): 42–73.

Yergeau, M. Remi. *Authoring Autism: On Rhetoric and Neurological Queerness.* Durham, NC: Duke University Press, 2018.

Young, Hershini Bhana. *Falling, Floating, Flickering: Disability and Differential Movement in African Diasporic Performance.* New York: New York University Press, 2023.

Zahaika, Dalia, et al. "Challenges Facing Family Caregivers of Children with Disabilities during COVID-19 Pandemic in Palestine." *Journal of Primary Care and Community Health* 12 (2021): 1–8.

김상희. "IL센터, 이대로 괜찮을까?" 비마이너, 2018년3월28일. http://beminor.com /detail.php?number=12032.

김성구. 신자유주의와 공모자들. 서울: 나름북스, 2014.

김재형. "'식민지 시기'부랑나환자'와 사회의 대응." 배제에서 포용으로— 형제복지원의 사회사와 소수자 과거청산의 과제 토론회(2018년 11월 19일 서울대학교) 자료집. 미간행), 2018.

김재형. 질병, 낙인─무균사회와 한센인의 강제격리. 서울: 돌베개, 2021.

김종인, 김재익. 자립생활실천론. 서울: 창지사, 2014.

김지혜. "'프라이버시와 차별'" 강의, 미간행, 장애여성공감, 2019년 3월 12일.

김현철. "'감금'에서 '감금지리'로: 언어화되지 않은 착취와 소외, 감정과 트라우마, 살들(fleshes)의 논의를 위해." 웹진글로컬포인트 no. 5 (2019). http://blog.jinbo.net/glocalpoint/78.

루인. "번호이동과 성전환─주민등록제도, 국민국가, 그리고 트랜스/젠더." 젠더의 채널을 돌려라. 서울: 사람생각, 2008, 25–46.

박정미. "식민지 성매매제도의 단절과 연속: '묵인-관리 체제'의 변형과 재생산." 페미니즘 연구 11, no. 2 (2011): 199–238.

박차민정. "AIDS패닉 혹은 괴담의 정치." 말과활 12 (2016): 35–48.

원미혜. "'보이지 않는 '경계'에서: 용산 성매매 집결지 중·노년층 여성의 이주 체험을 중심으로." 이화인문과학원탈경계인문학 7, no. 2 (2014): 233–71.

이익서, 최정아, 이동영. "장애인 자립생활모델에 대한 탐색적 고찰: 사회적 배제 관점을 중심으로." 한국사회정책 14, no. 1 (2007): 49–81.

이정은. "'난민' 아닌 '난민수용소,' 오무라(大村)수용소: 수용자, 송환자에 대한 한국정부의 대응을 중심으로." 사회와역사 103 (2014): 323–48.

정근식 외. 한센인 인권 실태조사. 서울: 국가인권위원회, 2005.

정종화, 주숙자. 자립생활과 활동보조서비스. 파주: 양서원, 2008.

조미경. "장애인 탈시설 운동에서 이뤄질 '불구의 정치' 간 연대를 기대하며." 시설사회. 서울: 와온, 2020, 279–89.

조미경. "탈시설 운동의 확장을 위한 진지로서의 IL 센터." IL과 젠더 포럼 자료집. 미간행, 2018.

조영길, 김정미, 노경수. 장애인자립생활개론. 서울: 학지사, 2016.

지은구. "바우처와 사회복지서비스: 복지서비스의 확대인가 퇴조인가?" 복지동향 11 (5/20/2008). https://www.peoplepower21.org/welfarenow/663627.

차승기. "수용소라는 안전장치─오무라 수용소, 폴리스, 그리고 잉여.'" 주권의 야만─밀항, 수용소, 재일조선인. 성공회대학교 동아시아연구소 기획, 권혁태·이정은·조경희 엮음. 파주: 한울아카데미, 2008.

천주교인권위원회, 공익인권법재단공감, 한국게이인권운동단체친구사이, 한국성적소수자문화인권센터. 구금시설과 트랜스젠더의 인권 토론회 자료집. 미간행, 2011년 4월 15일.

최정기. 감금의 정치. 서울: 책세상, 2005.

형제복지원구술프로젝트. 숫자가 된 사람들. 파주: 오월의봄, 2015.

황지성. "건강한 신체와 우생학적 신체들." 배틀그라운드: 낙태죄를 둘러싼 성과 재생산의 정치. 서울: 후마니타스, 2018, 215–42.

SONY CORÁÑEZ BOLTON is assistant professor of Spanish and Latinx and Latin American studies at Amherst College. He studies the intersections of Latinx and Filipinx cultural politics, literature, and embodiment through the lenses of postcolonial disability, queer of color critique, and transnational feminism. His forthcoming book, *Crip Colony: Mestizaje, US Imperialism, and the Queer Politics of Disability in the Philippines*, analyzes the disability politics of Filipinx mixed-race subjects during the historical transition from Spanish colonial to US imperial rule. Sony's work has appeared in *Journal of Asian American Studies*, *Revista Filipina*, *Verge: Studies in Global Asias*, and *Q&A: Voices from Queer Asian North America*.

SUZANNE BOST is a professor in the Department of English at Loyola University Chicago. She is the author of three books—*Mulattas and Mestizas: Representing Mixed Identities in the Americas, 1850–2000* (2003), *Encarnación: Illness and Body Politics in Chicana Feminist Literature* (2009), and *Shared Selves: Latinx Memoir and Ethical Alternatives to Humanism* (2019)—and she coedited, with Frances Aparicio, *The Routledge Companion to Latino/a Literature* (2012). She has also published more than two dozen articles on Latinx literature, feminist theory, illness and disability, and archival practices. Her current work focuses on decolonial feminisms and silence.

MEL Y. CHEN is associate professor of gender and women's studies and director for the Center for the Study of Sexual Culture at the University of California, Berkeley. Following *Animacies: Biopolitics, Racial Mattering, and Queer Affect* (Duke University Press, 2012), they are completing a second book titled *Chemical Intimacies*, on intoxication's involvement in archival histories of the interanimation of time, race, and disability. Besides publishing widely in journals, Chen coedits a Duke book series titled ANIMA, enjoys teaching to the odd note, and is part of a small and sustaining queer/trans of color arts collective in the San Francisco Bay Area.

NATALIA DUONG is a researcher, teacher, and performance maker whose work spans performance studies, Asian American studies, disability studies, and the environmental humanities. Her forthcoming book, *Chemical Diasporas*, examines the transnational spread of the chemical compound Agent Orange and the sensory and affective geographies created through its dispersal. Natalia received a PhD in performance studies with a designated emphasis in gender and women's studies from the University of California, Berkeley. Her writing can be found in *Catalyst: Feminism, Theory, Technoscience*; *Canadian Review of American Studies*; *Journal of Dramatic Theory and Criticism*; and *Dance Research*. Natalia is currently a University of California President's Postdoctoral Fellow at the University of California, Los Angeles.

LEZLIE FRYE is an assistant professor of gender studies and disability studies in the School for Cultural and Social Transformation at the University of Utah. Her research concentrates on the cultural history of disability, race, and gender in the United States since the 1970s, with a particular emphasis on histories of state violence, citizenship, and social movements. Lezlie received her PhD in 2016 from the American Studies Program, Department of Social and Cultural Analysis, at New York University and was the 2014–15 Predoctoral Research Fellow in the Fisher Center for Gender Studies at Hobart and William Smith Colleges. Lezlie is currently working on a manuscript titled "Domesticating Disability: Post–Civil Rights Racial Disenfranchisement and the Birth of the Disabled Citizen." Lezlie's academic work is preceded by over a decade of popular education, performance, activism, and organizing work that coheres around disability, racial, and economic justice.

MAGDA GARCÍA received her PhD from the Department of Chicana and Chicano Studies at the University of California, Santa Barbara, where her dissertation research on affect theory, Chicanx/Latinx literary and cultural studies, and the speculative was supported by a Ford Foundation Dissertation Fellowship. She is currently a University of California President's Postdoctoral Fellow in the Department of Ethnic Studies at the University of California, San Diego, where she is working on her manuscript, titled "Claiming La Bruja: Rage, the Speculative, and Contemporary Border Tejanx Feminist Affects." She is coeditor of *Transmovimientos: Latinx Queer Migrations, Bodies, and Spaces* (2021), alongside Ellie D. Hernández and Eddy Francisco Alvarez Jr. She is from the Rio Grande Valley of South Texas.

ALISON KAFER is the Embrey Associate Professor of Women's and Gender Studies and an associate professor of English at the University of Texas at Austin, where she also teaches courses in LGBTQ studies and disability studies. She is the author of *Feminist, Queer, Crip* (2013), which theorizes crip futurity and imagines futures for disabled people through cross-disability, cross-movement, and coalition politics. Her more recent work appears in *Catalyst: Feminism, Theory, Technoscience*; the *Journal of Literary and Cultural Disability Studies*; and *South Atlantic Quarterly*. She is currently working on a manuscript on disability and reproductive justice.

EUNJUNG KIM is an associate professor in the Department of Women's and Gender Studies and the Department of Cultural Foundations of Education and Disability Studies

Program at Syracuse University. She is the author of *Curative Violence: Rehabilitating Disability, Gender and Sexuality in Modern Korea* (Duke University Press, 2017, winner of Alison Piepmeier Award, James B. Palaise Prize). Her work has appeared in journals such as *Catalyst: Feminism, Theory and Technoscience*; *Sexualities*; GLQ; and *Social Politics*, and in edited collections, *Against Health*; *Intersectionality and Beyond*; *Asexualities*; and *Disability, Human Rights, and the Limits of Humanitarianism*. Her research and teaching is in transnational feminist disability studies theories, asexuality theories, and crip ecologies. She is a member of the disabled women's organization Jangaeyeosong Gonggam, WDE, in South Korea.

YOO-SUK KIM is an English/Korean translator and has translated materials mainly on Korean studies including the *Source Book for the Korean History of Science* (co-translation; forthcoming); human rights and social justice including Chung Chinsung's *Military Sexual Slavery of Imperial Japan: Historical Realities and Social Movements for Resolution* (forthcoming); and artists and art exhibitions including siren eun young jung, Jane Jin Kaisen, the National Museum of Modern and Contemporary Art, Korea (MMCA), and the Korean Pavilion at the Venice Biennale.

KATEŘINA KOLÁŘOVÁ is a researcher at the Sociological Institute of Czech Academy of Science and teaches in the Gender Studies Program at the School of Humanities, Charles University, Prague. Her work engages intersections of disability, crip, queer, and race theories; dialogue between postcolonial and decolonial studies with disability and queer studies; and feminist queer crip interrogations of microbial lives and microbiopolitics. The manuscript for her forthcoming book, *Rehabilitative Postsocialism: Disability, Race, Gender and Sexuality and the Limits of National Belonging*, won the 2019 Tobin Siebers Prize for Disability Studies in Humanities. With Martina Winkler, she coedited *Re/Imaginations of Disability in State Socialism: Visions, Promises, Frustrations* (2021), which maps disability politics under state socialism across Eastern Europe.

JAMES KYUNG-JIN LEE is professor of Asian American studies and English and the director of the Center for Medical Humanities at the University of California, Irvine. He is the author of *Pedagogies of Woundedness: Illness, Memoir, and the Ends of the Model Minority* (2022) and *Urban Triage: Race and the Fictions of Multiculturalism* (2004). He also co-guest-edited (with Jennifer Ho) a special issue of the *Amerasia Journal*, "The State of Illness and Disability in Asian America" (2013).

STACEY PARK MILBERN (1987–2020) was a queer Korean/white Southern femme disability justice movement worker, writer, and thought leader. From age sixteen in North Carolina, Stacey organized with other disabled youth of color in the South, with the Disabled Young People's Collective and at the national level. She was a prolific writer, beginning her blog *Cripchick* as a young adult, which led to her working with other emerging radical queer women of color writers in the SPEAK! Women of Color Media Collective. Her writing appeared in many anthologies, including *Disability Visibility: Stories from the 21st Century*, *Resistance and Hope*, and *Don't Leave Your Friends Behind*. After moving to

Oakland in 2010, she was foundational to much disability justice organizing, from cocreating the Creating Collective Access space at the Allied Media Conference to work with Sins Invalid, Bad CRIPP, and the #PowerToLive and NoBodyIsDisposable coalitions, organizing for disabled, elder, and fat survival and mutual aid during climate emergency events, power shutoffs, and COVID-19. She was part of the national successful fight to save the ACA and Medicaid during the Trump administration, sharing her own experiences as someone whose life was supported by paid care attendants, allowing her to live and work in community. She served as an appointed adviser to the Obama administration, coproduced the impact campaign for the Netflix film *Crip Camp*, and co-wrote Bernie Sanders's 2020 disability platform. In 2019 she founded the Disability Justice Culture Club, a disability justice community center in her accessible East Oakland home, as a gathering place for the disabled BIPOC community. She said, "I want to leave a legacy of disabled people knowing that we are powerful and beautiful because of who we are, not despite it," and she succeeded.

JULIE AVRIL MINICH is an associate professor in the departments of English and Mexican American & Latina/o Studies at the University of Texas at Austin. Minich is the author of *Accessible Citizenships: Disability, Nation, and the Cultural Politics of Greater Mexico* (2014), winner of the 2016 MLA Prize in United States Latina and Latino and Chicana and Chicano Literary and Cultural Studies. She is currently finishing a book titled *Radical Health: Justice, Care, and Latinx Expressive Culture*.

TARI YOUNG-JUNG NA has participated in the feminist antiwar movement, movements for and by women with disabilities, LGBT rights movement, HIV/AIDS human rights movement, refugee human rights movement, movement for the right to found families, movement for sexual rights and reproductive rights, and drug users' human rights movement for more than twenty years. As a member of Women with Disabilities Empathy, she has studied and searched for joint action regarding the problem of institutions that exist in society in diverse forms. In relation to this, she has jointly planned and published *Institutionalized Society* (2020). In recent years, she has provided support to the victim of an incidence of torture at the Hwaseong Immigration Detention Center and participated in the movement to close down immigration detention centers.

THERÍ A. PICKENS (she/her) authored *Black Madness :: Mad Blackness* (2019) and *New Body Politics* (2014). She edited *Arab American Aesthetics* (2018) and special issues of *African American Review* (2017) and *College Language Association* (2021). Her poems have appeared in *Prairie Schooner*, *Diode*, and *The Journal*. She is an avid bowler, home chef, and all-around badass.

LEAH LAKSHMI PIEPZNA-SAMARASINHA is a queer disabled and autistic nonbinary femme writer, educator, curator, and disability/transformative justice worker of Burgher/Tamil Sri Lankan and Irish/Galician/Roma descent. They are the author or coeditor of ten books, including *The Future Is Disabled: Prophecies, Love Notes and Mourning Songs*, *Beyond Survival: Stories and Strategies from the Transformative Justice Movement* (coedited with Ejeris Dixon), as well as *Tonguebreaker*, *Care Work: Dreaming Disability Justice*, *Dirty*

River: A Queer Femme of Color Dreaming Her Way Home, *Bodymap*, and *Consensual Genocide*; with Ching-In Chen and Jai Dulani, they coedited *The Revolution Starts at Home: Confronting Intimate Violence in Activist Communities*. A longtime performer with Sins Invalid, they are creating Living Altars/The Stacey Park Milbern Liberation Center, performance and retreat space by and for disabled QTBIPOC writers. They are the 2020 recipient of the Lambda Foundation's Jeanne Córdova Prize in Lesbian/Queer Nonfiction, recognizing "a lifetime of work documenting the complexity of queer experience," and a 2020–21 US Artists Disability Futures Fellow.

JASBIR K. PUAR is professor of women's, gender, and sexuality studies at Rutgers University. She is the author of the award-winning books *The Right to Maim: Debility, Capacity, Disability* (2017) and *Terrorist Assemblages: Homonationalism in Queer Times* (2007), which was reissued as an expanded version for its tenth anniversary (2017), translated into Spanish and French, and is forthcoming in Greek and Portuguese. Her scholarly and mainstream writings have been translated into more than fifteen languages. She is also coauthor of exhibitions for the Sharjah Architecture Triennial (2019) and the Sharjah Art Biennial (2023). She is the recipient of the 2019 Kessler Award from the Center for LGBTQ Studies (CLAGS) at CUNY, which recognizes lifetime achievement in and impact on queer research and organizing.

SAMI SCHALK is an associate professor of gender and women's studies at the University of Wisconsin–Madison. Her research focuses on the intersections of disability, race, and gender in contemporary American literature and culture. She is the author of *Bodyminds Reimagined: (Dis)ability, Race, and Gender in Black Women's Speculative Fiction* (Duke University Press, 2018) and *Black Disability Politics* (Duke University Press, 2022). Schalk is a Black disabled queer femme and a pleasure activist.

FAITH NJAHÎRA WANGARÎ (she/her) is a disabled wheelchair-riding scholar-activist with muscular dystrophy from Kenya. Her experience as a researcher, consultant in the humanitarian sector, and beyond has involved work on inclusive education, disability accessibility, sexuality, and health advocacy. She has given guest lectures at organizations and in university classrooms. She is a coproducer, with Shiilā Seok Wun Au Yong (2019), of the documentary film *For All the Brilliant Conversations*, a film about friendship, healing, and navigating trauma. Njahîra also contributed to *#YouthCan* (2020), a book collection of African stories in various sectors. She loves basking in the sun, dancing to music, being with loved ones, all the things that add to her joy. Njahîra founded Muscular Dystrophy Society Kenya in 2013 as a support platform for those with muscular dystrophy and their loved ones. She serves on the boards of the 1in9 Campaign (South Africa) and National Gay and Lesbian Human Rights Commission (Kenya). Njahîra holds a graduate degree from Syracuse University through the Open Society Foundation's Disability Rights and Inclusive Education scholarship program. Currently, she is a doctoral researcher interrogating healthcare professionals' interactions with persons with disabilities with the Centre for Human Rights at the University of Pretoria, South Africa.

Page numbers in italics denote illustrations.